SpringerWienNewYork

Tort and Insurance Law
Vol. 11

Bernhard A. Koch (ed.)

Terrorism, Tort Law and Insurance
A Comparative Survey

With Contributions by

Kenneth S. Abraham
Bertil Bengtsson
Giovanni Bisazza
Israel Gilead
Sabine Gutzwiller
Kevin P. Hilliard
Bernhard A. Koch
Helmut Koziol
Fabien Lafay
Christian Lahnstein
Thomas Lörtscher
Ulrich Magnus
Miquel Martín-Casals
Olivier Moréteau
Linda S. Mullenix
Johann Neethling
Claudio Parizzi
Jordi Ribot
Stefan Strahwald
Clive Walker
Peter H. Woodin
Alessio Zaccaria

SpringerWienNewYork

European Centre of Tort and Insurance Law
Landesgerichtsstraße 11
A-1080 Vienna
Tel.: +43 1 40127 1688
Fax: +43 1 40127 1685
E-Mail: ectil@ectil.org

Austrian Academy of Sciences
Research Unit for European Tort Law
Landesgerichtsstraße 11
A-1080 Vienna
Tel.: +43 1 40127 1687
Fax: +43 1 40127 1685
E-mail: etl@oeaw.ac.at

Printed in Austria

Springer-Verlag Wien New York is part of Springer Science + Business Media
springeronline.com

Typesetting: Composition & Design Services, Minsk
Printing and binding: Manz Crossmedia GmbH & Co KG, A-1051 Wien

Printed on acid-free and chlorine-free bleached paper
SPIN: 11669586

CIP data applied for

ISSN 1616-8623
ISBN 3-211-01867-0 Springer-Verlag Wien New York

Preface

The tragic events of September 11, 2001, have stirred international debate on how to cope with losses that terrorist acts inflict upon individuals and businesses. This study aims at providing insight into how selected jurisdictions deal with spreading such risks and what alternatives to traditional tort law tools (if any) they offer for such purpose. Special regard is given to fund solutions as available in some countries. Renowned experts from those jurisdictions were asked to respond to a questionnaire. Their country reports are presented in the first part of this book.

The results of this project were presented at a conference in Munich on February 27 and 28, 2003. The first day was devoted to special reports from the United States, and these are presented in a separate section below. This set of contributions particularly focuses on the consequences of the WTC attack from a practical and procedural point of view.

The volume concludes with contributions from a more general perspective, including an economic analysis of such issues, deliberations concerning liability insurance, as well as comparative reports.

I would sincerely like to thank all contributors for solving the difficult task of providing all essential information on a limited number of pages and for keeping to the tight deadlines that I set them. Furthermore, I owe thanks to Tanja Steindl for producing the index to this volume. Last, but not least, I am grateful to all staff members of the European Centre of Tort and Insurance Law and the Austrian Academy of Sciences' Research Unit for European Tort Law, especially to Sabine Gantner, Sophie Pedersen, Donna Stockenhuber, and Stefan Strahwald, for all their valuable assistance in producing this publication.

Innsbruck, November 2003 Bernhard A. Koch

Table of Contents

Definition of Terrorism

We are aware that there is a legal discussion about the term "terrorism" and, for the purpose of this project, we would like to adopt Alex P. Schmid's "Academic Consensus Definition", which is also proposed by the UN Office on Drugs and Crime as a basis for the analysis[*]:

> "Terrorism is an anxiety-inspiring method of repeated violent action, employed by (semi-) clandestine individual, group or state actors, for idiosyncratic, criminal or political reasons, whereby – in contrast to assassination – the direct targets of violence are not the main targets. The immediate human victims of violence are generally chosen randomly (targets of opportunity) or selectively (representative or symbolic targets) from a target population, and serve as message generators. Threat- and violence-based communication processes between terrorist (organization), (imperilled) victims, and main targets are used to manipulate the main target (audience(s)), turning it into a target of terror, a target of demands, or a target of attention, depending on whether intimidation, coercion, or propaganda is primarily sought"[**].

[*] See for further information: http://www.unodc.org/unodc/terrorism_definitions.html.

[**] A.P. Schmid/A.J. Longman, *Political Terrorism* (2nd edn. 1988), 28.

Questionnaire

A. General

1. Does your legal system have special legislation on terror attacks, in particular concerning liability or other indemnity?
2. Are there any special funds applicable providing alternative compensation for victims of terror attacks?
3. Have your judges ever had to address the issue of liability in connection with terror attacks in any leading cases?
4. Did the events of 11 September 2001 or any other recent terror attacks have any influence on your liability systems (interpretation, discussion about reforms, duty to take care)?
5. Does your country participate in any international conventions in connection with liability for terror attacks?

B. Strict Liability

1. Focusing on strict liability for means of transport and enterprises or facilities, would you say the owner, custodian or keeper is also liable if a terrorist initiates the damage?
2. Can terror attacks be classified as a defence like Act of God/*force majeure*/unavoidable event?
3. If there is another person liable besides or instead of the terrorist, for which kind of damages is he/she liable (for example also compensation for consequential damage like plundering following a terror attack)?

C. Fault Liability

1. At public facilities such as airports, train stations, sports stadiums etc., who is responsible that no terrorist enters and causes harm? The entity that runs the facility, enterprises that take advantage thereof (such as airlines or organizers of sports events), the state, or any other person(s)? How far do his duties of care go in that respect?
2. To what extent do individuals or entities have a duty of care to participate in the active avoidance of terrorist acts?

D. Cases

1. A terrorist hijacks an aeroplane and crashes into
   (a) a building
   (b) a nuclear plant.
2. A terrorist sets a bomb situated in an aeroplane and the plane crashes into
   (a) a residential area
   (b) a nuclear plant.
3. A terrorist drives with somebody's car or bus into a crowd of people.
4. A terrorist hides a bomb in a car which explodes within a crowd of people.

Country Reports

AUSTRIA
LIABILITY FOR ACTS OF TERRORISM UNDER AUSTRIAN LAW

Bernhard A. Koch and Helmut Koziol

I. General

A. Does Your Legal System Have Special Legislation on Terror Attacks, in Particular Concerning Liability or Other Indemnity?

1. Criminal Law

The Austrian Criminal Code (*Strafgesetzbuch*, StGB) has recently been amended by adding sections on terrorist activities and organizations as well as the financing thereof (§§ 278b–278d StGB). The central provision is § 278c StGB, which defines "terrorist acts" in its first paragraph as a special qualification of certain enumerated crimes regulated elsewhere in the Code such as murder, assault, compulsion, kidnapping, air piracy (which is a crime of its own, § 185 StGB), intentionally endangering the public, e.g. by potentially harmful abuse of radiation (§§ 171, 177b StGB), explosives (§ 173 StGB) or the like: These offences are considered acts of terrorism if they are "apt to cause a severe or lasting disturbance of public life or economy and if they were committed with the intent to gravely intimidate the public, or to coerce public authorities or international organisations to certain actions or omissions, or to seriously impair or destroy basic political, constitutional, economic or social structures of a state or international organisation".[1] 1

[1] This qualification reads in the original language as follows:
"wenn die Tat geeignet ist, eine schwere oder längere Zeit anhaltende Störung des öffentlichen Lebens oder eine schwere Schädigung des Wirtschaftslebens herbeizuführen, und mit dem Vorsatz begangen wird, die Bevölkerung auf schwerwiegende Weise einzuschüchtern, öffentliche Stellen oder eine internationale Organisation zu einer Handlung, Duldung oder Unterlassung zu nötigen oder die politischen, verfassungsrechtlichen, wirtschaftlichen oder sozialen Grundstrukturen eines Staates oder einer internationalen Organisation ernsthaft zu erschüttern oder zu zerstören."

2 While several provisions of the Criminal Code serve as *Schutzgesetze* (protective laws)[2] in a wider sense, whose violation is particularly considered in a tort law action, these new provisions on terrorism do not add to that catalogue since they merely extend the statutory range of punishment for behaviour which was already prohibited and sanctioned before.

3 Apart from these changes to substantive criminal law, the Austrian Code of Criminal Procedure (*Strafprozessordnung*, StPO), has been modified in order to facilitate criminal investigation in the field of terrorism. The most important amendment from the victims' perspective concerns § 145a StPO, which now also relaxes banking secrecy rules *inter alia* if an account is suspected of serving terrorist organisations or the financing of terrorist acts. The investigating magistrate can issue injunctions to freeze such accounts (§ 144a StPO), which may have the side effect of securing funds for compensation of victims.

2. Tort Law

4 Two provisions of Austrian tort law explicitly refer to terrorism: § 12 no. 3 *Rohrleitungsgesetz* (Pipelines Act, RohrlG) excludes strict liability for damage caused by pipelines if triggered *inter alia* by "terrorist attacks". § 12 RohrlG is mirrored by § 34 *Gaswirtschaftsgesetz* (Gas Industry Act, GWG), which uses the same wording for its defences to the liability of natural gas suppliers. Both provisions will be further dealt with below.[3]

B. Are There any Special Funds Applicable Providing Alternative Compensation for Victims of Terror Attacks?

1. Terror Pooling Agreement of the Austrian Insurers

5 As a consequence of the events of 11 September 2001, the Austrian insurance companies have decided to enter into a pooling agreement,[4] which has already been notified to the respective bodies, the financial market authority, the Ministry of Finance as well as the competition authorities in Brussels. It took effect on 1 October 2002, and will cover risks starting 1 January 2003. The terror pool provides for property cover against acts of terrorism.[5] The maximum base cover amounts to € 5 million per customer, who can increase this capacity to a maximum of € 25 million for extra premiums. The capacity of the pool currently amounts to € 200 million, of which € 50 million are covered by di-

[2] See H. Koziol, Mitigation of Damages under Austrian Law and Ideas for Future Regulations, in: J. Spier (ed.), *The Limits of Liability* (1996), 54; M. Karollus, *Funktion und Dogmatik der Haftung aus Schutzgesetzverletzung* (1992).

[3] See infra no. 35.

[4] H. Koziol, Haftung für Terrorschäden, [2002] *Die Versicherungsrundschau* (VR), 225 (233). Details can be found on the website of the Austrian Insurance Association (http://www.vvo.at), see also Th. Klöckner, Terror pool in Austria – Review of risk management approach to terrorism (at http://www.converium.com).

[5] The definition of terrorism follows the German Insurance Association proposition, see Th. Klöckner (supra fn. 4) for details.

rect insurers (according to their individual market share), the rest of it by reinsurers.

2. Compensation for Crime Victims

If someone is injured or killed as a direct victim or as a passer-by of an intentional crime,[6] the victim or his dependants can claim state compensation under the Austrian *Verbrechensopfergesetz* (Act on granting aid to crime victims, VOG) as long as they did not participate in the crime or expose themselves to such danger with gross negligence. Victims of terrorist acts are clearly also entitled to such support, which is limited to the consequences of bodily harm or death. The statute contains detailed provisions on the type and extent of compensation. Generally, a substantial share of the loss (in particular medical costs) will already be covered by social security, whose provider has a claim for reimbursement in limited circumstances (§ 4 VOG). Legislative measures taken by the European Union in the field of compensation for crime victims may affect this scheme in the future.[7] 6

3. Compensation for Damage Caused by Lawful Police Actions

According to the *Polizeibefugnis-Entschädigungsgesetz* (Law on compensation for damage caused by lawful police actions, PolBeG), someone harmed by weapons used in the course of legitimate coercive measures by the federal police authorities[8] can recover damages from the Federal Republic unless he is compensated by some insurance or under some other statutory scheme.[9] This also applies if someone is injured in the course of police actions aimed at fighting terrorist attacks, even if the action was not aimed at the victim directly. 7

Victims are not entitled to damages for pain and suffering (§ 2 subs. 1 PolBeG). If the harmful measures were taken for the prevailing interest of the injured party (if the victim was, for example, kidnapped by terrorists and injured in the course of his liberation), damages for personal injuries can be mitigated if equitable, while property damages are not recoverable at all (§ 2 subs. 2 PolBeG). 8

[6] The minimum punishment must exeed six months of imprisonment (§ 1 para. 2 VOG). It is not necessary that the offender be known.

[7] See B.A. Koch, European Union, in: H. Koziol/B.C. Steininger (eds.), *European Tort Law 2001* (2002), 473 (no. 25 et seq.), and the recent Commission Proposal for a Council Directive on compensation to crime victims, COM(2002) 562 final (available on http://europa.eu.int/eur-lex/en/index.html). Recital 15 of the latter draft explicitly refers to "terrorist offences".

[8] The actions, in particular the weapons used, have to fall under the *Waffengebrauchsgesetz* (Law on the use of weapons by police authorities). § 15 PolBeG extends such liability to damages caused by legitimate actions of prison officers or customs authorities.

[9] Liability is excluded if he unlawfully induced such actions himself (§ 1 PolBeG). On this compensation scheme in general, see M. Schauer, Zivilrechtliche Probleme des Polizeibefugnis-Entschädigungsgesetzes, [1989] *Juristische Blätter* (JBl), 763.

4. Compensation for Road Traffic Victims

9 If victims of a road traffic accident cannot recover damages from other sources, they can claim compensation from the *Fachverband der Versicherungsunternehmen* (association of Austrian insurance companies) pursuant to the *Verkehrsopfergesetz* (Law on the extended protection of traffic accident victims, VerkOG). This is particularly true if no liable person can be identified (§ 2 para. 1 no. 2 VerkOG), if the vehicle was used without the consent of the holder (who himself is not liable, § 2 para. 1 no. 3 VerkOG), or if insurance cover is excluded due to the tortfeasors intentional unlawful acts (§ 2 para. 1 no. 4 VerkOG), which consequently also covers cases where terrorists use motor vehicles to cause damage. The victims can claim indemnification of both personal harm as well as property damage, the latter only if in excess of € 220. Property damage is excluded altogether in the first mentioned case (§ 2 para. 1 no. 2 VerkOG).

C. Have Your Judges Ever Had to Address the Issue of Liability in Connection with Terror Attacks in any Leading Cases?

10 So far, there have been no court cases in Austria discussing civil liability for terrorist acts.

D. Did the Events of 11 September 2001 or any Other Recent Terror Attacks Have any Influence on Your Liability Systems (Interpretation, Discussion About Reforms, Duty to Take Care)?

11 Apart from the fact that Austrian tort law as a whole is currently under revision by an expert committee (which was instituted irrespective of these special events), who will certainly consider these peculiar aspects of liability as well, there have been only very specific amendments or proposals for legislation so far, including temporary measures as suggested by the ECOFIN Council providing short-term bridging cover for the airline industry.[10] The above-mentioned additions to the Criminal Code and the Code of Criminal Procedure[11] were indirectly also introduced in the wake of the World Trade Center attack inasmuch as they implement the respective decisions of the EU Council.[12] The most striking (and certainly most controversial) change to Austrian law was brought about by a recent amendment to the Act on the Prevention of Criminal Acts Against the Security of Civil Aviation, which will be outlined below.[13]

[10] E.g. art. XI. para. 1 no. 7 *Bundesfinanzgesetz* (Federal Finance Act, BFG) 2002, as amended by *Bundesgesetzblatt* (BGBl) I Nr. 156/2001.

[11] Supra no. 1.

[12] E.g. the Council Framework Decision of 13 June 2002 on combating terrorism, OJ L 164, 22 6. 2002, 3. See the Explanatory Commentary to the *Strafrechtsänderungsgesetz* (Criminal Code Amendments Act) 2002, 1166 *Beilagen zu den stenographischen Protokollen des Nationalrates* (BlgNR), XXI. *Gesetzgebungsperiode* (Legislative Period, GP).

[13] Infra no. 56.

E. Does Your Country Participate in any International Conventions in Connection with Liability for Terror Attacks?

Austria has ratified several international conventions relating to criminal law aspects of terrorism such as the European Convention on the Suppression of Terrorism as well as most UN treaties[14] (e.g. the Hostages Convention or the International Convention for the Suppression of Terrorist Bombings). The only international convention relating to civil law aspects of terrorism that Austria has ratified is the 1999 UN Convention for the Suppression of the Financing of Terrorism, whose art. 5 suggests civil liability as one of the possible measures to be taken by the signatories. Some of the above-mentioned recent changes to Austrian criminal law[15] were introduced in order to implement said convention. 12

II. Strict Liability

A. Focusing on Strict Liability for Means of Transport and Enterprises or Facilities, Would You Say the Owner, Custodian or Keeper is also Liable if a Terrorist Initiates the Damage?

1. Strict Liability Under Austrian Law in General

a) Statutory Enumeration of Specific Risks

There is no general clause of no-fault liability in Austrian law. Instead, certain particular risks are governed by specific legislation, be it in individual liability statutes or as singular provisions in more comprehensive codifications.[16] Courts nevertheless cautiously allow analogy either to these special statutory rules[17] or to the common core of all strict liabilities as a whole,[18] which gradually helps to overcome loopholes in the rather loose patchwork of risks that have already been dealt with by specific liability legislation.[19] 13

[14] This includes the 1963 Tokyo Convention on Offences and Certain Other Acts Committed on Board Aircraft, the 1970 Hague Convention for the Suppression of Unlawful Seizure of Aircraft, the 1971 Montreal Convention for the Suppression of Unlawful Acts against the Safety of Civil Aviation, the 1979 Convention against the Taking of Hostages, the 1980 Vienna Convention on the Physical Protection of Nuclear Material, and the 1997 Convention for the Suppression of Terrorist Bombings.

[15] See supra no. 1–3.

[16] See B.A. Koch/H. Koziol, Strict Liability under Austrian Law, in: B.A. Koch/H. Koziol (eds.), *Unification of Tort Law: Strict Liability* (2002), 9 (in particular no. 18 et seq.).

[17] On cases of analogous application of the *Eisenbahn- und Kraftfahrzeughaftpflichtgesetz* (Statute on liability for keeping railways and motor vehicles, EKHG), see P. Apathy, *Kommentar zum EKHG* (1992), § 2 no. 14 et seq; M. Schauer, in: M. Schwimann, *ABGB* VIII (2nd edn. 1997), § 2 EKHG no. 15 et seq.

[18] On the basis of such an analogy, the Supreme Court has already attached strict liability to the risks brought about by fireworks (*Oberster Gerichtshof* [Austrian Supreme Court, OGH] *Entscheidungen des österreichischen Obersten Gerichtshofes in Zivil- und Justizverwaltungssachen* [SZ] 46/36) or for factories emitting toxic fumes (OGH SZ 31/26) or producing ammunition (OGH SZ 25/84).

[19] H. Koziol, *Österreichisches Haftpflichtrecht*, vol. II (2nd edn. 1984), 575 et seq.; M. Schauer, in: M. Schwimann (supra fn. 17), § 2 EKHG no. 12 et seq.

b) Notion of Keeper in General

14 While ownership or possession as such are not required in order to establish strict liability under Austrian law, both can serve as indications for identifying the keeper (*Halter*) who is the relevant person when it comes to attributing loss according to the respective statutes, even though they do not necessarily use that particular term for naming the possible defendant.[20] Whoever is considered to be in control of the risk subject to a strict liability regime shall bear the consequences if the danger should turn into harm. It is not necessary, however, that he exercises actual control. Instead, it suffices if he is in a position *de facto* (and not necessarily *de iure*, even though the latter might be an indication of the former) to influence the degree of risk. Such control is typically coupled with some (not necessarily calculable) advantage that the defendant derives from the source of danger. If more than one person meets these requirements, all of them are jointly and severally liable.[21]

15 Apart from instances where terrorists use objects of their own (or someone permitted such use), they can also be keepers in the above-mentioned sense (and therefore be strictly liable) in case of an unauthorized use of dangerous objects since the right to dispose of such objects is not required for determining whether a person was in control thereof.[22] They will only be considered keepers, however, if they misappropriated the object with the intent to make more than singular short-term use of it since the notion of the keeper is built upon the idea that he can (at least theoretically) influence the risk, which requires a certain minimum time where such influence could be exerted.[23] Even if this period is too short in order to qualify the terrorists as keepers, they may nevertheless be liable for harm caused in the course of the unauthorized use of the dangerous object according to other provisions.[24]

16 As personal liability of the terrorists themselves may come as no surprise anyhow (and typically already follows from their acts performed with the intent to cause harm), the key question remains whether the fact that terrorists may be qualified as keepers under such circumstances can serve as a defence for the person whose object was used (and who would otherwise be considered to be the keeper in the absence of terrorist intervention). While the unauthorized use of the (original) keeper's object may in many cases deprive him of this quality relevant for establishing liability (and therefore release him), he may still be held jointly and severally liable with the terrorists, in particular if it was his own fault that they could make use of his property. This follows from the respective rules governing liability for motor vehicles which are mirrored in oth-

[20] See B.A. Koch/H. Koziol (supra fn. 16), no. 63 et seq.

[21] See also the explicit provisions in § 18 *Atomhaftungsgesetz* (Nuclear Liability Act, AtomHG), § 5 subs. 2 EKHG, § 148 *Luftfahrtgesetz* (Aviation Act, LFG).

[22] P. Apathy (supra fn. 17), § 5 no. 17; R. Reischauer, in: P. Rummel, *ABGB* II (2nd edn. 1992), § 1320 no. 7.

[23] Cf. P. Apathy (supra fn. 17), § 5 no. 18, § 6 no. 7; M. Schauer, in: M. Schwimann (supra fn. 17), § 5 EKHG no. 12; H. Koziol (supra fn. 19), 537 (fn. 156).

[24] See infra no. 20 et seq.

er strict liability statutes or at least applied by analogy. These provisions shall be presented in the following paragraphs.

2. Means of Transport

a) Motor Vehicles

Strict liability for motor vehicles is governed by the EKHG. Damages only have to be compensated by the keeper of the vehicle if caused while it was "in operation", which is interpreted extensively in court practice.[25] 17

While there is no doubt that a vehicle was in operation if it is used as a weapon itself (if a terrorist, for example, drives a bus at high speed into a group of people, or if he ignites the explosive load of a tanker), this is not true if it only served as a cover for a bomb: In such case, the typical risk of a car or bus covered by the EKHG does not emanate since an exploding bomb may cause equal harm if placed in a wastebin or other stationary location rather than a vehicle, whether it was moving or not.[26] 18

The mere fact that the terrorist acted intentionally does not exclude the applicability of the EKHG, since intentional acts do not rule out the statute's requirement of an "accident" as interpreted by the courts.[27] 19

Someone who drives a motor vehicle without the keeper's authorization is liable as though[28] a keeper (and therefore subject to strict liability), while the latter is freed from such responsibilities (§ 6 subs. 1 EKHG). The key aspect that shifts liability in this case is the fact that the unauthorized user effectively exerts a certain degree of control over the vehicle to the extent that the lawful keeper can no longer influence its actual use under the given circumstances. It is therefore not essential that the unauthorized user actually operates as the driver as long as the person steering the vehicle is acting under his instructions (whether voluntarily or not).[29] 20

If it was the (original) keeper's fault that such third person could make use of the car,[30] both of them are subject to joint and several liability (§ 6 subs. 1 EKHG). If, however, the unauthorized driver of the car was employed to oper- 21

[25] H. Koziol (supra fn. 19), 513 et seq.; P. Apathy (supra fn. 17), § 1 no. 8 et seq.; M. Schauer, in: M. Schwimann (supra fn. 17), § 1 EKHG no. 10–43; all with further references.

[26] H. Koziol, [2002] VR, 231.

[27] P. Apathy (supra fn. 17), § 1 no. 7; M. Schauer, in: M. Schwimann (supra fn. 17), § 1 EKHG no. 7; OGH SZ 56/51.

[28] If he deprived the keeper of the motor vehicle permanently (or at least for more than just singular short-term use), he may himself be liable *as* a keeper: cf. supra no. 15.

[29] M. Schauer, in: M. Schwimann (supra fn. 17), § 6 EKHG no. 5.

[30] The standard of care is fairly high: The keeper has to do anything reasonable under the circumstances that might be necessary to avoid unauthorized driving: P. Apathy (supra fn. 17), § 6 no. 17 et seq.; M. Schauer, in: M. Schwimann (supra fn. 17), § 6 EKHG no. 14–20; OGH [1997] *Evidenzblatt der Rechtsmittelentscheidungen* (EvBl, part of *Österreichische Juristen-Zeitung* [ÖJZ]) no. 79.

ate the vehicle (such as a chauffeur) or if the keeper had left him the car (though the driver abused such confidence),[31] then the keeper remains the sole person liable under the EKHG.[32] The person actually using the car in such case is only subject to a claim in tort, though the burden of proving fault is shifted onto him (§ 6 subs. 2 EKHG).

22 If, therefore, a terrorist, for example, causes damage by driving a bus into a group of people, he is not considered to be a keeper of the bus if he was employed by the company owning the bus, who remains the sole keeper under the EKHG and is consequently fully liable (up to the limits applicable under this statute). The owner of a car may also have to compensate the loss if he failed to lock the car; while the terrorist who takes advantage thereof will be jointly and severally liable, it is unlikely in practice that the owner will actually be able to seek contribution, so that he will effectively be left with the full loss (though subject to the statutory limits mentioned in the following paragraph).

23 According to § 15 no. 1 EKHG, damages for personal injury are limited to a maximum of € 291,000 per person (or alternatively to an annual rent of € 17,450). If more than one person is injured, the combined award must not exceed an overall total of € 872,000 (§ 15 no. 3 EKHG),[33] otherwise payments for each individual are to be reduced proportionately. § 16 EKHG limits compensation for destruction or impairment of property to a combined total of € 145,350.[34]

b) Trains

24 Liability for trains is governed by the same statute as the one for motor vehicles mentioned above, so that the same rules apply respectively. This is also true for the statutory limits to liability. As a noteworthy exception, § 16 no. 3 EKHG provides that damages to real property caused by trains is unlimited. Furthermore, the above-mentioned overall limit to compensation for injuries suffered by more than one person (§ 15 no. 3 EKHG)[35] does not apply in the case of train accidents.

[31] On these cases, see P. Apathy (supra fn. 17), § 6 no. 28 et seq.; M. Schauer, in: M. Schwimann (supra fn. 17), § 6 EKHG no. 27–38.

[32] On the liability of the keeper in such cases, see H. Koziol (supra fn. 19), 538 et seq.

[33] The overall cap is higher in case of accidents with certain buses. If the vehicle that caused the accident was transporting dangerous goods at the time, the maximum is augmented by an additional amount of € 1.3 million for damages resulting from such hazardous qualities.

[34] Again, in case the vehicle had dangerous goods on board, the keeper is liable for up to an additional € 1.3 million for any damages resulting just from such dangers.

[35] Supra no. 23.

c) Aircraft[36]

Liability of air carriers vis-à-vis their passengers and other contracting customers is to a large extent governed by international conventions ratified by Austria[37], furthermore by §§ 154 et seq. *Luftfahrtgesetz* (Aviation Act, LFG). 25

Tortious liability for damage caused to persons or property not aboard is governed by §§ 146 et seq. LFG. The keeper of an aircraft is strictly liable for any harm resulting from accidents in the course of its operation. As to the definition of "accident" in this context, the broad approach used in the context of liability for motor vehicles[38] equally applies here: It builds upon the notion of a sudden impact from without, which clearly encompasses terrorist attacks on or to the aircraft.[39] Furthermore, the bombing of aircraft or using aeroplanes to destroy constructions on the ground occurs "in the operation" of the aircraft, since terrorists thereby intentionally make use of the specific dangers of air transportation.[40] 26

Liability for the unauthorized use of aircraft is governed by the same principles as the above-mentioned rules applicable to motor vehicles[41]: § 147 LFG uses the same words as § 6 EKHG for aircraft accidents. The keeper of an aeroplane is therefore released from liability if terrorists effectively take over control of the aircraft, whether they steer it themselves or force the original pilot to act under their instructions.[42] If the terrorists gained control because of fault within the sphere of the keeper, the latter remains liable (jointly and severally with the terrorists). 27

Strict liability under the LFG is limited by maximum amounts listed in § 149 LFG, which depend upon the weight of the aircraft and reach up to € 6.5 million, of which one third is reserved for property damages, the other two thirds for personal injuries and death. The maximum one single victim can recover barely exceeds € 1 million. 28

d) Ships

While there is no statutory strict liability for ships, an analogous application of the respective statutes mentioned before could lead to a similar liability regime in court practice. So far, however, strict liability for ships has been denied[43] de- 29

[36] See generally H. Koziol, [2002] VR, 226–227.

[37] This includes, in particular, the Warsaw Convention. The Montreal Convention will be acceded to in accordance with EC decisions on this point: see B.A. Koch (supra fn. 7), no. 19 et seq.

[38] Supra no. 19.

[39] H. Koziol, Attentate mit Luftfahrzeugen: Haftung des Halters für nicht beförderte Personen und Sachen?, [2002] VR, 71 (72 et seq.).

[40] H. Koziol, [2002] VR, 226–227.

[41] Supra no. 20 et seq.

[42] H. Koziol, [2002] VR, 72.

[43] Courts thereby point at § 3 *Binnenschifffahrtsgesetz* (Law on private law aspects of inland navigation) and claim that there is no gap to be filled in light of this provision: OGH SZ 49/89; SZ 56/52; EvBl 1986/75; cf. P. Apathy (supra fn. 17), § 2 no. 16. This is not entirely convincing since it merely confirms the vicarious liability of the ship-owner for his crew and is not intended to establish any grounds of liability of its own. Otherwise, strict liability could never be introduced by way of analogy since there are of course rules on fault and vicarious liability in the ABGB which are of general application.

spite the above-mentioned admission of analogy in other cases[44], which underlines the fact that the spectrum of no-fault liabilities in Austrian law is rather incomplete. Terrorist acts involving the use of ships is, therefore, currently governed by traditional rules of fault liability.

3. Enterprises or Other Facilities

a) Atomic Power Plants or Similar Facilities

30 The AtomHG 1999 holds the entrepreneur ("Betriebsunternehmer")[45] of a nuclear facility liable for all damage to persons or property caused by the operation of the facility (§ 3 subs. 1 AtomHG 1999). He is equally liable for damage caused by nuclear material that is on its way to another facility or that came from another plant with his consent (§ 3 para. 2 AtomHG 1999). § 4 AtomHG 1999 provides for the liability of the carrier of nuclear material as long as he cannot prove that he did not know of the radioactive quality thereof. Furthermore, the keeper of a radionuclide is liable for any damage resulting from ionizing radiation (either by itself or in combination with other dangerous features thereof, § 9 AtomHG 1999). He can avoid liability by proving that he and his staff have observed all due care necessary to avoid harm under the circumstances.[46]

31 In contrast to prior law (*Atomhaftpflichtgesetz*, in force until 1998), whose § 9 included a defence for "war, armed conflicts, civil war, revolts or turmoil", the new statute abolished any such defences and now holds the operator of a nuclear facility absolutely liable for any realisation of nuclear risks, including those triggered by external influences such as *force majeure* or armed attacks.[47] The only remains of the prior defence are now reflected in § 6 AtomHG 1999, which obliges the operator to take out minimum insurance coverage for his potential liability. Such compulsory insurance must extend to *force majeure* events, but need not include risks arising from "war, armed conflicts, civil war, revolts or turmoil" (which were held to be uninsurable by the legislator[48]), which arguably includes terrorist attacks.

[44] Supra no. 13.

[45] The entrepreneur is defined in § 2 para. 4 AtomHG 1999 as the person or entity who operates the nuclear facility and who controls the economic success thereof. In any case responsibility lies with the person who holds the license to run the facility.

[46] While the wording of § 9 subs. 2 AtomHG 1999 corresponds to § 9 subs. 2 EKHG inasmuch as the required diligence is concerned ("jede nach den Umständen des Einzelfalls gebotene Sorgfalt"), the Explanatory Commentary to the new AtomHG 1999 speaks of the keeper's subjective fault (1357 BlgNR XX. GP, 26 et seq.), while the keeper of a vehicle is only exonerated if he complies with an objective standard of care (cf. infra no. 45). The latter must also be true for liability under § 9 AtomHG 1999.

[47] These two examples were expressly used in the Explanatory Commentary, 1357 BlgNR XX. GP, 15.

[48] Explanatory Commentary, 1357 BlgNR XX. GP, 23.

b) Facilities for Genetic Engineering

Whoever runs facilities for genetic engineering is liable for damages to persons or property resulting from operations or works with genetically modified organisms or after such organisms have been released, but before they have been actually marketed under a valid permit (§ 79a *Gentechnikgesetz* [Gene Technology Act, GTG]).[49] Liability is limited to harm caused by the altered properties of the organisms (either alone or in combination with other qualities thereof such as toxicity). 32

Liability is, however, excluded if the harm was caused by "war, similar hostility, civil war, revolts or an extraordinary, unavoidable natural event whose consequences could not have been prevented" (§ 79c no. 1 GTG), and even more so if caused by "a third person not taking part in the operation who acted with the intention to cause harm", but only "if all adequate measures of safety have been followed" (§ 79c no. 2 GTG). Effectively, therefore, the operator of such a facility will not be liable for acts of terrorism involving his facility or its products unless the terrorist was employed thereby, or if the operator failed to apply the utmost care in the operation and its security.[50] 33

c) Mains and Pipelines

Accidents caused by the effects of gas (other than natural gas) or electricity as conducted by mains are covered by § 1a *Reichshaftpflichtgesetz* (Reich Liability Act, RHPflG) 1943.[51] The holder of these mains is liable unless the damage occurred internally within a building or confined piece of land, or if it involved some electric appliance.[52] He is further subject to claims for harm caused by the mere existence of the mains unless the latter are in proper condition, which they are if they are intact and correspond to the current state of engineering. Liability is excluded in cases of *force majeure* (§ 1a subs. 3 no. 3 RHPflG), which is held to include terrorist attacks.[53] 34

§ 10 Pipelines Act (RohrlG) provides for strict liability in case of damage caused by pipelines.[54] The mere operation of pipelines is considered to be dangerous, though only operational risks are covered.[55] There is also an explicit exclusion of risks resulting from acts of terrorism: § 12 no. 3 RohrlG bars liability if caused by "war, armed conflicts, civil war, turmoil, revolts or terrorist 35

[49] See generally J. Stabentheiner, Die neue Gentechnikhaftung, [1998] ÖJZ, 521.
[50] J. Stabentheiner, [1998] ÖJZ, 521.
[51] A further provision is § 21 *Starkstromwegegesetz* (Act on power supply lines), which covers certain damage to the land where the installations are made upon. § 29 subs. 2 *leg. cit.* refers to the RHPflG.
[52] This exception does not apply, however, if the damage was caused by a sudden current surge which affects these internal installations. See H. Koziol (supra fn. 19), 417 et seq.
[53] H. Koziol (supra fn. 19), 421.
[54] Excluded are water mains or pipelines transporting natural gas as well as gas at an overpressure lower than 0.5 bar, furthermore all pipes within a commercial structure or mains serving only for the local distribution of gas.
[55] See H. Koziol (supra fn. 19), 428.

attacks". However, a high standard of care applies, so that this exclusion may not apply if the operator did not use the utmost care to prevent such harm.[56] It is difficult to predict how far such precaution must go in practice, though: One not only would have to consider the likelihood of terrorist attacks on the particular pipeline, but also take into account that it is primarily the duty of the public authorities to prevent acts of terrorism.[57]

36 §§ 34 et seq. GWG introduce strict liability for natural gas distributors subject to certain maximum amounts as listed by § 35 GWG[58] and coupled with an insurance requirement (§§ 14 para. 1 no. 2, 37 GWG). The defences listed in § 12 RohrlG are mirrored in § 36 GWG, so that the aforementioned rules apply accordingly.

d) Dams

37 While there is currently no explicit statutory rule on liability for dams, § 26 para. 2 *Wasserrechtsgesetz* (Act on the Use of Water, WRG) seems to apply at first sight: This provision holds that a person entitled to exploit water contained in a facility designed for its use is liable for any harm caused to real property or a building in the course of the lawful use of this facility or for the impairment of another right to use the water if such negative effect was unforeseeable at the time the facility was licensed. The meaning of this paragraph is different, however, and only covers harm caused by the lawful use of the facility and does not extend to terrorist attacks on it.[59]

38 One might further think of a general analogy to other strict liabilities.[60] Even if courts accepted such reasoning, they would apply the *force majeure* defence as outlined below, so that the operator of a dam most likely will not be held strictly liable under Austrian law (which does not rule out that he may have to account for negligent supervision of such construction).[61]

e) Other Facilities or Constructions

39 Apart from the instances of strict liability already mentioned, there is no further special legislation on liability for industrial plants, not even for particularly dangerous ones such as refineries or factories producing explosives.[62] If they cause harm, it may well be possible, however, that the Supreme Court

[56] This follows from the concept embodied in § 9 EKHG outlined above (supra no. 45): H. Koziol, [2002] VR, 229.

[57] Infra no. 50 et seq.

[58] Caps for personal injuries or death correspond to the amounts quoted in § 15 EKHG (but do not apply to medical costs or burial expenses). Damages to property must not exceed € 8,760,000 or, if and to the extent real property is harmed, an additional amount of € 9,490,000.

[59] H. Koziol (supra fn. 19), 330 et seq.; F. Kerschner, Zur Haftung nach § 26 Wasserrechtsgesetz und zum Deliktsstatut im IPR, [1983] JBl, 338.

[60] In favour F. Kerschner, [1983] JBl, 338 (at fn. 54) for dams and similar facilities with high potential of harm if attacked. On the possibility of analogy in general see supra no. 13.

[61] H. Koziol, [2002] VR, 230.

[62] § 2 RHPflG only slightly extends vicarious liability of the operator of a factory.

would consider a general analogy to other strict liabilities also in those scenarios.[63] This would not help the victims in cases of terrorist attacks, though, since such analogy would include the availability of the *force majeure* defence as mentioned before. The operator of such a facility would therefore only be liable in cases where he failed to apply the utmost care in protecting his facility against such attacks, which would be determined in light of the probability (*inter alia*) that it may become the target of terrorists.[64]

If harm to persons or property is caused by parts of a building blasted into the air by the explosion of a bomb, for example, the victims may at first sight have a chance to obtain compensation from the owner of the building under § 1319 *Allgemeines bürgerliches Gesetzbuch* (Austrian Civil Code, ABGB), which provides for the liability of the keeper of a building that collapses or of which parts fall off. This is not an instance of strict liability in a narrower sense, since it merely shifts the burden of proving fault onto the keeper: He goes free if he can prove that he has observed all due care as is reasonable under the circumstances in order to prevent harm, which is determined objectively.[65] While this is still advantageous for the plaintiffs, they may not succeed in cases of terrorist attacks, however, since liability under § 1319 ABGB requires that the harm can be traced to some defective condition of the building, which will typically be overridden as a cause of the injuries in cases of bombings. This reduces the possible causes of action to fault-based claims, e.g. on the grounds of inadequate surveillance of a building that may be attractive as a target for terrorists.[66] 40

4. Products

If terrorists poison foodstuffs or other goods (which includes e.g. tap water[67]) falling under the *Produkthaftungsgesetz* (Act on Product Liability, PHG), which is modelled on the European Product Liability Directive, the producer may be strictly liable for any harm caused thereby to consumers or innocent bystanders: If the product was poisonous or otherwise harmful at the time it was put into circulation, there is no doubt that it was "defective" within the meaning of § 5 PHG. The producer may most likely not avail himself of a defence listed in § 8 PHG, in particular because the state of scientific and technical knowledge at the time the product was put into circulation most likely would have enabled him to discover the existence of such defect (§ 8 no. 2 PHG). There is no general *force majeure* defence under the PHG.[68] 41

[63] Supra no. 13.
[64] H. Koziol, [2002] VR, 229.
[65] R. Reischauer, in: P. Rummel (supra fn. 22), § 1319 no. 15–17; H. Koziol (supra fn. 19), 400–401.
[66] On liability under § 1319 ABGB in the context of terrorism, see H. Koziol, [2002] VR, 228–229.
[67] Cf. the Report for the Commission of the European Communities on the Application of Directive 85/374/EEC on Liability for Defective Products (Study Contract No. ETD/93/B5 – 3000/MI/06) 5 (on an English case concerning the pollution of public water).
[68] H. Koziol, [2002] VR, 230.

B. Can Terror Attacks be Classified as a Defence like Act of God/Force Majeure/Unavoidable Event?

42 Some strict liability statutes explicitly refer to acts of terrorism as a defence of such kind: This is true for § 12 no. 3 RohrleitungsG as well as § 36 no. 3 GWG.[69] In statutes which do not mention terrorist acts specifically, but nevertheless admit the defence of *force majeure* (e.g. § 1a subs. 3 no. 3 RHPflG), it is argued that illegal attacks by third parties fall under this notion and therefore exonerate the keeper.[70]

43 Still, *force majeure* is sometimes treated differently to acts of third parties, even if the latter are as extraordinary and unexpected as terrorist attacks: While the most far-reaching strict liability statute in Austrian law, the Nuclear Liability Act (AtomHG), does not allow either case as a defence, it nevertheless differentiates between the two when it comes to imposing compulsory insurance cover: § 6 AtomHG requires coverage for *force majeure*, but not for war and the like, the latter including terrorist acts as argued before.[71] It is important to note, however, that this does not affect the absolute liability of the nuclear facility's operator, even if it was attacked by terrorists.

44 While the LFG equally does not include a *force majeure* defence, acts of terrorism will nevertheless not lead to liability of the airline, but for exceptional circumstances[72]: In most scenarios imaginable so far, the terrorists took over control of the aircraft, which relieves the airline from liability inasmuch as it is not at fault for such loss of control.

45 The most important strict liability statute, the EKHG (applicable to motor vehicles and trains), does not speak of "force majeure", but includes the defence of the so-called "unavoidable event", which is broader and therefore includes the notion of the former.[73] Under § 9 EKHG, the keeper escapes liability if the vehicle was not defective and "all due diligence according to the circumstances of the case" had been employed. The standard of care under this rule is very high, however it is not just ordinary care that has to be exercised according to the EKHG, but the utmost care ever possible to an experienced expert in a similar case.[74] While following the regular standards of care might relieve the defendant from personal liability, he is therefore not exonerated unless this highest possible diligence was employed.[75] While this defence extends to cases where the accident was caused by the victim himself, by some third per-

[69] Supra no. 35 and 36.
[70] Supra no. 34.
[71] Supra no. 31.
[72] See supra no. 25 et seq. and infra the responses to Cases I and II.
[73] H. Koziol (supra fn. 19), 547–548.
[74] See *generally* H. Koziol, *Österreichisches Haftpflichtrecht*, vol. I (3rd edn. 1997), no. 6/20 with further references; on § 9 EKHG in particular M. Schauer, in: M. Schwimann (supra fn. 17), § 9 EKHG no. 19–35. Alike provisions can be found in § 53 para. 4 ForstG or § 164 para. 2 MinroG.
[75] Cf. OGH 2 Ob 2178/96z (not yet published).

son or by animals, it does not apply if such third person or animal triggered an extraordinary operational hazard (so-called "außergewöhnliche Betriebsgefahr", § 9 para. 2 EKHG).[76]

The influence of terrorists will hardly ever be considered under § 9 EKHG, however if the vehicle was only used as a hiding place for a bomb, its peculiar dangerousness is not involved and therefore liability under the EKHG is not established in the first place. The keeper equally goes free – as explained earlier – if the terrorist gained control over the car either as a keeper[77] or in the sense of § 6 EKHG.[78] In those exceptional cases of § 6 EKHG where the keeper remains liable[79], he will hardly be able to avail himself of the "unavoidable event" defence of § 9 EKHG.[80] 46

C. *If There Is Another Person Liable Besides or Instead of the Terrorist, for Which Kind of Damages is He/She Liable (for Example also Compensation for Consequential Damage like Plundering Following a Terror Attack)?*

The standard principles of damages and causation apply, in particular the rules on consequential loss. The scope of compensable harm will further be determined by the protective purpose of the rule that the defendant has violated.[81] 47

For tortious acts to property, § 1324 ABGB provides for gradated damages according to the degree of fault. Therefore, if the tortfeasor acted with slight negligence, he only has to pay the "eigentliche Schadloshaltung", that is "actual loss", but neither lost profit nor non-pecuniary damage. Prevailing opinion holds that the latter is true for all cases of strict liability (unless expressly ruled differently by statute) and that therefore loss of profit will not have to be indemnified.[82] 48

If the keeper of a dangerous object is jointly and severally liable with the terrorist, the former's strict liability may be limited by statutory caps as explained before, while fault liability of the terrorist will always be unlimited. 49

[76] See O. Edlbacher, Die „außergewöhnliche Betriebsgefahr" im Spiegel von Lehre und Rechtsprechung, [1989] *Zeitschrift für Verkehrsrecht* (ZVR), 193.

[77] Supra no. 15.

[78] Supra no. 19 et seq.

[79] Supra no. 21.

[80] Cf. P. Apathy (supra fn. 17), § 9 EKHG no. 10.

[81] See in particular H. Koziol (supra fn. 74), no. 13/1 et seq.

[82] P. Apathy (supra fn. 17), § 1 no. 4; B.A. Koch/H. Koziol (supra fn. 16), no. 102 (where this common opinion is criticized).

III. Fault Liability

A. *At Public Facilities such as Airports, Train Stations, Sports Stadiums etc., Who Is Responsible that no Terrorist Enters and Causes Harm? The Entity that Runs the Facility, Enterprises that Obtain an Advantage Therefrom (such as Airlines or Organizers of Sports Events), the State, or any Other Person(s)? How far Do These Duties of Care Go in that Respect?*

1. The State's General Duty to Maintain Safety and Security

50 As a general rule, the state is responsible for maintaining the safety of its citizens, which includes the prevention of terrorist attacks.[83] According to § 20 *Sicherheitspolizeigesetz* (Law on Public Safety and Order, SPG), state authorities have to maintain public safety *inter alia* by defending against risks and by protecting legal interests against possible harm.[84] § 21 para. 1 SPG defines the former aspect in a rather broad sense by referring to "general dangers" that have to be prevented, which is further defined by § 16 SPG.[85] State authorities not only have to immediately put an end to dangerous attacks (§ 21 para. 2 SPG), but also need to observe any "groups" when there is substantiated fear in light of their structure or other characteristics that criminal attacks on public safety may follow, in particular violent acts motivated by ideology or religious beliefs (§ 21 para. 3 SPG, so-called extended risk investigation). § 28a SPG provides for other duties to investigate the likelihood of risks the state is obliged to prevent according to this statute.

51 § 22 SPG further explains the scope of necessary protection by introducing explicit duties to take precautionary measures. Apart from the protection of national institutions as well as representations and representatives of international persons, state authorities are therefore required to protect people who cannot defend themselves properly against dangerous attacks. They further have to safeguard objects which are unprotected against such risks because they are no longer under the control of those persons entitled thereto. § 22 para. 2 SPG establishes a general rule that state authorities need to prevent all probable attacks on life, health, freedom, morality, assets or the environment. If such an attack has to be feared, all persons concerned need to be informed and offered protection (§ 22 para. 4 SPG).

52 While this statute therefore provides for rather broad duties of public authorities to prevent illegal activities, liability of the state does not follow from the mere occurrence of incidents. The Austrian Statute on Government Liability (*Amtshaftungsgesetz*, AHG) naturally requires that the authorities have at least

[83] B.-Ch. Funk, Das neue Sicherheitspolizeirecht – Kodifikation und Reform einer klassischen Verwaltungsmaterie, [1994] JBl, 137.

[84] H. Koziol, [2002] VR, 227–228.

[85] According to § 16 para. 1 SPG, a "general danger" exists in particular if there is a likelihood of intentional crimes as further qualified by the StGB or if three or more people form a criminal association.

negligently violated a duty of care,[86] which is evaluated according to objective standards since authorities have to be considered experts in their field (§ 1299 ABGB).

As to the required standard of care, several factors have to be taken into consideration (as under the general law of torts)[87], including the value of the protected interests, the likelihood of harm, the expectations of the victim, the feasibility and reasonableness of preventive measures. This already indicates the difficulties in establishing liability according to these standards: The latter aspects in particular may be hard to assess since neither the probability of a terrorist attack nor the extent of the ensuing harm may be predictable, nor may available resources be reasonably increased indefinitely to prevent any such incident: If public authorities were not in a position to learn about terrorist activities in advance or to prevent them in light of their current staff or equipment but could have done so with better resources, the question arises to what extent budgetary means would have had to be assigned to such safety measures, which not only depends upon the overall finances but also on the predictability of the risk. In any case, can the state not be held liable for acts of legislation, which are excluded from governmental liability altogether?[88] A claim can therefore hardly be based on the state's failure to provide for adequate financial means since the budget is decided upon by the legislator (though liability may lie for inadequate preparation of parliamentary acts by the executive branch). 53

2. The State's Special Duty to Maintain the Security of Civil Aviation

The Act on the Prevention of Criminal Acts against the Security of Civil Aviation (*Bundesgesetz über den Schutz vor Straftaten gegen die Sicherheit von Zivilluftfahrzeugen*[89]) primarily obliges the state authorities to perform security checks on airports. § 1 of the said Act describes the scope of protection. According to this provision, public authorities are under a special duty to protect civil aircraft and the people aboard or entering the aircraft against dangerous attacks performed with the use of weapons, ammunition, explosives or the like.[90] It also obliges the operators of airports as well as airlines to contribute to such protection to the extent possible as outlined by further provisions of this Act. 54

The Federal Ministry of the Interior may, in agreement with the Ministry of Economics, delegate such duties to private entities who can be hired by con- 55

[86] R. Rebhahn, *Staatshaftung wegen mangelnder Gefahrenabwehr* (1997), in particular 471 et seq.

[87] See R. Rebhahn (supra fn. 86), 481 et seq.

[88] § 1 AHG limits the scope of this statute to the enforcement of laws.

[89] BGBl 824/1992.

[90] It is not entirely clear, however, if only those people mentioned are protected by the scope of this statute, or whether other persons such as airport staff or passers-by are equally covered. The latter is supported by the words of § 7 *leg. cit.*, which speaks of compensation "to whoever", while the former alternative is based upon the above-mentioned wording of § 1.

tract to perform such checks. If they are at fault in the course of the fulfilment of these duties, § 7 of the said Act holds the state vicariously liable for any harm resulting therefrom.

56 According to a recent amendment introduced in July 2002[91], liability of the state, which was previously unlimited (as all other cases of governmental liability under the AHG still are), can now no longer exceed "the amount of one million Euros". This ridiculously low figure has been introduced without the slightest indication whether it applies per incident, per airport, per annum or any other clarification of such kind. The same amendment extended the state's right of recourse against the entity to which security checks have been delegated: While it was previously in accordance with the principles of the Act on Government Liability that such recourse is impossible in cases of merely slight negligence of the delegee, this limitation has been deleted. It is highly likely that this unprecedented legislation will be declared unconstitutional, so that the old wording of the statute will ultimately have to be reinstated.

57 The question to what extent security checks were performed negligently cannot be answered easily. One would certainly have to consider the risks involved: The more dangerous the situation is, the more care has to be applied when checking passengers at the gate. A further aspect are the technical means available for identifying potential criminals going aboard, which not only extends to the equipment actually at hand, but also possibly improved industrial standards which should have been acquired in order to keep pace with the development of crime and terrorism rates. Furthermore, one should also consider how far such controls should reasonably go: How much intrusion into their privacy do law-abiding passengers have to bear in order to support the protection of the public at large? After all, searching passengers not only aims at maintaining their own safety, but also the security of other people, which is particularly obvious at airport terminals where security checks are performed not for individual flights, but for all people entering the gates.

58 Another issue may concern the failure of technical equipment used in the course of the security checks. Apart from instances of wrong use or lack of maintenance, which poses no significant problems, the question remains who is liable for technical malfunctioning, in particular if it was entirely unforeseeable. While it may go too far to introduce strict liability for such machinery[92], it can certainly be argued that it should be up to those in charge of the security checks to prove that no negligence within their sphere contributed to the failure of the system.

[91] BGBl I 104/2002. On the problems inherent in this new legislation, see H. Koziol, [2002] VR, 227.

[92] There are, however, already some narrow cases of strict government liability for failures of computers: See B.A. Koch/H. Koziol (supra fn. 16), no. 23, 52.

3. Public Events

The above-mentioned *Sicherheitspolizeigesetz*[93] also includes general rules on maintaining safety in public places (§ 27 SPG) as well as specific powers of public authorities to ensure and effectuate security at public events (e.g. § 41 SPG). 59

Federal laws such as the *Versammlungsgesetz* (Act on Assemblies, VslgG) and legislation of the Austrian provinces (such as the Viennese *Veranstaltungsgesetz* [provincial statute on public gatherings] and the *Veranstaltungsstättengesetz* [provincial statute governing locations where public gatherings are held]) deal with matters of organizing, regulating and permitting public gatherings and include several duties of the organizers of such events which may be of relevance in this context. 60

§ 11 VslgG for example lays down the general obligation of the organizers of public gatherings to maintain security at their events, which, however, does not preclude secondary duties of the public authorities to control compliance with statutory provisions or with specific directives of the competent agency. Since § 11 VslgG is intended to protect the audience from the dangers arising from within the gathering, it does not impose any special duty upon the organizers to specifically protect them from terrorist attacks as long as the regular standard of safety is maintained. The organizers therefore need to ensure that, for example, escape routes are accessible, that the appropriate number of doctors and ambulances[94] are available, that people entering a mass event are searched upon entering and the like, and will be liable if harm is caused or aggravated by failure to do so, but not beyond such duties. 61

There are other statutory provisions which regulate the layout and general safety requirements for buildings where public events are held.[95] While these provisions – again – primarily address risks originating from the event as such (e.g. the danger of fire in theatres), they are nevertheless also designed to ensure that the public can safely escape from such facilities in cases of emergency, which includes turmoil or other threatening situations following terrorist acts aimed at or carried out in the course of the event. If people, who would have remained unharmed had these provisions been obeyed, are injured, the keepers of the building or the organizers of the event[96] may be held liable for those negative consequences even though they may not be liable for the primary impact of the terrorist act per se. 62

[93] Supra no. 50 et seq.

[94] See e.g., § 24 of the Viennese *Veranstaltungsgesetz*.

[95] See e.g. the *Bundestheatersicherheitsgesetz* (Act on the safety at Federal Theatres) or provincial statutes regulating public buildings (including the above-mentioned Viennese *Veranstaltungsstättengesetz*).

[96] Cf. the following provisions of the above-mentioned Viennese *Veranstaltungsgesetz*: § 28 specifies the duties of the organizers of public events, and § 29 the duties of the keeper of the building or facility where the event is held.

63 Apart from the above-mentioned general duties of the state and the organizers of public events, the 1985 European Convention on Spectator Violence and Misbehaviour at Sports Events and in particular at Football Matches, which Austria has ratified, may bring about further specific obligations of both public authorities as well as private sports organizations to provide for a certain level of security at public sports events. Even though the Convention is primarily designed for coping with violence and misbehaviour amongst spectators (in particular hooligans), the various duties to safeguard the security of innocent viewers and other bystanders will invariably also lead to at least some protection against acts of terrorism. In cases of failure to abide by such standards, courts may likely consider those rules when attributing the negative consequences arising therefrom.

4. Weapons, Explosives and the Like

64 Federal acts such as the *Waffengesetz* (Act on Arms, WaffG) and the *Schieß- und Sprengmittelgesetz* (Act on Ammunition and Explosives) specify several duties of the state designed to control the use of weapons and explosives, which foresees licences for the production, acquisition and use thereof. The more dangerous the respective objects are, the tighter are the requirements for obtaining such licences. Inasmuch as the public authorities fail to observe these requirements or otherwise misapply the statutory provisions, the state will be liable for any negative consequences arising therefrom under the Statute on Government Liability. This might be relevant in the context of terrorism, for example, if an activist of a terrorist organization is granted a licence to hold weapons despite the fact that he does not meet the qualities listed in § 8 WaffG ("Verläßlichkeit" or reliability), or if he has to be considered dangerous within the meaning of §§ 12 or 13 WaffG, which oblige the state to temporarily or permanently withdraw a licence and immediately seize the weapons in his control.

65 Apart from such public duties to survey and control the use of weapons and explosives, the above-mentioned statutes and their implementing regulations specify in more or less detail duties of the permit holders to keep and secure these items.[97] Producers and vendors, but also private persons who fail to abide by these provisions will be held liable for violating such "Schutzgesetze".

[97] See e.g. § 3 *Zweite Waffengesetz-Durchführungsverordnung* (Second regulation implementing the Act on weapons, 2. WaffV) specifying the requirements for "safe keeping" of weapons, or the provisions in the *Schieß- und Sprengmittelmonopolsverordnung* (Regulation on the state monopoly for ammunition and explosives) and the attachments thereto particularizing the duties to store explosives and the like.

B. *To What Extent Do Individuals or Entities Have a Duty of Care to Participate in the Active Avoidance of Terrorist Acts?*

Unless the state's duty to maintain public safety has been delegated to a company or natural person[98], there is no general obligation on citizens to take active measures in order to prevent terrorist acts. There may, however, be a special duty arising under the circumstances if, for example, the likelihood of terrorist attacks on a specific building or facility is so evident that the keeper has to take extraordinary precautionary measures.[99] 66

Furthermore, there is a general duty expressed by § 95 StGB to help others in cases of emergency such as accidents or public danger: In order to avoid criminal (and civil) liability, one has to do everything possible and reasonable to rescue people from the danger of death or significant bodily harm. It is beyond reasonableness, however, if such aid should involve risks to life and limb of the rescuer or if other "important" interests are at stake (§ 95 para. 2 StGB). It is therefore necessary, for example, to inform the police if one learns of criminal activities likely to cause harm to other people[100], but there is no obligation to risk one's life in order to prevent terrorists from carrying out their plans. 67

IV. Cases

In all the following hypothetical cases, there is no doubt that the terrorist will be personally liable for his intentional acts. In case of suicidal acts, the estate of the terrorist will inherit his obligation to compensate the victims.[101] It is, however, highly unlikely that his assets – if one could ever get a hold thereof – would ever cover any substantial part of the whole loss he caused. This may be more true for the financial means of the terrorist organization backing the actual tortfeasor, which will jointly and severally be liable for supporting the latter in the planning and carrying out of the attack, but again, it may not be easy to seize such assets.[102] 68

1. A Terrorist Hijacks an Aeroplane and Crashes into

a) A Building

Apart from the claims of the victims aboard (or their dependants respectively), which are governed by the Warsaw Convention and §§ 154 et seq. LFG, liability of the airline as the keeper of the aircraft vis-à-vis claimants on the ground (including the owner of the building) may arise only if the airline or its staff were negligent in preventing the terrorist from taking over control of the aircraft, e.g. if international safety standards aboard were not obeyed: While in- 69

98 See e.g. supra no. 55.
99 Cf. supra no. 40.
100 Cf. OGH *Entscheidungen des österreichischen Obersten Gerichtshofes in Strafsachen und Disziplinarangelegenheiten* (SSt) 55/36.
101 R. Welser, in: H. Koziol/R. Welser, *Bürgerliches Recht* II (12th edn. 2001), 414.
102 But see supra no. 3.

tentionally steering the hijacked plane into a building per se does not rule out strict liability under §§ 146 et seq. LFG, the defence of § 147 LFG applies in this case which builds upon the fact that actual control of the plane was taken over by the terrorist without fault on the side of the airline or its staff.[103]

70 Since security checks at the airport are not within the responsibility of the airlines, but are the duty of the state according to the above-mentioned Act on the Prevention of Criminal Acts against the Security of Civil Aviation[104], the airline would not be liable for the fact that the terrorist could bring weapons aboard that could have been discovered at the gate unless it has violated a remaining duty, for example, if airline employees in charge of controlling baggage going onboard could have detected the bomb, or if the crew could have disarmed the terrorist aboard.

71 In case of inadequate security checks falling under the said statute, victims could therefore sue the state under the Act on Government liability for violating the necessary safety standards.[105] Another possible defendant in case of weak security checks is the company that actually performed them under a contract with the state, although their resources (and insurance cover) may not suffice to cover the totality of losses.

b) A Nuclear Plant

72 Apart from the possible defendants under variant a), the question arises whether the operator of the nuclear plant may also have to account for the additional harm arising because of the special dangers peculiar to his facility. Since the current *Atomhaftungsgesetz* was introduced with the legislator's intent (*inter alia*) to abolish the *force majeure* defence, the operator of the nuclear plant will remain strictly liable for any harm caused by the release of radiation (but not, for example, if only the building as such is affected and falling bricks damage persons or property, while the reactor remains safe).[106] This is even true in cases like the one at hand where the nuclear plant is targeted and radiation is set free with (at least conditional) intent of a third party (the terrorist).

[103] See supra no. 26 et seq. Another case where the defence of § 147 LFG does not apply is when the terrorist was employed by the airline as a pilot (§ 147 para. 2 LFG).

[104] Supra no. 54 et seq.

[105] The above-mentioned limitation (supra no. 56), which was recently introduced, does not apply in this case since people or property injured on the ground are not within the scope of this Act, though this is not entirely clear: see H. Koziol, [2002] VR, 228.

[106] Supra no. 30–31.

2. A Terrorist Sets a Bomb Situated in an Aeroplane and the Plane Crashes into

a) A Residential Area

73 Strict liability under the *Luftfahrtgesetz* for damage caused to third parties on the ground[107] is not subject to any defences apart from the above-mentioned case of a terrorist who takes over control of the aircraft (§ 147 LFG). Therefore, liability of the airline carrier is not excluded in this hypothetical since placing a bomb inside an aeroplane does not fall under said exception[108]. However, such liability is limited by maximum amounts as mentioned above[109].

b) A Nuclear Plant

74 Again, the same rules apply as in Case I. Since the operator of the nuclear plant cannot escape liability even in a case of intentional targeting, he will remain strictly liable in the instant hypothetical where his plant is hit accidentally.

3. A Terrorist Drives with Somebody's Car or Bus into a Crowd of People

75 Apart from liability for such intentional act, the terrorist in this hypothetical will also be strictly liable either as the (new) keeper of the car or like the keeper according to § 6 EKHG.[110]

76 If the owner (or other original keeper) made it possible that the terrorist took possession of the car (e.g. by leaving it open and unattended), he will still be liable next to the terrorist even though the latter assumed actual control, in which case both of them will be (jointly and severally) liable under the EKHG.[111] The victims will therefore be able to sue the original keeper for their full loss up to the statutory limits outlined above, leaving the keeper with a (rather theoretical) right of recourse against the terrorist (or the latter's estate, if he was killed in this attack).

[107] See generally supra no. 25–28.

[108] One may, however, argue, that the terrorist wanted to purposely influence the course and fate of the aircraft by placing a bomb inside the aircraft, and thereby most likely took over much more effective control over the plane than his colleague in Case 1 who actually went on the aircraft and threatened the pilot (or took over steering himself): In the latter case, the terrorist still runs the risk of being overpowered by the crew or the passengers, while the bomb – if constructed properly – explodes invariably unless detected beforehand. While it seems odd to treat those two cases differently, one must consider that the legislator must have been aware of those two alternatives, but only provided for a defence in the latter case, so that an analogous application in the former seems to be unavailable. See also the Explanatory Commentary to these provisions: 758 BlgNR XX. GP, 17: While the risks of terrorism are not mentioned at all, it is stated explicitly that *force majeure* is no defence to liability under §§ 146 et seq. LFG.

[109] Supra no. 28.

[110] Supra no. 20–22.

[111] H. Koziol, [2002] VR, 231.

77 If the original keeper of the vehicle had hired the terrorist for its operation (e.g. as a bus or cab driver), though ignorant of his peculiar dangerousness, the bus company or other employer remains the sole keeper and is therefore alone strictly liable for the harm caused (again, up to the statutory limits of the EKHG). Since the terrorist remains personally liable for his intentional acts (though only under fault liability), the keeper could (again, most likely not effectively) recover his contribution from the terrorist or his estate. Since courts tend not to take strict liability into account in cases of concurring fault liability, the right of recourse may even go up to the full amount paid out in compensation by the keeper.[112]

4. A Terrorist Hides a Bomb in a Car Which Explodes Within a Crowd of People

78 Whether or not the terrorist is the keeper of the car in the instant case (which he could be even if he had stolen the car[113]), he will be the only person liable (apart from the terrorist organization that sponsored this attack) in this case. Strict liability under the EKHG does not apply here since it requires that the car was "in operation", and that the typical risk of the car emanated. This is not true in the case of an exploding bomb (even if transported to the location of the explosion by car): The harm resulting therefrom does not differ significantly from a case where the bomb was placed e.g. hidden under a bench or in a wastebin.[114] The mere fact that the vehicle made it possible to put the bomb into this particular location does not suffice: Otherwise also the keeper of the taxi in which the terrorist was driven to the place of the attack would be liable, even if the terrorist had hidden the bomb outside the sphere of the cab after arrival.

[112] See B.A. Koch/H. Koziol (supra fn.16), no. 82.
[113] See supra no. 15.
[114] H. Koziol, [2002] VR, 231.

FRANCE
LIABILITY FOR ACTS OF TERRORISM UNDER FRENCH LAW

Olivier Moréteau[1] *and Fabien Lafay*[2]

I. Introduction

In the past two decades, France has been severely hit by a number of terrorist attacks, mostly by way of bombs placed in front of department stores, schools or synagogues as well as in the Paris underground. This generated a strong public reaction, which triggered the development and the improvement of a firm policy to prevent the occurrence of terrorist attacks and to ensure proper compensation of victims of such attacks whenever they occur.[3] Prevention is based on improved international co-operation and better co-ordination between various government agencies (*Division nationale de lutte antiterroriste*), which so far have prevented major attacks against the European Parliament and Strasbourg cathedral. The most visible public action is the *Plan Vigipirate*, co-ordinated by the Minister of the Interior and activated at times of crisis and major threat: the Gulf War 1991, terrorist attacks in Paris and Lyon in 1995 and 1996, Football World Cup 1998, attacks in Corsica November 2000 and following the events of 11 September 2001. It includes the reinforced protection of all buildings and places open to the public such as schools 1

[1] Professor of Comparative Law, Director of the Edouard Lambert Institute of Comparative Law, Université Jean Moulin Lyon 3.

[2] Teaching and Research Assistant, Université Jean Moulin Lyon 3. The authors are indebted to Stewart Newcombe for his comments and contribution.

[3] For more information in French on recent developments, see: M.-H. Gozzi, *Le terrorisme: essai d'une étude juridique* (1998); La loi sur la sécurité quotidienne et la lutte anti-terroriste, [2002] *Dalloz* (D.), 4; A. d'Hauteville, Victimes mieux aidées, mieux indemnisées: des perspectives nouvelles, [1989] *Revue de science criminelle et de droit comparé* (Rev. sc. crim.), 172; L'indemminsation des victimes d'actes d'attentat, [1987] *Revue générale des assurances terrestres* (RGAT), 328; C. Lienhard, Aperçu rapide sur la protection juridique des victimes d'attentats terroriste, [1996] *Juris-classeur périodique* (JCP), Actualités, no. 51–52; J.-F. Renucci, l'indemnisation des victimes d'actes de terrorisme, [1987] D., chron. 197; J. Pradel, Les infractions de terrorisme, [1987] D., chron. 39; T. Renoux/M. Roux, Responsabilité de l'Etat et droits des victimes d'actes de terrorisme, [1993] *Actualité juridique-droit administratif* (AJDA), 75. More generally, see Ph. le Tourneau/L. Cadiet, *Droit de la responsabilité et des contrats* (2002–2003), no. 763–774.

and universities, public administration buildings, railway stations, airports etc., by police and *gendarmerie* forces (*Vigipirate simple*) and military forces (*Vigipirate renforcé*), enforced after 11 September. Where prevention fails, an efficient compensation system, based on a special fund to indemnify persons suffering physical injury, and an extensive insurance coverage of damage to property, have been created and improved. Psychological help is also available to victims, under a system created after the terrorist attacks of 1986.

II. General

A. *Does Your Legal System Have Special Legislation on Terrorist Attacks, in Particular Concerning Liability or Other Indemnity?*

2 In addition to the prevention system mentioned in the introduction, France has set up an efficient system of compensation, mainly by the creation of a compensation fund, based on the pattern of the fund to compensate victims of road traffic accidents when the tortfeasor is unknown. As explained in II.B below, this fund may provide compensation even pending a criminal and civil action against persons suspected of having committed the terrorist act. It provides full compensation for physical injury and mental suffering. However, it does not cover damage to property.

3 Regarding damage to property, all persons living in rented premises must subscribe to an insurance called *multirisque habitation*, covering most risks to the building, its contents, and the consequences of tortious acts committed by the insured or his dependants. Private house and apartment owners also subscribe to such insurance, especially when the property is mortgaged. Coverage of risks linked to terrorist attacks is by law compulsory, but a person who contributes to a terrorist act is not entitled to compensation.[4] People may also benefit from a special insurance policy (*couverture individuelle accident*; *assurance des risques de la vie* etc.) or in appropriate cases from their car insurance scheme. Uninsured victims may also be compensated by a compensation fund.

4 Otherwise, ordinary tort law applies, including liability based on fault or negligence (art. 1382 *Code civil* [French Civil Code, C. civ.]), strict liability of the guardian of a thing causing the damage (art. 1384 § 1 C. civ.) and strict liability of car drivers causing a road traffic accident (law no. 85-677 of 5 July 1985). No specific amendment to these rules has been necessary. Indeed, the victim of a terrorist attack will never be in a situation where he will have to sue the tortfeasor directly because, in application of the normal rules of subrogation:

> where the victim is indemnified by the compensation fund, the action in tort vests in the fund which may recover according to the ordinary rules of tort;

[4] *Code des assurances* (Insurance Code), art. L 126-1.

where the victim is compensated by an insurance company, the action in tort similarly vests in the insurer.

Certain other rules, although not related to compensation, may be briefly mentioned. Exceptions are made to some protective rules of criminal procedure wherever a suspected terrorist is prosecuted, criminal jurisdiction is in the Paris courts wherever the terrorist act took place, deportation of foreign terrorists may be ordered in an absolute emergency, infringement of rights of privacy may be allowed to authorise tapping of telephone conversation etc. All this indicates the determination of the French authorities to fight terrorism in the past fifteen years or so. Even though right wing governments may go further in implementing a tougher policy creating more extensive exceptions to rules protecting fundamental rights of the accused, left wing governments have shown a similar determination. 5

B. Are There any Special Funds Available Providing Alternative Compensation for Victims of Terrorist Attacks?

A special fund was created by a law of 9 September 1986 (art. 9), a year when France was the subject of a number of terrorist attacks,[5] and the system was improved by a law of 6 July 1990.[6] It is now called the Compensation Fund for the Victims of Terrorist Action and other Offences (FGTI, hereinafter called the Compensation Fund or the Fund).[7] The Fund is administered by a board of thirteen members appointed for a period of three years. The Minister of Economy and Finances, who acts as supervisor, appoints the chairperson. Funding is provided by a levy on the premiums paid to insurance companies insuring damage to property (€ 3 per contract in 2003). 6

The Fund compensates all French citizens victim of a terrorist attack in France or abroad, as well as foreign victims of a terrorist attack in a French territory. In 1991, the scope of compensation was extended so as to compensate victims of serious offences (*infractions graves*) and, later on, victims of road traffic accidents occuring abroad. 7

The Fund provides full compensation for physical injury, pain and suffering and any consequential loss, but does not cover damage to property. In case of death, the victim's dependants are compensated for their economic loss. Compensation includes the coverage of all medical expenses as well as all additional expenses arising from physical impairment such as medical appliances and special fittings, costs related to nursing and assistance with housework, in 8

[5] Victims of terrorist attacks had organised themselves as a pressure group (*Association SOS Attentats*), requesting the legislature to intervene.

[6] Law no. 90-589 of 6 July 1990.

[7] *Fonds de garantie pour les victimes d'actes de terrorisme et d'autres infractions*. See *Code des assurances*, art. L 126-1 and L 126-2, L 422-1 to L 422-5 (legislative part), R 422-1 to R 422-10 (regulations) and A 422-1 (byelaws); *Code de procédure pénale* (Code of Criminal Procedure), art. 706-3 to 706-14 (legislative part) and R 50-1 to R 50-28 (regulations).

addition to welfare benefits. The victim may also claim additional compensation for damage to or loss of clothing, within certain statutory limits. As explained above under II.A, insurance companies compensate any other damage to property.

9 Certain rules of procedure are relevant here. Once informed of a terrorist attack, the State Prosecutor (*Procureur de la République*) initiates proceedings and must inform the Compensation Fund of the attack. If the attack occurs abroad, the consular authorities provide such information. The list of victims must be supplied within 48 hours.

10 All victims, or dependants in case of death, may file a compensation claim to the Fund directly, by means of registered letter.[8] The period of limitation is ten years from the event and a new claim may be introduced within the same ten-year period should the victim's situation deteriorate. The claim must identify the victim and give detailed information as to the date, place and nature of the terrorist attack and include the police report and statements by witnesses. Medical certificates and any evidence relating to the injury must be enclosed. Information relating to welfare coverage must also be included as well as the quantum of social benefits already received. Indication that the injury may have been caused by an industrial accident must also be supplied.

11 Within three months of receipt of the claim, the Fund must make an offer of compensation. Where the victim accepts the offer, there is a binding and directly enforceable agreement, compromising any existing or future action (*transaction*[9]). Payment will be made shortly thereafter, but an interim payment to cover exsiting costs will be made not later than one month after the application.[10] If the victim rejects the offer, a registered letter must be sent within fifteen days and the victim may start proceedings before the civil courts.

12 By way of subrogation, the victim's entire claim is assigned to the Fund.

13 Some important exceptions are made in order to afford better and more efficient protection to some basic principles of French law. The fact that the Fund must pay compensation, even though the terrorists have been identified and prosecuted, reveals a national duty of solidarity.[11] In the French legal system, the victim of a criminal offence may initiate a claim in damages before the criminal court, by laying a plaint and constituting himself a party to the action (*plainte avec constitution de partie civile*). The civil action (*action civile*) is decided after the criminal action (*action publique*). Where the victim elects to sue in damages before a civil court rather than laying a plaint before the criminal court, no judgment may be rendered by the civil court pending a criminal

[8] A special form is provided on http://www.fgti.fr.

[9] Art 2044 C. civ.

[10] Complete information is supplied on the Compensation Fund website: http://www.fgti.fr.

[11] As explained in a judgment of the Court of Appeal of Paris, 24 June 1992, *Gazette du Palais* (Gaz. Pal.) no.318–319 of 13–14 November 1992.

action initiated on the same facts: *le criminel tient le civil en l'état*. Exception is made to this principle in cases of terrorism. The civil court has no obligation to stay the proceedings and may award damages without waiting for the verdict of the criminal court, usually the *Cour d'assises* in case of terrorist attacks.[12] Likewise, interim payments and payments by the Compensation Fund may take place before any criminal judgment.[13] It is indeed crucial that victims receive compensation before the close of criminal proceedings, which often take place after very lengthy investigations and proceedings in terrorist cases. The Code of Criminal Procedure allows the Fund to recover against the terrorists by any type of court action, including a civil action before a criminal court.[14]

Yet, this does not have the effect of extinguishing all the victim's claims. As explained in II.C below, the victim may nonetheless take proceedings in order to obtain a higher amount. This appears to be an exception to the general rule that a settlement excludes all further claims. 14

The law of 1990 grants the victims of terrorism the status of civil victims of war (*victimes civiles de guerre*), with all the rights and advantages inherent in such status. This includes totally free medical care[15] and the benefit of a pension, in addition to compensation.[16] 15

C. Has Your Judiciary ever Had to Consider the Issue of Liability in Connection with Terrorist Attacks in any Leading Cases?

Due to the efficiency of the Compensation Fund, the number of cases reaching the courts is necessarily limited. However, interesting claims may arise where the victim of a terrorist attack, after having received, supposedly, full compensation from the Fund, claims additional compensation from the terrorist by means of a civil action. Such situations should not occur under normal circumstances. Indeed, the compensated victim assigns all claims to the Fund, by way of subrogation, so that the Fund should be the only party with a claim in damages against the terrorist. However, as mentioned in II.B above, French law allows victims to initiate criminal proceedings by way of *constitution de partie civile* in order to obtain compensation. 16

A case arose in 1992, where the *Cour d'assises spéciale de Paris* sentenced to life imprisonment a member of the terrorist group *Action Directe*, directly involved in a bloody bomb attack on the central criminal police station in Paris in July 1986. This was a widely reported case, the terrorist dismissing his lawyer during the hearings. The victims had already been compensated by the 17

[12] *Code des assurances*, art. L 422-3.

[13] For a case of interim payment, see *Deuxième chambre civile de la Cour de Cassation* (Cass. Civ. 2ème), 15 November 2001, [2001] D., *partie "informations rapides" du recueil Dalloz* (IR), 3586.

[14] *Code de procédure pénale*, art. 706-11 par. 2.

[15] With the exception of hospital expenses, the French national health system does not cover medical expenses in their entirety, a share being supported by the patient (*ticket modérateur*).

[16] Law of 6 July 1990, art. 26.

then newly created Compensation Fund. Nevertheless, some of them initiated a civil action before the criminal court, which was more generous than the Fund in granting higher damages. The Fund was also a civil party to the case,[17] in order to recover what had already been paid to the victims.[18] The *Cour d'assises*, in the civil part of the judgment, rejected the claim of the Fund to recover damages in respect of those compensated victims who did not introduce a civil action.

18 The Fund appealed to the *Cour de cassation*, the highest French court for civil and criminal cases. In a judgment of 20 October 1993,[19] the criminal panel of the *Cour de cassation* held that the Fund was entitled to recover by way of a civil action even for those victims who were satisfied with the compensation and did not take civil proceedings. The full benefit of subrogation granted to the Fund by the statute creates an independent cause of action. This part of the judgment of the *Cour d'assises* was therefore reversed.

19 However, the second ground of the Fund's appeal, against the order of the court disregarding the settlement, was dismissed. The *Cour de cassation* held that granting higher damages to those victims who took civil proceedings before the criminal court did not aggravate the Fund's position, since only the amount paid in excess of agreed compensation benefits the victims, without causing loss to the Fund.

20 This ruling raises an interesting question concerning the legal status of the agreement made between the victim and the Fund. Such an agreement is a settlement (*transaction*), enforceable as a final judgment.[20] As such, prima facie, it extinguishes the victim's cause of action, since the object of the settlement is to grant the victim full compensation. However, French law considers settlements to be a category of contract. The principle of privity of contract (*effet relatif du contrat*) therefore applies, but settlements are also binding on third parties. According to the *Cour de cassation*, the extinctive effect of settlements[21] is limited to the parties to the agreement, namely the Fund and the victim. It has the effect of discharging any claim the victim may have against the Fund, but not any claim which the victim may have against the tortfeasor (a euphemism for a terrorist), who is not a party to the agreement. The victim's right to a civil action against the terrorist is not extinguished. This raises a further question: is the criminal court, when deciding the civil action, bound by the settlement? The

[17] Although not a *partie civile* strictly speaking, but intervening in the action because of the right to subrogation to the victim's rights. See Ph. le Tourneau/L. Cadiet, *Droit de la responsabilité et des contrats* (2002–2003), no. 672.

[18] A right granted to the Fund by the *Code de procédure pénale*, art. 706-11 par. 2, as explained supra II.B.

[19] *Cour de Cassation, chambre criminelle* (Cass. Crim.), 20 October 1993, [1994] D., 280, note Anne d'Hauteville.

[20] See Law no. 86-1020 of 9 September 1986, art. 9-III referring to Law no. 85-677 of 5 July 1985, art. 18 to 21.

[21] See G. Viney/P. Jourdain, *Traité de droit civil, Les effets de la responsabilité* (2nd edn. 2001), no. 288 et seq.

Paris *Cour d'assises* ruled that it had jurisdiction to assess the damage suffered by each victim on the basis of the evidence. This, it held, allowed it to grant higher damages than those agreed with the Fund. Unfortunately (for the academic community, but not for the victims!), the *Cour de cassation* skirts the problem, simply pointing out that the judgment of the *Cour d'assises* did not cause loss to the Fund. One may comment that this is a French way of combining two rules: first, a universal rule that injury must be fully compensated, second, a more parochial rule that the assessment of damages is a question of fact and not of law. The result is that as the *Cour de cassation* is only entitled to review questions of law, and not of fact, that it has no power to review quantum of damages. Local courts of appeal have their own scales. Are the French courts to be blamed for transferring more money from terrorist pockets to severely impaired victims, with the additional gift of a legal riddle for surviving academics?

The *Cour de cassation* is not always so generous. In a case from Corsica, de- 21
cided in 1995, the first Civil Chamber gave a somewhat restrictive interpretation of the concept of terrorism, refusing compensation by the Fund to victims of a bomb explosion in a school, causing psychological shock to the doorkeeper, his wife and two children.[22] The general definition given by the Penal Code as amended by the law of 1986 is as follows: "The following offences constitute acts of terrorism where they are committed intentionally in connection with an individual or collective undertaking the purpose of which is seriously to disturb public order by means of intimidation or terror".[23] The *Cour*

[22] Cass. Civ. 1re, 17 October 1995, [1996] *RCA*, no. 72.

[23] *Code pénal*, art. 421-1 (translation http://www.legifrance.fr). The article then gives a list of the offences:

"1° wilful attacks on life, wilful attacks on the physical integrity of persons, abduction and unlawful detention and also as the hijacking of planes, vessels or any other means of transport, defined by Book II of the present Code;

2° theft, extortion, destruction, defacement and damage, and also computer offences, as defined under Book III of the present Code;

3° offences committed by combat organisations and disbanded movements as defined under articles 431-13 to 431-17, and the offences set out under articles 434-6, 441-2 to 441-5;

4° the production or keeping of machines, dangerous or explosive devices, set out under article 3 of the Act of 19 June 1871 which repealed the Decree of 4 September 1870 on the production of military grade weapons;

- the production, sale, import or export of explosive substances as defined by article 6 of the Act no. 70-575 of 3 July 1970 amending the regulations governing explosive powders and substances;
- the purchase, keeping, transport or unlawful carrying of explosive substances or of devices made with such explosive substances, as defined by article 38 of the Ordinance of 18th April 1939 defining the regulations governing military equipment, weapons and ammunition;
- the detention, carrying, and transport of weapons and ammunition falling under the first and fourth categories defined by articles 4, 28, 31 and 32 of the aforementioned Ordinance;
- the offences defined by articles 1 and 4 of the Act no. 72-467 of 9th June 1972 forbidding the designing, production, keeping, stocking, purchase or sale of biological or toxin-based weapons;
- the offences referred to under articles 58 to 63 of the Act no. 98-467 of 17th June 1998 on the application of the Convention of the 13th January 1993 on the prohibition of developing, producing, stocking and use of chemical weapons and on their destruction;

5° receiving the product of one of the offences set out in paragraphs 1 to 4 above."

de cassation agreed with the lower court that such acts require "a minimum of organisation", the existence of which falls within the trial court's discretion (*appréciation souveraine des juges du fond*). The Court went on to hold that the violent action was an isolated act, committed by unknown offenders lacking professionalism and not claiming responsibility for the attack. These words are not to be found in the statute. This case may reveal the reluctance of the courts to recognise the political character of some actions, so that small groups may not claim some form of political legitimacy.

D. Did the Events of 11 September 2001 or any Other Recent Terrorist Attacks Have any Influence on Rules Concerning Liability (Interpretation, Discussion About Reforms, Duty to Take Care)?

22 Following the unprecedented terrorist attacks of 11 September, a new term appeared in the professional terminology, that of "hyper terrorisme". Ten days later, a phenomenal explosion occured at the AZF factory in Toulouse, killing 29 people and injuring 2,400, besides devastating thousands of private and public buildings (the estimated damage is approximately one billion Euros): the explosion was apparently due to an accidental cause. No amendment was made to the rules of tort law, but the events generated a significant move in the insurance sector. A decree of 28 December 2001[24] amended the Insurance Code and defined the conditions under which property may be insured in case of terrorist attacks[25]. Minimum coverage is provided for in the case of "great risks": whichever should be the higher of € 20 million or 20% or the risk insured.[26]

23 The principal effect was a growing awareness of the huge amount of damage that may be caused by terrorist action. Through the Central Reinsurance Fund (*Caisse centrale de réassurance*, CCR), the State increased its guarantee for risks linked to air transportation and adopted tax measures to help insurance companies expand their reserve funds, so as to cover risks linked to terrorism. The most significant move was that the French insurance and reinsurance companies created a pool (Pool GAREAT) to cover damage to property caused by terrorist action. This mutual fund is backed up by the State through the CCR, up to an unlimited amount, at least until the insurance companies feed the fund completely, which is done by an increase on the premiums charged to industrial companies. The Pool GAREAT deals with policies insuring high industrial risks, for damages exceeding six million Euros. The system has been prolonged so as to cover 2003.

[24] Decree no. 2001-1337 of 28 December 2001.

[25] *Code des assurances*, art. R 126-2.

[26] *Grands risques*, as defined in *Code des assurances*, art. L 111-6.

E. *Does Your Country Participate in any International Conventions in Connection with Liability for Terrorist Attacks?*

France is a party to the European Convention on the Suppression of Terrorism signed at Strasbourg on 27 January 1977 and ratified in 1987. It is also a party to the United Nations multinational conventions for the suppression of terrorism. The International Convention for the Suppression of Terrorist Bombings (New York, 15 December 1997) was signed in 1998 and ratified on 8 August 1999. The International Convention for the Suppression of the Financing of Terrorism (New York, 9 December 1999) was signed on 10 January 2000 and ratified on 7 January 2002. 24

France participates with other European countries in multilateral actions against terrorism, including actions based on art. 31 of the Treaty on European Union (formerly art. K3). 25

Bilateral agreements exist with European countries, including Germany, Spain (Basque Country) and the United Kingdom (Channel Tunnel). More recently, bilateral agreements also came into force with Hungary, the Czech Republic and Romania. 26

So far as concerns the victim, this would be the proper place to conclude the report. However, there is much more to say from the perspective of the Fund and insurance companies, which are subrogated in the victim's rights. They have to face intricate tort liability issues. The French Civil Code, with its five rather short articles dealing with tort liability may give a false impression of simplicity. They have been developed by an impressive body of case law and supplemented by a number of specific statutory provisions. In addition, they only apply to litigation in the ordinary courts. Administrative courts, which deal with claims against the State or public entities, are apt to apply different rules and standards. Differences in substance come in addition to tricky jurisdiction issues. It is remarkably difficult to find books or articles offering a general overview of such problems, the *summa divisio* between private law and public law beeing stronger than that between common law and equity in Pre-Victorian Britain, with similar adverse consequences for the litigants. With rare exceptions, academics still adhere to this historical dichotomy which has been promoted and refined beyond the limits of logic.[27] 27

III. Strict Liability

A. *Focusing on Strict Liability for Means of Transport and Enterprises or Facilities, Would You Say the Owner, Custodian or Keeper is also Liable if a Terrorist Causes the Damage?*

French law imposes a duty on transporters to carry passengers safely to their destination (*obligation de sécurité*), in all contracts for the carriage of passen- 28

[27] For a comparative and critical approach, see the General Report, in: O. Moréteau/J. Vanderlinden (ed.), *La structure des systèmes juridiques* (2003).

gers.[28] This obligation requires the purpose to be achieved (*obligation de résultat* during the course of transportation and to some extent during embarkation and disembarkation.[29] Thus the carrier is strictly liable and may only be exonerated in a case of *force majeure* or the act of a stranger (e.g. a terrorist).[30] It becomes an obligation requiring the deployment of appropriate care to achieve the purpose of the contract (*obligation de moyens*) during stopovers and at other times in which case the carrier may only be made liable for negligence. In a case against British Airways, decided in 1999,[31] some French passengers had purchased tickets in France for a flight to Madras and Kuala Lumpur via London. On 2 August 1990, the aircraft made an unscheduled stopover at Kuwait City, the day Iraq invaded Kuwait. The passengers were taken to a hotel where they were held prisoner by the Iraqi army, for periods of one to three months. British Airways were held liable for breach of their contractual *obligation de moyens*[32]: the stopover, announced to the passengers at the time of departure from London, was not mentioned on the tickets. It was organised at a time when the outbreak of war and the invasion of Kuwait were very probable and in circumstances where the aircraft had enough fuel to continue the journey,[33] so that the passengers were exposed to a risk of war without cause.[34]

29 Where a bomb is carried into an airport or onto an aircraft, one may claim that the airport authority, the airline, or the company handling the luggage, is strictly liable on the basis of art. 1384 § 1 of the Civil Code. Strict liability is based on the *garde de la chose*, which means that the defendant must have the use, direction and control of the thing that causes the damage.[35] Exoneration is only possible in case of *force majeure* or act of a stranger.[36] However, where the object having caused the damage is activated by dynamism of its own (case of a soda or gas bottle),[37] there is a split in the guard and there are two possible guardians. The party handling the object is liable for any damage caused by harmful manipulation (*garde du comportement*), and the manufacturer retains the guard of the structure (*garde de la structure*) even though he is no longer in possession of it.[38]

[28] Cass. Civ., 21 November 1911, [1913] D., I, 249, note L. Sarrut; for more details see O. Moréteau, Codes as Straight-Jackets, Safeguards and Alibis: The Experience of the French Civil Code, [1995] 2 *North Carolina Journal of International Law*, 273 (284 et seq.).

[29] Subject to international conventions such as the Warsaw Convention of 12 October 1929 in the case of air transport.

[30] See infra III.B.

[31] Cass. Civ. 1re, 15 July 1999, D. 2000, 283, note Sophie Pech-le Gac

[32] The application of French law was not challenged by the airline.

[33] The airline may otherwise have pleaded necessity.

[34] In this case, although already compensated by the Fund, the victims were allowed to sue the airline, since they had not been informed in writing of their right to reject the offer made by the Fund during the period of two weeks, as explained in II.B above.

[35] *Chambres réunies de la Cour de Cassation* (Cass. Ch. réun.), 2 December 1941 (*Franck c. Connot*), [1942] *Recueil Dalloz critique* (DC), 25, note G. Ripert.

[36] See III.B below.

[37] See the famous *Oxygène Liquide* case: Cass. Civ. 2e, 5 January 1956, [1957] D., 261, note R. Rodière and Cass. Civ. 2e, 10 June 1960, [1960] D., 609, note R. Rodière.

[38] See *L'Oxygène Liquide* case (supra fn. 37) and G. Viney/P. Jourdain, *Traité de droit civil, Les conditions de la responsabilité* (2nd edn. 1998), no. 691–702.

This applies to a parcel or a bag containing a bomb: the carrier ignoring the content and not being involved in the terrorist action only has the *garde du comportement* but not the *garde de la structure*. Tort liability may otherwise be based on fault or negligence, due to lack of care in security checks but, as explained below,[39] the point is likely to be litigated in an administrative court and to be governed not by the Civil Code but by the administrative law of tort.

Harm caused to third parties by the crash of the aeroplane or by the fall of parts of it is governed by specific legislation contained in the Civil Aviation Code which puts strict liability on the airline[40] for any harm to the person or to property of third parties. As explained above, liability to passengers is based on the contract of carriage and the Warsaw Convention. The damage caused by the crash must be suffered on the ground and not in the air,[41] which excludes the collision with another aircraft.[42] The airline may not plead the defence of *force majeure*.[43] 30

B. Can Terror Attacks Be Classified as a Defence like Act of God/Force Majeure/Unavoidable Event?

The defence of *force majeure* or *cause étrangère* is available wherever the following requirements are satisfied: the terrorist attack must be an outside event, namely where the defendant is not involved in the attack, which must be unavoidable. Generally, the defendant has no means of preventing an unsuspected object from exploding or an incoming plane from crashing. The requirement of unforeseeability, very stringent in the past, has been relaxed, if not abandoned. It is sufficient if the defendant cannot prevent the occurrence of the event by taking reasonable precautions.[44] The standard of care may be higher in airport and railway stations, at times of insecurity, for instance when the *Vigipirate* plan is in force. 31

However, *force majeure* is no defence to an airline or to the charterer of an aircraft when strictly liable to third parties for damage caused on the ground by 32

[39] See infra IV.A.

[40] *Code de l'aviation civile* (Civil Aviation Code), art. L 141-2; the code uses the word "*l'exploitant*"; in the case of a charter party, the owners and the charterers are jointly liable to third parties: art. L 141-4.

[41] *Code de l'aviation civile*, art. L 321-3 et seq. and L 322-3.

[42] In such cases, the provisions of the Civil Code apply: *Code de l'aviation civile*, art. L 141-1.

[43] *Code de l'aviation civile*, art. L 141-2; see also art. L 141-3.

[44] *Cour de Cassation, chambre commerciale* (Cass. Com.), 1 October 1997, [1997] D. Affaires, 1217, no. 37: robbery case against a carrier. The Court of Appeal held that there was no *force majeure* since the damage was foreseeable. The judgment was reversed, since according to the *Cour de cassation*, "the irresistible character of the event constitutes in itself *force majeure*, where its effect may not be prevented despite its foreseeable character, (...) in circumstances where the carrier took all the requested steps to avoid the occurrence of the event." In a luxury hotel robbery case (Cass. Civ. 1re, 9 March 1994, *bulletin des arrêts de la Cour de Cassation, chambres civiles* (Bull. civ.) I, 91, translated in H. Beale/A. Hartkamp/H. Kötz/D. Tallon, *Cases, Materials and Text on Contract Law* (2002), 594), the defence of *force majeure* was rejected on that last ground: because the hotel owner had not taken sufficient care to control night entries, all reasonable precautions had not been taken.

the crash of the plane or parts of it. The only defence is *faute de la victime*, a term which covers default of the victim and contributory negligence of the victim.[45]

C. *If There Is Another Person Liable Apart from or Instead of the Terrorist, for What Kind of Damages is He/She Liable (for Example also Compensation for Consequential Damage such as Plundering Following a Terrorist Attack)?*

33 No case related to terrorism has been found but the problem has been considered in different contexts. For instance, a weapon abandoned in a public place is used to cause harm. French law is not clear in such a situation. There are cases where the initial tortfeasor is made liable for the whole damage,[46] others where only the second tortfeasor is made liable,[47] and last but not least, cases where both tortfeasors are made jointly liable, which seems the more logical and satisfactory solution. This is now the solution usually adopted, and it is applied to cases of negligently abandoned weapons.[48]

34 In the above examples, there are two successive acts leading to a single damage. In the case of plundering after a terrorist attack, the initial damage to property may be aggravated as a result of plundering, or totally new and independent damage may be caused by persons taking advantage of a chaotic situation. Such cases will be decided on causation.

35 From the victim's point of view, compensation for physical injury will be paid by the Fund and damage to property will be recovered from insurance companies, as explained above.[49] It is difficult to imagine cases where the victim may be in trouble due to the plurality of events. One may imagine the case of a passer-by who comes to the rescue and is assaulted by a gang of plunderers and who seeks to recover from the Fund on the grounds of terrorism. Compensation will be paid since the Fund indemnifies victims of offences other than terrorism,[50] but it is not certain that he will be considered a victim of a terrorist attack, hence entitled to all the rights, such as being treated as a civil victim of war.

36 Finally, it must be noted that where an airline, airport or other transportation authority may be held to be strictly liable, usually on the basis of a contractual relationship with the passenger,[51] it will often be possible to plead *force ma-*

[45] *Code de l'aviation civile*, art. L 141-2 and supra III.A.

[46] Case of the car driver injuring the victim who dies following medical negligence during the surgical operation: Cass. Crim., 15 January 1958, [1959] JCP II, 11026, note Esmein.

[47] Liability of a driver who caused an accident with a stolen car where the negligence of the owner favoured the theft: Cass. Civ. 2e, 4 March 1981, Bull. civ. II, no. 49.

[48] Cass. Civ. 2e, 13 June 1974, Bull. civ. II, no. 197; Cass. Civ., 11 January 1979, Bull. civ. II, no. 19.

[49] See supra II.A.

[50] See supra II.B.

[51] See supra III.A.

jeure.[52] The Fund and the insurance companies may try to recover both from the terrorist and the carrier, but are less likely to recover from the latter unless there is a clear case of negligence.

IV. Fault Liability

A. *At Public Facilities such as Airports, Train Stations, Sport Stadiums etc., Who Is Responsible that no Terrorist Enters and Causes Harm? The Entity that Runs the Facility, Enterprises that Obtain an Advantage Therefrom (such as Airlines or Organizers of Sports Events), the State, or any Other Person(s)? How Far Do These Duties of Care Go in that Respect?*

This is a difficult question, since the liability of the State or of certain public authorities, governed by administrative law and within the jurisdiction of administrative courts, may coincide with the liability of private individuals or entities, governed by the Civil Code and under the jurisdiction of ordinary courts. Like most continental countries, France has two court systems, which generates problems of jurisdiction, called *conflits de juridiction*. In addition, administrative courts do not apply the Civil Code to disputes within their jurisdiction. Thus, a defendant may be held liable by a civil court in a case where the claim would be dismissed if adjudicated by the administrative court. More frequently, both courts will hold the defendant liable but in general civil courts grant more generous damages than their administrative counterparts. Another jurisdictional difficulty arises from the right to initiate a civil action before criminal courts. It is good news for the victim to be entitled to direct and immediate compensation by the Fund[53] and by the insurance company.[54] As explained above, the issues discussed in this paragraph concern only the Fund and insurance companies trying to recover from the tortfeasor. 37

Let us start with facilities managed by State agencies or public authorities, which is the case of most public buildings, central and local government buildings, State schools and universities as well as churches, which are the property of municipalities. The difficulty arises from the fact that in French law, there are two types of public service. Where the public service is deemed to be administrative, administrative law applies and administrative courts have jurisdiction. However some *services publics* are held to be *industriels et commerciaux*, in which case they are governed by private law and the civil courts have jurisdiction. Disputes as to jurisdiction are solved by way of case stated by a Tribunal of Conflicts, which will not decide the case on the merits but decides only the issue of jurisdiction. For instance, chambers of commerce and industry have a mixed activity, both administrative and industrial and commercial. They often manage airports, for instance Aéroport Saint-Exupéry at Lyon. In 1976, the Tribunal of Conflicts ruled that the management by Aéroports de Paris of the equipment used for embarking and disembarking 38

[52] See supra III.B.
[53] See supra II.B.
[54] See supra II.A.

passengers and their luggage falls within the jurisdiction of the administrative courts, since such equipment "has the character of public works"[55]. The same solution applies to air traffic control.[56] In addition, airports are under the control of the police and the Customs.

39 Sport stadiums and public theatres are within the public domain. In 1968, the *Conseil d'Etat*, the highest French administrative court, held that the administrative court had jurisdiction in a case concerning the exploitation by the town of Vienne of its Roman theatre, where a famous jazz festival is organised every summer.[57] In any doubt, there is a presumption that the activity is administrative and comes within the jurisdiction of the administrative courts.

40 There is a line of cases holding that "unless expressly provided by statute, the State cannot be made liable for acts of terrorism occuring on French territory".[58] The State may be liable in the case of a terrorist attacks on the public domain if, but only if, the damage is the consequence of a riotous assembly or riot, which implies the activity of a crowd.[59]

41 It is remarkably difficult to make the State liable for breach of a duty to ensure safety in public places. Evidence of gross negligence (*faute lourde*) needs to be adduced.[60] The fact that the State did not manage to reduce the number of terrorist attacks in Corsica may not be considered as gross negligence generating State liability.[61] An insufficient number of police is no ground for action, nor is the fact that a protective fence was not high enough.[62] Where a suspicious parcel has been found, gross negligence of the police must be proved to make the State liable. If the police injures a person when trying to arrest terrorists, the State may be declared liable by the civil courts, since the police is no longer acting in the course of its administrative functions but within its so-called judicial activity, a subtlety that even a French lawyer might find hard to understand.[63]

42 Where a company contracts for the purpose of providing security or surveillance, there is a contractual *obligation de moyens*: no damages may be claimed unless negligence is proved.[64] Such companies have a duty to advise their cus-

[55] *Tribunal des conflits* (TC), 13 December 1976, *Epoux Zaoui*, 706, [1977] AJDA, 438, note J. Dufau.

[56] TC, 23 February 1981, *Crouzel*, 631, [1981] AJDA, 603.

[57] CE Sect., 26 January 1968, *Dame Maron*, 69, [1968] AJDA, 293.

[58] CE Sect., 29 April 1987, *Yener et Cons. Erez*, 151, [1987] AJDA, 450. A number of cases could be cited, all relating to claims by insurance companies.

[59] *Code des communes*, art. L 133-1, now *Code général des collectivités territoriales*, art. 92 (Law no. 83-8 of 8 January 1983). As stated in a conference at the Ecole nationale de la magistrature (*L'aide aux victimes d'attentats*, 14 January 1987, p. 7), both the *Tribunal des conflits* and *Cour de cassation* interpret these concepts very restrictively.

[60] CE Sect. 29 April 1987, *Yener et Cons. Erez* (supra fn. 58): attacks against the Ambassador of Turkey; police protecting the ambassador held not to be negligent.

[61] CAA (*Cour administrative d'appel*) Marseille, 5 July 2001, no. 98MA01316, unreported.

[62] CAA Marseille, 23 November 2000, unreported.

[63] TC, 7 June 1951, *Dame Noualek*, 636, [1952] Sirey (S.), 3.13.

[64] Cass. Civ. 1re, 5 February 2002, no. 99-21660, unreported.

tomers as to necessary security improvements and can be made liable if they fail to do so.

B. To What Extent Do Individuals or Entities Have a Duty of Care to Participate in the Active Avoidance of Terrorist Acts?

Generally speaking, the standard of diligence required of the State is rather low, since gross negligence must be established. The standard required of a private undertaking subject to civil law is higher.[65] 43

However, rules of criminal law and criminal procedure impose certain special duties, breach of which may give rise to a civil action in damages before a criminal court. Such duties include the following: 44

> Failure to denounce a crime, in itself an offence, is aggravated in case of terrorism.[66]
>
> Failure to prevent the commission of an offence is also an offence, provided that intervention implies only a limited risk to oneself.[67] Acquittal no longer means absence of liability, since the *Cour de cassation* has abandoned the principle of unity of civil and penal fault, reverting to the 19th century dualist doctrine.[68] However, it is hard to imagine a situation where a passive (and surviving) witness of a terrorist attack can be made liable for the consequences of such attack: the claim may be rejected because of lack of causation.[69]
>
> Wherever an offender is seen in the act of committing a serious offence (*crime* or *delit*), the Code of Criminal Procedure imposes on every citizen a duty to prevent the commission of such offence.[70]
>
> A party assisting, actively or passively, the commission of a terrorist action may be guilty (and therefore liable) as an accomplice, wherever he has knowledge of the terrorists' intention.[71]

V. Cases

In all four cases, the victim will recover from the Fund (physical injury and dependents' economic loss in case of death)[72] and from his insurance compa- 45

[65] See IV.A above.

[66] *Code pénal*, art. 434-1 and 434-2: five years imprisonment and a € 75,000 fine.

[67] *Code pénal*, art. 223-6. It is to be noted that in case of terror attacks, the terrorist withdrawing in the course of the criminal action may not be declared guilty on the ground of attempt: *Code pénal*, art. 422-1.

[68] Cass. Civ. 1re, 30 January 2001, Bull. civ. I, no. 19, [2001] *Rev. sc. crim.*, 613, note A. Giudicelli. In this case, despite the absence of conviction, the civil court held the defendant liable for lack of care.

[69] See paragraph B3 above.

[70] *Code de procédure pénale*, art. 73.

[71] Cass. Crim., 9 October 1941, [1941] DA, 374.

[72] See supra II.B.

ny (damage to property).[73] In all cases, the victim is unlikely to sue. The Fund and the insurance companies benefit from subrogation of the victim's right, to the extent that compensation is paid. Yet, as explained above, compensated victims may sometimes sue in order to recover increased damages.[74]

1. A Terrorist Hijacks an Aircraft Which Crashes into

a) A Building

b) A nuclear plant

46 The following persons or entities may be held liable:

the terrorists and their accomplices for all damage caused by their criminal action;

the airline to the passengers on board on the basis of the contractual *obligation de sécurité* (strict liability), yet with possible exoneration (*force majeure*);[75]

the airline or charterer of the aircraft (joint liability) to third parties for any damage to the person or property on the ground caused by the crash of the plane or parts of it; *force majeure* is no defence;[76]

pilots or crew members or the airline (vicarious liability), in so far as they may have helped the perpetration of the hijacking whether actively or passively.[77]

47 As regards the building, if it belongs to an enterprise covered by the Pool GAREAT and if the damage exceeds € 6 million, the Pool will intervene.[78]

48 If the buiding is a nuclear plant, the State may be liable for gross negligence if the *Vigipirate* plan is in force (*Vigipirate renforcé*).[79] The army has the duty to intercept the plane, but the President of the Republic or the Defence Minister must make the decision. Nuclear plants are supposed to be built to resist a plane crash and the risk is covered by insurance.[80] In case of radiation, the operating company may be made liable[81] as well as the builders, for damage caused to the environment.[82] Compensation may not exceed € 23 million for any single accident.[83]

[73] See supra II.A.
[74] See supra II.C.
[75] See supra III.A and III.B.
[76] See supra III.A and III.B.
[77] See supra IV.B.
[78] See supra II.D.
[79] See supra I.
[80] Decree no. 94-569 of 11 July 1994, art. 4.
[81] EDF (*Electricité de France*) is an industrial and commercial public service and is therefore governed by private law: CE Cont., 5 July 1989, unreported, http://www.legifrance.fr.
[82] Law no. 68-943 of 30 October 1968, as amended by the Law of 16 June 1990.
[83] As from 1 September 2002.

2. A Terrorist Sets a Bomb in an Aeroplane and it Crashes into

a) A Residential Area

b) A nuclear plant

The following persons or entities may be held liable: 49

- the terrorists and their accomplices for all damage consequential on their criminal act;
- the airline to the passengers on board on the basis of the contractual *obligation de sécurité* (strict liability), but with possible exoneration (*force majeure*);[84]
- the airline or charterer (joint liability) to residents or owners of the plant for any damage to the person or property on the ground caused by the crash of the aircraft or parts of it; *force majeure* is no defence;[85]
- the airport authorities to residents in the area devastated by the crash or owners of the nuclear plant for gross negligence in the security check and handling of luggage containing the bomb (action before the administrative court).[86]

In situation (a), a resident obtains compensation from the Fund and from his insurance company (*Assurance multirisque habitation*).[87] In situation (b), same as case 1(b), except that there will be no time to initiate military action. 50

3. A Terrorist Drives with a Third Person's Car or Bus into a Crowd of People

The victims will recover from the Fund only if the terrorist intention is proved. The liability of the terrorist will be based on fault and not on the special statute imposing strict liability on drivers of a vehicle involved in a road traffic accident.[88] Indeed, this is not an accident but a deliberate action.[89] 51

The owner of the car may be liable if he has facilitated the use of the car by his own negligence (car or bus left parked unlocked and unattended with ignition key left in a visible place). However, as noted earlier, French courts are reluctant to hold the owner liable in such cases.[90] 52

[84] See supra III.A and III.B.
[85] See supra III.A and III.B.
[86] See supra IV.A.
[87] See supra II.A.
[88] Law no. 85-677 of 5 July 1985.
[89] Cass. Civ. 2^{e}, 30 November 1994, Bull. civ. II, no. 243, [1995] *revue trimestrielle de droit civil* (RTDCiv), 132, note P. Jourdain.
[90] See supra III.C.

53 The owner of the vehicle may recover from his insurance company for the theft and subsequent damage to the car.

4. A Terrorist Hides a Bomb in a Car, Which Explodes Among a Crowd of People

54 The terrorist's intention may appear obvious but French courts require "a minimum of organisation" to classify the act as a terrorist action.[91] The terrorist will be held liable on the basis of his criminal action. The State may only be made liable if there was a riotous assembly or riot, but evidence of gross negligence is required. The State may also be made liable if a police officer, having been informed of the situation, did not take reasonable steps to prevent the explosion or to protect people, but it is necessary to establish gross negligence.[92] An individual in a position to prevent the crime without taking unreasonable risks may also be held liable.[93]

55 To conclude this report, the French system may appear as a model in terms of victim protection but as an *inferno* (including a paradise for lawyers) for subrogated indemnifiers trying to recover.

[91] Cass. Civ. 1re, 17 October 1995, cited supra II.C.
[92] As explained supra IV.A.
[93] See supra IV.B.

GERMANY
LIABILITY FOR ACTS OF TERRORISM UNDER GERMAN LAW

Ulrich Magnus

I. General

A. Does Your Legal System Have Special Legislation on Terror Attacks, in Particular Concerning Liability or Other Indemnity?

As yet, Germany has not enacted specific legislation on liability for terror attacks. However, the Victim Compensation Act of 1976 (*Opferentschädigungsgesetz,* OEG)[1] entitles victims of violent attacks under certain conditions to claim compensation from the Federal Republic of Germany or the Bundesländer (as to this Act see further infra no. 2). This Act can also provide some financial assistance in case of damage caused by terrorists. 1

B. Are There any Special Funds Applicable Providing Alternative Compensation for Victims of Terror Attacks?

The OEG entitles persons to claim compensation when they have been bodily injured through an intentional and wrongful violent attack against their person or against another person or when they were injured in legitimate defence against such attack (§ 1 par. 1 OEG).[2] The same right to compensation is granted when the injury is caused by intentional poisoning or by negligently 2

[1] Act of 11 May 1976 on the Compensation of Victims of Violent Acts (*Bundesgesetzblatt* [BGBl.] 1976 I 1181) as amended on 6 December 2000 (BGBl. 2000 I 1676). As to the recent amendments see: F. Wältermann, Zur Änderung des Opferentschädigungsgesetzes und weiterer Gesetze, [2001] *Neue Juristische Wochenschrift* (NJW), 733 et seq. Further amendments – of 2002 – were declared unconstitutional by the Federal Constitutional Court (Bundesverfassungsgericht, BVerfG, BGBl 2003 I 126).

[2] § 1 par. 1 OEG: „Wer im Geltungsbereich dieses Gesetzes oder auf einem deutschen Schiff oder Luftfahrzeug infolge eines vorsätzlichen, rechtswidrigen tätlichen Angriffs gegen seine oder eine andere Person oder durch dessen rechtmäßige Abwehr eine gesundheitliche Schädigung erlitten hat, erhält wegen der gesundheitlichen und wirtschaftlichen Folgen auf Antrag Versorgung in entsprechender Anwendung des Bundesversorgungsgesetzes. Die Anwendung dieser Vorschrift wird nicht dadurch ausgeschlossen, dass der Angreifer in der irrtümlichen Annahme von Voraussetzungen eines Rechtfertigungsgrundes gehandelt hat".

causing a danger for others through a criminal act committed with means dangerous to public safety (§ 1 par. 2 OEG). Whether the Act foresees compensation also for persons who have been injured while helping victims of terror attacks (policemen, fire-brigade, volunteers) is doubtful.[3] The Act does, however, not provide compensation for property damage or for mere economic loss. The victim must have suffered harm to his or her health.[4] It is further necessary that the attack took place either in Germany or aboard a German ship or aircraft. If all requirements are met, then compensation is granted by the federal state (*Bundesland*) where the violation occurred or where the victim habitually resided. Harm suffered aboard a ship or aircraft has to be compensated by the Federal Republic of Germany.[5] Compensation is granted in accordance with the provisions of the Federal Pensions Act.[6]

3 The "violent attack" required by § 1 par. 1 OEG would also cover terror attacks like that of September 11 since that attack was a wrongful act of violence directed against all those aboard the aircrafts as well as against all those in the World Trade Center buildings and in the near surroundings, either with the direct intention of killing or injuring all these persons or at least with the indirect intent of incurring their death or injury.[7] Therefore, if the attack had happened in Germany the people injured and the dependants of the victims,[8] would have been entitled to compensation under the OEG.

4 The OEG is applicable even if a person would be entitled to claim damages under normal tort law or other provisions of law (see also § 3 OEG). The agency granting compensation under the OEG then acquires the victim's claim against any tortfeasor by way of legal assignment (§ 5 OEG).

C. *Have Your Judges ever Had to Address the Issue of Liability in Connection with Terror Attacks in any Leading Cases?*

5 There are few cases addressing civil liability for such acts which can be classified as terror attacks in the sense as used here.

In 1904 the former Imperial Court (*Reichsgericht,* RG) decided a case in which a heavy road construction machine had been put on the rails of a railway line so that a train derailed.[9] The question was whether the railway company was strictly liable to the victims under § 1 Liability Act (*Haftpflichtgesetz,* HaftPflG) or was excused by *force majeure* as the same statute foresees

[3] As to the circle of protected persons see E. Kunz/G. Zellner, *Opferentschädigungsgesetz. Kommentar* (4th edn. 1999), § 1 no. 3 et seq.

[4] Cf. E. Kunz/G. Zellner (supra fn. 3), § 1 no. 31 et seq.

[5] See § 4 OEG. The state of habitual residence has to compensate the harm only if the place of occurrence cannot be determined.

[6] Act of 20 December 1950 on Pensions for Victims of the War (BGBl. 1950 I 791) as amended on 15 June 1999 (BGBl. 1999 I 1328).

[7] Indirect intent is sufficient; *Bundessozialgericht* (Federal Social Court, BSG) *Entscheidungen des Bundessozialgerichts* (BSGE) 81, 288; E. Kunz/G. Zellner (supra fn. 3), § 1 no. 28.

[8] See § 1 par. 8 OEG.

[9] RG in [1904] *Juristische Wochenschrift* (JW), 577.

as exemption from liability. Although the judgment does not state whether the machine had been put on the rail for terrorist purposes it makes clear that the railway company would be excused only if the instance had been absolutely unavoidable as e.g. in case of the throwing of a dynamite bomb.

In 1926 the RG was again seized of a case where a railway company was sued for damage caused through an act of an unknown person who had shifted a switch so that a train collided with another train.[10] Similar attacks had happened before for unknown motives and again the court expressed its opinion that such attacks can constitute *force majeure*, which exempts from strict liability, but only if even the highest possible degree of diligence would not have prevented the damage.

In 1988 the Federal Court had to decide on the liability of an energy company after unknown persons (probably opponents to the energy policy of the company) had destroyed the pylon of the electric wires of the company and after the wires, by falling down, had caused damage to third persons.[11] Again the court expresses the opinion that acts of sabotage can constitute *force majeure* but only if they cannot be prevented by applying reasonable means and the utmost care which can reasonably be expected.[12] In the case at hand *force majeure* was denied because the statute provided for an unrestricted strict liabilitiy in case electric wires fell down.

D. *Did the Events of 11 September 2001 or any Other Recent Terror Attacks Have any Influence on Your Liability Systems (Interpretation, Discussion About Reforms, Duty to Take Care)?*

Civil liability for terror attacks as such has not been discussed very much in Germany.[13] Thus far the question of insurability of terror damage has been the focus of discussion after September 11, whereas for instance the recent reform of the law of damages, which entered into force on 1 August 2002,[14] did not introduce any changes specifically directed towards terror damage. Neither can any changes in the interpretation of the present liability system, nor in the standard of duty of care, be observed. Legislative changes as a reaction to September 11 have been introduced e.g. in the Act concerning the powers of the secret service to better protect the public against international terrorist attacks and to better prevent those attacks.[15] 6

[10] RG in [1926] JW, 2290.

[11] *Bundesgerichtshof* (Federal Court, BGH) in [1988] NJW, 2733.

[12] BGH ibid.: „Sabotageakte auf Anlagen, für die eine Gefährdungshaftung besteht, können höhere Gewalt darstellen, da es sich dabei um von außen kommende betriebsfremde Eingriffe handelt. Voraussetzung ist dafür aber, dass sie mit zumutbaren Mitteln auch durch die äußerste, vernünftigerweise zu erwartende Sorgfalt nicht verhindert werden können".

[13] The discussion concentrates on criminal and administrative measures to punish and prevent terrorist acts; see, e.g., E. von Bubnoff, Terrorismusbekämpfung – eine weltweite Herausforderung, [2002] NJW, 2672; K. Nehm, Ein Jahr danach – Gedanken zum 11. September 2001, [2002] NJW, 2665.

[14] *Zweites Gesetz zur Änderung schadensersatzrechtlicher Vorschriften* (Second Act on Amendments of Provisions on the Law of Damages) BGBl. 2002 I 2674.

[15] In the so-called G 10 Act; see thereto B. Huber, Das neue G-10 Gesetz, [2001] NJW, 3296 et seq.

7 Concerning insurance matters, a new insurance company ("Extremus Versicherungs-AG") has been established in order to grant coverage in case of huge damage caused by terrorist attacks. The admission of this new company to the insurance market has been recently approved by the respective state authority.[16] The new company will offer insurance protection against terrorist damage to property and business interruption which exceeds € 25 million, up to € 3 billion. Beyond that limit the state will provide additional coverage up to the amount of € 10 billion.

E. Does Your Country Participate in any International Conventions in Connection with Liability for Terror Attacks?

8 Germany has ratified the European Convention on Compensation for Victims of Violent Acts.[17] The standard of the Convention corresponds to that of the OEG (see supra no. 1 and 2).

II. Strict Liability

A. Focusing on Strict Liability for Means of Transport and Enterprises or Facilities, Would You Say the Owner, Custodian or Keeper Is also Liable if a Terrorist Initiates the Damage?

9 In answering this question one must distinguish between the different means of transportation and also between different activities of enterprises:

10 With respect to *means of transportation* and leaving aside international conventions applicable in Germany, German law provides for strict liability of keepers of motor vehicles[18] and of aeroplanes[19] as well as of operators of railways.[20] The strict liability of the keeper of a motor vehicle or aircraft and of the operator of a railway can only be invoked when the damage that ensued was due to the operation of the vehicle ("*beim Betrieb*"). The misuse terrorists make of the means of transportation, as especially the tragic events of September 11 exemplify, could be regarded as outside the normal operation of vehicles and therefore also as outside the scope of the respective strict liability statutes. However, the Federal Court has decided that strict liability under the Road Traffic Act is incurred even if a car – its specific speed and weight – has been used as instrument to kill a policeman.[21] This decision though partly critizised[22] is approved by the prevailing view.[23] Its

[16] See the report in *Frankfurter Allgemeine Zeitung* (FAZ), 4 September 2002, 11 ("Terrorversicherung Extremus gegründet").
[17] Convention of 24 November 1983.
[18] § 7 par. 1 *Straßenverkehrsgesetz* (Road Traffic Act, StVG).
[19] § 33 par. 1 *Luftverkehrsgesetz* (Air Traffic Act, LuftVG).
[20] § 1 par. 1 HaftPflG.
[21] *Entscheidungen des Bundesgerichtshofs in Zivilsachen* (BGHZ) 37, 311.
[22] H. Kötz/G. Wagner, *Deliktsrecht* (9th edn. 2001), no. 388.
[23] See e.g. W. Filthaut, Die Gefährdungshaftung des Kfz-Halters und des Bahnbetriebsunternehmers für vorsätzlich verursachte Schäden, [1998] *Neue Zeitschrift für Verkehrsrecht* (NZV), 89; M. Fuchs, *Deliktsrecht* (2nd edn. 1997), 206; D. Medicus, *Schuldrecht II. Besonderer Teil* (10th edn. 2000), no. 881.

reasoning can be applied to other strict liability statutes which therefore in principle can be invoked even if terrorists use aeroplanes or other means of transportation as weapons.

The strict liability of the *car keeper* and the *operator of a railway* is however excluded if the damage is caused through *force majeure* (*höhere Gewalt*).[24] It is commonly understood that besides war, natural catastrophes etc. also unforeseeable acts of third persons, which cannot be prevented even with utmost care and foresight, qualify as *force majeure*.[25] Therefore the keeper of a car and the operator of a railway would not be liable if a terrorist used the car or train for a terror attack and caused damage, unless they could have prevented such activity, for instance by safely locking the unattended car or train or similar safety measures. For road traffic accidents this rule has been specifically enacted in § 7 par. 3 StVG.[26] 11

The *keeper of an aircraft* is on the contrary responsible even for damage through a malfunction of the plane due to *force majeure*.[27] But the statute provides that if somebody uses the aircraft without knowledge and consent of the keeper this person is strictly liable instead of the keeper unless the latter has negligently enabled the unpermitted use.[28] The keeper then remains strictly liable. It has not yet been decided which safety measures are necessary in order to prevent terrorists from the misuse of the aircraft. After September 11 the standard will however be rather high. Nevertheless, it is likely that the keeper of the aircraft will regularly not be liable. 12

German law does not provide for strict liability of *enterprises* in general but only of those conducting particularly dangerous activities. Therefore, enterprises (but also single persons) are strictly liable which operate *installations of energy lines* like electricity wires, pipelines, gas lines when the electricity, liquid or gas has caused damage to persons or property.[29] The operating enterprise is exempted from strict liability again in case of *force majeure* unless the damage is caused by falling down (electric) wires.[30] Thus, terrorist acts on 13

[24] § 7 par. 2 StVG; § 1 par. 2 HaftPflG. Both provisions have been amended very recently. Until 1 August 2002 the keeper of a car was excused in case of an "unavoidable event". The same was true for accidents of railways (tramways) on public roads (for other railway accidents only *force majeure* could exempt the operator from liability). The exemption from liability is now slightly more difficult for car keepers and railway operators than before; see also Reasoning ("Begründung") to the Draft Proposal of the Second Act on Amendments of Provisions on the Law of Damages (supra no. 5) *Bundestags-Drucksache* (BT-Drucks.) 14/7752, 71.

[25] BGHZ 7, 338, 339; BGHZ 62, 351, 354; BGH in [1953] NJW, 184; BGH in [1986] NJW, 2313; BGH in [1967] *Versicherungsrecht* (VersR), 138, 139; BGH in [1976] VersR, 963; BGH in [1888] VersR, 910 (with respect to § 1 par. 2 HaftPflG which contains the notion "höhere Gewalt"). See also the cases cited supra no. 5.

[26] As to the same rule in air traffic see § 33 par. 2 LuftVG and infra no. 11.

[27] E. Deutsch, *Unerlaubte Handlungen, Schadensersatz und Schmerzensgeld* (3rd edn. 1995), no. 387; H. Kötz/G. Wagner (supra fn. 22), no. 363.

[28] § 33 par. 2 LuftVG.

[29] § 2 par. 1 HaftPflG.

[30] § 2 par. 3 no. 3 HaftPflG; see also the BGH case cited supra in no. 5.

those installations would regularly exempt the operator from its strict liability since unforeseeable and unavoidable acts of third persons qualify also here as *höhere Gewalt*.[31] But the operator would remain strictly liable for damage caused through terror attacks when wire installations fall down as a consequence of the attack (e.g. on a pylon whose breakdown causes the wire to fall down).[32]

14 According to § 25 par. 1 Nuclear Energy Act (*Atomgesetz*, AtomG) the owner of a *nuclear installation* is strictly liable for damage caused by a nuclear incident of his installation as far as such damage would be covered by the Paris Convention on Third Party Liability in the Field of Nuclear Energy.[33] This strict liability of the owner even applies in case of "armed conflict, invasion, civil war, insurrection, or a grave natural disaster of an exceptional character" where under the Paris Convention strict liability would be excluded.[34] This is provided for by § 25 par. 3 AtomG. Therefore a terror attack on a nuclear plant would not relieve the operator of that plant from strict liability for the ensuing damage. Since art. 6 (b) Paris Convention channels the liability onto the operator of the nuclear installation the owner alone would be liable to persons injured by the incident. But the owner would have a right of recourse against the wilful tortfeasors since the terrorists would act with intent (art. 6 (f) (i) Paris Convention). For cases outside the Paris Convention strict liability is provided for as well (§ 26 par. 1 sent 1 AtomG). But here the owner is excused if he used the utmost care to prevent the damage. In such a case a terror attack would not trigger the owner's liability.

15 Enterprises which *pollute the water* (lakes, rivers, groundwater) and thereby damage others are strictly liable for the loss.[35] If they have actively brought substances into the water, no excuse is permitted; if the emmission of substances occurs by chance, *force majeure* is an excuse (§ 22 par. 1 and 2 WHG). If terror attacks on plants lead to the pollution of water and damage to others, the owner of the plant would therefore be exempted from strict liability for such damage since it cannot be said that he then actively polluted the water (unless he, through carelessness, enabled the attack to take place and thus the ensuing damage).

16 Enterprises which *pollute the environment* through certain installations via an environmental medium like air, water or soil and thereby cause bodily harm to others or damage to property are also strictly liable for the loss[36] but can invoke the excuse of *force majeure*.[37] Again, the notion of *force majeure* includes unforeseeable acts of third persons like terrorists[38] so that the owner of

[31] See the references in supra fn. 25.
[32] Cf. BGH in [1988] NJW, 2733 (supra no. 5).
[33] BGBl. 1975 II 957 et seq.
[34] Art. 9 Paris Convention.
[35] § 22 *Wasserhaushaltsgesetz* (Waterhousehold Act, WHG).
[36] § 1 *Umwelthaftungsgesetz* (Environmental Liability Act, UmweltHG).
[37] § 4 UmweltHG.
[38] J. Kohler in v. Staudinger, *Kommentar zum Bürgerlichen Gesetzbuch mit Einführungsgesetz und Nebengesetzen. Umwelthaftungsrecht* (2002), § 4 UmweltHG no. 12.

the installation would not be liable when terrorists misuse the installation to pollute the environment and injure third persons.

Enterprises which produce or work with *genetically modified* organisms are strictly liable for damage caused by those organisms to third persons.[39] This liability is not excluded in case of *force majeure*.[40] Therefore, if terrorists misuse genetically modified organisms and thereby cause damage, then nevertheless the operator of the enterprise, which has modified these organisms, remains strictly liable to third persons who have suffered harm. 17

Mining enterprises which by certain mining activities injure persons or damage property are strictly liable.[41] Again, *force majeure* is no excuse here.[42] Thus, where terrorists destroy a mining installation listed in § 2 par. 1 no. 3 BBergG the operator of the installation is strictly liable for the damage suffered by third persons insofar as the damage is due to typical mining dangers. 18

Pharmaceutical manufacturers are strictly liable for damage caused through their pharmaceuticals.[43] But the AMG provides for excuses, namely that the detrimental effects of the pharmaceutical do not originate from its development or manufacture (§ 84 par. 3 AMG).[44] If e.g. terrorists contaminated pharmaceuticals of a certain manufacturer and injured third persons, this excuse would probably work in favour of the manufacturer. 19

B. *Can Terror Attacks Be Classified as a Defence like Act of God/Force Majeure/Unavoidable Event?*

As the foregoing survey shows German law regards unforeseeable and unavoidable acts of third persons including terror attacks only partly as a defence in the sense of *force majeure* (*höhere Gewalt*). Persons who would otherwise be strictly liable are in some situations relieved from liability if such acts intervene. Partly, these intervening acts are no defence, namely for the operator of electric wires which have fallen down, for the operator of a nuclear plant, of a mining installation or of an enterprise concerned with genetically modified organisms. On the other hand the keeper of a motor vehicle, the operator of a railway or a polluting plant can rely on the *force majeure* defence. In fact, the keeper of an aeroplane is regularly also not liable for terrorist misuse of his plane.[45] The distinction between the two categories could perhaps be based on the argument that particularly dangerous activities or installations should leave the risk even of misuse with the operator. Nevertheless it does not appear too convincing that the keeper or operator is the right person to be liable when 20

[39] § 32 *Gentechnikgesetz* (Genetechnic Act, GenTG).
[40] J. Kohler (supra fn. 38), §§ 32, 34, 35, 37 GenTG no. 40.
[41] § 114 *Bundesberggesetz* (Federal Mining Act, BbergG).
[42] J. Kohler (supra fn. 38), § 114 BBergG no. 40.
[43] § 84 par. 1 *Arzneimittelgesetz* (Pharmaceuticals Act, AMG).
[44] The recent reform of the law of damages placed the burden of proof for this excuse on the manufacturer.
[45] See supra no. 12.

terrorists use his property or installation as means for their attack and he himself is to some extent a victim of the attack. Anyhow, in case of catastrophic terror attacks it will be mainly the public which has to bear the burden via the Victim Compensation Act.

C. *If There Is Another Person Liable Besides or Instead of the Terrorist, for Which Kind of Damages Is He/She Liable (for Example also Compensation for Consequential Damage like Plundering Following a Terror Attack)?*

21 As far as another person is strictly liable besides or instead of the terrorist (see supra no. 8 et seq.) the compensable loss is limited to compensation for bodily harm and direct property damage. All medical and repair costs can be claimed. The compensation of other consequential loss is restricted by the scope of protection of the respective strict liability statute.[46] Protection against plundering is regularly outside the protective purpose of those statutes which disregard *force majeure* as an excuse.

III. Fault Liability

A. *At Public Facilities such as Airports, Train Stations, Sports Stadiums etc., Who Is Responsible that no Terrorist Enters and Causes Harm? The Entity that Runs the Facility, Enterprises that Obtain an Advantage Therefrom (such as Airlines or Organizers of Sports Events), the State, or any Other Person(s)? How far Do These Duties of Care Go in that Respect?*

22 In principle the operator of the facility is responsible for its reasonable safety and security. Therefore, e.g. the Deutsche Bahn AG is responsible for controlling train stations in a reasonable manner. But also the organiser who uses the facility e.g. a sports stadium for a sports event is liable as well or even instead of the owner, keeper or operator of the facility. The extent of the duty to take care for safety and security depends on the circumstances and requires such measures as can be reasonably and economically expected. For instance, the organiser of a sports event must care for a sufficient number of staff that is present to control the situation, that hooligans are kept out or rival groups are kept apart[47] and the like. Since terrorists normally hide their intentions[48] effective preventive measures against their activities are difficult to apply. While airlines may be obliged to control each passenger the same seems impossible for railways or bus lines in particular at rush hours and rather difficult at large sports events. A certain, sometimes even superficial control, as is reasonable and adequate in the circumstances, must suffice.

23 The state can be made liable if its officials have neglected their duties ("Amtspflichten") towards citizens who have been injured by terrorists.[49] Such

[46] See J. Kohler (supra fn. 38), § 1 UmweltHG no. 74 et seq.
[47] OLG Düsseldorf in [1980] VersR, 1147, 1148.
[48] See also the UN definition adopted for this project.
[49] See § 839 *Bürgerliches Gesetzbuch* (German Civil Code, BGB) in connection with art. 34 *Grundgesetz* (Basic Law, GG).

duties may consist of a duty to warn if there are sufficient hints at terror attacks. In particular the police is obliged to prevent impending criminal acts as far as possible.[50] But again, also for the police it will be difficult if not impossible to prevent terror attacks whose secret preparation and unexpected commission is characteristic.

B. To What Extent Do Individuals or Entities Have a Duty of Care to Participate in the Active Avoidance of Terrorist Acts?

Individuals and enterprises have no specific duty to take an active part in the avoidance of terrorist acts. It is, however, a crime if somebody who gains reliable knowledge that specific criminal acts (which are listed in § 138 Criminal Code and contain most terrorist acts) are planned does not inform the authorities or the potential victim(s). § 138 Criminal Code has been regarded as a provision which does not directly protect the victim.[51] According to this view, the neglect of this duty has no bearing on civil liability; § 138 Criminal Code cannot be combined with § 823 par. 2 BGB to found a damages claim in tort. In contrast to this opinion it could and should, however, be argued that the criminal duty implied in § 138 Criminal Code to warn the victim of massive criminal acts which are threatened is a duty directed at the protection and in favour of the victim and therefore constitutes a "Schutzgesetz" ('protective act') in the sense of § 823 par. 2 BGB. 24

IV. Cases

1. A Terrorist Hijacks an Aeroplane and Crashes into

a) A Building

In alternative (a) the keeper of the aeroplane would not be liable for the ensuing damage. He would only be jointly liable – with the terrorist – if he had negligently enabled the terrorist to misuse the aircraft.[52] That case could e.g. arise where the keeper of the aeroplane did not organise for sufficient controls before the passengers entered the plane. 25

b) A Nuclear Plant

In alternative (b), if a nuclear incident resulted from the crash and persons were thereby injured, the owner of the nuclear plant alone would be liable for that damage since liability is channelled onto him.[53] But he would have a right 26

[50] See the examples BGHZ 12, 206 (failure to control a camp of asocial people); OLG Celle in [1975] VersR, 177 (failure to prevent criminal acts of participants of a demonstration).

[51] LG Hamburg in [1996] *recht + sport* (r + s), 396, 397; J. Hager, in: v. Staudinger, *Kommentar zum Bürgerlichen Gesetzbuch mit Einführungsgesetz und Nebengesetzen* (13th edn. 1999), § 823 no. G 42.

[52] See supra no. 12.

[53] See supra no. 14.

of recourse against all terrorists who were jointly involved in the commission of the tort.[54]

2. A Terrorist Sets a Bomb Situated in an Aeroplane and the Plane Crashes into

a) A Residential Area

27 In this case the terrorist does not personally use the aircraft as in case 1 but merely damages it (on the assumption that the bomb explodes when the plane is in the air). In alternative (a) therefore the exemption of the unpermitted use (§ 33 par. 2 LuftVG)[55] does not apply which would relieve the keeper from liability. But since the keeper of an aircraft is not exempted from strict liability even in case of *force majeure* it is rather likely that the courts would hold him liable.

b) A Nuclear Plant

28 In alternative (b) the same result as in case 1 (b) applies.

3. A Terrorist Drives Somebody's Car or Bus into a Crowd of People

29 Although the use of a vehicle as an instrument for murder would not exclude strict liability under § 7 par. 1 StVG if its keeper uses it in this function[56] the keeper is in general not liable if somebody used the vehicle without his permission and caused damage to others unless the unpermitted use was negligently enabled (§ 7 par. 3 StVG). Therefore, neither the car keeper nor the bus keeper would here be liable under the StVG for the unpermitted use of their vehicles unless they had negligently enabled the terrorist to use the car or bus.

4. A Terrorist Hides a Bomb in a Car Which Explodes Within a Crowd of People

30 The car keeper (on the assumption that he was in no way participating in, or supporting or knowing of, the bomb attack) would not be liable for the damage caused by the bomb. Although the car was in some sense involved as cause of the damage it is already questionable whether the damage occurred while the car was in operation since it was not the specific dangerousness of the car – its speed and weight – which was used to cause the damage.[57] But in any event the explosion, which is due to the activity of the terrorist, would constitute *force majeure* and exempt the keeper from his strict liability.

[54] § 25 par. 1 AtomG in connection with art. 6 (f) (i) Paris Convention.
[55] See supra no. 12.
[56] See supra no. 10.
[57] In contrast to case 3 and also in contrast to the case BGHZ 37, 311. See also supra no. 10.

ITALY
LIABILITY FOR ACTS OF TERRORISM UNDER ITALIAN LAW

Alessio Zaccaria and Giovanni Bisazza

I. General

A. *Does Your Legal System Have Special Legislation on Terror Attacks, in Particular Concerning Liability or Other Indemnity?*

The Italian legal system provides for some public interventions in favour of those who have suffered personal injuries as a consequence of specific types of crimes committed with violence. In particular, the increasing phenomena of terrorism and organized crime have led to the progressive introduction of a system of financial compensation – i.e. donations that were initially reserved to the victims of duty belonging to the security forces and were later extended in favour of the members of the judiciary and of the citizens who are seriously and permanently disabled as a consequence of the injuries caused by terrorist or mafia actions. 1

The key legislation which makes up this system is formed by the Law of 13 August 1980, no. 446; the Law of 20 October 1990, no. 302; the Law of 23 November 1998, no. 407. 2

As confirmed by Italian courts, these regulations are a form of public indemnity founded on the *ratio* of the fundamental right of social solidarity, which is expressed in art. 2 of the Italian Constitution. In particular, this article imposes on the State the fulfilment of the unbreakable duties of economic solidarity for the protection of the inviolable rights of the human being[1]. 3

[1] On this topic see *Corte di Cassazione* (Italian Supreme Court, C.) 632/1990; see also *Corte dei Conti* (Italian Court of Auditors, C. Con.), sez. I, 25 May 1992, no. 146 and C. Con., 15 April 1993, no. 876/a, which affirmed that "the norms of Law no. 446 of 1990 are essentially an expression of national solidarity"; *Consiglio di Stato* (Administrative Supreme Court, Cons. St.), sez IV, judgments of 14 May 1999 no. 845 and 846, where it is explained that Law no. 302/1990 aims at the introduction of a "form of community participation in the case of harm to citizens accidentally involved in episodes of organized crime, whose combat and repression are one of the State's principal objectives".

4 The Law of 13 August 1980, no. 466 (special donations in favour of categories of public employees and citizens, victims of duty or victims of terrorist actions), provides the concession of a donation of € 51,646 (increased to € 77,468 by art. 2 of Law no. 302/1990 for the events following the entry into force of the latter), in favour of judges, public order forces, civilian personnel who are part of the governmental administration of prisons and firemen, who, while on duty, as a direct result of injuries inflicted as a consequence of terrorist or criminal actions or on public duty, suffer a permanent disability of at least eighty percent of their working ability or such that entails, in any case, the end of the employment (the so-called victims of duty).

5 Law no. 302/1990 (norms in favour of victims of terrorism and organized crime) also awards to "whoever suffers a permanent disability, as a result of injuries inflicted as a consequence of terrorist acts or overthrowing of the democratic order which take place on the State's territory" (art. 1), a donation as high as € 77,468, in proportion to the percentage of disability found with reference to the working ability, quantified as € 774.68 for every percentage point. Where the permanent disability refers to at least two thirds of the working ability, the victim, instead of a donation in one amount, can opt for a one-off life annuity payment quantified as € 6.197 per month for each percentage point.

6 The same events which give entitlement to the donation granted by the above-mentioned law, also entitle, as provided by the Law of 23 November 1998, no. 407 (new norms in favour of the victims of terrorism and organized crime) whoever suffered a permanent invalidity of at least one quarter of their working ability, to a further donation consisting of a one-off life annuity payment of € 258 per month.

7 Where the victim should die as a consequence of his injuries suffered, the benefits granted by the above-mentioned laws are assigned to the victim's surviving family members.

8 The relation between the mechanism of public donations described above and the system of civil liability for damage caused to the victim or to his relatives is not quite clear.

9 Considering Law no. 460/1980, the meagre case law holds that the special donation in favour of the victim of duty (or in favour of his relatives) cannot reduce the amount owed in favour of damages due from whoever caused (or helped cause) the harmful event, as the so-called *compensatio lucri cum damno* could not be invoked, since the special donation granted by the last law mentioned above is given for solidarity purposes and is only occasioned, but does not causally depend on the illegal harmful event which has realized one of the hypotheses laid down by the law for the distribution of the compensation (C 90/632; C 91/8772).

10 This orientation follows the consolidated case law which holds that in order to invoke the compensation of the damage with the favourable conditions which

eventually derive from the harm, it is necessary that the prejudice and the patrimonial increase both descend in a direct and immediate manner from the same event, without taking into account, when determining the *quantum* of the damages, the patrimonial advantages eventually obtained by the injured on a different title (on the basis of such a criterion the application of the *compensatio lucri cum damno* has already been refused in relation to the invalidity annuity conceded to the victims of a tort, see C 70/1928; C 78/4863; 78/550; C 72/2892).

As a consequence of the exclusion of a chain of causation between the donation granted by Law no. 460/1980 and the tort system – see art. 2043 *codice civile* (Italian Civil Code, cc) – it appears that it is impossible for the State to bring an action against the author of the tort in order to obtain the repayment of the amount donated to the victim. However, notwithstanding this logical deduction, the few existing judgments on this point hold that in the hypothesis of the payment of the special donation granted by the Law of 13 August 1980, no. 446, brought into force by the Ministry for Internal Affairs following terrorist acts, the public administration may obtain a refund by taking civil action in criminal proceedings against the accused party (*Corte d'Assise di Roma* (Rome First grade Criminal Court) – Ordinance 7 March 1983; in the same direction see also *Cassazione penale*, – sez. I – [Italian Supreme Criminal Court, C. pen.] decision 14 May 1980). 11

Compared to Law no. 460/1980 which did not mention the point, Law no. 302/1990 – whilst reaffirming the principle that the benefits awarded are independent of the right to damages due to the injured subject or to other beneficiary subjects on behalf of those liable for the harmful events – provides that if the beneficiary has already been awarded damages, the corresponding sum must be subtracted from the amount of the donation, whereas, if damages have not yet been awarded, the State shall replace, for the corresponding amount of the donation, the beneficiary's rights towards those responsible. 12

Summarising, it seems that the special donation contained in Law no. 460/ 1980 is always accumulable with damages, except where the State administration later recovers the sum donated from the injured citizen. 13

The possibility of accumulating the damages with the donation granted by Law no. 320/1990 is, on the contrary, expressly excluded. 14

B. Are There any Special Funds Applicable Providing Alternative Compensation for Victims of Terror Attacks?

Except for the above-mentioned[2] legal system on the social compensation for victims of terrorism and organized crime, there are no special funds available providing for alternative compensation for victims of terror attacks. 15

[2] See the answer to question I.A. supra.

C. Have Your Judges ever Had to Address the Issue of Liability in Connection with Terror Attacks in any Leading Cases?

16 Art. 185, subs. 2 cc says that "any criminal offence, that has caused a patrimonial or non-patrimonial damage, obliges the offender and the persons who, according to the civil laws, are liable for the offender's facts, to pay damages".

17 This norm has always been applied in all cases – not so many actually – in which it was possibile to identify the authors of terrorist attacks, in favour of those vicitms who have taken civil action in criminal proceedings.

D. Did the Events of 11 September 2001 or any Other Recent Terror Attacks Have any Influence on Your Liability Systems (Interpretation, Discussion About Reforms, Duty to Take Care)?

18 Neither the events of 11 September 2001 nor any other recent terror attacks had any discernable influence on Italian's liability system.

19 These events have only led to the presentation of a few draft laws concerning mainly pension and fiscal profiles and to the enaction of the Law of 27 November 2001, no. 413 (that converted into law decree-law of 28 September 2001, no. 353). In the latter law the State – considering the extraordinary need and urgency to recognize an appropriate financial guarantee in favour of the national air transport undertakings and considering also the peculiar and contingent market conditions regarding the costs of insuring risks deriving from terrorist attacks – committed itself to supporting a system of state compensation for injuries suffered by third parties as a consequence of war or terrorist acts while an aeroplane is in service, in favour of national air transport entrepreneurs and in favour of airport management, with the exclusion of any action of recoupment, except in the case of intent or gross negligence of the said undertakings.

E. Does Your Country Participate in any International Conventions in Connection with Liability for Terror Attacks?

20 Italy does not participate in any international conventions in connection with liability for terror attacks. Italy is not, in fact, a contracting party in the only international convention that would seem to be applicable in the case of compensation for injury suffered as a consequence of terrorist attacks, the 1983 European Convention on the Compensation of Victims of Violent Crimes.

II. Strict Liability

A. *Focusing on Strict Liability for Means of Transport and Enterprises or Facilities, Would You Say the Owner, Custodian or Keeper is also Liable if a Terrorist Initiates the Damage?*

The Italian legal system provides both hypotheses of strict liability and hypotheses where the injuring party's fault is presumed. 21

1. Transportation Contract

The norms which govern contracts of carriage set *iuris tantum* presumptions of the carrier's liability. 22

With reference to the contract of transportation of passengers by land, art. 1681 subs. 1 cc provides that the carrier is liable for the harm which occurs to the passenger during the trip if he does not prove to have taken all the appropriate measures to avoid the harm. Analogous norms are contained in the legislation on maritime and air transportation, respectively in art. 409 and 942 *Codice della Navigazione* (Italian Navigation Code, c. nav.).[3] 23

The carrier's liability outlined this way is of a contractual nature, being based on the assumption of the obligation on behalf of the carrier to protect, during the performance of the transportation, the physical safety of the passenger[4], and it is meant in a particularly strict way, as the carrier must prove, in order to exclude his liability (according to art. 1681 cc), not only to have taken all the measures abstractedly suitable to avoid the damage with reference to the security norms for the type of service given, but also to have taken the necessary precautions to avoid the damage in the *concrete situation* in which the transportation was carried out.[5] 24

[3] Art. 409 c. nav. states: "il vettore è responsabile per i sinistri che colpiscono la persona del passeggero, dipendenti da fatti verificatisi dall'inizio dell'imbarco sino al compimento dello sbarco, se non prova che l'evento è derivato da causa a lui non imputabile" ("The carrier is liable for accidents which injure the passenger, provided that the accident took place between the beginning of the embarkation and the end of the disembarkation, unless the carrier proves that the accident is due to a cause which cannot be ascribed to him").
Similarly, art. 942 c. nav., dealing with air transport, says that "il vettore risponde per i sinistri che colpiscono la persona del passeggero, dall'inizio delle operazioni di imbarco al compimento di quelle di sbarco, a meno che non provi che egli e i suoi dipendenti e preposti hanno preso tutte le misure necessarie e possibili, secondo la normale diligenza, per evitare il danno" ("The carrier is liable for accidents which injure the passenger, provided that the accident took place between the beginning of the embarkation and the end of the disembarkation, unless the carrier proves that he and his agents have taken all necessary and possible measures, according to due diligence, to avoid the damage").

[4] It is however a consolidated opinion that the eventual injury can be the basis for a concurring action of civil liability: C 73/835; C 75/4032; C 74/3536.

[5] See C 93/10680; C 72/2658.

25 The carrier is also freed from liability if he can prove that the injuring event is to be connected to an event that is unrelated to his conduct, and therefore cannot be causally reconnected to the latter.

26 As a result, by examining the judgments of Italian courts, the cause that is alien to the carrier's activity, the proof of which frees the carrier from liability for injuries that occur to the passenger, can also consist in the third party's act (to whom terrorist attacks must also be reconnected).[6] In order to have an interruptive effect in the above-mentioned chain of causation, the third party's act, has to obviously present itself as an element that is totally alien to the carrier's activity during performance of the transportation contract. As a consequence, if the carrier gave the third party the possibility to cause the event, the carrier's liability could not be denied and the presumption of fault determined by the law would become operative.[7] In other words, the third party's act that was the direct cause of the harmful event does not exclude the carrier's liability if the remote cause of the harmful event was found in a pre-existing, simultaneous or supervening cause, which is imputable to the carrier.[8]

27 Thus, for example, in the case of a robbery on a coach with the killing of a passenger, the carrier was found to be liable on the basis of art. 1681 cc, for not having been able to prove to have taken all the suitable measures in order to avoid the event, considering that the driver had stopped at night in a place where he should not have stopped.[9]

28 A further example of concurring liability of the carrier with the third party act can be found in a judgment delivered by the *Tribunale di Venezia* (Venice First Grade Court) on the 11 February 1998. The case concerns a bomb that had been set off by some robbers on the postal carriage of a train, injuring the plaintiff who was travelling on another train in the opposite direction to the one where the bomb had exploded. In this case, the injury was ascribable to the National Railway Society that had decided to use the train on which the plaintiff was travelling in order to get closer to the robbed train, to make a reconnaissance. The National Railway Society was held responsible for the accident suffered by the passenger, as the conduct had a causal connection with the event causing the injury and it contrasted with the "obligation to take all the necessary measures and precautions fundamental to assure the safety of the transported passengers".

29 Considering the above, it can therefore be said that, insofar as a terrorist attack is undoubtedly a third party's act, alien to the organization of the transportation undertaking, and therefore suitable to interrupt the material chain of cau-

[6] C 75/1649; 71/2408; 70/2181; 52/2256; 49/165.

[7] C 62/577; C 57/445.

[8] See C 63/877.

[9] C 97/11161.

sation between the transportation activity and the harmful event occurring to the passenger, the carrier should not, as a principle, be considered liable for the damage suffered by the passengers.

The carrier could, however, be considered liable for the accident which occurred to the passenger following the terrorist attack, if, *from the concrete circumstances of the case*, it should result that the taking place of the terrorist attack was possible because of omitted necessary measures to protect the physical safety of the passengers, to be taken on behalf of the carrier (or his employees). 30

In this last hypothesis, the chain of causation between the transportation activity and the accident occurring to the passenger could not be considered interrupted by the intervention of the terrorist attack, which could be considered only as a concurrent cause of the accident, with the consequent operativeness of the liability presumption affirmed in art. 1681 cc. 31

In this case, the concurrent liability of carrier and terrorists would be governed by the rule of joint liability[10] settled in art. 2055 cc.[11] The injured passenger could therefore claim all damages from the carrier, who would then have a right of recourse against the terrorists. 32

2. Damage Caused by Aircraft to Third Parties on the Ground

As for the damage caused by aircrafts to third parties on the surface, art. 965 c. nav. affirms that the aircraft operator's liability, who is liable now *also in case of force majeure*, is excluded "when the air carrier proves that the damage was caused voluntarily, without any connection to the exercise of the aircraft by persons not belonging to the crew who are on board, and that neither the carrier nor his employees have been able to avoid such damage". 33

In this hypothesis, therefore, the carrier will be held liable if, considering the actual circumstance of the case, he could have, with the diligence required, foreseen or otherwise avoided the third party's harmful conduct. 34

[10] Cf. C 65/2133; 56/2720.

[11] Art. 2055 cc states that "Se il fatto dannoso è imputabile a più persone, tutte sono obbligate in solido al risarcimento del danno. Colui che ha risarcito il danno ha regresso contro ciascuno degli altri, nella misura determinata dalla gravità della rispettiva colpa e dall'entità delle conseguenze che ne sono derivate. Nel dubbio, le singole colpe si presumono uguali". ("If the act causing damage can be attributed to more than one person, all are liable *in solido* for the damages. The person who has compensated for the damage has recourse against each of the others in proportion to the degree of fault of each and to the consequences arising therefrom. In case of doubt, the degree of fault attributable to each is presumed to be equal".) English version of this article is taken from M. Beltramo/G. Longo/J. H. Merryman, *The Italian civil Code* (1969), 505.

3. Nuclear Energy

35 With regard to civil liability depending on the peaceful use of nuclear energy, Law no. 1860 of the 31 December 1962 (peaceful use of nuclear energy), art. 15, subs. 1, states that the the holder of a nuclear licence is strictly liable for any damage caused to persons or things by a nuclear accident.[12]

36 The person carrying out the activity cannot prove that he has taken all the prescribed measures, but he can be freed from liability only by proving that the nuclear accident is referable to one of the cases affirmed by art. 15, subs. 5, that is, to armed conflict, hostility, civil war, insurrection or natural disasters of an exceptional nature.[13] The list contained in the above-mentioned article is considered to be peremptory, and as a consequence the holder of a nuclear licence cannot invoke in a general way *force majeure*, including the third party act, as exempting him from nuclear liability.

37 It has been considered possible to adopt "a broad construction of the single voices with regard to the development of new phenomena, not expressly foreseen by the norm but however assimilable to the situation the norm disciplines".[14] Therefore, an attack by a terrorist organisation could also be invoked by the holder of a nuclear licence in order to avoid his liability.

4. Dangerous Activity

38 Finally, a further *iuris tantum* presumption of liability is stated by art. 2050 cc for he who performs a dangerous activity for the damage caused to third parties.[15]

39 This norm applies to all the activities marked as dangerous by the Law on Public Safety (*regio decreto* (r.d) 18 June 1931, no. 773), such as factories, deposits and transportation of substances which can explode or catch fire and the

[12] Art. 15, subs. 1, affirms that: "L'esercente di un impianto nucleare è responsabile, in conformità della presente legge, di ogni danno alle persone o alle cose causato da un incidente nucleare avvenuto nell'impianto nucleare connesso con lo stesso". ("The holder of a nuclear licence is liable, according to the present law, of any damage to persons or goods caused by a nuclear accident occurring in the nuclear plant connected to it").

[13] Art. 15, subs. 5, states as follows: "L'esercente un impianto nucleare non è responsabile dei danni causati da un incidente nucleare se tale incidente è dovuto direttamente ad atti di conflitto armato, di ostilità, di guerra civile, di insurrezione o a cataclismi naturali di carattere eccezionale".("The holder of a nuclear licence is not liable for the damage caused by a nuclear accident if such an accident is directly due to acts of an armed conflict, of hostility, of civil war, of inserruction or natural catastrophies of an exceptional nature").

[14] V. V. Di Martino, *La R. C. nelle attività pericolose e nucleari* (1979), 245.

[15] Art. 2050 cc states: "Chiuque cagiona danno ad altri nello svolgimento di un'attività pericolosa, per sua natura o per la natura dei mezzi adoperati, è tenuto al risarcimento, se non prova di avere adottato tutte le misure idonee ad evitare il danno" ("Whoever causes injury to another in the performance of an activity dangerous by its nature or by reason of the instrumentalities employed, is liable for damages, unless he proves that he has taken all suitable measures to avoid the injury"). English version of this article is taken from M. Beltramo/G. Longo/J. H. Merryman (supra fn. 11).

use of weapons (see *decreto del Presidente della Repubblica* (d.p.r) 15 August 1948, no. 1184, on criminal regulation for the control of weapons).[16]

The person who performs a dangerous activity, just like in the case of the carrier, can be freed from liability only by concretely proving to have taken all the appropriate measures to avoid the damage, according to the circumstances of the case. The third party's act, as a terrorist attack could be, can also have redeeming effects only if it is such as to exclude, in a certain way, the chain of causation between the dangerous activity and the harmful event, "and not when it is a concurring element in the causation of damage, by inserting itself in a situation of danger that has rendered it possibile because of the unsuitability of the preventive measures adopted".[17] 40

B. *Can Terror Attacks Be Classified as a Defence like Act of God/Force Majeure/Unavoidable Event?*

An answer to this question has been partly given in point II.A). 41

1. Transportation Contract

The presumption of liability, affirmed by the norms on the transportation of people, is based on the assumption of the cause-effect relation between the activity of performance of transportation and the accident occurring to the passenger. The third party's act (which includes, as mentioned above, a terrorist attack), that was an immediate and direct cause of the accident occurring to the passenger, and the occurrence of which was by no means made possible by the omitting of suitable measures, on behalf of the carrier, for the protection of the physical safety of the passengers, is an act that interrupts the above-mentioned chain of causation between the performance of the transportation and the accident occurring to the passenger, stopping the operativeness of the presumption of liabilty which lies on the carrier. 42

The *force majeure*, instead, excludes the person's fault for the damage that is causally related to the act (or the omission) of the person.[18] 43

The *force majeure* and the third party's act, therefore, are considered on different levels, the former referring to the subjective element of fault, the latter to the material element of the chain of causation between conduct and harmful 44

[16] The sphere of application of art. 2050 cc has gradually been specified by courts, which have identified as dangerous also all those activities entailing a relevant possibility that injury shall occur, because of their nature or the characteristics of the means used (C 90/7571; C 93/8069; C 88/6739; C78/2189). It has to be underlined that it has been stated that the judgment concerning the dangerousness of the activity must be given on the basis of an *ex post* factual finding, while keeping in mind the factual circumstances existing at the moment in which the activity is carried out, and that should have been known to the agent considering the activity carried out (C 95/9205).

[17] C 91/4710. C 98/5484.

[18] Cf. M. C. Bianca, *Diritto Civile 5, La responsabilità* (1994), 662.

event. Considering this, the terrorist attack does not seem to be classifiable as an act of *force majeure*.

2. Damage Caused by Aircraft to Third Parties on the Surface

45 For the same reasons illustrated above in point (2.a), the terrorist attack, being important in the sphere of material causality, does not seem to be classifiable as an act of *force majeure*. This seems to be confirmed by the wording of art. 965 c. nav. which, after having expressly affirmed the aircraft operator's liability in the case of *force majeure* as well, excludes the aircraft operator liability for damage caused by persons on board, alien to the crew.

3. Civil Liability Depending upon the Pacific Employment of Nuclear Energy

46 Referring to what has been said above (point 1.c), it can be observed that the list of causes that exclude the liability of the holder of a nuclear licence (art. 15 of Law no. 1860/1962), in which, following a broad construction, the terrorist attack can be inserted as well, seem to represent hypotheses which are suitable to exclude that the nuclear accident is causally referable to the use of nuclear energy. In this hypothesis too, therefore, it seems possible to affirm that the terrorist attack cannot be regarded as an act that affects the person's fault, and therefore as a case of *force majeure*.

4. Dangerous Activity

47 In this case too, as already explained above (see point 1.d), the terrorist attack is important in order to exclude the chain of causation between the dangerous activity and the harmful event. It follows that it would not seem possible to reconnect the terrorist attack among the causes of *force majeure*, which affect the evaluation on the existence of the subjective element of fault.

C. If There Is Another Person Liable Besides or Instead of the Terrorist, for Which Kind of Damages Is He/She Liable (for Example also Compensation for Consequential Damage like Plundering Following a Terror Attack)?

48 In the case in which, on the basis of the norms recalled above,[19] in addition to the terrorist organization, another person liable for the damage can be identified – even if it is a hypothesis which is rarely true, considering the normal unforeseeability of a terrorist attack – the latter will be liable, according to the general principle affirmed by art. 1223 cc,[20] for the damage connected to the

[19] See the answer to question II.A., supra.

[20] Art. 1223 cc, applicable also for civil liability affirms that: "Il risarcimento del danno per l'inadempimento o per il ritardo deve comprendere così la perdita subita dal creditore come il mancato guadagno, in quanto ne siano conseguenza immediata e diretta" ("The measure of damages arising from non-performance or delay shall include the loss substained by the creditor and the lost profits insofar as they are a direct and immediate consequence of the non-performance or delay"). English version of this article is taken from M. Beltramo/G. Longo/J. H. Merryman (supra fn. 11).

act attributable to him by a causal connexion which is legally relevant; that is, for damage that, according to common experience, it was objectively foreseeable would derive from his conduct. In such a case, the persons who are charged with the harmful event, even if on the basis of a different title,[21] will be liable *in solidum* towards the injured person,[22] who will be entitled to proceed indifferently against either one of the liable persons to obtain full compensation.[23]

As far as the discipline of the relation between persons causing the injury is concerned, art. 2055 cc affirms that he who has compensated the injured person has a right of recourse against the other joint wrongdoers, in a measure which is proportional to the degree of fault of each one (in case of doubt, the fault is presumed to be the same for each one), and to the extent of the consequences that followed from it. 49

The damage resulting from possibile plundering following the terrorist attack could not be considered among the objectively foreseeable at the moment of the illicit conduct, and therefore is not included among the damage which must be compensated by the person considered liable beside the terrorist organization. Furthermore, the plundering could be qualified as a completely new factor, apt to interrupt the legally relevant chain of causation. 50

III. Fault Liability

A. *At Public Facilities such as Airports, Train Stations, Sports Stadiums etc., Who Is Responsible for Preventing Terrorists from Entering and Causing Harm?*

Liability for terrorist attacks carried out through intrusion, inside public or open to the public facilities – such as airports, stations, stadiums, etc. – of members of terrorist organisations presupposes an existing legal duty to prevent such events. 51

The Italian legal system does not proscribe a general legal duty to prevent loss to others by positive conduct. 52

[21] The joint and several liability, therefore, exists also between persons to whom the same harmful event is imputable on the basis of different titles. See Cass. 95/7231.

[22] Art. 2055 cc states that "Se il fatto dannoso è imputabile a più persone, tutte sono obbligate in solido al risarcimento del danno. Colui che ha risarcito il danno ha regresso contro ciascuno degli altri, nella misura determinata dalla gravità della rispettiva colpa e dall'entità delle conseguenze che ne sono derivate. Nel dubbio, le singole colpe si presumono uguali". ("If the act causing damage can be attributed to more than one person, all are liable *in solido* for the damages. The person who has compensated for the damage has recourse against each of the others in proportion to the degree of fault of each and to the consequences arising therefrom. In case of doubt, the degree of fault attributable to each is presumed to be equal"). English version of this article is taken from M. Beltramo/G. Longo/J. H. Merryman (supra fn. 11).

[23] See C. 29 August 1987, no. 7118.

53 A *general* duty to prevent terrorist attacks could be attributed only to the State, as this duty is part of the duties of the police, that are among the State prerogatives: Art. 1 of the Law on Public Security (r.d 18 June 1931, no. 773), indeed provides that the public security authority look after the maintenance of public order, and the safety of citizens.[24] However, in reality, one must consider that the terrorist attack represents an unforeseeable and unavoidable event, the occurring of which cannot, in principle, be imputable to the State.

54 The evaluation concerning the existence of a possible liability of the State, in any event, must be carried out considering the circumstances of the case. In this regard, it can be observed that the public safety authority is part of the Ministry of the Interior; those who are part of it are therefore subject to the discipline set for civil servants contained in d.p.r 10 January 1957, no. 3 (concerning the regulation of the civil servants of the Italian State). Art. 22 and 23 of this law, in conformity with what is affirmed by art. 28 of the Constitution[25], provide for the personal liability of the civil servant who, in performing his office, causes injust harm to a third party, where injust harm means the harm following any violation of the third party's rights that the employee has committed with intent or gross negligence.

55 The public security officer or agent who omits, with intent or gross negligence, to carry out the controls assigned to him by his office for the safety of citizens (for example, inside an airport), could be considered liable for the damage following a terrorist attack, to the occurring of which he contributed by his omissive conduct. Considering what is affirmed in art. 2059 cc[26] and 185, subs. 2 cp,[27] as a hy-

[24] The law on the "New legal system of public safety administration" (1 April 1981 no. 121), confirms these attributions; art. 24 of this law, indeed, states that: "La Polizia di Stato esercita le proprie funzioni al servizio delle istituzioni democratiche e dei cittadini sollecitandone la collaborazione. Essa tutela l'esercizio delle libertà e dei diritti dei cittadini; vigila sull'osservanza delle leggi, dei regolamenti e dei provvedimenti della pubblica autorità; tutela l'ordine e la sicurezza pubblica; provvede alla prevenzione e alla repressione dei reati; presta soccorso in caso di calamità ed infortuni" ("The state police carries out its duties at the service of the democratic institutions and of the citizens while urging for their cooperation. It protects the freedom and rights of the citizens; it watches over the observance of the laws, the regulations and the provisions adopted by the public authority; it protects the public order and safety; it prevents and represses crimes; it brings aid in the event of calamity and accidents").

[25] Art. 28 of the Italian Constitution says: "I funzionari e i dipendenti dello Stato e degli enti pubblici sono direttamente responsabili, secondo le leggi penali, civili e amministrative, degli atti compiuti in violazione dei diritti. In tali casi la responsabilità civile si estende allo Stato e agli enti pubblici" ("State and public office employees and officers are directly liable, according to the criminal, civil and administrative laws, for the acts performed in violation of rights. In such cases the civil liability extends to the State and the public offices").

[26] Art. 2059 cc: "Il danno non patrimoniale deve essere risarcito solo nei casi indicati dalla legge" ("Non-patrimonial damages shall be awarded only in cases provided by law"). English version of this article is taken from M. Beltramo/G. Longo/J. H. Merryman (supra fn. 11).

[27] Art. 185, subs 2 cp: "Ogni reato, che abbia cagionato un danno patrimoniale o non patrimoniale, obbliga al risarcimento il colpevole e le persone che, a norma delle leggi civili, debbono rispondere per il fatto di lui" ("Any criminal offence, that has caused a patrimonial or non-patrimonial damage, obliges the offender and the persons who, according to the civil laws, are liable for the offender's facts, to pay damages").

pothesis of crime is here involved,[28] the duty of compensation should be extended to include moral damage as well.

The request for damages can also be addressed directly to the State administration, which, once it has compensated the injured party, has a right of recourse against the public employee (art. 22 d.P.R 1957 no. 3). 56

B. To What Extent Do Individuals or Entities Have a Duty of Care to Participate in the Active Avoidance of Terrorist Acts?

This question is largely answered in the previous point. The duty to prevent the occurrence of terrorist attacks is in fact recognizable only for the State. The evaluation concerning the fulfilment of this duty must be carried out considering the concrete circumstances of the case. 57

IV. Cases

1. A Terrorist Hijacks an Aeroplane and Crashes into

a) A Building

As has been said,[29] the carrier will not be liable for the death or personal injury suffered by the passengers. The hijacking of the aeroplane by the terrorists is considered a (third party) act which, being the only and exclusive cause of the harmful event, breaks the chain of causation between the transportation activity and the accidents suffered by the persons on board and it excludes the operativeness of the presumption of liability that weighs on the aircraft carrier according to art. 942 c. nav. 58

Nor will the damage caused to the building and the people inside it be imputable to the aircraft carrier, who, even if strictly liable for the damage caused to third parties on the ground, is not liable, as affirmed by art. 965 c. nav.,[30] for the damage caused by people on board who are alien to the crew. 59

For the damage following the crash, the single terrorist who is author of the hijacking is first of all liable. The cooperation of other persons who are part of the terrorist organisation could constitute a hypothesis of participation in crime,[31] with the consequent criminal liability of all the members of the terrorist organization who have knowingly contributed in any way, materially or psychologically, to any of the various phases of ideation, organisation and ex- 60

[28] Art. 40 cp states that: "Non impedire un evento che si ha l'obbligo giuridico di impedire equivale a cagionarlo" ("Not preventing an event that one has the legal duty to prevent is equivalent to causing it").

[29] See the answer to question II.A.

[30] See the answer to question II.A.

[31] Art. 110 cp: "Quando più persone concorrono nel medesimo reato, ciascuna di esse soggiace alla pena per questa stabilita....". "When more than one person concurrs in the same crime, each one is subject to the punishment laid down for it...".

ecution of the criminal action.[32] From this the duty of compensation of damage according to art. 185 cp above[33] would also follow for those who have in any way cooperated in the terrorist attack.

b) A Nuclear Plant

61 The position of the carrier as far as the damage caused to passengers and third parties on the ground is concerned is identical to the one illustrated in sub 1.a).

62 The holder of a nuclear licence could be held not liable for the nuclear damage if the provision of art. 15, subs 5, of the Law 31 December 1962, no. 1860, is construed broadly so as to include terrorist attacks as well among the causes excluding the liability of the holder of the nuclear licence.[34]

2. A Terrorist Sets a Bomb Situated in an Aeroplane and the Plane Crashes into

a) A Building

63 As for the accidents occurring to the passengers, the position of the terrorists and of the aircraft carrier does not differ from the one illustrated in sub 1.a). The carrier will therefore not be held liable given that from the examining of the concrete case it should not result that the terrorist was able to set the bomb inside the aeroplane by exploiting the omitted performance, on behalf of the carrier or his auxiliaries, of the duty of adopting the suitable measures to protect the physical safety of the passengers.

64 As for the damage caused to third parties on the ground, that is to the damaged buildings and the injured people, the carrier seems strictly liable, according to art. 965 c. nav., *in solidum* with the terrorist. In this case, in fact, as the damage is caused by a bomb situated inside the aircraft, the hypothesis of exclusion of liability of the carrier affirmed by art. 965 c. nav., that only concerns the damage caused by the voluntary conduct of people on board who are alien to the crew, will not be applicable. It must be noted however that Italian law, in this case, provides a limitation of the sum due to the injured person by the carrier for damages, which will not have to exceed a determined amount (limitations to the extent of the damage that can be compensated are also set in favour of the aircraft carrier with regard to the damage suffered by passengers).

b) A Nuclear Plant

65 The position of the terrorists and the carrier is identical to the one illustrated in case 2(a). The holder of the nuclear licence could be freed from liability for

[32] See F. Mantovani, *Diritto Penale, Parte generale* (3rd edn. 1992), 509 et seq.; G. Fiandaca/E. Musco, *Diritto Penale* (3rd edn. 2002), 436 et seq.

[33] See the answer to question I.C.

[34] See the answer to question II.A.

the nuclear damage following the crash, should the terrorist attack be included in the hypothesis of exclusion of liability.[35]

3. A Terrorist Drives in Somebody's Car or Bus into a Crowd of People

The terrorist and the other members of the terrorist organization that have co-operated in the criminal action[36] will be liable for all the damage. 66

A possibile liability of police agents could be affirmed only if, considering the concrete circumstances of the case, it can be affirmed that they had the duty to prevent the event (because, for example, they were aware of the danger) and that they did not take the measures that were reasonably possibile and necessary to avoid the disaster. 67

4. A Terrorist Hides a Bomb in a Car Which Explodes in a Crowd of People

See the answer to case 3. 68

[35] See the answer to case 1. b).
[36] See the answer to case 1. a).

South Africa
Liability for Acts of Terrorism Under South African Law

Johann Neethling

I. General

A. Does Your Legal System Have Special Legislation on Terror Attacks, in Particular Concerning Liability or Other Indemnity?

1 During the apartheid era South Africa had extensive legislation to combat terrorism as a criminal offence.[1] However, apart from a few exceptions, all these statutory measures were repealed by the new democratic Parliament. All that remains on the statute book nowadays is sec. 54 of the Internal Security Act 74 of 1982, which deals with criminal liability for terror attacks under the heading "Terrorism and related offences".[2] Sec. 54(1) deals with terrorism, sec. 54(3) with sabotage and sec. 54(4) with aiding perpetrators of terrorism or sabotage. Since effective anti-terrorism legislation is one of the available tools governments can use to fight terrorism, and South Africa's existing legislation in this respect is clearly defective,[3] the South African Law Commission embarked upon a project,[4] involving in-depth comparative research, to review sec. 54 of the Internal Security Act. In its report, which was released in August 2002, the Commission proposes extensive new legislative measures in the Anti-Terrorism Bill 2002, to combat terrorism through the criminal justice system.[5]

[1] See the Terrorism Act 83 of 1967. For important cases on the definition of terrorism in this Act, see *S v Ffrench-Beytach* 1972 3 *South African Law Reports* (SA) 430 (A); *S v Hosey* 1974 1 SA 667 (A); *S v Moumbaris* 1974 1 SA 681 (T); *S v Cooper* 1976 1 SA 932 (T).

[2] See C.R. Snyman, *Criminal Law* (2nd edn. 1989), 326–330, 322–335 for a discussion of sec. 54. Note, however, that these offences are no longer discussed in C.R. Snyman, *Strafreg* (3rd edn. 1992), mainly because prosecutions for committing them has according to the author for all practical purposes ceased (see v–vi).

[3] See also C.R. Snyman, *Strafreg* (supra fn. 2), v–vi.

[4] *Project 105: Review of Security Legislation (Terrorism: Section 54 of the Internal Security Act, 1982 [Act No. 74 of 1982]).*

[5] A terrorist act is defined as follows: It is "an act, in or outside the Republic,
(a) that is committed –
(i) in whole or in part for a political, religious or ideological purpose, objective or cause, and

However, neither sec. 54 nor the Bill make any mention of delictual liability or other forms of indemnity.

Since the interim Constitution of South Africa of 1993 provided a historic bridge between the past of a deeply divided society characterized by strife, conflict, untold suffering and injustice, and a future founded on the recognition of human rights, democracy and peaceful co-existence for all South Africans, the Promotion of National Unity and Reconciliation Act 34 of 1995 makes provision, *inter alia*, for the investigation of the nature, causes and extent of gross violations of human rights committed from 1960 to the cut-off date contemplated in the Constitution, emanating from the conflicts of the past, and – important for the purposes of this report – both the granting of amnesty to persons who make full disclosure of all the relevant facts relating to acts associated with a political objective committed in the course of the conflicts of the past during said period (including, of course, acts qualifying as terrorism), and the taking of measures aimed at the granting of reparation to the victims of violations of human rights.[6] 2

A person who has been granted amnesty in respect of any injurious act is, in terms of sec. 20(7)(a) of the Promotion of National Unity and Reconciliation Act, not liable (criminally or delictually) for such conduct. Vicarious liability of the State, an organisation or a person is also excluded. Because amnesty has now been granted to most perpetrators of what would have qualified as acts of terror during the past 40 years, delictual actions on account of such acts are almost non-existent. And even where they are brought to court to claim damages, the defence of prescription will probably succeed in most cases.[7] 3

(ii) in whole or in part with the intention of intimidating the public, or a segment of the public, with regard to its security, including its economic security, or compelling a person, a government or a domestic or an international organization to do or to refrain from doing any act, whether the person, government or organization is inside or outside the Republic, and

(b) that intentionally –

(i) causes death or serious bodily harm to a person by the use of violence;

(ii) endangers a person's life;

(iii) causes a serious risk to the health or safety of the public or any segment of the public;

(iv) causes substantial property damage, whether to public or private property, if causing such damage is likely to result in the conduct or harm referred to in any of subparagraphs (i) to (iii); or

(v) causes serious interference with or serious disruption of an essential service, facility or system, whether public or private, including, but not limited to an information system; or a telecommunications system; or a financial system; or a system used for the delivery of essential government services; or a system used for, or by, an essential public utility; or a system used for, or by, a transport system, other than as a result of lawful advocacy, protest, dissent, or stoppage of work that does not involve an activity that is intended to result in the conduct or harm referred to in any of subparagraphs (i) to (iii), but, for greater certainty, does not include conventional military action in accordance with customary international law or conventional international law."

[6] See sec. 26 and 27 of the Promotion of National Unity and Reconciliation Act.

[7] Cf. *Lombo v African National Congress* 30 May 2002 case no. 17/2002 (SCA).

B. *Are There any Special Funds Applicable Providing Alternative Compensation for Victims of Terror Attacks?*

4 There are no special funds available providing for alternative compensation for victims of terror attacks. Apart from the granting of reparation to the victims of violations of human rights under the Promotion of National Unity and Reconciliation Act 34 of 1995,[8] mention can be made of the special insurance through the South African Special Risks Association (SASRIA) against damage to property caused by, *inter alia*, terror attacks. In terms of the Reinsurance of Damage and Losses Act 56 of 1989, loss of or damage to property caused by the following acts are covered: any act (whether on behalf of any organisation, body, person or group of persons) calculated or directed to overthrow or influence any state or government, or any provincial, local or tribal authority, with force, or by means of fear, terrorism or violence; as well as any act which is calculated or directed to bring about loss or damage in order to further any political aim, objective or cause, or to bring about any social or economic change, or in protest against any state or government, or any provincial, local or tribal authority, or for the purpose of inspiring fear in the public, or any section thereof. Due to the short-term insurance industry not being prepared to underwrite the risks in question, the Government agreed, in the public interest, to act as reinsurer of last resort. In 1998 SASRIA was for various reasons converted into a public company by the Conversion of SASRIA Act 134 of 1998, but retaining the control of the State. In future the State may dispose of all or any of its shareholding in the company; and in this way also reduce the State's risk exposure.

C. *Have Your Judges ever Had to Address the Issue of Liability in Connection with Terror Attacks in any Leading Cases?*

5 As said,[9] because amnesty has been granted to most perpetrators of what would have qualified as acts of terror during the past 40 years, delictual actions on account of such acts are virtually non-existent. There are therefore no leading cases in which our judges had to address the issue of liability in connection with terror attacks.

D. *Did the Events of 11 September 2001 or any Other Recent Terror Attacks Have any Influence on Your Liability Systems (Interpretation, Discussion About Reforms, Duty to Take Care)?*

6 The events of 11 September 2001 or other recent terror attacks did not have any discernible influence on South Africa's liability systems.[10]

[8] See the answer to question I.A supra.

[9] Ibid.

[10] An international conference on *Ius commune: Suid-Afrikaanse en Europese Perspektiewe* was held at the University of Stellenbosch from 13 to 15 February 2002. At this conference some attention was given to the possible influence of the events of 11 September on the law of delict.

E. *Does Your Country Participate in any International Conventions in Connection with Liability for Terror Attacks?*

Although South Africa participates in several international conventions either dealing directly with or relating to various aspects of terrorism, these conventions do not deal with liability for terror attacks. They are the following: 7

- Convention on Offences and Certain other Offences Committed on Board Aircraft, Tokyo 14 September 1963
- Convention for the Suppression of Unlawful Seizure of Aircraft, The Hague 16 December 1970
- Convention for the Suppression Unlawful Acts against the Safety of Civil Aviation, Montreal 23 December 1971
- Convention for the Physical Protection of Nuclear Material, Vienna 3 March 1980
- Protocol for the Suppression of Unlawful Acts against the Safety of Fixed Platforms located on the Continental Shelf, Rome 10 March 1988
- Convention on the Marking of Plastic Explosives for the Purpose of Detection, Montreal 1 March 1991
- International Convention for the Suppression of Terrorist Bombings, General Assembly 15 December 1997 (SA 21 December 1999)
- International Convention for the Suppression of the Financing of Terrorism, General Assembly 9 December 1999 (SA 10 November 2001)
- OAU Convention on the Prevention and Combatting of Terrorism, Algiers 14 July 1999

II. Strict Liability

A. *Focusing on Strict Liability for Means of Transport and Enterprises or Facilities, Would You Say the Owner, Custodian or Keeper is also Liable if a Terrorist Initiates the Damage?*

As far as means of transport and enterprises or facilities are concerned, the South African legislature created strict liability[11] for fire damage caused by a locomotive or train,[12] damage caused by aircraft[13] and nuclear damage.[14] In 8

[11] See J. Neethling/J.M. Potgieter/P.J. Visser, *Law of Delict* (4th edn. 2002), 381–383; J. Neethling, South Africa, in: B.A. Koch/H. Koziol (eds.), *Unification of Tort Law: Strict Liability* (2002), 271, 273.

[12] Clause 2(1) of the Legal Succession to the South African Transport Services Act 9 of 1989 reads as follows: "When any property has been destroyed or damaged by a fire caused by a burning object coming from a locomotive or a train operated by the Company … the Company shall … be liable for the payment of compensation … and the claimant shall not be required to prove that the fire was due to negligence on the part of the Company or its employees."

principle, the owner of the train or aircraft, or the holder of a nuclear licence is therefore, apart from the terrorist (or his organisation),[15] also liable for the (fire, nuclear, etc) damage initiated by the terrorist – unless the conduct of the terrorist (intentional wrongdoing) may be raised as a complete defence against the victim's strict liability claim against the owner or licence holder. In this regard it should be noted that according to the courts the owner or licence holder may only raise those defences which are specifically mentioned in the relevant strict liability statutes;[16] no other non-statutory common law defence is available to such a person.[17] Accordingly, no defence is available to the owner of the train since the statute mentions none, while the owner of an aircraft may raise fault (intent or negligence) on the part of the prejudiced person as his only defence.[18] In the case of the holder of a nuclear licence, the following defences are at his disposal: that the damage is attributable to the unauthorised presence of the plaintiff or his property at or in the nuclear installation, or on the site of that installation; and intent on the part of the prejudiced person.[19] Since culpable (intentional or negligent) conduct on the part of a third person is not mentioned as a defence in any of these acts, it may not be raised against the claim of the victim based on strict liability. The intentional act of the terrorist will therefore not qualify as a defence.

9 But be that as it may, under South African law persons are regarded as joint wrongdoers if they are liable in delict for the same damage.[20] The words "lia-

[13] Sec. 11(2) of the Aviation Act 74 of 1962 provides: "Where material damage or loss is caused by an aircraft in flight, taking off or landing, or by any person in any such aircraft, or by any article falling from any such aircraft, to any person on land or water, damages may be recovered from the owner of the aircraft in respect of such damage or loss, without proof of negligence or intention or other cause of action as though such damage or loss had been caused by his wilful act, neglect or default."

[14] In terms of sec. 30(1) of the National Nuclear Regulator Act 47 of 1999 the holder of certain nuclear licences is strictly liable ("whether or not there is intent or negligence on [his] part") for all nuclear damage caused during his period of responsibility.

[15] If the terrorist organisation is not vicariously liable (see J. Neethling/J.M. Potgieter/P.J. Visser (supra fn. 11), 373 et seq. on the employer-employee relationship and motor car owner-motor car driver relationship), it may still be delictually liable for the damage caused by the terrorist on the following basis: A person who does not actually take part in the wrongful act which inflicts the harm but who assists, aids or abets the wrongdoer in any way to commit such an act, is in principle also liable *ex delicto* under South African law (see *McKenzie v Van der Merwe* 1917 AD 41 51; *Omega, Louis Brandt et Frere SA v African Textile Distributors* 1982 1 SA 951 (T) 954, 957; H.J.O. van Heerden/J. Neethling, *Unlawful Competition* (1995), 67).

[16] Cf. *Black v Kokstad Town Council* 1986 4 SA 500 (N) 502.

[17] See J. Neethling (supra fn. 11), 275–276; J. Neethling/J.M. Potgieter/P.J. Visser (supra fn. 11), 365.

[18] See sec. 11(3) of the Aviation Act; J. Neethling/J.M. Potgieter/P.J. Visser (supra fn. 11), 382.

[19] Sec. 30(6) of the National Nuclear Regulator Act; cf. J. Neethling/J.M. Potgieter/P.J. Visser (supra fn. 11), 382–283 as regards the similar provisions of the repealed sec. 61(4)(a) of the Nuclear Energy Act 131 of 1993.

[20] See in general J. Neethling/J.M. Potgieter/P.J. Visser (supra fn. 11), 269–271; N.J. van der Merwe/P.J.J. Olivier, *Die Onregmatige Daad in die Suid-Afrikaanse Reg* (6th edn. 1989), 292–307; J.C. van der Walt/J.R. Midgley, *Delict: Principles and Cases* (2nd edn. 1997), 212; J.M. Burchell, *Principles of Delict* (1993), 240–242. See also *Lloyd-Gray Lithographers (Pty) Ltd v Nedcor Bank Ltd t/a Nedbank* 1998 2 SA 667 (W) 671; *Nedcor Bank Ltd t/a Nedbank v Lloyd-Gray Lithographers (Pty) Ltd* 2000 4 SA 916 (SCA) 922–923.

ble in delict"[21] should be construed extensively and are therefore not limited to actual wrongdoers only.[22] Since liability in delict also includes strict delictual liability,[23] the terrorist (organisation) and the owner or licence holder will be regarded as joint wrongdoers[24] who are liable *in solidum* and the one who has paid the victim will in principle have a right of recourse against the other.[25] In this regard the Apportionment of Damages Act[26] makes it clear that the only criterion for the apportionment of damages between joint wrongdoers is the degree in which a joint wrongdoer was at fault in relation to the damage suffered by the plaintiff. However, it is uncertain how the damages will be apportioned – if at all – where the terrorist acted intentionally while the owner or licence holder merely acted negligently or was free of all blame. In the former case, although there is case law endorsing the view that the Apportionment of Damages Act has changed the common law in this respect and that apportionment may therefore take place,[27] the Supreme Court of Appeal[28] has thus far bypassed the issue by holding that the common law, which denies a right of recourse to an intentional wrongdoer, is still applicable in such cases. Where there is no fault on the part of the owner or licence holder but intentional con-

[21] Sec. 2(1) of the Apportionment of Damages Act 34 of 1956; *Kohler Flexible Packaging (Pinetown) Ltd v Marianhill Mission Institute* 2000 1 SA 141 (D) 145.

[22] J.C. van der Walt/J.R. Midgley (supra fn. 20), 214; J.M. Burchell (supra fn. 20), 241; see also *Maphosa v Wilke* 1990 3 SA 789 (T); *Becker v Kellerman* 1971 2 SA 172 (T); *Prinsloo v Du Preez* 1965 4 SA 300 (W).

[23] See J. Neethling (supra fn. 11), 269 et seq.; J. Neethling/J.M. Potgieter/P.J. Visser (supra fn. 11), 363 et seq.

[24] See *Maphosa v Wilke* 1990 3 SA 789 (T) for an example of where the Apportionment of Damages Act was applied in an instance of strict vicarious liability. Here the defendant negligently drove a truck into a stationary bus. The driver of the bus was also negligent. The plaintiff, the defendant's passenger, was injured and he instituted a claim. On the ground of the busdriver's negligence, the defendant joined both the *owner* (employer of the busdriver) and the *insurer* of the bus (in terms of the Compulsory Motor Vehicle Insurance Act 56 of 1972) as joint wrongdoers. The court had to decide whether the last-mentioned two parties could be joint wrongdoers (with the defendant). Du Plessis A.J. (797–799) answered in the affirmative since both – although they were not delictual wrongdoers – were liable *in delict* to the plaintiff for the (same) damage that the busdriver had caused: the employer on the ground of vicarious liability for the delict of his employee, and the insurer in terms of sec. 2(1) of the 1972 Act.

[25] Cf. sec. 2(6)(a) of the Apportionment of Damages Act; *Lloyd-Gray Lithographers (Pty) Ltd v Nedcor Bank Ltd t/a Nedbank* 1998 2 SA 667 (W) 673–674; J. Neethling/J.M. Potgieter/P.J. Visser (supra fn. 11), 270; J.C. van der Walt/J.R. Midgley (supra fn. 20), 217.

[26] Sec. 2(6)(a), 2(7), 2(8)(a) and 2(11) of the Apportionment of Damages Act.

[27] *Lloyd-Gray Lithographers (Pty) Ltd v Nedcor Bank Ltd t/a Nedbank* 1998 2 SA 667 (W) 672–673; cf. *Randbond Investments (Pty) Ltd v FPS (Northern Region) (Pty) Ltd* 1992 2 SA 608 (W) 616 et seq.; *Greater Johannesburg Transitional Metropolitan Council v ABSA Bank Ltd t/a Volkskas Bank* 1997 2 SA 591 (W) 609. According to these decisions, which can be supported, the difficulty of apportioning liability between such joint wrongdoers can be overcome by taking their "degrees of culpability" into account (see J. Neethling/J.M. Potgieter/P.J. Visser (supra fn. 11), 269n5; J.C. van der Walt/J.R. Midgley (supra fn. 20), 214, 217; J.M. Burchell (supra note 20), 240–241). This will enable the court to apportion the damages between the joint wrongdoers "in a just and equitable manner", having regard to the degree of their "fault in relation to the damage" (cf. sec. 2(6)(a), 2(7), 2(8)(a) and 2(11) of the Apportionment of Damages Act; see J. Neethling/J.M. Potgieter/P.J. Visser (supra fn. 11), 269n5; see also J.C. van der Walt/J.R. Midgley (supra fn. 20), 217).

[28] See *Nedcor Bank Ltd t/a Nedbank v Lloyd-Gray Lithographers (Pty) Ltd* 2000 4 SA 916 (SCA) 921–923; cf. *ABSA Bank Ltd v Bond Aquipment (Pretoria) (Pty) Ltd* 2001 1 SA 372 (SCA) 381.

duct on the part of the terrorist in relation to the damage, it is submitted that it would be just and equitable[29] not to apportion the damages between the wrongdoers but to hold the terrorist liable for the full damage.

10 In this regard the National Nuclear Regulator Act[30] expressly makes provision for the licence holder's right of recourse, while the Aviation Act states that where the damages recovered from the owner of an aircraft arose from damage caused solely by the wrongful, culpable act of a third person, the owner has a right of recourse against that person for the full amount,[31] but the latter may dispute the reasonableness of the damages recovered from the owner.[32] The owner may even join such a third person as a defendant in the original action.[33]

B. Can Terror Attacks Be Classified as a Defence like Act of God/Force Majeure/Unavoidable Event?

11 A terror attack may under South African law be classified as a defence like *vis major*, *casus fortuitus*, or an Act of God in the form of an unavoidable event – that is, impossibility as a ground excluding wrongfulness – in circumstances where it was reasonably impossible to avoid the terror attack and its harmful consequences.[34] But this defence will be applicable only where there was a legal duty[35] on a person to prevent the terror attack and he did everything reasonably possible to comply with the duty. In the area of liability for an omission this defence therefore provides justification for breach of a legal duty. However, as is indicated above,[36] *vis major* or *casus fortuitus* may not be raised as a defence against a statutory strict liability claim since it is not specifically provided for by the legislature.[37]

29 Cf. supra fn. 27.
30 Sec. 30(7).
31 Sec. 11(4).
32 Sec. 11(5)(b).
33 Sec. 11(5)(a).
34 See J. Neethling/J.M. Potgieter/P.J. Visser (supra fn. 11), 92.
35 See J. Neethling/J.M. Potgieter/P.J. Visser (supra fn. 11), 57 et seq. as to liability for an omission in our law, especially the factors which are indicative of a legal duty to prevent harm to another person – *inter alia*, control of a dangerous object or situation (such as an aircraft or a nuclear installation). See also the answer to question III.1 infra.
36 See the answer to question II.A.
37 In *Black v Kokstad Town Council* 1986 4 SA 500 (N) 502 the court made the following remarks: "In my view the defences open to the undertaker are limited to those provided in s 50(2). I do not think it is possible to hold that by necessary implication the defence of *casus fortuitus* or *vis major* is included in the defences provided to the undertaker in ss (2) … I am aware of the fact that the provisions of s 50(1) are a departure from our common law in that they establish a rule of absolute liability on the part of the undertaker in terms of the Act. The exceptions provided by the Legislature are of an extremely limited nature. Had they intended that *casus fortuitus* or *vis major* were to be a defence under this Act, they would in my view have said so. The Legislature has in fact done precisely this in certain other statutory enactments such as the Nuclear Installations Licensing and Security Act 43 of 1963. It is interesting to note that in the later Act, that is the Nuclear Energy Act 92 of 1982 which repealed the earlier Act, *vis major* has been removed as a defence … The defence of *vis major* has been specifically preserved in statutes creating liability in other countries and [defendant] referred me to … the German and French systems in this regard. In them this defence has been specifically given to the

C. If There Is Another Person Liable Besides or Instead of the Terrorist, for Which Kind of Damages Is He/She Liable (for Example also Compensation for Consequential Damage like Plundering Following a Terror Attack)?

In terms of the relevant acts,[38] the owner of a train will be strictly liable for damages for property destroyed or damaged by fire, the owner of an aircraft for material damage caused to a person by the aircraft (which is not limited to property damage and may therefore also include pure economic loss, for example, loss of maintenance as a result of the death or injury of a breadwinner), and the nuclear license holder for all nuclear damage. It is therefore doubtful whether these persons will be liable for consequential damage following a terror attack which does not qualify as resultant fire damage, or nuclear damage, or damage caused by the aircraft. A clear example of such consequential damage would be the plundering or looting by thugs after the terror attack. Apart from the fact that this type of damage is not covered by the wording of the relevant acts, according to general principles of the law of delict (tort), legal causation[39] would also be absent.[40] The looting would in all probability qualify as a *novus actus intervenience* which interrupts the chain of legal causation.[41] According to the flexible approach to legal causation in South African law which takes account of policy considerations based on fairness, reasonableness and justice,[42] it will not be fair, reasonable or just – even though the looting may have been reasonably foreseeable[43] – to impute or attribute the looting damage to the owner or licence holder.[44] 12

operator in terms of the relevant acts. There are other statutory enactments in this country which impose absolute liability and also do not include *vis major* or *casus fortuitus* as a defence, for example the Aviation Act 74 of 1962 and the South African Transport Services Act 65 of 1981... [Defendant] also endeavoured to persuade me that *casus fortuitus*, which is something referred to as an act of God, can be covered by the provisions of s 50(2). I am not persuaded that the wording of that subsection is sufficiently wide to cover damage caused by lightning...".

38 See supra fn. 12, 13 and 14.

39 Which is a requirement for liability also in instances of strict liability (J. Neethling (supra fn. 11), 276; J. Neethling/J.M. Potgieter/P.J. Visser (supra fn. 11), 201–202).

40 See in general on legal causation under South African law, J. Neethling/J.M. Potgieter/P.J. Visser (supra fn. 11), 183 et seq.; J. Neethling, Element of causation in South African law of delict, in: J. Spier (ed.), *Unification of Tort Law: Causation* (2000), 94–97.

41 J. Neethling/J.M. Potgieter/P.J. Visser (supra fn. 11), 204–207; cf. *Road Accident Fund v Russel* 2001 2 SA 34 (SCA); *Napier v Collett* 1995 3 SA 140 (A); *OK Bazaars (1929) Ltd v Standard Bank of South Africa Ltd* 2002 3 SA 688 (SCA) 699.

42 J. Neethling/J.M. Potgieter/P.J. Visser (supra fn. 11), 186–189. In *Standard Chartered Bank of Canada v Nedperm Bank Ltd* 1994 4 SA 747 (A) 765 the court made it clear that "the absence or presence of a *novus actus intervenience* plays a role in the application of the flexible approach to legal causation".

43 Although an event will as a rule qualify as a *novus actus intervenience* only if the event was not reasonably foreseeable (J. Neethling/J.M. Potgieter/P.J. Visser (supra fn. 11), 207), the Appeal Court emphasied that the application of the criterion of reasonable foreseeability in the flexible approach to legal causation will only be acceptable if fairness, reasonableness and justice prevails in the end (*Smit v Abrahams* 1994 4 SA 1 (A) 18; see also J. Neethling/J.M. Potgieter/P.J. Visser (supra fn. 11), 188).

44 Note, however, that in *Meevis v Sheriff, Pretoria East* 1999 2 SA 389 (T) the court decided that the robbery of the plaintiff's jewels while they were in the defendant's possession did not constitute a *novus actus intervenience*, and held the defendant liable for the value of the jewels. But this case is to be distinguised from the terror-looting situation, mainly because the jewels were unlawfully in possession of the defendant (see J. Neethling, Onregmatige beslaglegging op goed: Die *actio legis Aquiliae*, kousaliteit en strikte aanspreeklikheid, [1999] *Tydskrif vir Hedendaagse Romeins-Hollandse Reg* (THRHR), 636 (639–640).

III. Fault Liability

A. *At Public Facilities such as Airports, Train Stations, Sports Stadiums etc., Who Is Responsible for Preventing Terrorists from Entering and Causing Harm?*

13 To determine, from a delictual point of view, which person (such as an airline, the owner of an airport, or the organiser of a sporting event) or the State is responsible to ensure that no terrorist enters a public facility (such as airports, train stations and sport stadiums) and causes harm will depend on whether that person or the State has a legal duty to prevent such entry. This encompasses the area of liability for an omission.[45] The premise in South African law is that there is not a general duty to prevent loss to others by positive conduct since the imposition of such a duty would place too heavy a burden on individuals in society.[46] Therefore, one has to determine in each case whether there is a legal duty to act positively to prevent or avoid loss. This conclusion of law depends upon a consideration of all the circumstances of each particular case and on the interplay of many factors which have to be considered. The issue, in essence, is one of reasonableness, determined with reference to the legal perceptions of the community;[47] in other words, an application of the *boni mores* criterion for wrongfulness in our law.[48]

14 Certain factors which, according to the legal convictions of the community, may indicate the existence of a legal duty to act positively to prevent harm, have been recognised and developed by the courts, but there is no *numerus clausus* of such factors.[49] For our purposes, the following factors may be of importance: (i) control of a dangerous object or situation; (ii) a special relationship between the parties; (iii) creation of an impression that the interests of the public will be protected; and (iv) relevant rules of law.[50]

[45] J. Neethling/J.M. Potgieter/P.J. Visser (supra fn. 11), 57 et seq.

[46] See also J.C. van der Walt/J.R. Midgley (supra fn. 20), 52; J. Neethling, Tort law in South Africa – The mixing of the general and the particular, in: J. Smits (ed.), *The Contribution of Mixed Legal Systems to European Private Law* (2001), 85–86.

[47] See e.g. *Carmichele v Minister of Safety and Security* 2001 1 SA 489 (SCA) 494; *Minister van Polisie v Ewels* 1975 3 SA 590 (A) 597; *Administrateur, Transvaal v Van der Merwe* 1994 4 SA 347 (A) 358; *Minister of Law and Order v Kadir* 1995 1 SA 303 (A) 317–318; *Knop v Johannesburg City Council* 1995 2 SA 1 (A) 27; *Government of the Republic of South Africa v Basdeo* 1996 1 SA 355 (A) 367; *Moses v Minister of Safety and Security* 2000 3 SA 106 (C) 113–114; J. Neethling/J.M. Potgieter/P.J. Visser (supra fn. 11), 57–58.

[48] See as to this criterion J. Neethling/J.M. Potgieter/P.J. Visser (supra fn. 11), 37 et seq.; J. Neethling, Wrongfulness in South African law of delict, in: H. Koziol (ed.), *Unification of Tort Law: Wrongfulness* (1998), 102–103; P.Q.R. Boberg, *The Law of Delict, Vol 1, Aquilian Liability* (1984), 30 et seq.; J.C. van der Walt/J.R. Midgley (supra fn. 20), 54 et seq.; N.J. van der Merwe/P.J.J. Olivier (supra fn. 20), 49 et seq.

[49] See e.g. *Administrateur, Transvaal v Van der Merwe* 1994 4 SA 347 (A) 363–364; *Cape Town Municipality v Baccerud* 2000 3 SA 1049 (SCA) 1055–1057.

[50] See J. Neethling/J.M. Potgieter/P.J. Visser (supra fn. 11), 55, 63 et seq.

(i) To ascertain whether a legal duty rests on a person to prevent someone being harmed by a particular (potentially) dangerous situation, the person must first of all actually be in control of the situation; and secondly, the facts and circumstances of the particular situation must indicate that the defendant should have exercised control, that is, should have taken steps to prevent damage.[51] Mere control of property and failure to exercise it with resultant harm to others, is therefore not per se wrongful. The question should always be whether the defendant ought reasonably and practically to have prevented harm to the plaintiff. In other words, whether it is reasonable to expect of the defendant to have taken positive measures to prevent the harm.[52] Various factors may play a role in answering this question: these include the knowledge or awareness of the defendant of the dangerous situation; the value to the defendant or to society of the harmful conduct; the degree of risk that harm would ensue; the nature and extent of probable harm; the (reasonable, practical) measures available to the defendant to prevent the harm, taking account of the chances that these measures would be successful, the relative ease or difficulty with which the measures could have been implemented, and the cost of the measures weighed against the extent of the harm;[53] and, very importantly, the values underpinning the constitutional Bill of Rights.[54] 15

Returning now to the question of who is responsible for preventing terrorists from entering public facilities and causing harm, it is clear that under South African law the answer will first of all depend on who is in actual control of the facility. Depending on the relevant facts, it may be the owner of, for example, the airport, train station or sport stadium, or it may be some other (juristic) person or the State who has actual control, such as the organiser of a sporting event, the police, or even a private security company who has contractually taken control of security operations at, for example, an airport.[55] Once this question is settled, the next question is whether this person ought reasonably 16

[51] *Administrateur, Transvaal v Van der Merwe* 1994 4 SA 347 (A) 359–361; J. Neethling/J.M. Potgieter/P.J. Visser (supra fn. 11), 63–64.

[52] *Carmichele v Minister of Safety and Security* 2001 1 SA 489 (SCA) 494; *Administrateur, Transvaal v Van der Merwe* 1994 4 SA 347 (A) 361.

[53] See *Administrateur, Transvaal v Van der Merwe* 1994 4 SA 347 (A) 361; J. Neethling/J.M. Potgieter/P.J. Visser (supra fn. 11), 64n126; cf. further *Mpongwana v Minister of Safety and Security* 1999 2 SA 794 (C) 802–805 (J. Neethling, Die regsplig van die polisie om die reg op die fisies-psigiese integriteit te beskerm, [2000] THRHR, 150 [153–154]); *Moses v Minister of Safety and Security* 2000 3 SA 106 (C) 115–117 (J. Neethling, Die regsplig van die staat om die reg op die fisies-psigiese integriteit te beskerm: Die korrekte benadering tot onregmatigheid, nalatigheid en juridiese kousaliteit, [2001] THRHR, 489 [491–492]); *Van Eeden v Minister of Safety and Security* 2001 4 SA 646 (T) 649–651 (2003 1 SA 389 [SCA]); *Seema v Lid van die Uitvoerende Raad vir Gesondheid, Gauteng* 2002 1 SA 771 (T) 277 (J. Neethling/J.M. Potgieter, Die regsplig van die staat om die reg op die fisies-psigiese integriteit teen aantasting deur derdes te beskerm: twee teenstrydige beslissings, [2002] THRHR, 273 [276–277]); *Minister of Safety and Security v Van Duivenboden* 2002 6 SA 431 (SCA).

[54] This will be discussed infra.

[55] Cf. *Compass Motors Industries (Pty) Ltd v Callguard (Pty) Ltd* 1990 2 SA 520 (W); *Longueira v Securitas of South Africa (Pty) Ltd* 1998 4 SA 259 (W); J. Neethling/J.M. Potgieter/P.J. Visser (supra fn. 11), 71n161.

and practically to have prevented any terrorist from entering the facility. Again, this will depend on the relevant facts, taking account of the factors mentioned above. Since terrorist activities in South Africa practically came to a standstill after 1990 – except for sporadic instances of terror acts in the Western Cape by a Muslim group – the degree of risk that harm will result from terrorist activities at, for example, sport stadiums, train stations or airports, is at present relatively small. Nevertheless, it can be assumed that complete inaction will not be reasonable, especially in the light of the nature and extent of probable harm should an attack occur. The person in control will therefore be expected – and therefore have a legal duty – to introduce some protective measures. Measures such as the presence of police or security personnel as well as surveillance through TV cameras at these facilities will probably suffice. The number of personnel or the extent and intensity of the surveillance will naturally depend on available resources (human and financial). Of course, if the person in control knows about (the possibility of) a terror attack, the picture will change completely and appropriate further (reasonable and practical) measures will have to be taken, such as alerting the police, a search (for weapons) of people entering a sport stadium, the reinforcement of security personnel, et cetera.

17 In the light of the events on 11 September 2001, a strong case can be made out that aircraft have a high degree of risk of terror attacks and that the person in control of the boarding of aircraft (probably the owner of the airport/private security company and the relevant airline) therefore have a legal duty to safeguard aircraft from such attacks. The legal expectations of the community will accordingly be that all (reasonable and practical) measures should be taken to prevent any terrorist from entering an aircraft. In this regard the minimum requirements should be that all baggage and passengers be scanned for weapons by reliable electronic equipment, and that passengers as well as their hand luggage be searched, before entering an aircraft (as is the practice nowadays).[56]

18 If there was a legal duty to prevent terrorists from entering a public facility, harm resulting from the omission to control the dangerous situation is *prima facie* wrongful. To avoid liability, it has to be clear either that the defendant's apparent wrongful omission was lawful (for example, as a result of the presence of a ground of justification, such as impossibility),[57] or that he did not act

[56] As said (no. 13 supra and no. 31 infra), if (terror) damage was caused through an aircraft in flight, taking off or landing, the owner of the aircraft is strictly liable but he has a right of recourse against the terrorist (organisation). If the person in control of safeguarding the boarding of the aircraft was not the owner thereof, such a person will in principle also be liable in delict for the negligent breach of his legal duty, and be regarded as a joint wrongdoer (with the owner of the aircraft and the terrorist) for the (same) damage. Where the terror attack happened while the aircraft was stationary, the owner is not strictly liable but the person in control of safeguarding the boarding of the aircraft (whether he be the owner of the aircraft or not), will likewise be regarded as a joint wrongdoer with the terrorist (cf. also the answer to question II.A. supra).

[57] See the answer to question II.B. supra on impossibility as a ground excluding wrongfulness.

negligently (in other words, that he had taken all practical steps that a reasonable person would have taken).[58]

(ii) A special relationship between the (possible) victim(s) of a terror attack and a third person may be indicative of a legal duty on the latter to prevent the attack.[59] But it is not clear under which circumstances a particular relationship between parties will in fact give rise to a legal duty. Recent case law involving the police seems to suggest that such a relationship will exist between the police and a possible victim if the police were informed and therefore knew about the threatening attack.[60] The police then has a legal duty to take all reasonable and practical steps to ward off the attack on the public facility involved. 19

(iii) Where a person (the possible victim of a terror attack) acts in reasonable reliance on the impression created by another person that the latter will protect the person or property of the former, a legal duty may rest on the latter to prevent harm to the former.[61] Security personnel employed by the owner at a public facility may therefore create the impression that the public will be protected against (terror, criminal) attacks and in this way be indicative of a legal duty on the owner to take reasonable steps for such protection. 20

(iv) In certain instances the law (either common law or statute) places an obligation upon a person to perform certain acts. If he fails to do this to the detriment of others, the common law or statutory duty is a factor that must, in the factual matrix of the case, be taken into account to determine whether, for the purposes of the law of delict, there was a legal duty on that person to act.[62] This is especially 21

[58] J. Neethling/J.M. Potgieter/P.J. Visser (supra fn. 11), 65–66.

[59] See J. Neethling/J.M. Potgieter/P.J. Visser (supra fn. 11), 69; cf. N.J. van der Merwe/P.J. Olivier (supra fn. 20), 46; J.C. van der Walt/J.R. Midgley (supra fn. 20), 72.

[60] Cf. e.g. *Carmichele v Minister of Safety and Security* 2001 1 SA 489 (SCA) 498–499; *Van Eeden v Minister of Safety and Security* 2001 4 SA 646 (T) 654; *Mpongwana v Minister of Safety and Security* 1999 2 SA 794 (C) 802; *Minister of Safety and Security v Van Duivenboden* 2002 6 SA 431 (SCA).

[61] This guideline is deduced from *Compass Motors Industries (Pty) Ltd v Callguard (Pty) Ltd* 1990 2 SA 520 (W). In this case a security firm was in control of certain premises in performance of a contract to minimise the chances of theft and damage. The court held that the security firm could be held delictually liable by a third party for the loss of property on the premises. But the court went perhaps too far in suggesting that a legal duty may be deduced from the mere existence of a business, i. e., where people may not even be aware of existing protective measures. The mere existence of a business (such as a shop or motor car dealership) should not in itself be regarded as creating the impression that safety measures for the protection of the interests of visiting third parties exist. See J. Neethling/J.M. Potgieter/P.J. Visser (supra fn. 11), 71–72; cf. also *Longueira v Securitas of South Africa (Pty) Ltd* 1998 4 SA 259 (W).

[62] See e.g. *Minister van Polisie v Ewels* 1975 3 SA 590 (A); *Nkumbi v Minister of Law and Order* 1991 3 SA 29 (E) 34–35; *Kadir v Minister of Law and Order* 1992 3 SA 737 (C) 739–741 (but cf. *Minister of Law and Order v Kadir* 1995 1 SA 303 (A) 317 et seq.); *Administrateur, Transvaal v Van der Merwe* 1994 4 SA 347 (A) 361; *Mpongwana v Minister of Safety and Security* 1999 2 SA 794 (C) 800; *Dersley v Minister van Veiligheid en Sekuriteit* 2001 1 SA 1047 (T) 1058–1060; *Minister of Safety and Security v Van Duivenboden* 2002 6 SA 431 (SCA); *Van Eeden v Minister of Safety and Security* 2003 1 SA 389 (SCA); J. Neethling/J.M. Potgieter/P.J. Visser (supra fn. 11), 66–68.

applicable with regard to the statutory duties of the police to prevent crime (terror attacks) and to maintain law and order.[63] There is also a statutory duty on members of the public to furnish information on (suspected) terrorists to the police.[64]

22 In conclusion it should noted that in particular instances the existence of a legal duty may often be ascribed to a single factor, but in other cases several factors play a role. The legal duty of the police to prevent a terror attack may be deduced from the statutory duty to prevent crime, from the special relationship between the police and possible victim(s) as well as from the fact that the police have taken actual control of a dangerous situation. This emphasises the fact that all the relevant circumstances of a particular case must be considered to determine whether a legal duty to act is present. In the final analysis one is dealing with the determination of the reasonableness of the defendant's failure to act in the light of all the circumstances of the case.[65]

23 Against this background attention must now be given to the influence of the Constitution of South Africa, 1996 on delictual liability, also in the area of harm caused by terrorism. The Constitution is the supreme law of this country and entrenches certain fundamental rights in chapter 2 (the Bill of Rights). The Bill of Rights is applicable to all law – therefore also the law of delict – and binds not only the State[66] but also, if applicable, natural and juristic persons.[67] This vertical and horizontal application of the Bill can take place directly or indirectly. Direct vertical application means that the State may not infringe any fundamental right except insofar as such infringement is reasonable and justifiable.[68] Direct horizontal application connotes that the courts must give effect to applicable fundamental rights by applying and developing the common law to the extent that legislation fails to do so.[69] By the indirect operation of the Bill of Rights is meant that all private rules, principles or norms – including those regulating the law of delict – are subject to and must thus be given content in the light of the basic values of the Bill of Rights. In this regard the courts have an obligation to develop the common law in accordance with the spirit, objects and purport of the Bill of Rights.[70]

63 See the cases in the previous note.

64 Sec. 54(4) of the Internal Security Act 74 of 1982.

65 See J. Neethling/J.M. Potgieter/P.J. Visser (supra fn. 11), 72.

66 See sec. 2 and 8(1) of the Constitution; J. Neethling/J.M. Potgieter/P.J. Visser (supra fn. 11), 19; J.C. van der Walt/J.R. Midgley (supra fn. 20), 6; J. Neethling, *Persoonlikheidsreg* (4th edn. 1998), 92.

67 Sec. 8(2) and (3) of the Constitution; J.C. van der Walt/J.R. Midgley (supra fn. 20), 6; J. Neethling (supra fn. 66), 92–93n378; J.M. Burchell, *Personality Rights and Freedom of Expression. The Modern Actio Iniuriarum* (1998), 65 et seq.

68 In other words, if the right is limited in accordance with sec. 36(1) of the Constitution.

69 Sec. 8(3) of the Constitution; J. Neethling/J.M. Potgieter/P.J. Visser (supra fn. 11), 20n129; J. Neethling (supra fn. 66), 92n378.

70 Sec. 39(2) of the Constitution; *Carmichele v Minister of Safety and Security (Centre for Applied Legal Studies Intervening)* 2001 4 SA 938 (CC) (for discussions of this case, see B. Leinius/J. R. Midgley, The impact of the Constitution on the law of delict, [2002] *South African Law Journal* (SALJ), 17 et seq.; M. Pieterse, The right to be free from public or private violence after *Carmichele*, [2002] SALJ, 27 et seq.; J. Neethling/J.M. Potgieter, Toepassing van die Grondwet op die deliktereg, [2002] THRHR, 265 et seq.); see too J. Neethling (supra fn. 66), 93n379; J. Neethling/J.M. Potgieter/P.J. Visser (supra fn. 11), 23.

The entrenchment of fundamental rights in the Constitution enhances their protection,[71] in particular also through the constitutional imperative[72] which obliges the State to respect, protect, promote and fulfil the rights in the Bill of Rights. The right to security of the person (including the right to bodily and psychological integrity) may serve as illustration.[73] A strong case can be made out that the entrenchment of this right is indicative of, for example, a legal duty which rests on the State (police) to take reasonable steps to prevent the assault (intentional infringement of the physical integrity) of a person by a third party (which will, of course, include causing personal injuries through terror attacks).[74] The indirect application of the Bill of Rights also supports this view. The promotion of the spirit, objects and purport of the Bill of Rights should take place through the development of the general delictual principles,[75] especially the element of wrongfulness, which should be defined more broadly[76] so as provide better protection to the values (such as the physical integrity) underpinning the Bill of Rights. This means that, in future, the courts will probably not be too hesitant to find that the State had a legal duty to protect its citizens against a terror attack; provided, of course, that the recognised factors which point to the existence or not of a legal duty and therefore the reasonableness or unreasonableness of the State's conduct, still have an important role to play in this finding.[77] Apart from the liability of the State, the direct and indirect horizontal application of the Bill of Rights will naturally 24

[71] Such enhancement may e.g. consist in increasing the quantum of damages for infringement of a personality right (cf. *Afrika v Metzler* 1997 4 SA 531 (NmHC) 539).

[72] Sec. 7(2) and 205(3) of the Constitution.

[73] Sec. 12 of the Constitution; see J. Neethling (supra fn. 66), 103 et seq.; J. Neethling/J.M. Potgieter/P.J. Visser (supra fn. 11), 332–333.

[74] See *Carmichele v Minister of Safety and Security (Centre for Applied Legal Studies Intervening)* 2001 4 SA 938 (CC); J. Neethling/J.M. Potgieter, [2002] THRHR, 265 (270–271); J. Neethling, [2000] THRHR, 150 et seq.; J. Neethling, [2001] THRHR, 489 et seq.; J. Neethling/J.M. Potgieter, [2002] THRHR, 273 et seq.; G. Carpenter, The right to physical safety as a constitutionally protected human right, in: G. Carpenter (ed.), *Suprema lex: Opstelle oor die Grondwet aangebied aan Marinus Wiechers* (1998), 139 (146–158); P.J. Visser, Enkele gedagtes oor die moontlike invloed van fundamentele regte ten aansien van die fisies-psigiese integriteit op deliktuele remedies, [1997] THRHR, 495 (499–500). Cf. also the following relevant decisions: *Seema v Lid van die Uitvoerende Raad vir Gesondheid, Gauteng* 2002 1 SA 771 (T); *Van Eeden v Minister of Safety and Security* 2001 4 SA 646 (T) (2003 1 SA 389 [SCA]); *Carmichele v Minister of Safety and Security* 2001 1 SA 489 (SCA); *Moses v Minister of Safety and Security* 2000 3 SA 106 (C); *Mpongwana v Minister of Safety and Security* 1999 2 SA 794 (C); *Minister van Polisie v Ewels* 1975 3 SA 590 (A); *Mtati v Minister of Justice* 1958 1 SA 221 (A); *Nkumbi v Minister of Law and Order* 1991 3 SA 29 (E); *Minister of Safety and Security v Van Duivenboden* 2002 6 SA 431 (SCA).

[75] Examples from case law are *Marais v Groenewald* 2001 1 SA 634 (T) 646; *Ntamo v Minister of Safety and Security* 2001 1 SA 930 (TkHC) 841–842; *Olitzki Property Holdings v State Tender Board* 2001 3 SA 1247 (SCA) 1256–1257, 1263; *Faircape Property Developers (Pty) Ltd v Premier, Western Cape* 2000 2 SA 54 (C) 64–67; *Amod v Multilateral Motor Vehicle Accidents Fund (Commission for Gender Equality Intervening)* 1999 4 SA 1319 (SCA) 1327–1330.

[76] *Carmichele v Minister of Safety and Security (Centre for Applied Legal Studies Intervening)* 2001 4 SA 938 (CC) 963; J. Neethling/J.M. Potgieter, [2002] THRHR, 265 (271–272); J. Neethling/J.M. Potgieter/P.J. Visser (supra fn. 11), 23.

[77] See J. Neethling/J.M. Potgieter, [2002] THRHR, 272; J. Neethling/J.M. Potgieter/P.J. Visser (supra fn. 11), 22.

also have an influence on the existence and content of the legal duty of persons in control of public facilities to protect the public against terror attacks.

B. To What Extent Do Individuals or Entities Have a Duty of Care to Participate in the Active Avoidance of Terrorist Acts?

25 This question has to a great extent really been answered under question III.1. The general delictual principles of liability for omissions stated there are of course also relevant here and should *mutatis mutandis* therefore be applied. As far as the legal duties of individuals or entities to participate in the active avoidance of terrorists acts are concerned, the following should nevertheless be added. Although practice has shown that the recognised factors strongly indicate the existence of a legal duty, in the final analysis, as said, one is dealing with the determination of the reasonableness of the defendant's failure to act in the light of all the circumstances of the case. In other words, it is not imperative that the omission in question falls into one of the crystallised categories. The following example may suffice. X discovers a terrorist bomb in the toilet of a restaurant. In determining whether a duty rested on him to warn the other people in the restaurant, X's conduct cannot be classified under any of the stereotyped categories which indicate a legal duty. Consequently, recourse must be had to the general test for wrongfulness. By means of the *boni mores* test a balancing process must take place between the interest of X (mere trouble to warn) and the interests of the other people in their lives and physical integrity. In the light of this extreme imbalance of interests, mere inaction on the part of X will not merely evoke moral indignation but should also be regarded as wrongful according to the legal convictions of the community. A legal duty therefore rested on X to take steps to warn the other people. However, the scales may favour X if, for example, it should appear that it would place his own life in danger were he to warn the others (because the bomb was on the verge of exploding).[78]

IV. Cases

1. A Terrorist Hijacks an Aeroplane and Crashes into

a) A Building

26 As said,[79] apart from the liability of the terrorist (organisation) for intentional harm, the owner of the aeroplane is strictly liable for the damage caused by the crash. The intentional wrongdoing of the terrorist may not be raised as a defence by the owner of the plane against any delictual claim as a result of the crash. Furthermore, if the person in control of the boarding of the aeroplane was not the owner of the plane, he may also be liable if he acted negligently in the execution of his legal duty to prevent the terrorist from entering the plane. The terrorist, the owner of the plane and the person in charge of the boarding

[78] Cf. J. Neethling/J.M. Potgieter/P.J. Visser (supra fn. 11), 72–73.
[79] See the answers to questions II.A. and III.A. supra.

of the plane, will therefore be regarded as joint wrongdoers since they are all liable in delict for the same damage.[80] Any possible claim based on fault liability against the owner, occupier or other person responsible for the safety of the building will on the other hand probably be dismissed on the ground of impossibility in the form of an unavoidable event, or on the absence of negligence on the part of such a person.[81] There would probably also not be a legal duty on crew or passengers (if any) to overwhelm the terrorist because of the risk to their own lives.[82]

b) A Nuclear Plant

The positions of the terrorist (organisation), the owner of the aircraft and the person in control of the boarding of the plane are the same as in (a), but here the holder of the nuclear licence is also strictly liable for the nuclear damage. In principle, there are therefore four joint wrongdoers. 27

2. A Terrorist Hijacks an Aeroplane and Crashes into

a) A Building

b) A Nuclear Plant

There does not seem to be any difference in law between the situation in the previous question and that in the present question. In (a) the terrorist (organisation), the owner of the plane and (possibly) the person in control of the boarding or loading of the aeroplane (for negligently failing to discover the bomb) will be regarded as joint wrongdoers. In (b) the holder of the nuclear licence should be added to the list of joint wrongdoers. 28

3. A Terrorist Drives in Somebody's Car or Bus into a Crowd of People

The terrorist (organisation) will be liable for the full damage. Other persons (such as the police or a member of the public) can be liable only if they had a legal duty to act (perhaps because they knew about the danger) and negligently failed to implement reasonable and practical measures to ward off the disaster.[83] 29

4. A Terrorist Hides a Bomb in a Car Which Explodes in a Crowd of People

Ditto. 30

[80] The task of apportioning the damages between the joint wrongdoers will, as indicated (see the answer to question II.A. supra) clearly not be an easy one.

[81] See the answer to question III.A. supra (text, supra fn. 57–58); cf. the answer to question II.A. supra.

[82] See the answer to question III.B. supra.

[83] See the answers to questions III.A. and III.B. supra.

SPAIN
LIABILITY FOR ACTS OF TERRORISM UNDER SPANISH LAW

Miquel Martín-Casals and Jordi Ribot*

I. General

A. Does Your Legal System Have Special Legislation on Terrorist Attacks, in Particular Concerning Liability or Other Indemnity?

1 The Spanish legal system has specific legislation against terrorism in different areas.

2 The Penal Code 1995 (*Código Penal*, CP) punishes as "crimes of terrorism" those criminal offences that aim to "subvert the constitutional order or to seriously disturb the public peace" (cf. art. 571–580 CP) or to "contribute to these ends by terrorizing the population or part of it" (cf. art. 577 CP).[1] Furthermore, it considers that "armed gangs, terrorist organisations or groups" are illicit associations (cf. art. 515 2° and 520 CP[2]), and punishes those persons who run such organisations or groups or take part in their activities or cooperate with them (cf. art. 516, 571 and 576 CP).

3 Art. 9.2 of the Organic Act LO 6/2002, of 27 June, of Political Parties[3] has laid down the possibility of declaring a political party as illegal and dissolving it if it "complements and gives political support to the activity of terrorist or-

* University of Girona.

[1] Art. 576 to 579 CP have been amended by the Organic Act 7/2000, of 22 December (*Boletín Oficial del Estado* [BOE] no. 307, 23.12.2000) in order to specifically deal with the so-called "urban terrorism" by extending crimes of terrorism to conduct that does not involve a risk to life or physical integrity and even if fire or destruction have not been brought about by means of explosives or weapons.

[2] Cf. art. 2.7 and 38.2 a) *Ley Orgánica* (LO) 1/2002, *de 22 de marzo, reguladora del derecho de asociación* (BOE no. 73, 23.3.2002).

[3] LO 6/2002, *de 27 de junio, de partidos políticos* (BOE no. 154, 28.6.2002) upheld by STC 48/2003, from 12 March.

ganisations in order to attain their ends of subverting the constitutional order or seriously disturb the public peace".[4]

The anti-terrorist legislation provided by art. 55.2 of the Spanish Constitution has introduced many peculiarities in criminal proceedings with the aim of easing the task of the security forces and of guaranteeing the effectiveness of the court system.[5] Among other devices, it has introduced specific central courts which are competent for prosecuting and judging the crimes of terrorism (for instance, the so-called *Audiencia Nacional* and the *Juzgados Centrales de Instrucción*, in charge of the preliminary investigation of cases of terrorism).[6] 4

With regard to tort liability ensuing from terrorist attacks there are no specific general rules and the provisions encompassed in the Penal Code dealing with the so-called "tort liability resulting from crimes or misdemeanours punished by the law" apply. In this area a fundamental distinction must be drawn between: 5

A) Persons who are *directly* liable. Pursuant to art. 109.1 CP "the execution of an act described by the law as a crime or a misdemeanour entails the obligation to repair the harm thereby caused in the terms provided by the legislation" and, according to art. 116.1 CP "every person who is criminally responsible for a crime or a misdemeanour is also civilly liable in the act which gives rise to damage". Moreover, authors and accomplices are jointly and severally liable directly for their shares and subsidiarily for the shares of the rest of the responsible persons (art. 116.2 I CP). 6

B) Persons who are *subsidiarily* liable. Art. 120 CP provides for subsidiary liability of certain persons. Noteworthy are, among others, the natural and legal 7

[4] It will be understood that a political party meets these conditions whenever, for instance, it regularly includes persons who have been sentenced for crimes of terrorism in its governing bodies or in its electoral lists (lit. c) art. 9.3); regularly cooperates with bodies or groups of persons who systematically act in accord with a violent or terrorist organisation, or who give shelter or support to terrorism (lit. f) art. 9.3); also whenever they promote, hedge, or participate in activities aiming at rewarding, paying honour or distinguishing either terrorist or violent actions or persons who commit them or cooperate with them (lit. h) art. 9.3) or whenever they hedge actions of disorder, intimidation or social coercion linked to terrorism or violence (lit. i) art. 9.3). Applying these provisions, *Sentencia Tribunal Supremo* (STS) 27 March 2003 has declared illegal the political parties Herri Batasuna, Euskal Herritarrok and Batasuna, has ordered their dissolution and has consequently begun the process of liquidation of their assets according to art. 12.1 c) LO 6/2002.

[5] Cf. art. 11 to 23 LO 9/1984, de 26 de diciembre (BOE no. 3, 3.1.1985) (which was partially declared unconstitutional by *Sentencia Tribunal Constitucional* (STC) 199/1987, of 16 December and LO 4/1988, of 25 May (BOE no. 26.5.1988), which introduced new provisions into the Criminal Proceedings Act (*Ley de enjuiciamiento criminal* [LECr]) and amended others. However, the new art. 504 bis LECr was declared unconstitutional by STC 71/1994, of 3 March).

[6] LO 7/2000 has introduced an Additional Provision into LO 5/2000, *de 12 de enero, de responsabilidad penal de los menores*, which provides for specific rules with regard to minors taking part in urban terrorist actions or in any sort of terrorist activity. One of these measures is the establishment within the *Audiencia Nacional* of a Central Court for Minors (*Juzgado Central de Menores*).

persons who are the owners or in charge of establishments in which crimes or misdemeanours are committed, when the persons who run or administer them or the employees have infringed the policy rulings or provisions issued by the authorities relating to the crime or misdemeanour committed (art. 120.3 CP) and, also, the natural or legal persons who are engaged in any sort of business are liable for the crimes and misdemeanour committed by their employees, representatives or agents while performing their duties or rendering their services (art. 120.4 CP)[7].

8 The "terrorism risk" and the damage caused by terrorist attacks to persons and to property can be insured[8]. However, it is not uncommon that accident and damage to property insurance policies specifically exclude this risk[9] [see infra sub a)]. The only damage that, until the events of September 11, 2001, private insurers used to cover was the loss of profits as a consequence of a terrorist attack [see infra b)].

a) Insured Persons and Properties, When the Policy Excludes Compensation for Damages Flowing from a Terrorist Attack

9 Direct damage to persons or property as a consequence of terrorist attack is in practice always covered by the "Consortium for Insurance Compensation" (*Consorcio de Compensación de Seguros*). The Consortium is a public corporation in the Ministry of the Economy designed to cover the risks defined in its Statute (*Estatuto Legal del Consorcio de Compensación de Seguros*[10] [ECCS]).[11] The risk of damage caused by *terrorism* is one of the so-called *extraordinary risks* covered by the Consortium[12] in exchange for a compulsory charge collected on behalf of the Consortium by private insurers in all accident and damage to property policies (see art. 7 ECCS).

10 The basic conditions for the Consortium's coverage in this case are the following:

[7] See infra Question I.D.

[8] Cf. art. 44 *Ley 50/1980, de 8 de octubre, de contrato de seguro* (Insurance Contract Act), as amended by *Ley 21/1990, de 19 de diciembre, de adaptación del Derecho español a la Directiva 88/357/CEE, sobre libertad de servicios en seguros distintos al de vida y de actualización de la legislación de seguros privados* (BOE no. 304, 20.12.1990). See F. Sánchez Calero, Comentario del art. 44, in: F. Sanchez Calero (ed.), *Ley de contrato de seguro. Comentarios a la Ley 50/1980, de 8 de octubre, y sus modificaciones* (2001), 738–753.

[9] See F.J. Tirado Suárez, El seguro privado y los actos terroristas en Derecho español, in: *Estudios de Derecho Mercantil en Homenaje al Profesor Manuel Broseta Pont*, vol. III (1995), 3767–3803 at 3769–3770.

[10] This was passed by art. 4 of the Act 21/1990 and modified by *Ley 30/1995, de 8 de noviembre, de ordenación y supervisión de los seguros privados* (BOE no. 268, 9.11.1995) and by *Ley 34/2003 de 4 de noviembre, de modificación y adaptación a la normativa comunitaria de la legislación de seguros privados* (BOE no. 265, 5.11.2003).

[11] More information on its website http://www.consorseguros.es/notainfo/fnotainfo_ing.htm.

[12] Together with the damage caused as the result of a "rebellion, sedition, mutiny or crowd uprising" (art. 6.1 b) ECCS). The other two types of extraordinary risks are the effects of natural forces (such as earthquakes, extraordinary flooding or falling of sidereal bodies) and the acts of the police or of the armed forces in peacetime (see art. 6.1 a) and c) ECCS). In all of them the Consortium is in practice always acting as a direct insurer.

1) Damage must be "caused violently as the result of terrorism" as defined in relevant regulation ("[A]ny violent action carried out with the aim of destabilising the established political system or causing fear or insecurity in the social surroundings in which it takes place"[13]).

2) The damage must relate to *insured* persons or property, the policy ought to be in force and the terrorism risk shall not be covered by it.

3) The terrorist attack must occur in Spain and concern risks placed in Spain. Relevant regulation considers risks placed in Spain whenever the terrorist attack harms an automobile registered in Spain, real state located in Spain, chattels placed in immovable property located in Spain and, in any other case, when the insured is resident in Spain (art. 6.1 IV ECCS). However, personal injuries suffered abroad shall be compensated by the Consortium when the injured is resident in Spain (art. 6.1 II ECCS).

The Consortium will cover the amount corresponding to the insured sums (art. 8.2 ECCS). However, the compensation solely covers damage caused *directly* by the event (cf. art. 6.1 II ECCS). The Consortium does not provide compensation for indirect events or losses of whatever sort derived from direct or indirect harms (see art. 6.2 (i)) ECCS: "[siniestros] indirectos o pérdidas de cualquier clase derivados de daños directos o indirectos". That used to mean that the system of protection against extraordinary risks covered only *material* losses, regarded as being the destruction or deterioration of the property insured and *direct* losses. This was explained by the fact that the aim of the system was to safeguard the productive structure of the country, and enable activity to be started up again quickly after an exceptional event. Loss of profits and other indirect damage were thus deemed to be items that may be covered by voluntary insurance.[14] 11

However, a noteworthy change has been introduced in legislation in the aftermath of the events of 11 September 2001.[15] Art. 6 ECCS[16] has recently broadened the system of protection against extraordinary risks in order to include – "with the extent and the limits to be established in a [future] regulation"– also the *loss of profits resulting from the direct damage* ("pérdida de beneficios consecuencia de [los daños directos en las personas y los bienes]"). When the new Regulation will finally be drafted and come into force, the Consortium's protection of terrorism risks to insured goods will therefore include loss of profits as well as direct damage to persons and to property. 12

[13] Cf. art. 4 *Real Decreto* (RD) 2022/1986, *de 29 de agosto, que aprueba el Reglamento de riesgos extraordinarios sobre las personas y los bienes* (BOE no. 235, 1.10.1986).

[14] See Chapter VII of *The Consorcio de Compensación de Seguros. The Extraordinary Risks Coverage*. Document available at http://www.consorseguros.com/extra/ingles/friskscoverage.cfm

[15] See the explanation of the amendment in *Boletín Oficial de las Cortes Generales* (Congreso), Serie A, no. 69, 17 May 2002, *Enmienda* no. 146. Nevertheless, the modification is still not legislation in force and will not come into force until a date to be determined by the same Regulation referred to in art. 6 ECCS (cf. Final Provision 3 Ley 44/2002) see infra.

[16] Amendment introduced by art. 11 3º 4 *Ley 44/2002, de 22 de noviembre, de medidas de reforma del sistema financiero* (BOE no. 281, 23.11.2002).

b) Insured Persons and Properties when the Policy Includes Compensation for Damages Flowing from a Terrorist Attack

13 According to the general rules of the insurance contract, the insurer must compensate the insured person for the damage included in the insurance policy up to the maximum of the insured amount. In that case, the intervention of the Consortium would be limited to the case of bankruptcy of the insurer (art. 8.1 b) ECCS). Nevertheless, as stated before, in practice private insurers never cover direct damages to persons or to property flowing from a terrorist attack. The only exception used to be the loss of profits resulting from the terrorist attack, but even this head of damage is going to fall into the extraordinary risks coverage of the Consortium when the new Regulation comes into force [see supra sub a)].

14 Meanwhile, as a result of 11 September 2001,[17] Spanish insurance companies have had to seek the intervention of the Consortium in order to obtain reinsurance of the terrorism risk regarding loss of profits. Alleging public interest reasons (art. 3.2 ECCS), the Consortium has accepted to assume it as an interim measure and an agreement was signed by the Consortium and the insurer's organization UNESPA on 31 January 2002. The agreement is open to the accession of individual insurance companies.[18]

15 In both cases [supra sub a) and b)], the Consortium's protection involves only liability for damage to insured persons or property. Third-party insurance liability relating to damage flowing from a terrorist attack is neither included in the extraordinary risks coverage nor in the reinsurance agreement adopted by the Consortium and UNESPA.[19] Nevertheless, pursuing the Royal Decree-Act 14/2001, of 28 September,[20] the Consortium exceptionally assumed – from 24 September 2001 and during a period of 30 days starting from the date of the anticipated expiration of reinsurance contracts existing before 11 September 2001[21] –

[17] Regarding the consequences of 11 September 2001 in the insurance market, see J.W. Stempel, The Insurance Aftermath of September 11, [2002] *Tort and Insurance Law Journal* vol. 11, 817. In Spanish literature see J. Alarcon Fidalgo, Terrorismo y Seguro. Redefinicion de coberturas, nuevos escenarios de riesgo, control de cumulos, calculos de PML, [2001] *Revista española de seguros*, 663–674.

[18] *Convenio de reaseguro de pérdida de beneficios para el riesgo de terrorismo.* It is available in Spanish at http://www.consorseguros.com/terrorismo/pdf/convenio.pdf.

[19] See also Response no. 20 regarding the agreement about reinsurance of loss of profits related to terrorism risk, in http://www.consorseguros.com/terrorismo/fterro.htm: "The Consortium is not thinking about assuming the reinsurance of the risk of civil liability flowing from terrorist attacks and neither to extend to it the coverage of extraordinary risks".

[20] RD-ley 14/2001, *de 28 de septiembre, por el que se establece el régimen del reaseguro por cuenta del Estado de los riesgos de guerra y terrorismo que puedan afectar a la navegación aérea* (BOE no. 234, 29.9.2001). This Royal Decree was validated by the resolution of the Lower Chamber of the Parliament (*Congreso de los Diputados*) adopted on 31 October 2001 (BOE no. 269, 9.11.2001).

[21] Art. 3.2 Royal Decree provided that the term could be prolonged by the Spanish Government, taking into account the circumstances that had justified the adoption of the measure. The term has been thus extended several times until 31 October 2002, when the private insurers had come back to the business.

the reinsurance of the risks of "war and terrorism" which could concern air traffic and the liability insurance *for the damage suffered by non-travellers* bought by Spanish airlines or by "Aeropuertos Españoles y Navegación Aérea (AENA)", the public company in charge of airports in Spain.

B. Are There any Special Funds Applicable Providing Alternative Compensation for Victims of Terrorist Attacks?

The Spanish State assumed for the first time the obligation to compensate victims of armed gangs and terrorist groups in Royal Decree (RD)-Act 3/1979, of 19 January, on the protection of citizens' security[22], which was developed by RD 484/1982, of 5 March[23], and which has ever since been expanded in order to increase the protection of the victims of terrorist attacks[24]. 16

This subject matter is currently governed by art. 93 of Act 13/1996, of 30 December, on fiscal, administrative and social measures[25], according to which: 17

> "bodily harm and damage to property caused by crimes of terrorism or on occasion of their commission to persons who are not responsible for them will be compensated by the State *to the extent and within the conditions provided by the norms that develop this provision*".

This development is currently contained in the Regulation on Benefits and Compensation to Victims of Terrorist Crimes (*Reglamento de ayudas y resarcimientos a las víctimas de delitos de terrorismo* [RAVT]), which was passed by RD 288/2003, of 7 March.[26] Its art. 1.2 provides that the victims will receive benefits from the State under the following heads: 18

> a) Personal injury, both bodily and mental, as well as medical expenses resulting from treatment… (…)

[22] RD-Ley 3/1979, *de 19 de enero, sobre protección de la seguridad ciudadana* (BOE no. 28, 1.2.1979; correction of mistakes in BOE no. 31, 5.2.1979).

[23] BOE no. 60, 11.3.1982.

[24] The subsequent regulations have been passed by RD 336/1986, *de 24 de enero* (BOE no. 43, 19.2.1986), RD 1311/1988, *de 28 de octubre* (BOE no. 265, 4.11.1988), RD 673/1992, de 19 de junio (BOE no. 156, 30.6.1992), RD 1211/1997, *de 18 de junio* (BOE no. 182, 31.7.1997), amended by RD 1734/1998, de 31 de julio (BOE 215, 8.9.1998) and RD 59/2001, *de 26 de enero* (BOE no. 24, 27.1.2001) and the currently in force RD 288/2003, *de 7 de mayo* (BOE no. 65, 17.5.2003). See a detailed summary about the legal development of the rules in force in M. R. Lloveras, Indemnizaciones a las víctimas del terrorismo. Evolución normativa y aplicación jurisprudencial, [2002] *InDret* 3 (www.indret.com), 8–10.

[25] BOE no. 315, 31.12.1996. Besides the Central State, some Autonomous Communities have also passed Acts providing for compensation for victims of terrorist attacks: *Ley de la Asamblea de Madrid 12/1996, de 19 de diciembre, sobre ayudas a las víctimas del terrorismo* (BOE no. 93, 18.4.1997, amended by *Ley 7/1997, de 17 de febrero* [BOE no. 207, 29.8.1997]); *Decreto de la Comunidad Autónoma del País Vasco 214/2002, de 24 de septiembre, que regula el Programa de Ayudas a las Víctimas del Terrorismo* (BO País Vasco no. 185, 30.9.2002; modified by *Decreto 313/2002, de 30 de diciembre* [BO País Vasco 31.12.2002, no. 249]) and *Decreto Foral (Navarra) 254/1988, de 27 de octubre, que regula la concesión de ayudas a los afectados por atentados terroristas* (BO Navarra no. 137, 11.11.1988).

[26] BOE no. 65, 17.3.2003.

b) Property damage caused to the usual dwelling[27] of physical or natural persons, to commercial and industrial establishments, and to political parties', trade unions' and social organizations' headquarters.

c) The expenses for provisional accommodation while repairs on the usual dwelling are carried out.

d) Damage caused to private vehicles as well as damage suffered by vehicles assigned to ground transport of persons or goods, except those of public ownership.[28]

19 A part of legal scholarship contends that these benefits correspond to an obligation of the State resulting from its duty to safeguard peace and public safety[29] or at least as a means of redistributing the risk stemming from the existence of armed groups opposed to the State[30]. Nevertheless, case law has made it very clear that this duty to compensate comes from a legal obligation of the State, which has a specific nature and which the State imposes on itself as an expression of solidarity with the victims.[31] Accordingly it does not identify either with liability of public bodies or with the protection offered by social security.

20 On the other hand, in addition to the benefits and compensation provided by these regulations, every permanent disability or death resulting from a terrorist attack gives rise to the entitlement to an extraordinary pension for terrorist attacks from the social security.[32]

[27] See art. 24.1 RAVT (limiting compensation to 50% of property damages when the dwelling is not the victim's usual home, up to a maximum of € 90,151.82).

[28] See art. 29 I RAVT which requires the vehicle to be insured, at least through the Road Traffic Act's compulsory insurance.

[29] Instead of many, see M. Fernández Martín-Granizo, La obligación de indemnizar por parte del Estado en los supuestos de daños a las personas causados por bandas o grupos armados (*Real Decreto-Ley 3/1979, de 26 de enero*), [1980] *Anuario de Derecho Civil* (ADC) 23, 867–913 at 888; Tirado Suárez (supra fn. 9), 3796 no. 60, and further references there.

[30] See G. García-Álvarez, in: J. Bermejo Vera (ed.), *Derecho Administrativo. Parte Especial* (4th. edn. 1999), 1211, following L. Martín-Retortillo, De la eficiencia y economía en el sistema de responsabilidad patrimonial de la Administración. De las indemnizaciones derivadas de hechos terroristas, [1987] *Revista Vasca de Administración Pública*, 19.

[31] See STS 2ª 19 December 1997 (RJ 1997\8799), 3ª 3 June 1985 (RJ 1985\3202), 3ª 24 October 1986 (RJ 1986\6627), 3ª 21 May 1987 (RJ 1987\3423), 3ª 27 May 1988 (RJ 1988\4208), 3ª 18 February 1991 (RJ 1991\1046), 3ª 16 November 1993 (RJ 1983\5421), 3ª 27 March 1998 (RJ 1998\2942), 3ª 1 June 1999 (RJ 1999\5637) and 3ª 1.2.2003 (RJ 2003\2230). In legal scholarship see J. L. Martínez-Cardós Ruiz, La obligación estatal de indemnizar los daños causados por las bandas armada, [1985] *Revista española de Derecho administrativo* 48, 563–580 at 572–573; M.V. de Dios Vieitez, Resarcimiento por el Estado de los daños que originan los delitos de terrorismo, [1987] *Actualidad Penal* 1, 473–482, 513–520 at 515–516; J.A. Domínguez Luis, La responsabilidad patrimonial del Estado en relación con las acciones terroristas, [1989–1990] *Revista de la Facultad de Derecho de la Universidad Complutense*, 197–224 at 212; O. Mir Puigpelat, Indemnizaciones a las víctimas del terrorismo, [2000] *InDret* 1, 7–8.

[32] *Disposición Adicional* (DA) 28ª *Ley 31/1991, de 30 de diciembre, de presupuestos generales del Estado* (BOE no. 313, 31.12.1991). The detailed regulation can be found in RD 851/1992, *de 10 de julio* (BOE no. 184, 1.8.1992), amended by *Real Decreto 38/1998, de 16 de enero* (BOE no. 15, 17.1.1998 [correction of mistakes in BOE no. 19, 22.1.1998]) and RD 134/2002, *de 1 de febrero* (BOE no. 29, 2.2.2002).

Together with this system of public benefits, Act 32/1999, of 8 October, on solidarity with the victims of terrorism[33] (LSVT), has granted victims of terrorism the right to obtain from the State the payment of the amounts corresponding to the damages awards that the authors of terrorist attacks and other persons responsible for these attacks should have paid as compensation for damage caused. Pursuant to art. 2.1 LSVT: 21

> "The victims of terrorism or of acts perpetrated by one or more persons pertaining to armed gangs or groups or who act with the aim of seriously disturbing social peace and public safety will be entitled to obtain compensation from the State, which as a way of an exception will pay the corresponding damages awards on account of tort liability and according to the provisions of this Act".

The grounds of the State's payment obligation are not to be found in any assumption of subsidiary liability of the State (art. 2.3 LSVT), but in the principle of solidarity towards the victims and, in this case, against the insolvency of the persons who are liable in tort for the damage caused (cf. Preamble LSVT). It has its grounds in the idea that the State places itself as a guarantor of the damages awards that the victims are entitled to receive. For this reason and in contrast to other payments already mentioned, the victims will receive the damages awards provided by this Act as long as the tortfeasors have not paid damages (art. 9.1) and only if, prior to obtaining the payments provided by this Act, they transfer to the State the claims that entitle them to obtain compensation from the tortfeasors (art. 8.2 LSVT; cf. also art. 5.2 b) and 9 RSVT). 22

The only recoverable damages are those corresponding to bodily or mental injuries suffered by the victims (art. 2.1 LSVT) and as long as the terrorist attacks that have caused them have taken place[34] between 1 January 1968 and 9 October 1999 (art. 2.2 LSVT).[35] Art. 2.2 RSVT clarifies that property damage 23

[33] *Ley 32/1999, de 8 de octubre, de solidaridad con las víctimas del terrorismo* (BOE no. 242, 9.10.1999), amended by *Ley 14/2000, de 29 de diciembre, de Medidas Fiscales, Administrativas y del Orden Social* (BOE no. 313, 30.12.2000 [correction of mistakes in BOE no. 155, 29.6.2001] and by *Ley 2/2003, de 12 de marzo* [BOE no. 62, 13.3.2003]). These rules were developed in RD 1912/1999, *de 17 de diciembre, que aprueba el Reglamento de ejecución de la LSVT* (BOE no. 305, 22.12.1999 [correction of mistakes in BOE no. 19, 22.1.2000])[RSVT], as well as in RD 1974/1999, *de 23 de diciembre, que aprueba el Reglamento de la Real Orden de Reconocimiento Civil a las Víctimas del Terrorismo* (BOE no. 307, 24.12.1999).

[34] On Spanish territory, even if that is not expressly required by the Act. See additional provision 2 LSVT (introduced by Ley 2/2003) that allows to grant "exceptional allowances" to Spanish citizens who have been victims of terrorist attacks perpetrated abroad since 1 September 2001 according to the provisions of future regulation.

[35] This deadline has been successively revised due to the break in the truce by the terrorist organisation ETA. The additional provision 9.1 *Ley 14/2000*, extended it to the terrorist attacks which occurred between 9 October 1999 and 31 December 2001, art. 44 *Ley 24/2001, de 27 de diciembre, de Medidas Fiscales, Administrativas y del Orden Social* (BOE no. 313, 31.12.2001), redrafted this additional provision 9 of the *Ley 14/2000*, in order to extend it to those which occurred between 1 January 2002 and 31 December 2002 and art. 48 *Ley 53/2002, de 30 de diciembre, de Medidas Fiscales, Administrativas y del Orden Social* (BOE no. 313, 31.12.2002) has once again redrafted this additional provision 9 of the *Ley 14/2000* to extend the deadline to those which occurred between 1 January 2003 and 31 December 2003.

and non-pecuniary losses suffered by the victims as a result of terrorist attacks are not recoverable according to this Act even when they have been awarded in a final judgment. The State is obliged to pay the amounts of damages awarded by the decision, updated according to the index of constant value of the peseta compared to 1999 (art. 12 RSVT) and, at least, the legally fixed amounts.[36]

24 With regard to the compatibility of the different claims available to the victim for the damage resulting from a terrorist attack a distinction must be drawn:

25 In personal injury, leaving aside very specific exceptions, the principle of full compatibility applies. Accordingly, the victim will be able to obtain both the benefits provided by RAVT (art. 94.7 Act 13/1996 and art. 6 RAVT) and the compensation on account of the tortfeasors' liability and under the heading of tort liability (art. 6.5 LSVT)[37]. Only complementary benefits addressed to cover expenses such as medical treatment, prosthesis or surgery are made dependant on the fact that "they have not been covered either by a public or by a private system of insurance", and in this case, before applying for compensation as provided by LSVT (art. 7.2 LSVT) the benefit pursuant to RAVT (art. 1.2 a) y 6 RAVT) must be claimed.[38] Finally, extraordinary pensions resulting from terrorist attacks are only incompatible with ordinary social security pensions that can be requested by the same beneficiaries for the same damaging events.

26 With regard to property damage, whereas the provisions of LSVT do not extend to it, the provisions of RAVT establish that the different heads of property damage covered by this regulation are compensated, in contrast to what happens with personal injury, only when they have not been covered by private insurance or by the Consortium for Insurance Compensation or when certain amounts are not covered[39] (cf. art. 3, 24.3, 27 and 28 RAVT).

27 Both in the case of personal injuries and in the case of property damage, the benefit and compensation awards provided by these rules are compatible with the claims that the victim of the terrorist attack may bring against the public administration if the attack, apart from giving rise to tort liability of its author, can also give rise to tort liability of the public administration pursuant to the "Legal Regime of Public Administrations and General Administrative Proce-

[36] According to the following headings: a) Death (€ 138,232.78); b) Severe permanent disability (€ 390,657.87); c) Absolute permanent disability (€ 96,161); d) Full permanent disability (€ 48,080.97); e) Partial permanent disability (€ 36,060.73); f) Permanent injuries which do not give rise to disability (awards assessed by means of the system applicable to injuries suffered as a result of traffic accidents [cf. Table II Annex LSVT, and art. 23 RSVT]).

[37] Cf. also art. 2.4 RD 1912/1999. It must be stressed that the Preamble of LSVT expressly recognises that "this Act does not aim at improving the benefits already offered by the rules in force". See also DA 9ª.2 Ley 14/2000, as amended by art. 48 Ley 53/2002.

[38] Against compatibility see, however, E. García de Enterría/T.R. Fernández, *Curso de Derecho Administrativo*, vol. II (7th. edn. 2000), 423. Also implicitly Lloveras (supra fn. 24).

[39] See supra Question I.A.

dure Act" (LRJAP).[40] This is a result which is beyond any doubt with regard to the benefits provided by the rules governing the benefits to victims of terrorist attacks,[41] and has also been upheld by legal scholarship with regard to the claims of the victims against the State pursuant to the provisions of LSVT.[42]

A noteworthy decision with regard to the damage caused by the public administration on the occasion of terrorist attacks is *Sentencia Audiencia Nacional* (SAN) 24.9.1999 (RJCA 1999\4137). In this case the controlled detonation of a car bomb set by ETA caused over € 18,000 worth of damage in the neighbouring property. This property damage was covered by the Consortium for Insurance Compensation which – besides covering the extraordinary risks resulting from terrorist attacks (see supra Question I.A.) – also has the legal duty to cover the extraordinary risks resulting from "action of the armed forces or of the security forces of the State in peacetime" (art. 6.1 c) ECCS). The decision acknowledges the right of the Consortium to subrogate – in the same way that any insurer would do – the claims of the victim against the tortfeasor who, in this case, is considered to be the police while performing their tasks.

C. *Have Your Judges ever Had to Address the Issue of Liability in Connection with Terrorist Attacks in any Leading Cases?*

Spanish case law specifically related to the topic of tort liability on the occasion of terrorist attacks is very scarce and is confined to the very few judgments in which the Spanish courts have held that the public bodies are liable for not having taken the measures required in order to prevent the terrorist attack itself or that it caused damage to the citizens. 28

The starting point of this case law is the idea that the duty to guarantee public safety does not turn the State into a guarantor for any harm ensuing from terrorist attacks that citizens may suffer. For this reason the intentional act of the terrorist, in principle, breaks the eventual causal link existing between the damage suffered and the operation of a public service such as the police.[43] Nevertheless, courts have occasionally considered that, under the given circumstances, an actual possibility of preventing or reducing the harm existed and, therefore, the public administration, irrespective of the liability in tort of the authors and their accomplices, also becomes directly liable towards the 29

[40] *Ley 30/1992, de 26 de noviembre, de régimen jurídico de las Administraciones Públicas y del Procedimiento Administrativo Común* (BOE no. 285, 27.11.1992 [correction of mistakes in BOE no. 311, 28.12.1993 and no. 23, 27.1.1993]), amended by the Act 4/1999, of 23 January 1999 (*Ley 4/1999, de 13 de enero, de modificación de la Ley 30/1992*, of 26 November, *de Régimen Jurídico de las Administraciones Públicas y del Procedimiento Administrativo Común* [BOE no. 12, 14.1.1999]).

[41] See STS 5ª 27 December 1988 (RJ 1988\9706), 3ª 27 May 1998 (RJ 1998\2942) and SAN 19.1.2000 (RJCA 2000\124). In legal writing, see S. Díaz Alabart, La responsabilidad estatal por los actos de bandas armadas y terroristas, [1990] ADC, 429–473 at 464 and Lloveras (supra fn. 24), 15.

[42] Cf. Mir Puigpelat (supra fn. 31), 9.

[43] See J.A. Domínguez Luis, Responsabilidad patrimonial y acción terrorista. Concurrencia de nexo causal por inactividad de la Administración, [1996] REDA 90, 285–298 at 292. See infra Question I.C.

victims.[44] This is the case, for instance, in three decisions of the Supreme Court in which the ground for the finding in the plaintiff's favour with its corresponding damages award, was police passivity when the police could have acted or was already acting with regard to a terrorist threat.

In STS 3ª 27 December 1988[45] the parents of a child brought a claim against the Ministry of the Interior seeking a 22 MPTA (€ 132,222) damages award. In the proceedings it had been shown that during the night between the 25 and 26 June 1982, coinciding with a terrorist campaign of ETA against the installations of the nuclear plant in Lemóniz which was owned by the electric company IBERDUERO, a suspicious backpack placed in front of the office of this company in Rentería had been detected. Local police, thinking that it might contain an explosive device, called the National Police deactivation service, cordoned off the area and kept it under surveillance all night. Since the National Police deactivation service had not shown up, despite repeated calls, the local police decided to put an end to these measures in the early hours of the morning. A few hours later the son of the plaintiffs saw the backpack and kicked it thereby causing it to explode. The Supreme Court held that the State was directly liable in tort since it considered that it was clear that "the security forces of the State (i.e. the National Police), which were the forces that had the technical means to prevent such crimes from happening within reach, despite having been alerted in time, did not act as could have been ordinarily required of them".

The judgments STS 3ª 31 January 1996[46] and STS 3ª 18 July 1997[47] refer to two claims for tort liability brought against the Ministry of the Interior by victims of the terrorist attack that ETA perpetrated in 1987 in Barcelona in the shopping centre Hipercor. Against the line of argument of the State, which contended that the damage was unforeseeable and unavoidable, the Supreme Court confirmed the opinion of the *Audiencia Nacional* court and decided against the State considering that the police had not reacted properly to the warning of the existence of a bomb and that it had omitted the precautionary measures required in order avoid the massacre, due to the fact that it entertained doubts about the plausibility of the warning.[48]

30 Another decision (STS 3ª 27 March 1998)[49], involved a post-office civil servant who was injured by the explosion of a letter-bomb addressed to the 1992 General Commission of the World Exhibition in Seville. The Supreme Court

[44] In this regard see a good summary in Lloveras (supra fn. 24), 15–16.

[45] RJ 1988\9706.

[46] RJ 1996\474.

[47] RJ 1997\6083.

[48] See also SAN 19.1.2000 (RJCA 2000\124). Being very critical with this approach, J. Barcelona Llop points out than in these cases a standard for optimal police action is applied to facts that took place at a historical moment when this standard was not adopted, since in those days false bomb threats were frequent and such an attack on a shopping centre had never been perpetrated before. Accordingly, he contends that the rules of experience were against taking this bomb warning seriously (Responsabilidad derivada de actuaciones policiales in: L. Martín Rebollo (ed.), *La responsabilidad patrimonial de las Administraciones públicas* (1996), 160). However, in favour of the position adopted by the court see Domínguez Luis (supra fn. 43), 296–297.

[49] RJ 1998\2942.

held that the State had been negligent for not having technical security equipment for the detection and inspection of explosive objects available in the headquarters of the Exhibition. These measures were required because both the 1992 Barcelona Olympic Games and the Seville World Exhibition were known targets for the terrorist gangs and, therefore, public officials could have foreseen such an attack.

This later decision differs from the rationale held in STS 3 June 1985[50] which – along the lines of other decisions referring to the public body in charge of the security of harbours and port installations[51] – acquitted the State in a case where a bomb exploded in the headquarters of "El Papus", a satirical magazine. In spite of the fact that the attack took place shortly after the police protection that had been established, following threats from right-wing gangs, had been discontinued, the Supreme Court held that "it seems obvious that such a special protection of private premises cannot be maintained for an unlimited period of time if the limitation of the human resources available is taken into account" and that as a result of the withdrawal of police protection the plaintiff should have adopted self-protection measures in order to prevent the harm from occurring.

D. *Did the Events of 11 September 2001 or any Other Recent Terrorist Attacks Have any Influence on Your Liability Systems (Interpretation, Discussion About Reforms, Duty to Take Care)?*

During 2002 the increase in legal action against political groups and entities linked to the entourage of ETA increased remarkably.[52] 31

In the area of tort liability the reinterpretation of art. 120.3 and 120.4 CP carried out by the courts in this setting is noteworthy.[53] By invoking these provisions, the writ of the *Juzgado Central de Instrucción núm. 5*, of 3 July 2002[54] has ordered the preventive seizure of the assets, credits and subventions of the Basque political party *Herri Batasuna-Euskal Herritarrok-Batasuna* to cover its eventual *joint and several*[55] liability in tort for the damage caused by the members of the illegal organisation SEGI in disturbances and riots that took place in the streets of the Basque Country from July 2001 to May 2002 and which has been preliminary assessed to amount to over € 24 million.[56] 32

The basis for this decision is to be found in pieces of circumstantial evidence such as that Batasuna allowed SEGI to use some of its premises for the

[50] RJ 1985\3202.

[51] See infra Question III.A.

[52] With regard to other measures see supra Question I.A.

[53] See supra Question I.A.

[54] *La Ley* 2002, 5813. Full text available in: http://www.lainsignia.org/2002/julio/ibe_043.htm.

[55] See Lloveras (supra fn. 24), 21.

[56] On 26 August 2002, the *Juzgado Central de Instrucción* no. 5, issued another writ in which, among other measures, the suspension of the political party *Herri Batasuna-Euskal Herritarrok-Batasuna* was decided for a three-year period on the grounds of an alleged crime of participation in a terrorist organisation (*Actualidad Jurídica Aranzadi* Ref. 548/17). This political party has been declared illegal on the grounds of LO 6/2002 by STS 27 March 2003 (see supra fn. 4).

preparation of protest demonstrations, as well some documents from which "the mutual instrumentation among several structures of the same terrorist complex lead by ETA" resulted. The writ established the principle of "complementarity" between legal and illegal organisations, in the sense that "their results amount to a benefit for the whole group for they contribute to the sole and common illicit aim which is no other than the subversion of the constitutional order or a serious disturbance of the same". When the court relates these circumstances to tort liability it considers that, in a similar way that as the legal structures that pertain to the terrorist complex put its assets and entitlements at the disposal of the common criminal organisation led by ETA in order to meet the internal needs of the group, they "must be also held liable for the damaging result to the life, freedom and property that the criminal acts of the members that make up the group cause and which could be avoided or diminished through a determined action against them". This criterion is summed up by saying that "this joint benefit that the criminal acts of the illegal structures and its members yields to the complex of legal and illegal structures of the MLNV ([*Movimiento de Liberación Nacional Vasco*], i.e. Basque National Liberation Movement) must give rise to liability according to the risk which, in any case, has not been prevented or has been consented to or, even more, fostered, by HB-EH-BATASUNA, which amounts to a sort of cover company in which those who act are managers according to the law but following the guidelines of the managers who in fact run the parent company: ETA".[57]

E. Does Your Country Participate in any International Conventions in Connection with Liability for Terrorist Attacks?

33 The most important are the following:[58]

- Convention on Offences and Certain Other Acts Committed on Board Aircraft, signed in Tokyo on 14 September 1963, ratified by Instrument of 25 August 1969.[59]
- Convention for the Suppression of Unlawful Seizure of Aircraft, signed in the Hague on 16 December 1970, ratified by Instrument of 6 October 1972.[60]
- Convention for the Suppression of Unlawful Acts against the Safety of Civil Aviation, signed in Montreal on 23 September 1971, ratified by Instrument of 6 October 1972.[61]

[57] J.M. Fuster-Fabra Torrellas, *Responsabilidad civil derivada de actos de terrorismo* (2001) has argued in favour of the tort liability of the political party *Herri Batasuna*, for the damage caused by the terrorist organisation ETA, among others, on the following grounds: the confusion of identities of both organisations within the framework of terrorist action (p. 92), the theory of "lifting the veil" of commercial companies (p. 93); the applicability of art. 120.3º and 4º CP, referring to vicarious tort liability resulting from crimes (pp. 119 et seq.), and the omission of the duty to avoid the commission of certain crimes (pp. 58 et seq.).

[58] See J. Alcaide Fernández, *Las actividades terroristas ante el Derecho internacional contemporáneo* (2000), 33 et seq.

[59] BOE no. 308, 25.12.1969.

[60] BOE no. 13, 15.1.1973.

[61] BOE no. 9, 10.1.1974.

- Protocol on the Suppression of Unlawful Acts of Violence at Airports Serving International Civil Aviation, supplementary to the Convention for the Suppression of Unlawful Acts against the Safety of Civil Aviation, signed in Montreal on 24 February 1988, ratified by Instrument of 8 April 1991.[62]
- Convention on the Prevention and Punishment of Crimes against Internationally Protected Persons, including Diplomatic Agents, adopted by the General Assembly of the United Nations on 14 December 1973, ratified by Instrument of 26 July 1985.[63]
- European Convention on the Suppression of Terrorism, concluded in Strasbourg on 27 January 1977, ratified by Instrument of 9 May 1980.[64]
- International Convention against the Taking of Hostages, adopted by the General Assembly of the United Nations on 17 December 1979, ratified by Instrument of 9 March 1984.[65]
- Convention on the Physical Protection of Nuclear Material, signed in Vienna on 3 March 1980, ratified by Instrument of 20 April 1987[66] and developed by Royal Decree 158/1995, of 3 February.[67]
- Convention for the Suppression of Unlawful Acts against the Safety of Maritime Navigation, signed in Rome on 10 March 1988, ratified by Instrument of 15 June 1989.[68]
- Protocol for the Suppression of Unlawful Acts against the Safety of Fixed Platforms Located on the Continental Shelf, concluded in Rome on 10 March 1988, ratified by Instrument of 15 June 1989.[69]
- Convention on the Marking of Plastic Explosives for the Purpose of Detection, signed in Montreal on 1 March 1991, ratified by Instrument of 23 February 1994.[70]
- International Convention for the Suppression of Terrorist Bombings, adopted by the General Assembly of the United Nations on 15 December 1997, ratified by Instrument of 22 April 1999.[71]
- International Convention for the Suppression of the Financing of Terrorism, adopted by the General Assembly of the United Nations on 9 December 1999, ratified by Instrument of 1 April 2002.[72]

[62] BOE no. 56, 5.3.1992 (correction of mistakes BOE no. 134, 4.6.1992).
[63] BOE no. 33, 7.2.1986.
[64] BOE no. 242, 8.10.1980 (correction of mistakes BOE no. 208, 31.8.1982).
[65] BOE no. 162, 7.7.1984.
[66] BOE no. 256, 25.10.1991.
[67] RD 158/1995, de 2 de febrero, *sobre la protección física de los materiales nucleares* (BOE no. 54, 4.3.1995).
[68] BOE no. 99, 24.4.1992.
[69] BOE no. 99, 24.4.1992.
[70] BOE no. 288, 2.12.1998.
[71] BOE no. 140, 12.6.2001.
[72] BOE no. 123, 23.5.2002.

II. Strict Liability

A. *Focusing on Strict Liability for Means of Transport and Enterprises or Facilities, Would You Say the Owner, Custodian or Keeper is also Liable if a Terrorist Initiates the Damage?*

34 In Spanish law the instances of strict liability that must be examined here with regard to the means of transport are traffic liability for *motor vehicles* [infra sub 1] and liability for damage caused by *air traffic* [infra sub 2]. With regard to strict liability for damage caused by enterprises or facilities, the liability of the operator of *nuclear installations* [infra sub 3] must be mentioned and also, in more general terms, the liability of *public bodies* for damage caused on occasion of the operation of installations that constitute a public service [infra sub 4].

In the case of strict liability for work accidents it is worth noting that the law provides that the accident caused by "*force majeure* alien to the work" (art. 115.4 a Social Security Act [LGSS, *Real Decreto Legislativo 1/1994, de 20 de junio, por el que se aprueba el texto refundido de la Ley General de la Seguridad Social*, BOE no. 154, 29.6.1994]) or that can be attributed to "tort or criminal liability... of a third party" who "has no relation to the work" (art. 115.5 b *e contrario* LGSS) will not be legally considered as a "work accident". However, case law labels the terrorist attack suffered by a worker while heading to his or her workplace (accident *in itinere*)[73] or during the performance of his or her work (the so-called *accidente en misión*) as a work accident.[74] In spite of the involvement of a third party who is acting with intent, case law considers that a direct relationship between the working activity and the damage ensued remains.[75] However, it must be stressed that the pattern of liability for work accidents has already been evolving for a long time towards a model of social security, even though the protective regulation of the Social Security still includes elements and conditions that pertain to a model of liability of the employer which, on this point, have already been surpassed.

1. Road-Traffic Liability

35 Art. 1.1 *Ley de responsabilidad civil y seguro en la circulación de vehículos a motor* (Road Traffic Liability Act, LRCSCVM)[76] provides that "[T]he driver of motor vehicles is liable, by virtue of the risk created by his or her driving, for the damage caused to persons or to property in the course of circulation". The risky activity specifically regulated by the LRCSCVM is the circulation

[73] *Sentencia Tribunal Central de Trabajo* (STCT) 14 December 1981 (RJ 1981\5081) and STS Social 21 December 1982 (1982\7877).

[74] STS Social 3 May 1988 (RJ 1988\4979).

[75] Cf. R. Escudero Rodríguez/M. Noguera Guastavino, Acción protectora (I). Contingencias protegidas, in: L.E. de la Villa Gil (ed.), *Derecho de la Seguridad Social* (2nd. edn. 1999), 312.

[76] As established by Additional Provision 8 (DA 8ª) of the Ley 30/1995, de 8 de noviembre, *de ordenación y supervisión de los seguros privados* (BOE no. 268, 9.11.1995) (Act on the ordering and supervision of private insurance [LOSSP], which modifies the Act of Use and Circulation of Motor Vehicles).

of motor vehicles (*hecho de la circulación*). Even though with regard to the insurance of the vehicle courts construe this concept in quite a broad way,[77] we think that it is very unlikely that it can encompass either the placement of an explosive device inside a car in order to transport it and make it explode in a certain place,[78] or the use of a car as a weapon or instrument to harm or damage persons or property with terrorist aims. Likewise, the damage caused by a car that is blown up as the result of the detonation of a bomb would not be related to the circulation of motor vehicles either.

Accordingly, case law includes within the concept of "hecho de la circulación" the cases of intent which aim at obtaining a certain result and, therefore, it holds that insurance companies have to compensate the damage caused. However, it always requires that the vehicle has not been used *exclusively* as an instrument for committing a crime by means of an action that has absolutely nothing to do with the circulation of vehicles. For this reason it considers that compensation must be given in those cases in which the vehicle was used as a means of transport on public or private roads open to everybody and caused harm to a person intentionally[79] as, for instance, in the most typical cases involving harm caused by offenders making their getaway.[80] By contrast, the harm caused by lawbreakers who use a stolen car as a battering ram to break the doors of the shopping centres open or who use it to commit murder or assault are regularly not included within this concept. In these latter cases, the Consortium for Insurance Compensation must not compensate, not even subsidiarily, for the damage caused by the stolen motor vehicle.[81]

2. Air Carriers' Liability

Currently all European Community air carriers are liable according to the provisions of the Council Regulation (EC) No. 2027/97 of 9 October 1997.[82] Art. 1 of this Council Regulation provides that "This Regulation lays down the obligations of Community air carriers in relation to liability in the event of accidents to passengers for damage sustained in the event of death or wounding of a passenger or any other bodily injury suffered by a passenger if the accident which caused the damage so sustained took place on board an aircraft or in the course of any of the operations of embarking or disembarking." With regard to the grounds of liability, art. 3.1 a) establishes a two-track system providing for strict liability for the damage that does not exceed the amount of 100,000 SDR (Special Drawing Rights) (approx. € 125,000) and for fault liability with presumed fault – which, therefore, admits proof of due care by the 36

[77] See M. Martín-Casals/J. Ribot/J. Solé, Spain in: H. Koziol/B.A. Koch (eds.), *Unification of Tort Law: Strict Liability* (2002), no. 59, 296.

[78] Obiter SAP Sevilla 30.12.2000 (ARP 2000\3109).

[79] STS 24 May 1997 (RJ 1997\4323).

[80] STS 2ª 24 October 1997 (RJ 1997\7768), 2ª 4 November 1998 (RJ 1998\7777) and 2ª 8 April 2002 (RJ 2002\5093).

[81] See SAP Valencia 21.3.1998 (ARP 1998\1517)

[82] Concerning air carrier liability in respect of the carriage of passengers and their baggage by air (as amended by Regulation (CE) 889/2002, of the European Parliament and the Council, of 13 May 2002 [OJEC L 140, 30 May 2002, 2]).

defendant – for the excess over this amount.[83] The new wording of art. 3 introduced by Council Regulation No. 889/2002, of 13 May 2002 but still not in force, provides by reference to art. 21.2 b) of the Montreal Convention[84] that the air carrier will be exonerated from the liability resulting from damage exceeding the limit of 100,000 SDR only if "such damage was solely due to the negligence or other wrongful act or omission of a third party".

37 In domestic law and as far as the subject matter has not been covered by the Council Regulation (EC) No. 2027/97, the *Ley de la Navegación Aérea* (Air Navigation Act, LNA) applies. This Act provides for the strict liability of an air carrier for the damage caused to the passengers, goods and luggage by the action of the aircraft as well as for that inflicted in the course of any of the operations of embarking or disembarking (art. 115 I LNA), and also for the damage to persons or to property located on the ground by the action of the aircraft, while in the air or on the ground, or by any objects that become detached from it or that are thrown out of it (art. 119 I LNA).

38 Art. 120 states that "[T]he recoverability of the loss has its objective grounds in the accident or the damage and will be appropriate up to the limits of liability established in this Chapter…". Art. 120 LNA states in general terms – i.e. for damage caused to passengers or goods in the course of transport or to persons or to property located on the ground – that the recoverability of the loss will be appropriate up to the limits of liability established by the Act and "in any event, *even in the case of chance accident and even if the carrier, operator or their employees can justify that they acted with due care*". Legal doctrine understands this article in the sense that air carriers are strictly liable in cases of *force majeure*, even when the damage can be attributed to the action of a third party (for instance, the accident was caused by a lack of foresight by the air traffic controllers).[85] This Act did not incorporate the defence established by the Rome Convention of 7 October 1952 on Damage Caused by Foreign Aircraft to Third Parties on the Surface,[86] which provides that "any person who would otherwise be liable under the provisions of this Convention shall not be liable if the damage is the direct consequence of armed conflict or civil disturbance, or if such person has been deprived of the use of the aircraft by act of public authority" (cf. art. 5). By contrast, it included into domestic law the rule, which is similar to art. 4 of the Convention, the main difference being that whereas in the Convention joint and several liability is provided, the Spanish rule establishes subsidiary liability. In this sense, art. 122 LNA provides that "If a person makes use of an aircraft without the consent of the car-

[83] See on the system established by the Council Regulation (EC) No. 2027/97 and its relationship with Spanish and International rules, M. Botana Agra, *La ilimitación de la responsabilidad del transportista aéreo comunitario por daños a los pasajeros en caso de accidente: un estudio del Reglamento (CE) 2027/1997* (2000).

[84] *Convention for the Unification of Certain Rules for International Carriage by Air* of 28 May 1999, adopted by the European Community on 5 April 2001 (OJEC L 194 18 July 2001, 38).

[85] L. Díez-Picazo, *Derecho de daños* (1999), 133–134.

[86] Instrument of ratification of 1 March 1957 (BOE no. 117, 17.5.1961).

rier or owner, the former shall be liable with no limit for the ensuing damage and the latter shall be *subsidiarily* liable for damage within the limits of liability provided by this Chapter, unless he proves that he has exercised due care to prevent such use." Therefore when the accident is the result of an act of a third party who does not make use of the aircraft (for instance, by placing a bomb inside it) the carrier or the owner will be liable within the legal limits of liability. By contrast, if a third party seizes the aircraft illegally and causes harm inside or outside of it, the carrier and the owner could be exonerated from liability as long as they could prove that they could not prevent the terrorist from seizing the aircraft.

3. Nuclear Damage

The *Ley de Energía Nuclear* (Nuclear Energy Act, LEN)[87] provides for strict 39
liability for nuclear damage without specifying which acts or type of accidents demarcate the application of the Act. In principle, every nuclear damage, whatever may be the cause that gave rise to it, would involve the application of this Act. Moreover, the terrorist attack is not a defence that the defendant can bring against the plaintiff who suffered nuclear damage. *Force majeure* is a defence in liability for nuclear accidents, but limited to the facts enumerated under art. 45 III LEN and art. 4.1 *Reglamento sobre cobertura de riesgos nucleares* (Regulation on Nuclear Risks Insurance, RRN),[88] i.e. "war conflicts, hostilities, civil wars, insurrections or natural catastrophes of exceptional character".[89]

4. Public Services and Installations

In the case of liablity of the public bodies who are in charge of facilities or run 40
premises to provide services in which terrorist attacks occur (for instance, terrorist attacks against ammunition stores or magazines, sabotage to electricity cables or water, gas or toxic substances pipes or to radio or TV stations) the general rules established by art. 106 Spanish Constitution (CE) and 139 LR-JAP do apply: These rules provide for strict liability for any harm "that results from the normal or abnormal operation of public services". In order to estab-

[87] *Ley 25/1964, de 29 April, reguladora de la energía nuclear* (BOE no. 107, 4.5.1964). This Act deals with liability for nuclear damage caused in the following cases: a) by accidents occurring in the nuclear installation; b) by accidents occurring during other activities when radioactive materials are being used; c) by accidents occurring during the transportation, on Spanish soil, of nuclear materials that are being sent to another country or that have been sent from a foreign country destined for a nuclear installation that is based on Spanish soil (art. 46 and 47 LEN).

[88] Approved by D 2177/1967, *de 22 de julio* (BOE no. 223, 18.9.1967).

[89] Corresponding to the rule established by art. 9 of the Paris Convention on Civil Liability for Nuclear Damage of 29 July 1960 (ratified by Spain through the Instrument of 10 October 1961 [BOE 28, 2.10.1961]). Art. 1 II RRN confirms that the participation of a third party does neither exclude nor limit the liability of the operator, since "the obligation to compensate for nuclear damage placed upon the operator of a nuclear plant or any other installation producing or working with radioactive materials or having devices which can give rise to ionising radiations *will persist regardless of the fact whether a third party has been held liable or not.*"

lish the liability of the public body, the plaintiff must prove causation between the operation of the public service and the damage suffered, but art. 139 LRJAP takes into account *force majeure* as a defence against strict liability (see also art. 106 CE and 141.1 LRJAP).

41 However, the intentional act of a third party does not automatically amount to *force majeure*. On the one hand, in spite of the fact that administrative courts required for a long time that the link between the operation of the public bodies and its services and the damaging event should be not only direct but also exclusive,[90] current case law considers now that in these cases the public body must compensate at least the proportional part of the damage which, despite the act committed against the third party, can still be attributed to it.[91]

42 It has been contended that the rationale that underpins this result is that liability of public bodies is strict.[92] However, it must be noticed that in the cases decided in this sense, together with the act of a third party, an *abnormal* operation of the public service has taken place. When the intentional interference of a third party is totally alien to the service and entails an event which could not have been avoided by using the measures and the means that can be ordinarily required form this service, the public body is not held liable and this action of a third party is treated as an instance of *force majeure*.

43 This last consideration applies to claims brought against the State for the action of security forces in terrorist attacks. The terrorist attack is an intentional act of a third party and, with no doubt it has been possible due to the inadequacy of the measures that the security forces have adopted. As a general rule, however, it cannot engage liability of the State on the grounds that its forces have not prevented it, since is an act that is unforeseeable and in most cases even when it is foreseeable is unavoidable. In this sense, legal scholarship points out that the minimum level of effective operation that can be required from the police service does not allow for the consideration that every time

[90] García de Enterría/Fernández Rodríguez (supra fn. 38), 397.

[91] The most quoted precedent to this change of position is STS 3ª 5 November 1974 (RJ 1974\4510), which held the Spanish State liable because the government of Equatorial Guinea, in retaliation for some news broadcast by Spanish public television, imposed high fines on several Spanish companies based within its territory. Cf. García-Álvarez (supra fn. 30), 1223 and García de Enterría/Fernández Rodríguez (supra fn. 38), 400. More recently public bodies have been held liable for damage that was attributable to a third party but to which the operation of a public service had also contributed (so, for instance, cases in which a prisoner who had escaped or who was on leave kills or injures someone, STS 6ª 25 May 2000 [*La Ley* 2000, 8832] or in which assault against inmates takes place in prisons, STS 6ª 13 March 2001 [*La Ley* 2001, 3861] and 23 February 1999 [*La Ley* 1999, 2957]).

[92] STS 3ª 28 October 1986 (RJ 1986\6635) held the State liable for not adopting effective measures in order to prevent out of control counter-demonstrators from attacking persons demonstrating in favour of abortion and pointed out that "this being an instance of strict liability of public bodies, the simple omission while providing a service has the same consequences as providing a service, since both constitute a normal or an abnormal operation [of the public service]". See also García de Enterría/Fernández Rodríguez (supra fn. 38), 401.

that a terrorist attack has taken place an abnormal operation due to an omission has occurred.[93]

STS 26 September 2000 (RJ 2000\8024) is a very enlightening decision in this respect.[94] Here the plaintiff had brought a claim against the Spanish State seeking a damages award over € 48,000 for the damage caused to goods of his property on the occasion of a terrorist attack against the premises of the tax services of the customs located in the harbour of Barcelona. In his appeal to the Supreme Court the plaintiff held that the provisions governing the strict liability of public bodies had not been applied to the case. The Supreme Court replying to this argument held that "even when admitting strict liability of the State it is necessary for the required causal link between that damaging result and the operation of the public body and its services to exist". Although it did not consider the exclusiveness and directness of this link necessary, it held that this fact "does not in any way imply that the State must become an insurer for all the damaging events resulting from criminal activities, since when this takes place, and is not accompanied by an abnormal operation of the public body, it breaks the casual link that is a condition for establishing liability in tort of the State". 44

Along the same lines, in a prior judgment, STS 15 November1985 (RJ 1985\5587), the Supreme Court rejected awarding compensation over € 3 million claimed by the owner of a ship under the French flag which was sunk in a terrorist attack while docked in the harbour of *Pasajes*. In this case, however, the Supreme Court did not mention the eventual strict liability of the public body in charge of the harbour and focused its attention on the task of "demarcating the scope of the functions of surveillance and security incumbent on the public body in charge of the harbour inside of the port installations, with regard to persons and property, and among which the docked ships must be included, in order to preserve them from actions of third persons who, taking advantage of an eventual lack of care in the surveillance, might harm them". The Supreme Court held that the damage could not be attributed to the public body since "it seems that it must be understood rationally that the nature of the terrorist attack that caused the disaster, by the display of a means of destruction such as the ones that were used by elements specialised in the technique of aggression, exceeds the ordinary functions of administrative surveillance and security addressed to keeping the harbour running". Moreover, taking into consideration how the attack was launched – by divers fixing the explosive charges onto the hull of the ship – "it necessarily escapes the most ordinary attentive surveillance that can be required of the guard in charge of policing the port installations." 45

[93] In this sense, with regard to liability of public bodies, see García-Álvarez (supra fn. 30), 1210. The State will be held liable in tort and will have to compensate for the damage, which occurred only when, taking into account the circumstances of the case, it can be considered that the terrorist attack or its results were avoidable. See supra Question A.3.

[94] See also Lloveras (supra fn. 24), 17.

B. Can Terrorist Attacks Be Classified as a Defence like Act of God/Force Majeure/Unavoidable Event?

46 See supra Question II.A.

C. If There Is Another Person Liable Besides or Instead of the Terrorist, for Which Kind of Damages Is He/She Liable (for Example also Compensation for Consequential Damage like Plundering Following a Terrorist Attack)?

47 Direct or subsidiary liability of the person who is held strictly liable for an accident caused by a terrorist attack extends to all heads of damage without drawing a distinction with regard to the type of resulting damage (economic or non-economic loss). This is due to the fact that in Spanish law the specific norms dealing with strict liability are not characterised by confining liability to certain heads of damage.[95]

48 However the caps to the awards of damages established in certain cases of strict liability imply that sometimes there will not be enough to cover full compensation for all the damage caused and that priorities based on the type of the protected interest must be established. Thus, "the damages awards due to personal injuries will be given preference for collection over any other which can be claimed on the grounds of the disaster if the person who is held liable cannot meet all of them" (art. 119 III LNA and 4 IV RD 37/2001, of 19 January).[96]

49 On the other hand, harm related to the accident caused by the terrorist attack will be compensated for only inasfar as it can be considered a direct and close result of the action. If, by contrast, damage is too remote or is the result of intentional or negligent acts of third parties or of circumstances unrelated to the risk created by the person initially liable, tort liability of the person strictly liable cannot be extended in such a way that it also encompasses this harm. In this sense, plundering in the aftermath of the terrorist attack can be solely attributed to the persons who committed this specific crime or, at most, to the security forces that did not cordon off the place adequately. Other cases, as for instance in the case of the fall of takings following a terrorist attack, due to its impact on potential visitors, or in the case of losses for the standstill of economic activities as the result of a terrorist attack suffered by another person are, in our opinion, losses for which the courts would not award compensation by arguing either that they are indirect or too remote or that their existence and amount is not clear or uncertain.

[95] See Martín-Casals/Ribot/Solé (supra fn. 77), no. 134–135, 311.

[96] BOE no. 29, 2.2.2001. See also art. 51 LEN, which provides for the preference of the full payment of personal injury over the payment of any property damage.

III. Fault Liability

A. *At Public Facilities such as Airports, Train Stations, Sports Stadiums etc., Who Is Responsible for Preventing Terrorists from Entering and Causing Harm?*

Currently it is usual that public facilities are managed by an entity other than the public body owning the facilities or the premises. Usually this other person is a legal person governed by public law (AENA, port consortia, bodies for the management of infrastructures) or a private legal person controlled by the State (RENFE) or other public bodies (FEVE, *Ferrocarrils de la Generalitat*). These bodies or companies can engage – and they usually do – private security services for the surveillance and control of the premises (security guards and cameras, detection equipments, etc). Sports or amusement facilities are usually handed over, temporarily or permanently, to private sports corporations or clubs or non-profit sports societies that take the responsibility for organising sports activities and for the security within the facilities.[97] 50

Despite the use of private security services for the facilities and premises for public use, the law provides that the Ministry of the Interior (or the equivalent body of the autonomous community when this is the case) is in charge of the "planning, coordination and general control of the security of persons, buildings, facilities, activities and objects of special interest, and propose and provide for the adoption of security measures or the approval of whichever rules might be necessary" (art. 3.2 *Ley orgánica 1/1992, de 21 de febrero, de seguridad ciudadana*[98] [LSC]). Therefore it is incumbent upon the Ministry of the Interior to provide for the adoption of the safety measures in facilities and premises, in accordance with the rules provided in regulations,[99] which are required "to prevent the commission of offences that may be committed against them, *when they give rise to direct risk to third parties or when the installations are especially vulnerable*" (art. 13.1 LSC).[100] The Ministry is also in charge of adopting the required security measures for the safety of meetings, demonstrations or public performances (art. 16.1 LSC). 51

[97] Cf. art. 66 et seq Ley 10/1990, de 15 de octubre, *del Deporte* (BOE no. 249, 17.10.1990).

[98] BOE no. 46, 22.2.1992.

[99] The development of this subject-matter through regulations can be found in the RD 1338/1984, *de 4 de julio, sobre medidas de seguridad en entidades y establecimientos públicos y privados* (BOE no. 167, 13.7.1984) which, however, provides for the mandatory character of certain measures only with regard to banks, savings banks and other banking institutions, jewellers, petrol stations, chemists, offices selling lottery tickets and companies transporting money and securities. See F. Alonso Pérez, *Seguridad Ciudadana. La Ley Orgánica 1/1992, de 21 de febrero, sobre la protección de la seguridad ciudadana* (1994), 293 et seq.

[100] Art. 13.4 LSC provides that "[T]he holders of premises and installations will be responsible for adopting or installing the mandatory safety measures, in accordance with the rules that govern them, as well as for their effective operation and for obtaining the protective and preventive result of each measure, regardless of the responsibility which can fall upon their employees in this regard".

52 With regard to tort liability, the ordinary standard of care according to the circumstances of time and place provided by art. 1104 Spanish Civil Code (CC) applies when specific regulations providing for the required standards of security are lacking or as a complement to them. The standard provided in art. 1104 CC involves the adoption of the safety measures addressed to avoid the risks that at a given moment may affect facilities and premises, striking a reasonable balance between the means assigned to security and the potential danger under which the installation is placed.[101]

53 As has already been pointed out,[102] the security forces do not have the duty to avoid the commission of terrorist attacks at all costs and by any means, and this also applies to terrorist attacks on public or private facilities and premises. The general duty to prevent and avoid terrorist attacks turns into a more specific duty to adopt certain measures for safety and control which are particularly addressed to prevent terrorists from launching terrorist attacks when there is an actual and direct threat against these sorts of installations or when other terrorist attacks have turned them into a terrorist target. This is the opinion that results from the already mentioned judgment of the Supreme Court (STS 3ª 27 March 1998) which held that the State was liable for not having adopted the measures required to control the delivery of the post and parcels addressed to the headquarters of the World Exhibition 1992 in Seville, when it was known that believable threats against the Exhibition had occurred and that sending letter bombs is a usual type of terrorist attack.

54 STS 11 March 1988 (RJ 1988\1961), dealing with a terrifying fire in the Hotel "Corona de Aragón" in Saragossa that took place on the 12 May 1979 and in which 76 persons died and a great number were injured, found that the companies that were the owners of the hotel were not liable in spite of the fact that it had been proven in the proceedings that, due to the lack of care of some of their employees, a small fire which took place in the kitchen of the hotel contributed to the disaster. The rationale underpinning this decision is that the court considers that the catastrophic results cannot be explained "but for the addition to the original cause of the fire of some strange element, placed by unknown persons, an element which could have been pyrogallol or even napalm… something that would explain why in a very few minutes a fire with thick smoke and at a high temperature broke out and, also in a very few minutes, spread to the other rooms and parts of the hotel." The Supreme Court held that "*in the cases in which the interference is intentional and has not been brought about by the original agent … an actual break in the causal link will occur*" which will lead to no liability of the defendants and will not prevent the plaintiff from bringing a claim against other persons who may be held liable with regard to the conduct of these unknown third persons who, by plac-

[101] Art. 13.2 LSC sets forth, in general terms, that "the competent officials shall be able to exempt from the implantation or maintenance of mandatory safety measures in the premises when the circumstances of the case make them unnecessary or inappropriate".

[102] See supra Question II.A.4.

ing inflammable or explosive substances which lead to a significant spreading of the initial fire, broke the causal link.

This decision only examines the scope of the negligence of the defendants with regard to the fire that started in the kitchen but, since it does not even mention any sort of special safety measures in order to prevent anyone from bringing inflammable materials or explosives similar to those that allegedly[103] caused the disaster[104] onto the premises, it seems that such measures were not required. Therefore, it must be understood that the adoption of specific safety measures in order to avoid the commission of crimes, in general, and particularly, terrorist attacks, cannot be required in those activities that do not regularly involve the risk of third parties committing offences. By contrast, adopting such specific safety measures could be mandatory when the facilities and premises involved are already dangerous and, therefore, when analysing the risks that they involve, it is necessary to take into consideration the additional risk posed by possible crimes of third parties and, among them, terrorist attacks.[105] 55

In this sense, for instance, art. 8, 10, 11 and 12 of the Royal Decree 158/1995, of 3 February, on the physical protection of nuclear materials,[106] provide that the measures of physical protection "will aim at protecting the nuclear materials against malicious or improper acts", and establish different rules according to the type of which these materials belong. For materials belonging to class I the use of a "highly protected zone" is compulsory, its safety personnel "will be adequately connected with the corresponding security forces", and "access will be limited to persons expressly authorised by the owner".

More usually, however, the specific facilities' rules refer only to the conditions of safety and to the means of preventing accidents that are the result of

[103] In fact, the hypothesis of a terrorist attack was only considered as proven in the civil proceedings by the decision of the Court of First Instance. This decision was directly appealed against in cassation, which dealt with legal questions only, and which was decided by the already mentioned STS 4 March 1988. Starting from this hypothesis, the State Council has occasionally recognised that the relatives of some victims are entitled to the benefits currently governed by RAVT (*Dictamen* 15 March 1990) and by LSVT (*Dictamen* 30 March 2000). By contrast, the decisions of the courts of other jurisdictions do not share the hypothesis of the introduction of explosives by terrorists (see SAN 23 January 1993, STS 3ª 17 February 1996 [RJ 1996\2250] and *Sentencia Tribunal Superior de Justicia* (STSJ) Catalonia 21 December 2001 [*Aranzadi Social* (AS) 2001\712]). In its day, the special court for terrorist crimes did not find any indication of the existence of a terrorist attack and returned the proceedings to the ordinary penal courts which dismissed the case.

[104] In fact it was not considered either whether the companies that owned the hotel had adopted the necessary and appropriate measures for the safety of their customers in the case of a fire of these characteristics, even if not caused by a terrorist attack. In the sense that it is important to take all these circumstances into account see SAP Zaragoza 2.4.2002 (*Aranzadi Civil* (AC) 2002\578), dealing with the liability of a residents' association for not having the technical means required to put out a fire caused by cars parked in the garage.

[105] In this sense, S. Cavanillas Múgica, Comentario de la sentencia de 11 de marzo de 1988, [1988] *Cuadernos Cívitas de Jurisprudencia Civil* 17, 388.

[106] RD 158/1995, *de 3 de febrero, sobre la protección física de los materiales nucleares* (supra fn. 67). In general, see art. 8.2 *Reglamento sobre instalaciones nucleares y radiactivas*, passed by RD 1836/1999, de 3 de diciembre (BOE no. 313, 31.12.1999).

the regular activities carried out therein.[107] Only in cases where there are devices or elements which are very dangerous or which can be used for illicit purposes are the applicable provisions that safety protocols are used in order to prevent the intentional interference from third parties regularly required.[108]

56 In summary, not adopting specific safety measures will lead to tort liability of the defendant in the case of damage caused by a terrorist attack if a) an actual threat against the facilities or installations that he operates has already taken place and b) if these facilities or installations can be described as dangerous, since this quality involves specific measures to prevent terrorist attacks or intentional harm by third parties being taken even in the absence of specific rules that make this requirement. It must be stressed, however that, when these safety regulations exist, the defendant will not be able to exonerate himself or herself from liability by proving that he or she has satisfied the regulations if, according to the circumstances in which the damage occurred, he or she should have prevented the plaintiff from suffering harm.[109]

B. To What Extent Do Individuals or Entities Have a Duty of Care to Participate in the Active Avoidance of Terrorist Acts?

57 From the point of view of liability in tort this question leads to an analysis of which cases and under which conditions a person who, in spite of the fact that he was not involved in the planning or execution of a terrorist attack, but who at least could have done something in order to prevent the attack from happening or causing harm, can be held liable in tort for the fact of not having acted actively.

58 The general clause of tort liability provided by art. 1902 CC mentions the omissions but, in contrast to other legal systems, the Spanish legal system lacks specific rules of tort liability for omissions. Hence legal scholarship and case law take the rules included in the Penal Code as the starting point.[110] Pursuant to art. 11 CP an omission is put on equal footing with an action when "there is a specific legal or contractual obligation to act or when the person

[107] As an example see the general guidelines for industrial safety set out in art. 9 a 11 *Ley 21/ 1992, de 16 de julio, de industria* (BOE no. 176, 23.7.1992).

[108] See especially the *Instrucción técnica complementaria núm. 1* of the *Reglamento de explosivos* (passed by RD 230/1998, de 16 de febrero [BOE no. 61, 12.3.1998]) which refers, among other aspects, to the conditions of security services, safety, communications, etc in installations such as factories, workshops, warehouses and in the transport of explosives.

[109] This is a yardstick, which is repeated by case law of civil courts in general, and which specifically refers to environmental damage. RD 1254/1999, de 16 de julio, *sobre prevención de accidentes graves en los que intervengan sustancias peligrosas* (BOE no. 172, 20.7.1999) especially sets out, for instance, that the manufacturer has the general duty to "adopt the measures set forth in this Royal Decree and all the other measures which are necessary in order to avoid serious accidents and reduce their impact on persons, property and the environment". In fact, to attribute criminal responsibility in the case of nuclear accidents (art. 341 ff CP) it is not even necessary to allege that regulation or administrative acts have been infringed. Cf. P.M. de la Cuesta Aguado, Imprudencia y energía nuclear, [2000] *La Ley* 2, 1790–1797, 1796.

[110] Instead of many, see Díez-Picazo (supra fn. 85), 289.

who omits to act has given rise to an opportunity of risking the protected interest by means of a preceding act or omission". Therefore liability depends on the existence of what criminal legal scholarship call "posición de garante" (guarantor's position), either because legally or contractually this person has the duty to protect the endangered interest, or because this person has the duty to control a source of danger which has been created by his own act or omission. Hence it results that the persons or entities who legally or contractually have assumed the duty of protection with regard to these sorts of risk or who have favoured the occurrence of the terrorist attack have the duty to act positively and take reasonable steps within their reach in order to avoid it.

Beyond this duty, the Penal Code offers a second element for clarifying the scope of the duty that falls on private individuals when it typifies as a crime the omission of the duty to prevent third parties from committing certain crimes. Specifically, when it sanctions the person who "*with his immediate involvement and with no risk for himself or for others* would have been able to prevent someone else from committing a crime that affects the life, the physical integrity or health, or the freedom or sexual freedom of a person and has not done it" (art. 450.1 CP). Additionally it must be said that art. 5 LSC provides for a general duty on citizens to cooperate in order to prevent others from committing crimes and that, undoubtedly, this duty also applies to terrorist attacks. Pursuant to this provision public officials may request citizens to give their help and cooperation if it is needed, and as far as it is indispensably needed for the fulfilment of their duties, "*as long as it does not involve a personal risk for themselves*". As can be noted, the demarcating elements of these eventual positive general duties are, firstly, that there is an effective possibility of cooperation and, secondly, that it is possible to do it without running personal risks.[111] 59

IV. Cases

General Note: The answer is given assuming that the damage has taken place within Spanish territory. 60

1. A Terrorist Hijacks an Aeroplane and Crashes into

a) A Building

Direct and *joint and several liability* of the authors and accomplices who have been sentenced for these facts by a criminal court (art. 109.1 and art. 116.1 CP). 61

[111] See art. 6.2 of the Convention on Offences and Certain Other Acts Committed on Board Aircraft, signed in Tokyo on 14 September 1963, and ratified by Instrument of 25 August 1969, which sets forth that "the aircraft commander may require or authorise the assistance of other crew members or may request or authorise, *but not require*, the assistance of passengers to restrain any person whom he is entitled to restrain ...".

62 Moreover:

63 Air carrier liability:

64 For the *damage suffered by the passengers* of the aircraft. Strict liability for death and personal injuries up to the maximum amount of 100,000 SDR (approx. € 125,000) for each victim. With regard to personal injuries exceeding the amount of 100,000 SDR and with regard to property damage, the fault of the defendant is presumed but the defendant can escape liability by proving that he or she acted with due care. When the new wording of art. 3, introduced by the Council Regulation No 889/2002, of 13 May 2002 enters into force, by reference to art. 21.2 b) of the Montreal Convention, strict liability will also include damage to the luggage and the air carrier will be exonerated from the liability resulting from personal injuries exceeding the limit of 100,000 SDR only if "such damage was solely due to the negligence or other wrongful act or omission of a third party".

65 For the *damage to persons or to property located on the ground* caused by the action of the aircraft, a distinction must be drawn between international and national air traffic:

66 a) The liability of the operator of an aircraft registered in another State will be capped according to art. 11 of the Rome Convention of 7 October 1952, on Damage Caused by Foreign Aircraft to Third Parties on the Surface. However, the operator will not be liable if he proves that he took all the required steps to prevent the terrorist from making use of the aircraft without his consent (art. 4 Rome Convention). In this case liability is joint and several.

67 b) The liability of the air carrier or owner of a Spanish aircraft will be subsidiary and have the caps provided by art. 119 LNA, which have been updated by art. 4 RD 37/2001, of 19 January, except "if the persons who make use of the aircraft do it without the consent of the air carrier or the owner" and these show that it was impossible for them to prevent the terrorist from seizing the aircraft. If both conditions are met, the air carrier and the owner are exonerated from liability.

68 Liability for *compensation funds* (which applies both to victims who are the passengers and to victims who have suffered the impact of the aircraft on a building).

69 *Insured persons and assets* when the risk was not included in the insurance policy: a terrorist attack would mean that the insured sum must be satisfied by the Consortium of Insurance Compensation (art. 6.1 b) and 8.2 ECCS).

70 *Any victim is:*

71 a) *Entitled to the compensation sums provided in favour of the victims of terrorism* for personal injury, both bodily and mental, as well as compensation

for the medical expenses if they are not otherwise covered (art. 1.2 a) and 6 RAVT); also entitled to compensation for the damage caused to his or her home and to commercial or industrial establishments and for the expenses for temporary accommodation and ensuing damage, but only when he fails to receive compensation from a private insurer or from the Consortium, or when part of the damage is not covered by this compensation (cf. art. 3, 24.3, 27 and 28 RAVT).

b) *Entitled to receive compensation from the State under the heading of damages award for tort liability and on account of liability in tort of the authors and accomplices* of the terrorist attack. Compensation is granted for bodily and mental injury suffered by the victims (art. 2.1 LSVT) and the sums awarded correspond to the amounts established by the judgment that rules for tort liability of the terrorists updated according to the cost of living (art. 12 RSVT) or, at least, to the amounts legally established. The damages awards are compatible with the compensation previously mentioned under a) and the collection of these awards entails that all the actions in tort that the plaintiffs may have against the defendants are transferred to the State. 72

b) A Nuclear Plant

See supra case 1. 73

The difference between this hypothetical case and the previous one is the additional responsibility of the operator of the nuclear plant with regard to damage consisting in *nuclear damage* which is the direct result of the collision of the aircraft with the nuclear plant. In principle, the operator of the nuclear plant will be held liable regardless of what was the source that has given rise to a materialisation of the nuclear risk. Moreover, the operator can exonerate himself from liability only for the cases expressly provided by art. 45 III LEN and 4.1 RRN, i.e. "war conflicts, hostilities, civil wars, insurrections or natural catastrophes of exceptional character", and it seems that the facts described in our hypothetical case do not fit in any of these cases. 74

Within the amount provided by the caps (25,000 MPTA [approx. € 150 million] and 1,000 MPTA [approx. € 6 million], cf. art. 57 LEN), "the payment of damages awards will be governed by the following priority rules: 1st. Personal injury, which will be compensated at least by the amount resulting from the schedules provided by the insurance for work accidents (...). 2nd. Property damage, which will be compensated once payments of the awards for personal injuries have been satisfied" (art. 51 LEN). When coverage is provided but the compulsory injury does not suffice to compensate for all personal injuries sustained "the State will take the legal steps to cover the difference" (art. 51.1 *in fine* LEN) while, with regard to property damage "a pro rata compensation in accordance with the importance of the property damage suffered by each victim will be carried out". 75

2. A Terrorist Sets a Bomb Situated in an Aeroplane and the Plane Crashes into

a) A Residential Area

76 The same answer as in case 1.a. applies, except for the possibility of exoneration from liability for the damage caused on the ground by proving that it was impossible to prevent the terrorists from placing the bomb in the aircraft, since this case cannot be covered by the wording "illegitimate use" to which both art. 4 of the Rome Convention and art. 119 LNA make reference.

b) A Nuclear Plant

77 The same answer as in case 1.b.

3. A Terrorist Drives in Somebody's Car or Bus into a Crowd of People

78 *Direct* and *joint and several liability* of the *author* and the *accomplices* who are condemned for these facts by a criminal court (art. 109.1 and 116.1 CP).

79 The *compulsory insurer* of the vehicle used to commit the attack does not have the duty to discharge the minimum compensation legally provided since the damage is not part of the risky activity specifically regulated by the LRCSCVM (art. 6 I). According to case law, intentionally causing harm with a motor vehicle is not included in the compulsory insurance coverage, which is legally connected to the traffic of motor vehicles. Therefore, if the vehicle belongs to the tortfeasors, the insurer is exonerated from liability; when the vehicle has been stolen and, in principle, the Consortium of Insurance Compensation would be subsidiaryily liable pursuant art. 8.1 c) LRCSCVM, the Consortium is exonerated from liability covered by compulsory insurance as well (SAP Valencia 21 March 1998 [ARP 1998\1517]).

80 Liability of *compensation funds*:

81 *Insured persons and property* when the risk of terrorism was not covered by the policy: the terrorist attack entails the coverage of the insured sums going to the Consortium of Insurance Compensation (art. 6.1 b) and 8.2 ECCS).

82 *Any victim is:*

83 a) *Entitled to compensation (benefits) established in favour of the victims of terrorist attacks* for personal injury, both bodily and mental, as well as compensation for the medical expenses if they are not otherwise covered (art. 1.2 a) and 6 RAVT).

84 b) *Entitled to compensation by the State under the heading of tort liability and on account of liability in tort of the authors and accomplices* of the terrorist attack. Compensation is awarded for *bodily* or *mental injuries* suffered by the

victims (art. 2.1 LSVT), either by paying the sums awarded by the judgment once they have been updated (art. 12 RSVT) or, at least, by paying the minimum amount legally provided. These damages awards are compatible with the benefits provided by RAVT and their collection entails transferring all the actions in tort that the victim may have against the tortfeasors to the State.

4. A Terrorist Hides a Bomb in a Car Which Explodes in a Crowd of People

The same answer as supra under number 3. 85

Although as *obiter dicta*, some decisions mention that placing a bomb in a car in 86
order to move it and make it explode in the desired place cannot be considered an "hecho de la circulación" for the purposes of giving rise to strict liability pursuant to LRCSCVM and to the duty to compensate according to compulsory insurance (for instance, SAP Sevilla 30 December 2000 [ARP 2000\3109]).

SWEDEN
LIABILITY FOR ACTS OF TERRORISM UNDER SWEDISH LAW

Bertil Bengtsson

I. General Remarks

1 The questions concerning liability for terror attacks have, until now, hardly been discussed in Swedish literature at all, nor have they caused any activity on the part of the legislator. As far as I know, the courts have never had to decide upon the subject. For such reasons there are several uncertain points in Swedish law as regards the influence of such unforeseen events upon the liability rules.

2 Above all, this is true about the application of rules of strict liability in these cases. As will appear in the following paragraphs, there are certain exceptions for *force majeure* (vis major, acts of God) contributing to the damage and similar defences; however, it is rather doubtful whether all actions of terrorism will fall under these concepts.

3 As for liability for fault, the main rules of the Tort Liability Act (1972:207) are clear: liability for physical damage to persons or property presupposes fault by the person liable or his employee. However, here, as well as in other situations, the concept of negligence implies a practical problem. The question is whether terrorist acts could reasonably have been foreseen and prevented. Of course, this depends upon the circumstances in the individual case, and it is not possible to discuss the question in detail in this paper. It should only be underlined that after the events of the 11 September 2001 the demands upon the authorities as well as upon enterprises responsible for the control of means of communication, public facilities, other structures or works will no doubt be more exacting than before. Earlier precedents concerning negligent surveillance (which of course do not concern prevention of terrorism in a strict sense) will probably have little importance.

4 Already here, some remarks should be made concerning two general concepts of importance in this connection. As mentioned before, a terrorist action can

often be regarded as a kind of *force majeure* which, at least according to some legislation, will exclude strict liability. However, the definition of this defence is not quite clear and varies to some extent in different countries. In Sweden, it has been described as an external event of great dimensions that occurs seldom and is not possible to control or influence; the event is not always difficult to anticipate, only to forestall.

Another general principle that may be invoked by the defendant in most of these situations is the principle of *adequate causality* ("adequate Kausalität") well-known from continental law (cf. "remoteness of damage" in English law). It is expressed in different ways in Scandinavian literature: if the damage is to be compensated, it should not be too difficult to foresee, not too atypical, not too remote. On the other hand, the damage need not be impossible to prevent provided that it had been anticipated. In this respect, the concept differs from *force majeure*. In any case, this may be an important defence when compensation is claimed for terrorist attacks, on the basis of strict liability or liability for negligence. 5

However, recent developments will probably have changed the attitude of the courts to the problem. Today, an attack is not altogether unexpected, even if it might be regarded as a kind of *force majeure*, and the risk can no longer be considered so very strange and extraordinary that liability *prima facie* should be ruled out. 6

An important factor when dealing with terrorist risks is to what extent they can be covered by insurance, above all liability insurance. Some remarks upon this will be made below (XII). 7

Of course, the Swedish government and Swedish authorities take part in international cooperation aiming at reducing the risk of terrorist acts of different kinds. As this report deals only with the present rules, this work shall not be discussed here. 8

II. Air Crashes

According to the Aviation Damage Act (1922:282), which concerns injury and damage caused to persons and property not transported by plane, the liability is strict without any exception for *force majeure* or similar events (sec. 1). In principle, the liable party is the owner of the plane; however, if anyone uses another person's plane without his permission, he is liable instead of the owner for damage caused during his use (sec. 3). The reasons alleged by the legislator for the strict liability was above all that it is reasonable and equitable that the damage should be borne by the owner of the aeroplane even if it is caused neither by any fault of his employees nor by any defect of the plane, especially as the owner can insure himself against the liability. 9

If a plane crashes as a consequence of a bomb exploding in the plane, it seems clear that the owner is liable for the damage caused on the ground. There is no 10 express exception for such situations in the text of the Act, and the event cannot be regarded as an atypical risk; the reasons for strict liability will have such weight also in this case that it is unlikely that a court would exempt the owner from the liability on the basis of some unwritten principle of liability. (As to mitigation of the liability, see XI below.)

11 The situation when a plane is hijacked is more complicated. As mentioned above, the owner is relieved from liability when somebody uses the plane without his permission. However, the meaning of "use" in this case is not quite clear. Evidently, if a terrorist steals a plane and causes a plane crash, the owner is not responsible for the damage; but it can be doubted whether the owner will escape liability if a terrorist suddenly appears in the cockpit and forces the pilot to steer into a building or, after overpowering the pilot, takes charge of the steering himself with such results. Can this be regarded as a use of the plane in the sense of the Act? There may be arguments for strict liability in this case, too. Here, however, we have got an express provision in the Act that makes it possible to exempt the innocent owner from the responsibility. Whether the damage is covered by the owner's liability insurance or not (cf. XII below), it is quite possible that the courts will interpret "use" in an extensive way and dismiss the claim, at least when the terrorist handles the steering more than momentarily.

12 The Aviation Act (1957:297) deals, among other things, with damage caused to persons and property *transported* by the plane. According to chapter 9, sec. 17, the carrier is liable for any injury to passengers occurring as a consequence of events on board the plane, injuries caused by the health of the passenger excepted. A similar liability is imposed in case of damage to luggage. As for transported goods, there are several exceptions from the liability, among others for acts of war or armed conflict. In case of a terrorist attack, the carrier will evidently be strictly liable for injuries to the passengers (and damage to their luggage). Concerning liability for transported goods, the essential problem is whether terrorist acts connected with the present "war against terrorism" can be regarded as acts of war or armed conflict. It is difficult to anticipate the attitude of the courts in this respect. One aspect that may be of importance is whether the terrorist action is the result of some kind of conspiracy or stands out as an isolated act by a single fanatic (though it can be rather difficult to establish whether other persons are involved). Another important factor may be the size of the destruction actual or intended. If a big passenger plane is attacked, there are reasons to consider the event equal to an act of armed conflict, whether firearms are used or not. However, the carrier (and his insurer) will in any case be exempted only from liability for goods transported, not for liability against the passengers.

III. Nuclear Disasters

13 According to the Atomic Liability Act (1968:45), based upon the 1960 Paris Convention and other conventions, the owner of a nuclear power station is

strictly liable for damage caused by nuclear explosions, except when the damage occurs by acts of war and similar acts of armed conflict, civil war or ressurection or is caused by serious natural disasters of an exceptional character. In such cases, only persons who have caused the damage intentionally are liable (but not, for instance, owners of aeroplanes that have crashed into a nuclear plant causing an explosion).

Here, too, the scope of the liability for terrorist acts depends upon the concept of war or armed conflict (see II above). Of course, the circumstances surrounding the event will have considerable importance. At least a full-scale attack against the power station by violence against the people on guard, or an attack by air, may be regarded as equal to the exceptions mentioned in the Act. The interpretation of the courts will no doubt be influenced by decisions by courts in foreign countries applying the Paris Convention in similar cases. 14

IV. Railway Disasters

The Railway Traffic Act (1985;192) prescribes strict liability for the railway against passengers injured as a consequence of the railway service; however, the railway is free from liability if the injury has been caused by circumstances not related to the service itself and the railway could not have avoided them nor prevent their consequences, even if it had taken all the measures that reasonably could be demanded (chapter 2, sec. 2). This provision is considered equal to a *force majeure* clause. If a bomb explodes in a train, the railway will probably be exempted in most cases, whereas it is open to some doubt whether the provision would be applied if an attack upon the train driver results in a railway disaster. Even today, the risk of such events is not considered very significant, and both types of attack may be regarded as instances of *force majeure* unless there is some kind of negligence on the part of the railway in the particular case. In any event, it is open to discussion what preventive measures can be reasonably required in a possible situation where there is a general threat of terrorist attacks in the country. 15

Under the same conditions, the railway is liable for damage to accompanied luggage. As for transport of goods, there are several exceptions from liability, among others one similar to the provision concerning injuries to passengers mentioned above. 16

V. Road Disasters

The Traffic Damages Act (1975:1410) can be regarded as a hybrid between tort and insurance legislation. This Act prescribes a particular type of compulsory road traffic insurance, placing the risk upon the owners of motor vehicles in almost the same way as if they had a strict liability. The insurance provides compensation for personal injuries caused by motor vehicle traffic in almost all cases, irrespective of fault on the part of the driver or the owner or any other person; the owner and the driver, too, are entitled to compensation from the insurance under the same rules as third parties. Exception is made for certain 17 types of contributory negligence and intent on the part of the victim, but not for *force majeure* or similar events. The outcome is that as far as personal injuries are concerned, there is hardly any ordinary liability in tort for traffic disasters; all claims are directed against the insurance company. As for damage to property, there are exceptions from the coverage in respect of damage to the insured vehicle itself and property carried in or on that vehicle; here, ordinary liability principles are applicable. Further, special rules apply to damage caused to other vehicles. A maximum amount of 300 million Swedish crowns in compensation is payable in consequence of the same event.

18 This system implies that compensation from the traffic insurance will be paid for personal injuries up to the maximum amount in all cases of terrorist attacks upon buses and other motor vehicles leading to a traffic disaster, as well as when such vehicles are used for attacks upon other vehicles, buildings or people in the street. However, the insurance will not pay for disasters caused for instance by a bomb exploding inside or outside a bus or car that is not moving in traffic.

VI. Disasters at Sea

19 As for sea transport, the carrier has no strict liability even for injuries to passengers according to the Maritime Act (1994:1009). However, negligence is presumed if the injury occurred in connection with the sinking of a ship, collision, stranding, explosion or fire or as a consequence of a defect of the ship. In such cases, the carrier is liable unless he proves that the injury has not been caused by fault on the part of himself or anyone that he is responsible for (chapter 15, sec. 20). A similar rule is applied in case of damage to accompanied luggage. In case of terrorist acts, e.g. the explosion of a bomb causing a ship to sink, the carrier can escape liability if he exercised due care when controlling the activities of people aboard. However, the demands upon the captain and the crew can be rather rigorous (see X below).

VII. Pollution

20 The Environmental Code (1998) prescribes strict liability for different types of pollution caused by the use of real property, *inter alia* air pollution and water pollution (chapter 32, sec. 1 and 3). There is no exception for *force majeure* or similar events, only for such interference as reasonably should be tolerated in view of the circumstances in the locality or in view of its general occurrence. As for adequate causality, the Supreme Court considered, in a case from 1981 concerning water pollution caused by the act of a third party, that the act was not so strange and unforeseen as to exempt the responsible municipality from liability ([1981] *Nytt juridiskt arkiv*, 622). However, the case concerned a negligent act by an industry using the drainage system, and it is open to some doubt if sabotage by a terrorist would be regarded in the same way.

VIII. Blasting Operations and Explosions

According to the Environmental Code, there is also strict liability for damage caused by stones and other objects cast about in blasting operations or as a consequence of activities otherwise involving a particular risk of explosion (chapter 32, sec. 4). The liability can be imposed on the operator as well as on the owner of the premises where the activity takes place. There is no exception for *force majeure* and similar causes in this case, either. Here, too, there will be unlimited liability for damage caused by terrorist acts, provided that there is adequate causality. (Concerning possibilities of reducing the compensation for small firms and private persons see XI below.) 21

IX. Water Dam Disasters

An important catastrophe risk in many parts of Sweden is the bursting of dams used for regulating waterpower, which may cause extensive material damage as well as injuries to persons. According to the Environmental Code (chapter 11, sec. 18), the owner of a power station responsible for the maintenance of the dam has a strict liability if it bursts, unless the owner can prove that the cause was an act of war or similar act under armed conflict, civil war or rebellion. The interpretation of this exception has been discussed above (see II). However, concerning dam disasters the government stated in the *travaux preparatoires* of the legislation that there were not sufficient reasons for excepting sabotage acts in general. This attitude may be a reason for the courts to interpret the exception in a restrictive way in case of a terrorist action. 22

X. Liability for Fault

Even if the particular legislation mentioned above will present the most intricate legal problems, it is evident that ordinary rules concerning fault liability will have considerable importance also in case of terrorist attacks. The question will usually be whether the enterprise or the public agency responsible for the control has neglected to take measures against the risk of terror attacks. The duties will often be determined in detail by internal instructions varying for different types of activities and different types of property. However, attention should be paid to some general legislation concerning the prevention of terrorism. 23

Above all I should mention the Act on Protection of Property of Public Importance (1990:217) which particularly aims at protection against sabotage, terrorism and espionage. If it is necessary for such purposes to limit the public access to a building, an area, a ship or an aircraft or the right to use such property, it can be declared to be a protected object. Such objects can be premises used for public administration of different types or for military purposes, military ships and aircraft, buildings or areas used or intended for commanding the civil defence, for energy supply, for water supply, for radio transmissions, for telecommunications, for transports or for military industries or areas otherwise used by military forces. In a state of war, also other types of property can 24 be declared to be protected objects. In general, admission to protected objects can be prohibited. Police, military personnel or other particularly commissioned personnel can be used to guard such objects. Detailed rules are given concerning the powers of such security guards. Anyone carrying on activities of essential importance for the military or civil defence can be ordered to arrange surveillance, put up fences or take similar measures to prevent, among other things, sabotage and terrorism. Even more rigorous rules are prescribed for prohibited areas used for military purposes.

25 Evidently, this legislation prescribes a very strict control concerning the protected objects, and even slight negligence in fulfilling the duties of surveillance will result in liability for the responsible entity if it has rendered a terrorist act possible.

26 Of course, there is also a duty to control passengers on planes, boats, trains and buses and visitors to industries in other cases. The details of this duty will vary according to the circumstances. If there is a threat of a terrorist act, the demands upon the responsible party will increase. Here, prescriptions by authorities will play an important part. As for nuclear plants, the Swedish Nuclear Power Inspectorate is preparing new instructions which will be influenced by the threats emerging after the events of September 11. The safety arrangements on airlines have been extended after these events, according to instructions from the Air Traffic Authority, but no similar change has taken place concerning the safety of trains or ships. Certain shipping companies and ports have tightened their control on their own initiative. The breach of such private instructions will not always be regarded as negligence on the part of the company or port; the essential question is whether the provisions implied reasonable precautions against the terrorist risk.

XI. Amount of Compensation

27 In general, the same rules concerning compensation are applicable in cases of strict liability and when the liability is based upon negligence (unless the legislation contains rules of maximum amounts, as is the case with the Aviation Act, the Atomic Liability Act and the Maritime Act, according to international conventions). Liability for personal injuries as well as for damage to property comprises in principle the whole of the economic damage. In case of personal injury, full compensation is payable except insofar as the injured person, due to the injury, receives benefits from social insurance and certain types of collective insurance. The compensation includes non-pecuniary damages such as pain and suffering, permanent disability and harm and particular other inconveniences caused by the injury. Liability for personal injuries is not reduced even if the victim has been negligent, unless the negligence is gross. In case of loss of life, any person who was entitled to receive a maintenance allowance from the deceased or was otherwise dependent upon the deceased is entitled to compensation; this compensation is not reduced even in case of contributory fault except if the deceased acted intentionally, that is to say in suicide cases.

If the death causes a shock to a person close to the deceased (above all husband, wife, parents and children), this person can be compensated for injury to his health. As for damage to property, full compensation is paid, too, but here even slight negligence is a ground for reduction.

Certain rules concerning mitigation of liability should also be mentioned. According to a general provision in the Tort Liability Act, (chapter 6, sec. 2) the court can mitigate liability of any kind if it is unduly heavy, taking account also of the interest of the person suffering the injury or damage and other circumstances. The intention is that this rule shall be applied above all when claims are directed against private persons of limited means or against small enterprises, provided that the liable party is not protected by liability insurance (or the claim exceeds the maximum amount of the insurance). However, it can (at least theoretically) also be invoked by other liable parties if the claim will have ruinous consequences, unless a reduction of the compensation would conflict with the aims of the legislation or with international conventions. This reservation will prevent any mitigation in most cases of strict liability mentioned before; however, the rule may be invoked for instance in cases of blasting operations and similar dangerous activities at least when small firms are liable (see VII above). Liability of the state or the municipality will never be mitigated on this ground. 28

Further, the vicarious liability of employers and public agencies can be adjusted insofar as it concerns damage to property if this is reasonable having regard to existing insurances or availability of insurance (chapter 3, sec. 6). This provision, which until now has had little importance, aims, *inter alia*, at the situation when insurers having paid compensation for an aircraft or a big ship use their right of recourse against some responsible party who is not fully protected by liability insurance. It may have some practical importance if a terrorist act causes extensive material damage which is not covered by the maximum insurance sum. 29

XII. Insurance Against Terrorist Risk

To a considerable extent, the future development concerning terrorist risks will probably depend upon the possibility of insurance, above all liability insurance. Swedish tort law is influenced by such considerations in several respects. If it is practicable to distribute the loss by liability insurance, or, in some cases, by property insurance on the part of the victim, this is traditionally a weighty argument to the legislator as well as to the courts when locating the risk. 30

Concerning terrorist risks, the terms of insurance vary to some extent among Swedish insurers. In general, injuries and damages caused by war and similar armed conflicts are excluded. In other respects, the attitude has changed as a consequence of the development after September 11, in particular in the reinsurance market. It is true that until now there has been no particular exception 31 concerning terrorism in life, health or accident insurance or consumer insurance, although the possibility to exclude nuclear, biological and chemical injuries caused by terrorists has been discussed. As for business insurance, most insurers prefer to tackle the problem in another way, by prescribing a maximum amount for all consequences of the same terrorist act or a maximum amount for each victim. At least one big company has excluded certain direct or indirect consequences of a terrorist act, including unforeseen interruption of the supply of electricity, gas, water or heating and damage caused by biological or chemical contamination. Most of these exceptions aim particularly at property insurance, but in general they will apply also in liability insurance. In liability insurance for aircraft, there is an exception for terrorist acts which, however, may be omitted in commercial aviation. Of course, this increased protection is very expensive.

32 On the whole, the insurance situation is rather unstable, and one should allow for a growing reluctance to cover terrorist risks.

XIII. Conclusions

33 Here, it has been assumed that the defence of adequate causality (or remoteness of damage) will no longer hold in typical cases of terrorist actions. The present awareness of terrorist risks will probably have extended liability insofar as terrorist acts are no longer regarded as such abnormal and unforeseen events that exempt a defendant according to the principle of adequate causality. This can, in a way, be regarded as a paradoxical consequence of the efforts of the authorities to call attention to the risk and the increased control on the part of public and private entities. Evidently, the principle in question is not an appropriate means of keeping the liability within reasonable bounds so as to facilitate insurance cover. Instead, the defence of *force majeure* might be used at least in case of new legislation upon the subject. On the other hand, even this defence is of no use if the authority or private firm responsible for the control neglected precautionary measures that could reasonably be required. Of course, the duty to take such measures is much more urgent today than before September 11.

34 As pointed out above, the possibility of insurance will be an important factor. If the liable parties can protect themselves in this way, this can influence not only the requisites for liability without fault but also the attitude to liability for negligence. It will no longer appear too harsh to demand a strict control on the part of a carrier or an industry, and the liability may be extended even to remote consequences of terrorist acts. On the other hand, if accident insurance or property insurance affords good protection to the victim, strict liability is not so important. However, insurers are becoming increasingly reluctant to cover these risks, at least in business insurance. Of course, the possibility that the state will give a guarantee for compensation in case of typical terrorist actions can be discussed, but until now there is no sign that the legislator will resort to such solutions. Thus, the further development in this field is very uncertain in several ways.

XIV. Cases

In the questionnaire, some cases are mentioned that should illustrate the present state of law in the particular countries. As appears from the above, the solutions in Swedish law will probably be the following: 35

2. A terrorist hijacks an aeroplane and crashes into

a) A Building

The owner of the aeroplane will be liable unless the terrorist can be regarded as the "user" of the plane (see II above). 36

b) A Nuclear Plant

The owner of the plane will be liable acccording to (a), but only towards the owner of the nuclear plant (not towards third parties suffering damage by a nuclear explosion; see III above). 37

3. A Terrorist Sets a Bomb Situated in an Aeroplane and the Plane Crashes into

a) A Residential Area

The owner of the aeroplane will be liable (here, the terrorist has not "used" the plane). 38

b) A Nuclear Plant

The owner of the aeroplane will be liable towards the owner of the plant, but not towards third parties (see 1 b). 39

4. A Terrorist Drives with Somebody's Car or Bus into a Crowd of People

The traffic insurance will pay (see V above). 40

5. A Terrorist Hides a Bomb in a Car Which Explodes Within a Crowd of People

The victims will get no compensation from the traffic insurance, as the injuries were not caused by traffic with the car. 41

Switzerland
Liability for Acts of Terrorism Under Swiss Law

Thomas Lörtscher, Claudio Parizzi and Sabine Gutzwiller

I. General

A. Does Your Legal System Have Special Legislation on Terror Attacks, in Particular Concerning Liability or Other Indemnity?

1 Switzerland has no special legislation governing liability or compensation for terrorist attacks in the sense of a federal law on terrorist attacks. However, the liability regulations of special legislation schemes may be applied to certain terrorism scenarios, namely in the following areas:

- Road traffic: Road Traffic Act (*Strassenverkehrsgesetz*, SVG) of 19 December 1958
- Railways: Third Party Liability Law for Railways (*Eisenbahnhaftpflichtgesetz*, EHG) of 28 March 1905
- Nuclear power plants: Nuclear Energy Liability Act (*Kernenergiehaftpflichtgesetz*, KHG) of 18 March 1983
- Aviation: Civil Aviation Act (*Bundesgesetz über die Luftfahrt*, LFG) of 21 December 1948
- Public authorities: Public Authority Liability Regulations (*Verantwortlichkeitsgesetz*, VG) of 14 March 1958
- Explosives: Explosives Act (*Sprengstoffgesetz*, SSG) of 15 March 1977
- (See further comments under Section II, Strict liability)

B. Are There any Special Funds Applicable Providing Alternative Compensation for Victims of Terror Attacks?

2 There is a special fund, based on the Victim Assistance Act (*Opferhilfegesetz*) of 4 October 1991, which states that any victim of a criminal act is entitled to compensation from a special fund in case of damage to physical, sexual or mental in-

tegrity. However, compensation from this fund can only be claimed if the victim is in need of financial support and if this support cannot be claimed from a third party (principle of subsidiarity). In addition, the Swiss social insurance system provides assistance and compensation in case of an accident, i.e. also for injuries caused by a terrorist attack. Compensation from different funds or systems is co-ordinated, i.e. overcompensation is not allowed.

C. Have Your Judges ever Had to Address the Issue of Liability in Connection with Terror Attacks in any Leading Cases?

There have been no such cases in Swiss court practice in connection with liability for terrorist attacks. 3

D. Did the Events of 11 September 2001 or any other Recent Terror Attacks Have any Influence on Your Liability Systems?

The attack of 11 September 2001 had no influence on the Swiss liability system. In the aftermath of this event, there was broad discussion on insurance coverage for aviation and property risks, but this was not limited to Switzerland, as the insurance industry was no longer willing to provide insurance coverage at given terms. Furthermore, new criminal legislation to suppress terrorism is pending. 4

E. Does Your Country Participate in any International Conventions in Connection with Liability for Terror Attacks?

Switzerland does not participate in any international convention in connection with liability for terrorist attacks. The most important convention in the area of terrorism to which Switzerland is a signatory is the 1977 European Convention on the Suppression of Terrorism. It also plans to ratify two new UN agreements on combating terrorist financing and terrorist attacks. 5

II. Strict Liability

A. Focusing on Strict Liability for Means of Transport and Enterprises or Facilities, Would You Say the Owner, Custodian or Keeper is also Liable if a Terrorist Initiates the Damage?

1. Means of Transport

a) Road Traffic

According to the SVG, the keeper of a vehicle is responsible for any damage to persons or any material damage caused by said vehicle in operation. The term "operation" in principle means that a vehicle is in motion (art. 58 SVG). 6

The SVG prescribes strict liability. However, the keeper is not responsible if he/she can prove that the accident was caused by an act of God or by gross 7 negligence of the injured party or of a third party (art. 59 SVG). Therefore, if a terrorist is using his own vehicle, he is strictly liable as keeper of this vehicle. If other keepers are involved in an accident caused by a terrorist, they are not liable if they can prove the gross negligence of the terrorist.

8 Special conditions in art. 75 of the SVG specify that in case of the theft of a vehicle (e.g. by a terrorist) for the sole purpose of using the vehicle (and not for the purpose of appropriation), both the thief and the keeper of the vehicle are liable (joint and several liability) for any damage caused by the stolen vehicle. However, the keeper and his/her insurer have the right of recourse against the persons that have stolen the vehicle. Given that such drastic abuse of a vehicle was not taken into consideration at the time the legislation was drawn up, it cannot be ruled out that a court would deviate from the strict interpretation of art. 75 in its ruling.

b) Air Traffic

i) Airport

9 The Swiss Confederation has granted the operating concession for Zurich Airport to Flughafen Zurich AG. According to regulations approved by the Federal Ministry for Civil Aviation on 1 June 2001, the liability of the airport operator is governed by the VG of 14 March 1958. This law prescribes strict liability. Requirements for liability to be present are unlawfulness and adequate causation.

10 According to art. 4 of the regulations governing operations (*Betriebsreglement*), the airport operator is not liable for damages caused by events beyond its control or by actions taken by third parties. This also applies in principle to damages caused by falling aircraft, for which the airline company is liable (see point (ii) below).

11 When examining the existence of unlawfulness in connection with terrorist attacks, it is namely a question of whether the airport operator is facing alleged neglect of duty (omission) with regard to security measures within its control. Above and beyond this, border protection controls are the responsibility of the police. They are subject to liability legislation in the canton of Zurich (*Haftungsgesetz des Kantons Zürich*), which, similar to the federal regulations on the liability of public authorities, prescribes strict liability, but is only enforced if the police officer has breached official duties through alleged failure to perform checks.[1]

12 Neglect of duties (omissions) that are within the control and the area of responsibility of the airport operator are only unlawful to the extent that air traffic safety and security obligations, such as regarding luggage and passenger

[1] See *Entscheidungen des Schweizerischen Bundesgerichts* (BGE) 123 II 577.

checks, are breached. In this respect the airport operator is legally assigned the role of guarantor. According to the regulations governing operations, art. 98 et seq., the airport operator is obliged to perform effective access checks. Furthermore, the operator is obliged to seal all access points to non-public areas by means of security measures. In view of the increased risk of terrorist attacks in the aviation industry, checks must be in line with generally accepted standards of airport security. Here again, the limitations of proportionateness and reasonableness of the security measures apply; these are determined by the level of the current risk situation.

Generally speaking, airline operations on the ground and in the air are assumed to be subject to an increased risk with regard to terrorist attacks on aircraft. This means that the conditions of foreseeability and adequate causal relationship are fulfilled in the case of insufficient checks being performed. 13

ii) Airline Companies

Airline companies are strictly liable for bodily injury or property damage on the ground caused by falling aircraft. Art. 64 LFG imposes strict liability. In view of the high operating risk of aircraft, it is not possible for the airline to argue an act of God in its defence[2] and it also cannot claim that the terrorist attack was something unforeseeable and inevitable. Art. 64, § 2, lit. b specifically states that the airline company shall also be held liable for damage caused by persons on board the aircraft. This also applies to terrorists. Nevertheless, in this case the amount of liability is limited to the amount of legal security to be provided by the airline. According to art. 125 of the Civil Aviation Decree (*Luftfahrtverordnung*, LFV), this may be up to CHF 75 million, depending on the size of the aircraft. 14

Liability according to the LFG is not applicable to passengers. The respective liability is governed by the applicable international Warsaw and Montreal conventions. Whilst the Warsaw Convention stipulates liability limits and exculpatory proof of the carrier, the 1999 draft of the Montreal Convention, which Switzerland still has to ratify, provides for unlimited liability for bodily injury (art. 21). Swiss airline companies are already voluntarily offering unlimited liability for bodily injury suffered by passengers as part of their conditions of carriage, in line with the IATA Intercarrier Agreement of 1995. This liability is strict up to an amount which corresponds to 100,000 Special Drawing Rights (approximately CHF 200,000). With regard to amounts in excess of these limits, the carrier can exculpate itself by proving that such damage was not due to the negligence or other wrongful act or omission of the carrier or its servants or agents. In the case of terrorist attacks carried out by a passenger, the exculpation would usually be valid. 15

[2] A. Keller, *Haftpflicht im Privatrecht* (5th edn. 1993), 241.

c) Railways

16 The focus here is on whether the Swiss Federal Railways (SBB) is liable as owner and operator of its railway stations. Insofar as it exercises the sovereign function of the railway police, strict liability is applied in accordance with the regulations on public authority liability.[3] However, strict liability also requires unlawfulness and the foreseeability of terrorist attacks as an element of adequate causation. Insofar as there is no concrete evidence of a threat, however, it is not possible to talk of an acute risk at railway stations as is the case for airports with regard to terrorist acts. In this respect, railway stations are subject to clearly fewer extensive safety and security obligations than airports. The principles of proportionateness and reasonableness of police intervention limit the amount of force and checks deemed necessary to carry out official duties.

17 With regard to damage from terrorist acts involving rail traffic, the liability situation is governed by the EHG. This states that strict liability is imposed on rail companies. However, they are exempted from liability where an act of God or gross negligence on the part of a third party or the injured party exists (art. 1 EHG). The law talks only of "negligence on the part of a third party or the injured party" without mention of "gross". The SBB is, however, only released from its liability if the negligence of the third party or the injured party is, from the point of view of adequate causation, the sole cause of the accident.[4] For example, a terrorist bomb attack would fulfil these criteria without doubt. Particularly strict criteria are imposed on an act of God as grounds for a break in the causal relationship, as rail companies have to cope with extreme weather conditions over the years and are consciously exposed to them.[5]

18 One peculiarity of the EHG is that strict liability applies unlimitedly only to bodily injury and to property damage caused in relation to bodily injury. The rail company is only liable for other property damage in the event of fault (see Section III Fault liability). With regard to the liability of the SBB under the contract of carriage in private law, the contractual and non-contractual principles of liability apply, which are likewise based on fault.

2. Enterprises/Facilities

a) Nuclear Power Plants

19 Art. 3 KHG stipulates that the owner of a nuclear power plant is liable without limitation for nuclear damage caused by nuclear materials from its plant. Only when the injured party causes the damage intentionally or through gross negligence is the owner of the plant released totally or partially from its liability (art. 5 KHG). However, an act of God (e.g. earthquake) or any type of third

[3] BGE 102 Ib 314, BGE 93 I 290.
[4] BGE 87 II 306 et seq., BGE 102 II 366.
[5] See A. Keller (supra fn. 2), 231 et seq.

party negligence (e.g. terrorist attack) are not a reason for exculpation of liability, as it is only the extreme risk that operating a nuclear plant represents which makes such devastating damage possible in the first place.[6]

b) Explosives Plants

In accordance with art. 27 SSG, the owner of a plant of this type is liable for any damage caused by the explosion of explosive materials. However, it may be released from this liability if it is able to prove that the damage was caused by an act of God or gross negligence by the injured party or by a third party. An unforeseen (but provable) terrorist attack would, depending on the interpretation (see Section B), be taken as an act of God or gross negligence by a third party, thereby releasing the operator of the plant from its liability. The owner of the plant must nevertheless comply with all security and storage obligations, otherwise it will be held strictly liable, e.g. if terrorists succeed in misappropriating explosive material from the plant and it emerged that security measures were inadequate. 20

B. *Can Terror Attacks Be Classified as a Defence like Act of God/Force Majeure/Unavoidable Event?*

An act of God is understood as a fortuitous, unforeseeable, extraordinary event which involves unavoidable violence from an external source. An act of God is thereby a fortuitous event of high intensity.[7] An act of God basically breaks the causal relationship and rules out liability. In the case of strict liability, however, particularly stringent conditions must be met for an event to qualify as an act of God, as it would otherwise not be possible to achieve the intended protection that these regulations are supposed to afford. As mentioned earlier, a break in the causal relationship by an act of God, which would release the liable party from liability, is in no way possible under the tight KHG liability provisions. 21

According to general legal interpretation, an act of God is, on account of the criteria of unforeseeability and unavoidability, simply an act independent of human agency.[8] However, classifying terrorist attacks similar to those experienced in 2001 is quite difficult. Basically, the following can be said: if terrorist attacks are carried out in a crisis hit country, in which attacks have been carried out in the past, and there were indications of these attacks, it would be difficult to speak of the unforeseeability of a new attack. On the other hand, if a terrorist attack, of which there was no specific indication, were to be carried out in Switzerland, it would be possible to talk of an act of God. Numerous contractual terms and conditions also draw the same conclusion, for example, tour operators or telecom companies explicitly subsume the risk of terrorist attacks under the term act of God. On a practical level, it is of little signifi- 22

[6] See A. Keller (supra fn. 2), 315.

[7] BGE 28 II 253, 81 II 443, BGE 90 IV 270.

[8] BGE 111 II 433 et seq.

cance whether the break in the causal relationship caused by the attack is attributed in specific cases to an act of God or gross negligence on the part of a third party.

C. If There Is a Person Liable Besides or Instead of the Terrorist, for Which Kind of Damage Is He/She Liable (for Example also Compensation for Consequential Damage like Plundering Following a Terror Attack)?

23 According to Swiss law, the damage is the "difference between the assets of a legal entity existing at the specific point in time and the amount that these assets would represent if the damaging event had not occurred".[9]

24 The damaging event must therefore be the cause of the damage, i.e. there must be a causal relationship between both elements. This must further be "adequate", i.e. an event is only taken to be the cause of a result if the event is capable of contributing to the result that occurred during the normal course of events and in line with general experience. From this angle, even extraordinary consequences can be considered adequate.[10] A distinction is drawn between bodily injury, property damage and pecuniary loss. These can be further divided into direct and indirect damage. The question of how liability for direct/immediate and indirect/consequential damage is dealt with depends ultimately on the purely practical issue of the number of links in the chain of causation and their legal significance. The deciding factor is therefore whether there are circumstances between the loss event and damage, for which the damaging party is not responsible, that make the damage a remote consequence.[11] In other words, there must be adequate causation between the damaging event and the damage incurred for each link of the chain, no matter how remote. If this is the case, the damaging party is basically liable for consequential or indirect damage, such as looting following a terrorist attack.

III. Fault Liability

A. At Public Facilities such as Airports, Train Stations, Sports Stadiums etc., Who Is Responsible that no Terrorist Enters and Causes Harm? How Far Do the Duties of Care Go in that Respect?

25 Basically a strict liability regime is applied to most instances of liability in connection with public facilities and public transport (aviation and rail, use of motor vehicles, nuclear installations) (see information provided in Section II). The duty of care only plays a role insofar as the breach of safety obligations or official duties forms the basis of liability for neglect of duty (omission) to which public authority liability is applied (rail and airport police, airport operator) (see II above).

[9] BGE 76 II 297, 104 II 199.
[10] BGE 96 II 396.
[11] See Th. Guhl/A. Koller, *Das Schweizerische Obligationenrecht* (8th edn. 1991), 64 et seq.

B. To What Extent Do Individuals or Entities Have a Duty of Care to Participate in the Active Avoidance of Terrorist Acts?

Traditional fault liability has a secondary practical role insofar as it concerns the liability of third parties (individuals or organisers) for acts carried out by terrorists. 26

Basically, fault liability according to Swiss tort law requires adequate causation, unlawfulness and negligence in addition to the occurrence of a loss. This essentially deals with the possible omissions of third parties who could have prevented the terrorist attack with the required duty of care. However, insofar as the third party could not have foreseen the terrorist attack or at least the specific threat of an attack, omissions do not provide a basis for adequate causal relationship. For unlawfulness and negligence in this respect, attention should be paid to the risk prevention principle ("Gefahrensatz") applied in law. This states that wherever a dangerous state is created or maintained there is a duty to implement security measures.[12] However, this principle applies only if the defendant can be considered to have assumed the role of a guarantor. Apart from individual cantonal criminal legislation on assistance in emergencies ("Nothilfeleistung"), Swiss law does not prescribe a general duty of action to avert danger[13]. The "principle of authorised inaction" applies.[14] 27

As mentioned the duty of care under the risk-prevention principle is applied only if a legal entity assumes the so-called role of guarantor. For entities under private law, this role of guarantor can result from criminal norms or a contractual relationship. However, only in rare cases can these duties of protection be applied with regard to the prevention or mitigation of the consequences of terrorist attacks. Improbable chains of events are disregarded from the outset. The most obvious cases are the guarantor roles assumed by tour operators or organisers of major events, such as sporting events and street parades.[15] If an indication of a risk of a terrorist attack is evident with regard to such events, all reasonable security measures must be taken (e.g. access and body searches at entrances to football stadiums, security barriers; in the case of specific risk of a terrorist attack, cancellation of the event if necessary). The type and extent of measures that must be undertaken depend on the specific circumstances. An objective definition of negligence applies. The law requires an average amount of care and attention, the care which is necessary in view of the given conditions and specific circumstances, such as with regard to the dangerousness of an activity or situation. These conditions are, with the exception of activities relating to airline operations, without doubt only applicable in exceptional cases with regard to the avoidance of terrorist attacks under extremely specific circumstances and with evidence of danger. 28

[12] BGE 121 III 358, 113 II 247; A. Schnyder, in: *Kommentar zum Schweizerischen Privatrecht* (2nd edn. 1996), art. 41 *Obligationenrecht* (Swiss Law of Obligations, OR) no. 18.

[13] BGE 80 II 26/39, 74 II 158/162.

[14] BGE 115 II 19; A. Schnyder (supra fn. 12), art. 41 OR no. 37.

[15] BGE 70 II 215.

29 The same applies to financial institutions who have to observe duties of care when accepting monies. It is seldom possible to recognise a terrorist, and the specific foreseeability of terrorist financing as a requirement of adequate proximate cause might only be present in exceptional cases.

IV. Cases

1. A Terrorist Hijacks an Aeroplane and Crashes into

a) A Building

30 The airline is liable without fault under strict liability in accordance with the LFG for the resulting property damage and bodily injury. The airline cannot be released from liability on account of an act of God or gross negligence of a third party. However, the liability limit mentioned under II ii) would be applicable.

b) A Nuclear Plant

31 The airline and the owner of the nuclear plant are jointly and severally liable for the resulting property damage and bodily injury. The airline cannot be released from its liability on account of an act of God or gross negligence of a third party. For the airline the liability limit would apply (see II ii).

2. A Terrorist Detonates a Bomb Located in an Aeroplane and the Plane Crashes into

a) A Residential Area

32 Identical to case 1 a). No liability limit if the terrorist was not on board.

b) A Nuclear Plant

33 Identical to case 1 b). For the airline, no liability limit if the terrorist was not on board.

3. A Terrorist Drives Another Person's Vehicle into a Crowd of People

34 If the terrorist stole the vehicle for the purpose of driving into a crowd of people, both the keeper of the vehicle and the terrorist are liable (joint and several liability). The keeper and his/her insurer have the right of recourse against the terrorist, which might be of theoretical value only (art. 75). If the vehicle was not stolen, but its keeper did not know of the terrorist's intention to drive the vehicle into a crowd, the keeper is not liable as he/she will be able to prove that a third party (i.e. the terrorist) acted with gross negligence (art. 59).

4. A Terrorist Hides a Bomb in a Car Which Explodes in a Crowd of People

The explosion of a bomb in a parked vehicle, whether stolen or not, does not meet the requirements of a vehicle in operation. It is not a traffic accident and thus strict liability based on the SVG does not apply. The general rules of fault liability are applicable. 35

If the bomb explodes in a moving vehicle, this is considered a traffic accident, triggering strict causal liability in accordance with the SVG, even if a bomb explosion does not represent a typical risk resulting from the operation of a vehicle. The mere fact that the vehicle is in operation and causes damage in traffic is sufficient grounds for the application of strict liability in accordance with art. 58 SVG. 36

UNITED KINGDOM
LIABILITY FOR ACTS OF TERRORISM: UNITED KINGDOM PERSPECTIVE

Clive Walker*

I. Introduction

1 The sub-form of political violence known as "terrorism" should be viewed as at the pinnacle of risks and liabilities, for it seeks to perpetrate harms which threaten not just single enterprises or individuals or even groups of them linked either by location or type but the entire population and the political economy. Academic and professional interest in the impact of terrorism has no doubt been heightened by the events of September 11.[1] Given that these attacks occurred in another jurisdiction[2] and that their recent origin means that their impacts are as yet not resolved, most of the relevant laws and practices prevailing in the United Kingdom predate the recent attacks. Accordingly, the focus of the law has been on a conflict of much greater longevity, namely, the campaigns by Republicans in Northern Ireland in favour of a United Ireland. As regards legal outcomes, the impact of this conflict can be seen in two stages, which will therefore provide some case studies for this paper.

2 The first study concerns the impact in the province of Northern Ireland itself. That impact was evident from the early 1970s onwards and resulted in direct state intervention to deal with civil liability. The second phase arose in Britain and concerns the IRA bombings in the City of London in 1992 and 1993 (plus

* Professor of Criminal Justice Studies and Head of School, School of Law, University of Leeds. Part of the research for this paper was funded by a grant from the Airey Neave Trust. The author thanks the Trust and also the co-researcher on that project, Dr. Martina McGuinness, Sheffield University. Parts of the chapter also appeared in C. Walker/M. McGuinness, Risk, political violence and policing the City of London, in: A. Crawford (ed.), *Crime, Insecurity, Safety and the New Governance* (2002).

1 See C. Walker, *Guide to the Anti-Terrorism Legislation* (2002).

2 Their extra-territorial nature may be relevant to the advent of legal development, but the United Kingdom has been directly affected in two ways. One concerns companies and individuals directly suffering loss or injury. The other is that the world insurance and reinsurance markets are centred on London, consequently, large losses inevitably have impact on the operation of the United Kingdom financial sector.

the London Docklands and Manchester bombings in 1996). The response to civil liability on this occasion was more indirect and mainly took the attempts to shore up the confidence of the City of London reinsurance market. The events pursuant to the attacks of September 11 follow a similar pattern to the second study and so can be presented as a postscript to it. However, there is a list of other legislation which provides for civil liability in the contingency of major harm or loss relating to vital public services or critical installations. These will also be detailed as "Special Sectoral Liabilities".

By adopting this focus, it is intended to elucidate several themes of liability. 3
They include aspects of risk which become novel or heightened in late modern society, as well as the manner in which a blur of public and private actors respond to these heightened liabilities. The nature of the risk and response also connects with the themes of the interplay of transnational and local – how the nature of financial markets produces global opportunity and risk.

There may be two observations about liability arising from terrorism. The first 4
is that this type of crime clearly mixes forms of traditional liability – property damage and loss and injury to life and limb – with behaviour which is not typically tortious but is highly politicised. The destruction and injury are not to be taken too personally by the victims – the attack is symbolic, and the real impact is to be on the state, again differing from the normal tortfeasor. This observation about the nature of terrorist-related torts should lead to a state response which is equally mixed in its aspects, and often is mixed not only in terms of addressing liability and loss but also in terms of the reformulation of economic and political policies and especially policing and security policies.[3] This shows the essentially organic nature of the processes of the "risk society" – "an epoch in which the dark sides of progress increasingly come to dominate social debate".[4] They also require new responses; as Beck states, "risks presume industrial, that is, techno-economic decisions and considerations of utility."[5]

The second observation is that this type of attack can also tell us as much 5
about contemporary political economies as well as about the manifold nature of threat to them, since it can open up the social matrix surrounding the environment in which it occurs.[6] Accordingly, the appropriate targets selected for this type of attack must be politically as well as economically important.

[3] See C. Walker (supra fn. 1).
[4] U. Beck, *Ecological Enlightenment* (1995), 2.
[5] U. Beck, *Risk Society* (1992), 98.
[6] S. Jasanoff, *Learning from Disaster* (1994), 2.

II. Northern Ireland – Direct Legal Intervention

A. History

6 By far the most important source of terrorism in the British Isles has been Irish Nationalism.[7] Rather than rehearse the full details of the most recent campaign which existed in Ireland since 1969 and in Britain since 1973, this commentary will be confined to IRA strategy as it has affected laws relating to civil liability. However, it should be noted that the campaign has witnessed several phases, some being more important than others in terms of triggering legal change and including an intermittent cease-fire since 1994. For example, car bombings in the early 1970s, which often had counter-productive results in terms of human casualties, were in part supplanted by the perfection of the use of incendiary devices in the mid-1970s, which focused attention on property damage and so had an important impact on the drafting of the compensation legislation issued in 1977. This first case study will focus upon the direct state provision for compensation for property damage caused by terrorism.

7 In both jurisdictions in Ireland, there has been a long tradition, enshrined in statute, of state compensation for criminal damage to private property arising from political violence. The contemporary legislative response in Northern Ireland is the Criminal Damage (Compensation) (Northern Ireland) Order 1977.[8] Though part of its historical background is based in forms of collective punishments of communities which have failed to control their rebels,[9] the more direct precursors were the Grand Jury (Ireland) Act of 1836[10] (as amended by the Local Government (Ireland) Act in 1898), the Criminal Injuries (Ireland) Act 1920, the Criminal Injuries Act (Northern Ireland) 1956 and the Criminal Injuries to Property (Compensation) Act (Northern Ireland) 1971.

8 Impetus for shaping the contemporary legislation came from the political crisis in which Northern Ireland found itself from 1968 onwards. The Northern Ireland Minister of State for Home Affairs noted in 1971 that although a couple of years previously, county councils were able to absorb the impact of compensation payments without significant effect on local rates, the height-

[7] M. Farrell, *Northern Ireland: The Orange State* (2nd edn. 1980); K. Kelley, *The Longest War* (1984); G. Hogan/C.P. Walker, *Political Violence and the Law in Ireland* (1989); C.P. Walker, *The Prevention of Terrorism in British Law* (2nd edn. 1992); P. Bew/P. Gibbon/H. Patterson, *Northern Ireland 1921–94* (1995); T. Wilson, *Ulster: Conflict and Consent* (1989); P. Bishop/E. Mallie, *The Provisional IRA* (1994); M.A. Poole, Political violence – the overspill from Northern Ireland, in: A. O'Day (ed.), *Political Violence in Northern Ireland* (1997); P. Taylor, *Brits: the War against the IRA* (2000); T.P. Coogan, *The IRA* (2000).

[8] *Statutory Instrument* (SI) No. 1247 (N.I. 14). See D.S. Greer/V.A. Mitchell, *Compensation For Criminal Damage* (1982).

[9] Tumultuous Risings Act 1765 sec. 3 5 Geo 3 c.8 (Ir) (a person suffering loss could require a levy to be raised in the area); Tumultuous Risings Act 1771 11 & 12 Geo 3 c.5 (Ir) sec. 10, 11 (collective fines); Tumultuous Risings Act 1775 15 & 16 Geo 3 c.1 (Ir) sec. 8 to 14, as amended by 36 Geo 3 c32 (Ir) (collective levy); Peace Preservation (Ireland) Act 1870 sec. 39.

[10] 6 and 7 William IV, c.116. Its long title was "An Act to consolidate and amend the Laws relating to the Presentment of public Money by Grand Juries in Ireland".

ened violence of the time left those same county councils facing financial ruin should they be obliged to carry out the same role.[11] Additional impetus to the decision to reform came from the Macrory Report on Local Government in Northern Ireland[12] which recommended that the scheme for criminal injuries compensation should also be a provincial service.[13] As a result, the 1971 Act saw one of the last steps taken in the total abandonment of the treatment of loss from terrorism as a matter of concern and responsibility for the locale. The Northern Ireland Government accepted total responsibility for all costs of damage and loss arising from civil disturbances and malicious damage.[14] Although the 1971 Act had only been in force since 1973, by 1975 it was felt necessary to review the legislation again, both in terms of its underlying principles and its operation.[15] To this end a committee under the chairmanship of Sir James Waddell was appointed and instructed to make recommendations to the Secretary of State for Northern Ireland. In the event, the 1977 Order did not radically alter the regime of the 1971 Act. Certainly it introduced no variation in the principle of publicly funded compensation for property. Investigation by the Waddell Committee into alternatives to the existing Northern Ireland scheme revealed that none appeared viable.[16]

B. Criminal Damage (Compensation) (Northern Ireland) Order 1977

Art. 1 and 2 specify the title, commencement and interpretation of various terms contained in the new Order. From the commencement date (1 April 1978), the Secretary of State is liable to pay, to those with an interest in the property, for damage to it, or its unlawful removal. The particular circumstances under which compensation is payable are in those cases where an applicant has suffered loss as a result of physical damage to property in the following circumstances: 9

(i) looting; that is the unlawful removal of property from a building in the course of a riot. To qualify three or more must tumultuously and riotously assemble together unlawfully, and maliciously or wantonly cause damage.[17]

(ii) property unlawfully, maliciously or wantonly damaged where three or more persons are unlawfully, riotously or tumultuously assembled together.[18]

[11] *House of Commons* (HC) (*Northern Ireland* [NI]) *Debates* (Debs.) vol. 82, column 1526.

[12] *Report of the Review Body on Local Government in Northern Ireland* (Command Paper 546, 1970).

[13] Ibid, para. 74.

[14] This acceptance of responsibility was tempered by provision in sec. 9(2) for recovering the cost from the rates.

[15] *Report of a Committee to Review the Principles and Operation of the Criminal Injuries to Property (Compensation Act) (Northern Ireland)* (1971), vii.

[16] *Waddell Report*, 5–7.

[17] Criminal Damage (Compensation) (Northern Ireland) Order 1977, art. 6(a).

[18] Art. 5(1)(a). In effect, a common law unlawful assembly must be proven: *WAC McCandless (Engineers) Ltd v Secretary of State* [1986] *Northern Ireland Law Reports* (NI), 55. In *Gilmore v Secretary of State* [1995] NI, 46 a claim failed where the applicant's car had been taken by three persons; the car had been unlocked with the keys in the ignition, so there was no evidence

(iii) property unlawfully, maliciously or wantonly damaged as a result of an act committed maliciously by a person acting on behalf of, or in connection with, an unlawful[19] association.[20]

(iv) the Chief Constable issues a certificate to the effect that he believes an act was committed maliciously by a person acting on behalf of, or in connection with an unlawful association.[21] This certificate is sufficient evidence for an application for compensation unless there is proof to the contrary.

(v) malicious and wanton damage caused to agricultural buildings and property.[22] In this case, there is no requirement to prove the involvement of three or more persons or an unlawful association.[23] This formula was a matter of some contention in the British Government's eyes. While bowing to pressure from local MPs and organisations, this "special treatment"[24] for farmers was not intended to continue indefinitely (but has in fact done so).

10 Any person who has an interest in the property which has been damaged and who suffers a loss of more than £ 200 because of that damage may apply for compensation. Where compensation of more than £ 200 is payable a statutory deduction of £ 200 will be made from the total compensation due.[25]

of force being used in the taking of the car, nor was there any evidence of any purpose to commit any crime of violence. But in *McGeown v Secretary of State for Northern Ireland* [1987] NI, 262, a car owner was compensated where the car had been taken by force from his garage; it was subsequently found wrecked in the Turf Lodge estate in west Belfast, the wrecking being seen as an inevitable consequence of the forcible taking. By contrast, though in *McGuinness v Secretary of State* [1981] 9 *Northern Ireland Judgement Bulletins* (NIJB), it was accepted that a car had been hijacked in Belfast by the IRA, when it was found damaged in the Republic of Ireland, there was no sufficient evidence of when, how, or where the damage was caused, nor any evidence that the car was still in the possession of the IRA when it was caused. But where it is clear that the youths who forcibly took the car were also responsible for crashing it in the Republic, then compensation could be payable: *Wells v Secretary of State for Northern Ireland* [1981] NI, 233.

19 An "unlawful association" is any organisation engaged in terrorism, including any organisation proscribed under the ambit of what is now the Terrorism Act 2000 Pt.I: Art. 2.

20 Art. 5(1)(b).

21 Art. 5(2).

22 Art. 4(1). As for the meaning of agricultural property, in *Gillespie v Secretary of State for Northern Ireland* [1990] NI, 392, a track digger which had been adapted for, and solely employed in, agricultural use fell within art. 4, though it could have non-agricultural uses. J. Carswell felt that though art. 4 was anomalous, "The justification for continuing it in modern times was said to be that such property is necessarily scattered and cannot easily be watched and protected...". A stricter attitude had been shown in *Stewart v Secretary of State for Northern Ireland* [1983] NI, 335, where a thoroughbred brood mare was not "livestock" of an agricultural nature.

23 This is a complete reiteration of the provisions for agricultural property contained firstly in the 1956 Act and then the 1971 Act, albeit an agricultural building is now defined under the Rates (Northern Ireland) Order 1972.

24 HC Debs. vol. 935, col. 1520.

25 Art. 10(6), as amended by Criminal Damage (Compensation) (Northern Ireland) Order 1977 (Amendment) Order 1990 SR 25.

It was the Government's intention to provide compensation for "damage" to property, rather than for "loss" of property.[26] By art. 3(1): "compensation shall be payable by the Secretary of State for damage caused as a result of an act committed on or after 1st April 1978 to any property or for the unlawful removal on or after that date of property in the circumstances described in Article 6." Thus, claims may relate to the cost of repairs or reinstatement or reduction in market value of property, fixtures and fittings and also damage to vehicles and other goods such as stock. Nevertheless, compensation for consequential loss (such as loss of profits or rental of alternative accommodation or bank interest arising from extra costs) continues to be available, as it had been under previous legislation, provided it can be related to the damage to property. Thus, in *Public Works (Belfast) Limited v Secretary of State for Northern Ireland*,[27] the High Court would allow compensation for losses directly flowing from the bombing of a canteen at a construction site, such as delay in the work programme owing to delays for meal breaks, but would not allow disruption arising from shock or fear on the part of employees. Where compensation is payable, applicants will also be entitled to the reasonable costs incurred in making out and verifying claims. Compensation is expressly not available for any damage to, destruction or theft of coins, bank notes, foreign currency, postal orders, money orders, or any postage stamps; or any articles of personal adornment, including watches and jewellery unless kept by the owner as part of stock in trade;[28] or property taken from a damaged vehicle or building except in certain circumstances such as if the property was stolen from a damaged building in the course of a riot.[29] 11

It will be noted that the scheme does not specify that it relates only or primarily to commercial damage. However, the scheme is most relevant to that category because commercial property is generally not covered by insurance companies for loss arising from criminal damage in Northern Ireland. Conversely, domestic property and contents may be insured. Therefore if the damaged property is domestic and insured, a claim should be made to the relevant insurance company as well as the Agency. In these circumstances the insurance company makes payments to the applicant based on the insurance cover provided and compensation awards are paid by the Agency to the insurers. 12

In order to make an application under the 1977 Order, the applicant must serve a notice of intention upon the Secretary of State, the local divisional police commander and whichever other persons prescribed.[30] In practice, most individuals or organisations making a claim under the current legislation tend to do so through a solicitor.[31] The notice of intention required under the Order is a particular form (form C1) created originally by the Northern Ireland Office 13

[26] Ibid.
[27] [1987] NI, 322.
[28] Art. 10.
[29] Art. 6.
[30] Art. 7(1).
[31] Charter Statement (Compensation Agency), 8.

and now issued by the Compensation Agency (the administrative agency operating the scheme).[32] This notice contains all relevant facts and information pertaining to the circumstances of the loss for which compensation is being sought. In order to allow for a prompt investigation of the damage to be carried out by the Agency's loss adjuster as soon as possible after damage occurs, it must be served within 10 days to the prescribed bodies. Again, in practice a solicitor will serve the notice of intention form on the Compensation Agency, a copy to the police in the area in which the damage occurred, and if there is a suggestion of paramilitary involvement, a further copy on Lisnasharragh Police, Montgomery Road, Belfast who deal with the issuance of Chief Constable's certificates. Although there is a time limit of 10 days for carrying out this preliminary action, this is fairly flexible. Indeed, the 1977 Order allows for an extension of this initial 10-day period up to six months, at the Secretary of State's discretion,[33] or the court on appeal.[34]

14 Generally when serving the preliminary notice on the Compensation Agency, the applicant's solicitor will request an application for compensation form (C2). This application must be made within four months, but again this time constraint may be extended up to, but not longer than, a year, at the discretion of the Secretary of State or the court.[35] Should the Secretary of State (or the Compensation Agency acting on his behalf) require additional information from the applicant, it must be furnished, otherwise the claim will be decided on the basis of the information in the Agency's possession.[36] Delay in the settlement of claims, due to a lack of information from the applicant, or the applicant's representative had been a problem under the 1971 Act.[37] Applicants are advised that the information required to substantiate a claim may include title deeds, leases, stock records, financial accounts, and invoices for work carried out.

15 The information in the compensation form together with further details contained in additional forms – notice for particulars (property) or motor vehicle – forms the initial basis for assessing compensation. Should the claim be substantial, from a financial point of view, the Compensation Agency may appoint a loss adjuster. Similarly, the applicant may appoint his own loss assessor to assist in the negotiation of the claim.[38] In many other cases the solicitor will negotiate directly with the Compensation Agency on behalf of the applicant.

[32] See http://www.compensationni.gov.uk.
[33] Art. 7(3). This was an amendment brought in as a result of recommendations by the Waddell Committee (supra fn. 16), 87, 88.
[34] Art. 15.
[35] Art. 8(1), 15.
[36] As under the 1971 Act, compensation can be reduced if the applicant has failed to take adequate precautions to prevent loss or has contributed in any way to increasing the likelihood of loss. See art. 9.
[37] HC Debs. vol. 935, col. 1521.
[38] "Reasonable" legal costs and expenses incurred by the applicant of a successful claim are paid by the Secretary of State: art. 12(2).

Terms for the assessment, reduction, or exclusion, of compensation are made more explicit under the 1977 Order than had been the case previously. It was clear from the Waddell Report that ambiguities in the 1971 Act[39] had caused difficulties.[40] Consequently art. 9 in the 1977 Order places an onus upon the applicant to show that they have taken all reasonable precautions to reduce or avoid loss and that they have complied with statutory requirements as to safety. An example would be the proper regulation and storage of flammable materials.[41] The Secretary of State will also take into account any unlawful use of the property by the applicant or anyone with his/her consent and any provocative or negligent behaviour which contributed directly or indirectly to the loss or which increased the chances of it being sustained 16

Further clarification is inserted in art. 10(3) to the effect that (the only exception being the Secretary of State's judgement that it would be in the public interest[42]), no present or past member of an unlawful association, or anyone who has, or is, engaged in any kind of terrorist activity may receive compensation. It is arguable that the width of this disqualification is not proportionate to the needs of public policy under art. 1 of Protocol 1 of the European Convention.[43] As might be expected, compensation is also not payable where the applicant planned, assisted in, or actively and willingly facilitated, the act which resulted in the damage (or looting) or was associated or connected with the person(s) who caused it[44] or where the applicant fails to co-operate with the police in identifying and apprehending offenders.[45] 17

Compensation is also not payable where the loss incurred has been, or can be recovered under any other statutory provision or common law.[46] One possibility here is where the loss is related to terrorism but arises from counter-measures by state agents. Compensation in that circumstance is provided whenever (a) real or personal property is taken, occupied, destroyed or damaged, or (b) any other act is done which interferes with private rights of property under the terms of the Terrorism Act 2000, sec. 102 and Schedule 12.[47] The nature of private rights has been explained in *R (McCreesh) v County Court of Judge of Armagh*[48] and in *R (Secretary of State for Northern Ireland) v County Court Judge for Armagh.*[49] The cases demonstrate that special loss (such as to busi- 18

[39] Art. 4(1)

[40] *Waddell Report*, chap. 10.

[41] HC Debs. vol. 935, col. 1521.

[42] Art. 12.

[43] Compare cases arising under the Offences against the State Act 1939 sec. 34 (disqualification from public office): *Cox v Ireland* [1992] 2 *Irish Reports* (IR), 503; *Murphy v Ireland* [1996] 3 IR; *McDonnell v Ireland* [1998] 1 IR, 141; G. Hogan/C. Walker (supra fn. 7), 265–266.

[44] Art. 12(2).

[45] Art. 10(8).

[46] Art. 10(3).

[47] C. Walker (supra fn. 1), chap. 7. See previously, sec. 55 and 56 of the Northern Ireland (Emergency Provisions) Act 1996: G. Hogan/C. Walker (supra fn. 7), 71–73.

[48] [1978] NI, 164.

[49] [1981] NI, 19.

ness profits) arising from interference with a public right (such as a road closure) is not recoverable.[50] Under paragraph 3, claims must be brought within 28 days (previously four months), and they are determined at the first instance by the Secretary of State (paragraph 4), with an appeal as to refusal to pay or the amount of payment to the county court (paragraph 5). Compensation may be refused or reduced where false statements are made or there is not full disclosure (paragraph 6 – these actions may also be offences under paragraph 12). In addition, compensation may be refused on public policy grounds under paragraph 9 in respect of an act done in connection with, or revealed evidence of the commission of, a scheduled offence or a non-scheduled offence under the Terrorism Act for which the claimant is convicted. It is again arguable that the width of this disqualification is not proportionate to the needs of public policy under art. 1 of Protocol 1 of the European Convention.

19 As a direct result of another recommendation from the Waddell Committee, a new provision was introduced to provide more adequate terms for the repair or reinstatement of buildings.[51] The aim of this was to plug a loophole which had facilitated abuse of the scheme by certain property owners, and effectively allowed them to take compensation payments without using the moneys to repair or reinstate buildings. Effectively they were making profit from the scheme, thus running contrary to the principle of indemnity which underlies the entire compensation arrangements (and also the public policy of restoration despite the terrorist onslaught). It was even alleged that this loophole had allowed paramilitary organisations to profit to the tune of £ 5 million.[52]

20 Art. 12 to 14 are concerned with general provisions, such as the application of payments for debt legislation to criminal damage compensation and the effect of certain agreements (such as mortgages) where property is maliciously damaged.

21 The appeals procedure is detailed under art. 15 which is materially the same as the 1971 Act version, still allowing appeal by an unsuccessful or dissatisfied applicant to the county court at any stage of the application process. A time limit of six weeks exists, from the time that the applicant receives the adverse decision and within which he must lodge his complaint.[53] Art. 16 and 17 provide for the recovery of moneys from the offender and from the applicant if he or she is subsequently awarded damages or compensation by a court or even if a court case is settled with payment to the claimant. Definitions and rules con-

[50] *R (Secretary of State for Northern Ireland) v Recorder of Belfast* [1973] NI, 112.

[51] Art. 11.

[52] Reported by *The Sunday Telegraph* and cited in parliamentary debate, HC Debs. vol. 935, col. 1524. The *Belfast Telegraph*, 23 June 1977, also carried an article about contract bombing by paramilitaries, that is the payment by individuals of a portion of compensation monies received in the event of a paramilitary organisation causing damage or destruction to an agreed property. See J. Adams, *The Financing of Terrorism* (1986).

[53] See further *Tansey v Secretary of State for Northern Ireland* [1981] NI, 193; *Coyle v Secretary of State for Northern Ireland* [1987] NI, 64.

cerning evidence, offences and payments into the Consolidated Fund are provided for in art. 18–20, whilst the final article outlines the power of the Secretary of State for Northern Ireland to make regulations in relation to the legislative scheme.

C. Administration

Operating under the ambit of the Northern Ireland Office, compensatory ar- 22
rangements are now dealt with by the Compensation Agency, the first Executive Agency established in the Province.[54] This body has taken over the role previously held by an administrative branch of the Office in directly administering compensation claims for criminal damage as well as criminal injuries. The Chief Executive is charged not just with the operation of the Agency but also with creating its annual Business Plan and then running the Agency within its allocated resources. The Framework Document identifies the aims of the Agency as four-fold:

(i) to support the victims of violent crime by providing compensation for serious injuries and financial loss;

(ii) through the provision of financial compensation for damage and consequential loss resulting from malicious damage to property to sustain business confidence;

(iii) to provide compensation for members of the public who suffer loss or damage resulting from action taken under the Northern Ireland (Emergency Provisions) Act 1996;[55]

(iv) to ensure that the Agency's resources are managed economically, efficiently and effectively at all levels.[56]

In 2000–01, £ 9.3 million was paid in compensation for criminal damage, with 23
a further £ 4.9 million to meet claims under the Terrorism Act (and the previous anti-terrorism legislation).[57] These figures are much lower than in previous years owing to the paramilitary cease-fires. For example, in 1972–73, the figure was £ 26,592,312, in 1982–83 £ 31,058,498, and in 1992–93 £ 75,927,801 (the highest ever annual total).

D. Comment

The overall shape of laws in Northern Ireland relating to compensation for 24
damage and loss arising from terrorist action have been characterised by state intervention which, as it finally came to rest in 1977, followed a centralising vector. Thus, the responsibility for criminal damage was initially borne by the

[54] The Compensation Agency was established on 1 April 1992.
[55] Sec. 55 and 56 allow compensation for loss or damage arising out of actions carried out under the 1996 Act by the security forces, such as powers to search and the requisition of property.
[56] Page 6.
[57] *Annual Report 2000–01*, 38.

local community in the nineteenth century. But increased levels of violence in the 1950s, directed against the established Northern Ireland Government and perceived as provincial "acts of war",[58] led the local government to argue that the principle of localism was no longer appropriate and that as the cause of these attacks stemmed from responsibilities and concerns of central (Northern Ireland or British or even Dublin) government, such as security and foreign relations, so it was only right and proper that some central government or other should bear the cost. The early legislation went "back to the time when there was no police system as now understood, and when it was held to be the responsibility of the inhabitants of any area to keep the peace of that area."[59] That situation had changed irrevocably, and so the call for the centralisation of compensatory arrangements was acknowledged by the Northern Ireland Government as a reasonable argument. However, that Government was still of the opinion that it was neither in the public interest nor practical to abandon the principle of localism entirely.

25 The completion of the transference of financial responsibility from the local, in terms of the mass of ratepayers across the Province, to central government exclusively for compensatory arrangements came with the 1971 Act.[60] Although there was provision under sec. 9(3) for recovery of expenses incurred under the Act,[61] through the raising of a rate or levy by the Treasury, this was mere window-dressing. How could a British Government place a special levy or rate to contribute to the expenses incurred under compensatory arrangements without handing a propaganda coup to the IRA and also running the risk of engendering disquiet and reducing public confidence especially amongst Unionist rate-payers? Furthermore, Keynesian welfare economics were still *de rigueur* at this time. Even in 1983, the then Secretary of State for Northern Ireland, James Prior, sardonically commented, "In Northern Ireland we're all Keynesians."[62]

26 The 1977 Order did nothing to weaken the principle of central government responsibility. Given the non-availability of insurance for criminal property damage in Northern Ireland, it was difficult to conceive an alternative approach. As the Waddell Report noted in 1976:[63]

> "During stable spells in Northern Ireland in the past insurance companies have been willing to provide cover against damage from riot and civil commotion on payment of an additional premium. Few householders or businessmen took advantage of the opportunity to insure, in some cases, no doubt, because the compensation scheme provided a form of safety net and, in others, because they were unaware of the possibility. The fa-

[58] HC (NI) Debs. vol. 40, col. 2617 1 November 1956.
[59] HC (NI) Debs. vol. 40, col. 2614 1 November 1956.
[60] Sec. 1(1) refers to "compensation payable out of public funds".
[61] There is no similar provision under the 1977 Order.
[62] *The Irish Times*, 15 June 1983.
[63] Chap. 4.

> cility was withdrawn in 1969 but those who with foresight bought this additional protection when times were normal have in the main been able to renew it at the same rate of premium. New cover against damage from riot or civil commotion has, however been unobtainable since 1969 except possibly by some industrial undertakings who erect or acquire premises in Northern Ireland and who had always made a practice of obtaining extended cover on their premises wherever they might be."[64]

The Report paints a picture of caution, some confusion, and inconsistency within the insurance market regarding criminal damage arising from riot and civil commotion. The position regarding acts of terrorism is unclear, although the implication is that there was some provision, albeit diminishing, by the insurance market. Hence the Committee comments, 27

> "How far the caution of insurers is due to the hazards created directly by terrorism and how far it may be influenced by uncertainty about their prospects of recovery through subrogation is difficult to say."[65]

However the Report does make it clear that in its view insurance companies would be unlikely to maintain any provision for insurance if the statutory insurance scheme was abandoned. The formal withdrawal of the insurance market from this area of cover did in fact take place in 1977, when the British Insurance Association announced "an overriding exclusion clause designed to free insurance companies from any liability in cases which came within the 1977 Order."[66] One might reasonably argue that traditional statutory compensatory arrangements mitigated against the development of a clear and comprehensive response by the private insurance market to the issue of criminal damage. On the other hand, it is equally rational to suggest that this would never have happened anyway in view of the extraordinary levels of political violence which have been a continuing and significant feature of Northern Irish life. 28

The Compensation Agency and its administration of the 1977 Order is representative of the contradictions inherent in the governance of Northern Ireland. The forms and appearances of late modern managerialism may be present, but the substance is still a modernist, state-centred, and welfarist approach. 29

III. Great Britain – Indirect Legal Intervention

A. *History*

Irish Republican terrorism has been perpetrated intermittently in Britain since the mid-nineteenth century,[67] but it failed to have any discernible impact on the laws relating to damage and harm until the 1990s, when the Provisional 30

[64] Para. 53.
[65] Para. 61.
[66] D.S. Greer/V.A. Mitchell (supra fn. 8), 28.
[67] C. P. Walker, *The Prevention of Terrorism in British Law* (2nd edn.1992).

IRA began to turn its attention to large-scale attacks on prime commercial target. The questions therefore arise, why were commercial targets selected during this time and what did the strategy involve?

31 As for why commercial targets were selected, the objective of the attacks differed markedly from the many previous attacks within Britain. Rather than front-line targets (such as from political life or the security apparatus), the attempt was made to disrupt and diminish the commercial and corporate life primarily of the City of London and then later other important commercial sites. The prime target is functionally and legally in the private rather than public sphere and so appears to be a less attractive symbol for terrorist attention. Nevertheless, unsustainable damage to the City would result in general public concern and pressure on the government from the corporate and financial lobbies. This disruption and consequent concern and pressure could not be achieved by bomb damage itself. However, by offering a credible threat of potential attack, it might prove possible to achieve indirect disruption through the undermining of the confidence of investors, especially foreign investors, and through raising the costs for office-based operations, including through insurance costs.

32 In terms of explaining the shift of emphasis upon economic targets, the main interpretation must be one of opportunism in the light of the growing importance of these particular economic targets within the post-Fordist state. The markets associated with the financial exchanges in the City of London became prime candidates for growth in the post-Fordist world,[68] which means that in terms of symbolism and attendant publicity, they have become appropriate targets for terrorism.[69] The City of London is one of the world's three major international financial centres, Tokyo and New York being the others. London differs from its two major competitors in that it is primarily an international centre.[70] Financial services are a major United Kingdom industry which accounts for approximately one-fifth of the Gross Domestic Product. In an interview with Martin Dillon, a senior member of the IRA explicitly stated the IRA's thinking:[71]

> "It's really about getting their attention. London is one of the major cities in Europe and when we make it unstable that's when the talking begins."

33 It would be an overstatement to imply that the IRA's strategy was entirely focused or coherent from the outset.[72] Nevertheless, with hindsight, three distinct strands can be identified.

[68] B. Jessop, Post-fordism and The State, in: A. Amin (ed.), *Post-Fordism. A Reader* (1994).

[69] O. Kelly, The IRA threat to the City of London, [1993] 9 *Policing*, 88; P. Rogers, *Economic Targeting and Provisional IRA Strategy* (1996), 24.

[70] R. Brealey/J. Ireland, *The Competitive Position of London's Financial Services: Final Report* (1995).

[71] M. Dillon, *25 Years of Terror: The IRA's War Against the British* (1995), 271.

[72] E. Mallie/D. McKittrick, *The Fight for Peace* (1996), 148.

The first strand concerned bomb attacks on City of London targets. The two most notable were, first, in 1992, the day after the General Election, the bombing at St Mary Axe, in which three died and 100 were injured.[73] Approximately 14 buildings suffered significant structural damage with the worst hit buildings being the Baltic Exchange and the Chamber of Shipping at an estimated cost of £ 350 million in damage. On the 24 April 1993 there was another large explosion in the City, outside the NatWest building in Bishopsgate, when a large bomb on a tipper truck killed a photographer, injured 94 persons and also resulted in damage initially estimated by the Association of British Insurers (ABI) at more than £ 300 million, mainly to prestigious commercial City buildings.[74] The end of the first Provisional IRA cease-fire in February 1996 was marked by a return to the emphasis on the financial and business sector with a 500 pound bomb at Canary Wharf which killed two and slightly injured up to 100 persons. 34

The second strand, also with economic implications, involved disruption of the transport system in London and elsewhere, which again gathered pace and ferocity as time went on. It included attacks on the rail system, especially the London underground, and road transport also came under fire, most notably with a large bomb at Staples Corner in April 1992. 35

The third strand related to the targeting of other economically strategic locations both inside and outside London. These included targets relating to the tourist industry, such as, in March 1994, three mortar attacks on Heathrow Airport. Later, there was a car bomb at the Arndale Shopping Centre in Manchester in June 1996. A large part of the city centre had to be closed for months, and damage was later assessed at £ 250 million, with uninsured losses at £ 175 million. 36

The bombing in 1992 produced a response from the government, concentrated around the Reinsurance (Acts of Terrorism) Act 1993.[75] 37

Reinsurance is the mechanism for spreading the risk of insurance. It is in essence the insuring of insurers who cannot perfectly calculate in advance the necessary premiums to cover all claims. Miscalculations might arise through false values being placed on assets or costs or through a false calculation of the probability of claims over a period of time or the value of claims. In a reinsurance contract the insured is an insurance company or underwriter and is referred to as the "reinsured", or the "ceding company", and the insurer, a specialist insurance company or underwriter, is referred to as the "reinsurer". In 38

[73] O. Kelly, (1993) 9 *Policing*, 88.

[74] City of London Police, *Annual Report for 1993* (1994), 32.

[75] W.J. Gloyn, Insurance against terrorism, (1993) 90(22) *Law Society's Gazette*, 20 (23); W.B. Bice, British government reinsurance and acts of terrorism, (1994) 15 *University of Pennsylvania Journal of International Business Law*, 441; C. Walker/M. McGuinness, Risk, political violence and policing the City of London, in: A. Crawford (ed.), *Crime, Insecurity, Safety and the New Governance* (2002).

plain terms, the reinsurer absorbs the impact of particularly hard blows to insurers, and by providing this service a whole range of people and organisations are protected. In particular, the reinsurance contract enables the insurer to spread any premium increases consequential on significant insured losses over a period of time, and possibly a range of insureds.

39 It was the bomb at St Mary Axe which precipitated the crisis in the reinsurance market. The level of loss to the insurance and reinsurance sector was unprecedented for this type of policy cover. The first signs of trouble came in a statement in October 1992 by one of the world's largest reinsurers, Munich Re, to the effect that it would prefer to exclude terrorism from its reinsurance treaties. It was not just the possibility of large losses which were the problem, but the difficulty of calculating those future losses when they would be affected by a purposive third party (the IRA) whose actions were intentionally reflexive with the viability of the insurance market and whose capacity for destruction seemed enormous. Thus, the premium to cover such a risk would have to be so high as to be wholly unattractive in the market place. By November 1992, it was clear that reinsurance renewals would not provide cover for terrorism. The issuance of a model terrorism exclusion wording by the ABI to its members on 12 November confirmed that, effective from the 1 January 1993, cover was no longer available to businesses.[76]

40 Immediately, pressure mounted on the government to take action, as the consequences of the absence of cover began to be contemplated. On the 21 December 1992, Michael Heseltine, Secretary of State for Trade and Industry, announced that the government had decided in principle to act as insurer of last resort. It was the government's intention that its involvement would be for a finite period of time (that is so long as exigencies required it) and should result in no additional burden to the taxpayer. The vehicle for government intervention was to be a new reinsurance company, Pool Re, which limited cover to that related to buildings, contents, computers, engineering and business interruption sections of commercial insurance policies. Cover was to be bought back in return for an additional premium which would then be paid into a mutual pool managed and staffed by insurance industry personnel on behalf of over 200 insurance companies and almost 100 Lloyd's of London syndicates; the government agreed to meet 90% of any subsequent claims not covered by the pool – insurance companies would meet the remaining 10%. It became clear later that cover would also be available for blocks of flats, often owned by commercial holding companies, whose total sum insured was in excess of £ 2.5 million. Once the scheme had been agreed, the ABI advised members to limit cover, unless the special premium was paid. The scheme was backdated to 1 January 1993.

[76] G. Souter, London Reinsurers Expect Restrictions Due to Catastrophes, (1992) 26(43) *Business Insurance*, 10.

B. The Reinsurance (Acts of Terrorism) Act 1993

The legislation consists of just three brief sections. The passage of the Bill provided little opportunity for detailed scrutiny, and no debate was ever held on the Pool Re agreements (especially the Retrocession Agreement entered between the Secretary of State for Trade and Industry and Pool Reinsurance Company, by which the Secretary of State undertakes to indemnify Pool Re in respect of Pool Re's "Ultimate Net Loss" in excess of its retention). The arrangements under the Act were ratified by the Treasury and approved by Parliament on 30 July 1993 as were the credit facility and guarantee. The following points should be noted from the 1993 Act itself. 41

Sec. 1 outlines the reinsurance powers of the Secretary of State: 42

> "1.– (1) There shall be paid out of money provided by Parliament such sums as may be necessary to enable the Secretary of State to meet his obligations under –
> (a) any agreement of reinsurance which, with the consent of the Treasury, is entered into (whether before or after the passing of this Act) pursuant to arrangements to which this Act applies..."

The vehicle for the transaction of the arrangement, Pool Re, is nowhere mentioned in the Act. But it is clear that if moneys are to be made available from the Consolidated Fund, this means that it is primarily the individual taxpayer who is providing the security for any financial liabilities incurred by the Secretary of State. 43

Sec. 2 outlines the reinsurance arrangements to which the Act applies. 44

> "2. – (1) This Act applies to arrangements under which the Secretary of State, with the consent of the Treasury, undertakes to any extent the liability of reinsuring risks against-
> (a) loss or damage to property in Great Britain resulting from or consequential upon acts of terrorism: and
> (b) any loss which is consequential on loss or damage falling within paragraph (a) above; and to the extent that the arrangements relate to events occurring before as well as after an agreement of reinsurance comes into being, the reference in section 1(1) above to the obligations of the Secretary of State shall be construed accordingly.
> (2) In this section 'acts of terrorism' means acts of persons acting on behalf of, or in connection with, any organisation which carries out activities directed towards the overthrowing or influencing, by force or violence, of Her Majesty's government in the United Kingdom or any other government de jure or de facto.
> (3) In subsection (2) above 'organisation' includes any association or combination of persons."

45 It is first made clear that the reinsurance agreements which the Secretary of State shall enter into are those pertaining to property damage alone; injury to persons is already dealt with by other state compensation schemes. Unfortunately, the Act does not closely define "damage" or "property". As far as "property" is concerned, it becomes evident from the agreements actually entered into under sec. 1 that it is commercial buildings which are the core concern. One result is that two possible forms of damage which might not be covered are losses to vehicles and losses to utilities' equipment (street furniture, water pipes, telephone wires and the like). On the other hand, care is taken to specify that cover is provided not only for "damage" as a result of acts of terrorism, but also consequential loss.

46 The definition of an "act of terrorism" under the Act differs from that in what was then sec. 20 of the Prevention of Terrorism (Temporary Provisions) Act 1989 (PTA) (now added to, and replaced, by sec. 1 of the Terrorism Act 2000). It seems they have arisen because the legislative draftsmen were told to have regard to the model terrorism exclusion clause issued in November 1992 by the ABI. The 1993 Act is much narrower than the Terrorism Act which makes little attempt to delimit the possible perpetrators. Adding the qualifier of the perpetrator having a connection with an organisation eliminates any acts which might be carried out by individuals with eccentric, singular or unaffiliated purposes. In the days of loose networks such as Al Qa'ida this gap has become a matter of concern.[77] An organisation includes "any association or combination of persons" for the purposes of the legislation. This leaves a number of questions. Is there a minimum number of members for a group to constitute an organisation; must the organisation be known previously by the authorities? What of anarchist groups for which chaos and disorganisation is the goal and theoretically the *modus operandi*? Would a collection of anarchists, such as have from time to time attempted to "Stop the City" constitute an organisation? In at least one other important respect the 1993 Act definition of "act of terrorism" might be narrower than that contained in the Terrorism Act. The latter contains a reference to the terrorising of persons – the use of violence for putting the public or any section of the public in fear. One can argue that as the Reinsurance Act concerns itself solely with damage to commercial property, reference to the public is redundant, hence its exclusion and the sole focus on the terrorising of governments. It is also stated explicitly that an organisation's activities do not have to be directed at the government of the United Kingdom only, a precursor to the extended definition in the Terrorism Act 2000.

47 Finally, the geographical bounds of the reinsurance scheme are specified by sec. 3(2). The coverage extends to the whole of the United Kingdom but with the exception of Northern Ireland, where other, more generous arrangements were already in place in the shape of the Criminal Damage (Compensation) (Northern Ireland) Order 1977.

[77] A. Riley, Hidden peril of the lone terrorist, *The Times Law* 10 September 2002, 5.

C. Administration

By the end of 1994, after the IRA cease-fire on 31 August, premiums pooled into the fund reportedly stood at £ 410 million. In November 1994, Pool Re, satisfied that the mutual's loss experience was sufficiently low, offered a potential discount of 40% on policyholders' premiums at renewal time. This system was retained the following year. By this time Pool Re was feeling sufficiently confident to raise the loss threshold to £ 75 million. The continuation of the cease-fire also led the company to reduce rates so that in 1996 the premiums charged were 20% lower than those set in 1993. Both these savings would be lost however in the event that the £ 75 million limit was crossed (the trigger point at which the year's 20% discount on rates and 40% premium reduction was to be revoked). The bomb at London Docklands in 1996 did eventually result in losses of £ 105 million. It is also very notable that most of the 1996 insured losses were with Pool Re, suggesting that commercial reinsurers had not entered the market significantly up to that time. 48

There was a major material difference between the South Quay bomb in the London Docklands area and previous London attacks. This lay in the social extent of the damage. As well as the impact upon commercial property (around £ 107 million), there was extensive loss sustained by non-commercial property. More than 10,000 residents lived within half a mile of the explosion, and approximately 650 homes, located mostly on the Barkantine estate and belonging to Tower Hamlets council sustained structural damage. The bill facing Tower Hamlets council was high. Tower Hamlets council complained that it was faced with £ 70 million worth of repair works, but it had been provided with a government grant of just £ 6 million to carry out demolition work. Later it was agreed to increase the Department of the Environment funds to £ 30 million to cover the additional costs of demolition and refurbishment. 49

On 15 June 1996 the IRA detonated a bomb in the centre of Manchester, containing an estimated one to one and a half tons of fertiliser explosives. Damage and loss was enormous, though as always difficult to quantify at the time. The owners, P & O (who sold on to Prudential in late 1997) were insured with Pool Re, and speaking at the end of September 1996, Leslie Lucas, the chief executive of Pool Re, estimated that the bill to Pool Re would be in the region of £ 400 million (it was later put at £ 285 million). Manchester City Council calculated that the Council could be left to find £ 3 million to cover loss due to damage and lost income. 50

On visiting Manchester on 3 July 1996, Michael Heseltine, the Deputy Prime Minister announced a number of measures aimed at alleviating the repercussions of the explosion. Firstly, there was to be a £ 20 million injection from the United Kingdom's allocation of European Structural Funds, a reallocation of funds originally earmarked for other parts of the United Kingdom. There was also to be a further £ 1 million to come from the current European programme to prepare a master plan for the future redevelopment of the city centre. From 51

United Kingdom government coffers would come an immediate contribution of £ 150,000 to support an international urban design competition, and substantial aid by mid-1997 was reckoned at £ 43 million. Manchester City Council has also made attempts to obtain additional government financial assistance under the "Bellwin rules",[78] now set out under sec. 155 of the Local Government and Housing Act 1989.

52 At least in Manchester's case, the city was wealthy enough to provide some self-help. After the bombing, the "Lord Mayor of Manchester's Emergency Fund" was set up as a non-charitable fund so as to assist the self-employed and small businesses which would not normally fall within the permitted benefactors of a registered charity.

53 For both Tower Hamlets and Manchester councils the gap in funds lay primarily in the costs to the Council of cleaning up after the bomb together with the anticipated hike in insurance premiums anticipated as a result of the bomb. Zurich Mutual estimated that councils had paid a premium of up to £ 10 million and their renewal bills could face increases of £ 6 million. In the end a fund of just £ 2.5 million was made available to both Manchester and Tower Hamlets in January 1997 to cover extra policing costs and consequential loss.

54 These challenges in 1996 for the 1993 Act showed up some of its limitations. Pool Re is essentially facilitative. It ensures that insurance against terrorism damage is always available, but the costs are increased (discounts returned only in late 1997) and many property owners may decide against coverage. In addition, the private insurance path inevitably brings delay. But where the loss is to an important public space such as a shopping centre, neither problem can be allowed to determine entirely the response. As a result, the Department of Trade and Industry (DTI) effectively sidestepped its own reinsurance scheme by its direct grants to redevelop Manchester.

55 As for its efficiency, Pool Re has operated at modest cost to government. There are no doubt process costs associated with its administration, though an indirect system of reinsurance avoids the creation of a large state infrastructure. In this way, the 1993 Act can rely on the workforce of assessors, clerks and so on within commercial insurance companies. But, at the bottom line, there has to date been no notified recourse to government funds by Pool Re.

56 Looking at effectiveness, there was overall success in the sense that there was no foreign exodus from the City. There were real concerns that the IRA activity could have had this impact. For example, in April 1993, the London-based

[78] See HC Debs. vol. 367, col. 750w 3 May 2001. The "Bellwin" scheme of emergency financial assistance allows assistance to a local authority for uninsurable costs following a disaster or emergency that involves destruction of, or danger to, life or property. The grant is normally paid at a rate of 85 per cent of an authority's qualifying expenditure above a set threshold. The threshold is the provision that a prudent authority might reasonably be expected to make for contingencies and emergencies (approximately 0.2 per cent. of its revenue budget).

Japanese Chamber of Commerce and Industry was reported as writing to the Home Secretary expressing concerns about the dangers of further attacks and that Japanese companies would look for safer alternatives in Europe if security were not improved.[79] But the measures taken, both security and insurance related, did seem to steady nerves and thereby achieved the fundamental objectives of insurance of increasing business stability through reducing investment risk and the uncertainty of financial exposure and more fundamentally averting the political anxiety about uninsurable chaos. Insurance cover in respect of terrorist damage remained available, though at a price which not all could afford. In addition, insurance companies have managed to maintain liquidity and no collapses have resulted from terrorist damage. Even in 1993, there were profits for leading insurance companies.

At the same time, this achievement is undermined by other forms of state sub- 57
vention, especially the Department of Environment grants to Manchester, or even (allegedly) the Insurance Premium Tax (described below).[80] In addition, there remain inherent problems with the 1993 Act scheme, namely that it concentrates risk within Britain (especially as the government is the ultimate recessionnaire), and it concentrates risk within commercial property insurers who act as insurers and then as members of Pool Re, effectively as reinsurers of themselves.

Another important aspect of effectiveness, the aim of time-limited interven- 58
tion by the DTI, has not been secured. It was hoped that the private market in reinsurance for terrorist attack would gradually reassert itself as confidence returned. The events in 1996 strongly suggest that this has not happened and that some redesign might be necessary if this aim is to be taken seriously. The picture of the failure of the private sector to re-enter the market is largely, but not entirely, true. From 1994 there had been a small and selective reinsurance market available, and some of the losses at Manchester were borne by reinsurers other than Pool Re. This grew later in 1996 and afterwards, encouraged by rigidity in Pool Re's terms and the prospects of peace, firms such as Hiscox became active in the market, though they still do not offer unlimited coverage.

Taking the circumstances of risk as a whole, considerations of effectiveness 59
might also have suggested some increase in the discounts given to properties wherever they might demonstrate increased security precautions. This condition (which might have to be set out in statute in order to achieve competitive equality in an international market) would not only have the effect of reducing risk, but it would also encourage insureds to take a more proactive role in risk amelioration by rewarding individual responsibility in regard to approved building strengthening or security measures. This link to the assumption of responsibility for security would build on experience in regard to mainstream

[79] J. Mullin/F. Kane, The scared mile, *The Guardian* 3 August 1993.

[80] Finance Act 1994 sec. 48. See J. Macleod/P. Milnes, Insurance premium tax, [1996] *British Tax Review*, 155; http://www.hmce.gov.uk/business/othertaxes/ins-prem-tax.htm.

crime, where it has been recognised that insurance can "constitute a powerful means by which financial incentives or disincentives can be offered for the adoption of crime prevention measures".[81] It would also avoid the shifting of risk back to the public sector by undue reliance upon police prevention.

60 In response to these ideas, Pool Re and the DTI produced guidance on security practice in 1994, showing an awareness of the importance of this issue. However, there is little evidence to suggest that this concern has been backed up in hard terms through the application of discounts for good practice or through warranties and conditions. Of course the encouragement of target-hardening in this way then brings up the vexed question of the displacement of large risk. Unlike a storm or earthquake, large risk in the guise of terrorist attack is responsive to change in the environment, whether political, security or economic. It seems a tenable inference that security measures applied in one part of the country – such as increased security in the City of London – encouraged reactions elsewhere: namely, Heathrow, Docklands and Manchester.

61 After 1997, there have been no further major attacks and so, by 2002, the reserves of Pool Re had reached £ 1.5 billion.[82] However, reflection upon the attacks of September 11 prompted some revisions of the scheme ahead of any possible replication in Britain. Thus, calls were made of the scheme to be extended from loss from explosion or fire to chemical or biological attack or incidental other damage from an attack elsewhere (such as flooding if the Thames Barrier were damaged). Following a review established in December 2001, the Treasury announced changes in July 2002 along these lines.[83] The changes include extension of Pool Re cover from "fire and explosion" only, to an "all risks basis", to ensure that a terrorist attack involving, for example biological contamination, impact by aircraft, or flood damage could be covered. The increased cover will result in higher premiums for the period covered. There will be an option to backdate to 1 January 2002. The existing exclusion for nuclear risks will also be removed. However, exclusion will remain for war risks and for computer hacking and virus damage (because of difficulties of proof). The rates of retention will be capped per event (under which insurers bear the first amount – usually around £ 100,000 – of any claims for an event covered by Pool Re, for each head of cover) and per event (at £ 30 million) and per annum (at £ 60 million), and insurers will be allowed to set the premiums for the underlying policies according to normal commercial considerations. The changes on retention are designed to offer space in the insurance market for commercial capacity; by raising the retention, the possibility is enhanced for insurers to seek commercial reinsurance to cover these retentions. Changes to the governance arrangements include a Public Interest Director on the board of Pool Re, who

[81] R. Litton, *Crime and Crime Prevention for Insurance Practice* (1996), 1.

[82] *The Times*, 6 June 2002, 3.

[83] HC Debs. vol. 389, col. 960w 23 July 2002 Ruth Kelly. See further http://www.hm-treasury.gov.uk/newsroom_and_speeches/press/2002/press_73_02.cfm.

will provide an annual report to the Treasury. These changes will take effect from 1 January 2003.

Any supposed achievements of Pool Re must be firmly situated within the contexts – economic, political and otherwise – which have developed since 1993. There are three worthy of mention. 62

The first is the circumstance of the IRA cease-fires. The first lasted from 1994 63
to 1996. The second was announced in July 1997. As well as the current cease-fire, the period interim to the two cease-fires experienced a period of relative quiescence on the part of the IRA both in Britain and Northern Ireland. The impact as far as the 1993 Act is concerned is that it has not been tested to anything approaching destruction. Though Docklands and Manchester did offer a severe test, like St Mary Axe and Bishopsgate, they have been followed by a lull which has allowed for the spreading of payments rather than a constant stream of massive losses. After the Belfast Agreement, the cease-fire has been restored and largely observed – certainly no major damage or loss has been perpetrated, despite some attempts by Republican dissident groups such as the Real IRA.

The second point is that the policy initiative was received in especially propi- 64
tious circumstances. One was that the economy was generally on the upturn during the period so that the ability to pay higher insurance premiums was also on the increase. Another was that the policy was largely applied within the singular circumstances of the City of London. This community (whose economic guise is more or less coterminous with its political and policing guises – all share the same territory and cross-membership) is able to take quick, decisive and concerted action in a way which more diversified polities cannot. This feature, which persists despite the global tendencies of the financial markets, was particularly important in terms of resisting the pressures towards relocation and of presenting a common front against the outside threat. More practically, it allowed the mobilisation of mutual assistance and the rapid conclusion of decisions about policing and urban design at the time of crisis caused by the bombings without the usual problems of consultation, dissent and exclusion. The commodification of security came naturally to this community.

The policing response is the third circumstance to be mentioned. This re- 65
sponse to the more physical aspects of the bombing campaign is worthy of a further study in itself[84] and cannot be more than mentioned here, but its importance is great. The features of the response reflect the likely approaches predicted by Ericson and Haggerty[85] – the management of criminal risk through surveillance, information gathering, information communication and informa-

[84] See C. Walker/M. McGuinness (supra fn. 75).

[85] R.V. Ericson/K.D. Haggerty, *Policing the Risk Society* (1997), 1–5. See also T. Jones/T. Newburn, *Private Security and Public Policing* (1998).

tion brokering both by the police themselves and powerful non-police power-holders – which in the case of the City of London, include the Corporation, and the financial institutions. It is reasonable to suppose that heightened security resulted in the elimination of the City as a soft target for terrorist attack, and CCTV footage has also been used to detect terrorism.[86] But one consequence is displacement or deflection to equally alluring targets within the striking distance, such as Heathrow or Docklands. In this sense, one can hark back to Beck's hypothesis of the inescapable and pandemic nature of risk, but with a caveat. Resources can be used to buy out of risk manifestation in certain circumstances, at the expense of others. Another cost is that special powers have been extended and embedded in the law on a permanent basis. As Beck argued, in the risk society "the state of emergency threatens to become the normal state".[87]

D. Comment

66 In order to comprehend how Pool Re operates and its appropriateness, one must look beyond the structure of the company *per se* and examine its political and economic environment. This environment may contain two significant shaping features which have coalesced around the evolution of the Pool Re arrangements.

67 The first is an understanding of the nature of risk in high modernity. One aspect of that nature is the emergence, or at least recognition, of new forms of risk which reflect progress and knowledge.[88] This is demonstrated by the physical vulnerability of the City. Its success makes it an attractive target to terrorists. Before the 1990s targets of terrorists were direct symbols of government. It was unforeseen that the concentration of business and finance in the Square Mile would mean that a terrorist explosion would result in an amount of damage disproportionate to the size of the bomb. Insurers, reinsurers, business, government and property owners became aware of the potential for loss arising from large risk. Knowledge brought both security and insecurity. Insurers and reinsurers decided that the distribution of risk was too heavily weighted against them and consequently eliminated the risk to themselves by withdrawing cover for property arising out of terrorist incidents. This impacted on business and property owners by creating added insecurity for them. As ever, the risk was not eliminated, only transferred.[89]

68 The second feature relates to the nature of the state which responds to risk. Pandemic nature of risk poses severe problems for the nation state and requires it to seek global rather than national solutions, and to respond by reflexive strategies of management and dispersal rather than solution and termination – especially through the compilation and dispersal of knowledge. So, in

[86] See City of London Police, *'CameraWatch' Closed Circuit Television Scheme* (1994).
[87] U. Beck (supra fn. 5), 79.
[88] Ibid., 97.
[89] N. Luhmann, *Risk: A Sociological Theory* (1993), 165.

the crisis of 1992 onwards, the reinsurance system did involve the exercise of old-fashioned state sovereignty in the form of an Act of Parliament. But through that there was spun a web of public/private relationships, building on well-established policy networks. These were especially pronounced in the City of London, where the City of London Corporation is itself a cipher for private rather than public interests. At the same time, the UK government recognised the potential of globalisation and the possible relocation of financial institutions. It therefore sought solutions which worked with the deregulated and globalised financial markets.[90] That those solutions were grounded in insurance is also interesting. In this way, decisions were taken of political significance to shift what might be seen as public social issues – security and protection – into private contractual issues.[91]

Viewed in this history, the choice of the structures adopted in the Reinsurance Act 1993 seem largely appropriate as being politically and economically consistent with the general thrust of governmental evolution. A scheme which incorporated models and personnel from the private sector activity on the part of the insurance industry and continued personal responsibility and risk management on the part of the insureds fitted well with government demands for both the encouragement of market-based enterprise and also the assumption of individual risk rather than welfarism. Of course, one can at the same time point to contradictions and anomalies. Ultimately, there was state support for business insurance, and there was also state involvement in the administration of the scheme. But in intention at least, the idea was to limit state intervention so far as practicable whether in terms of operational matters, subvention or the very existence of the arrangements. And the state intervention was arguably narrower than alternative schemes within the insurance market, such as a special levy on all insurance contracts, both business and personal, so as to create a fund for the payment of terrorist damage. That design would have involved substantial direct state intervention with costs in terms of administration and the creation of the temptation for terrorists to confront the state. And it would be unattractive politically, since the effect would be to subsidise the international finance and corporate sectors. It has been suggested that this alternative or addition has in fact been adopted. So, as well as extra premiums under the Pool Re scheme which came into being under the 1993 Act, the government also announced in the Budget in November 1993 that it would raise funds by a special levy on all household and motor vehicle policies in Britain and expected to raise £ 750 million and to add £ 18 per year to an annual household insurance bill on average. The subsequent Finance Act 1994 (sec. 48) duly introduced the Insurance Premium Tax as a levy on insurance premiums. Whether the Insurance Premium Tax really is a lasting testament to the power of IRA bombs to impact on the taxation system may be debatable. Certainly, 69

[90] See H.J. Johnson, *Global Financial Institutions and Markets* (2000); S. Valdez, *An Introduction to Global Financial Markets* (3rd edn. 2000).

[91] See K. Abraham, *Distributing Risk* (1986); M. Feeley/J. Simon, Actuarial Justice: the Emerging New Criminal Law, in: D. Nelken (ed.), *The Futures of Criminology* (1994); T. Baker/J. Simon (eds.), *Embracing Risk* (2002).

the tax still exists and its rate has actually increased, but the Chancellor of the Exchequer who first announced it in 1993, Kenneth Clarke, made no explicit link with the terrorist campaign.[92] Instead, the new tax was presented, along with a new air passenger duty, as a way of broadening the indirect tax base.

70 By contrast, the grander and more supportive scheme of direct compensation for terrorist property damage in Northern Ireland would not have suited the then Conservative government's post-Fordist discourse, especially in the flagship sectors of financial services in general and the City of London in particular. Though some argued that the Northern Ireland system should have been extended to Britain, it was not an attractive option for two reasons. First, the potential liability assumed by the government under such a mechanism would be enormous by any standards. Even in a relatively small business market such as Northern Ireland, losses incurred by the government still managed to reach £ 616.7 million in the period 1968 to 1991/92. Secondly, this solution would have been ideologically very unpopular. The cost of direct compensation in Britain would be a noticeable additional burden on taxation which would be politically dangerous both as a signal to the terrorists and also in terms of the official policy of Ulsterisation. Although the government was nominally the insurer of last resort under the 1993 Act, it was its aspiration that the reinsurance arrangement established should be self-funding.

71 Equally, the alternative of doing nothing was unappealing. Should businesses be left without insurance cover for terrorism because of the withdrawal of reinsurance, financial ruin was a real possibility in view of the magnitude of potential loss from damage and dislocation in the event of a bombing. Those businesses which could survive financially would still be severely economically disadvantaged. Those who could attempt to budget for such an eventuality would do so at the cost of the effective loss of working capital and a consequential loss of flexibility and effectiveness in the market. Facing this scenario and assessing the level of risk, how many City organisations would choose to relocate? For the wider ramifications upon the insurance industry, the government was concerned about the effect upon companies' solvency margins. Aside from financial considerations, an insurance collapse would have attacked the very notion of the legitimacy and sovereignty of the state, subjected the British government to embarrassment on an international level, not to mention handing the IRA another propaganda coup.

72 Looking at a broader perspective, one can see the establishment of Pool Re as, if not the ideal government response to the threat of large risk, then equally not the worst. It was one part of a three-pronged strategy in response to the threat, the other two being the Northern Ireland peace process (culminating in the Belfast Agreement in 1998),[93] plus a national security policy. Arguably

[92] HC Debs. vol. 233, col. 932 30 November 1993.

[93] British Irish Agreement reached in the multi-party negotiations (Cm.3883, London, 1998). See R. Wilford (ed.), *Aspects of the Belfast Agreement* (2001).

these decisive actions by the British government demonstrate that talk of a hollowed-out nation state is premature. Only an active and sovereign state could have taken on the holistic role that the British government assumed.

IV. Great Britain – A Postscript

Irish troubles notwithstanding, international terrorism has also been a constant feature of British life since the 1970s. The most serious incident for many years was the loss of 270 lives (44 of which were British) in the Lockerbie air crash of 1988,[94] though the number of British citizens killed in the World Trade Center in September 2001 is reckoned to be 67.[95] The costs of the September 11 attacks will have an enormous impact on the London insurance and reinsurance markets, since many of the policies relating to buildings in New York are issued by companies based, or with a strong presence, in London.[96] To give an indication of the trading situation, Swiss Re announced in February 2002 that it would be experiencing its first annual loss since 1866.[97] Many of the claims are as yet unsettled and can to some extent be spread over time and so be met by increased premiums over time. However, an even more acute and urgent problem arose in the airline industry. 73

As a result of the reassessment of risk after September 11, insurance costs for airlines were reported to have risen from $ 1.7bn to $ 6bn.[98] It was also reported that commercial insurance became unavailable for war risk beyond a minimal level.[99] With the prospect of airlines being grounded by leasing companies which would not allow their aircraft to be operated with a $ 50 million cap while the "the first war of the twenty-first century"[100] conjured by US President Bush was being pursued, the UK government acted quickly to arrange from 24 September 2001 the Troika Insurance Company Limited.[101] The legal basis for the arrangements was unclear, and one Minister[102] alluded to the Maritime and Aviation Insurance (War Risks) Act 1952, which allows for the 74

94 See R. Wallis, *Lockerbie* (2001).

95 *The Times*, 15 October 2002, 1: 33 were killed in the Bali bombing.

96 An estimate of costs is $ 40 billion: *The Times*, 10 September 2002, 15. See further J.D. Wright, Insurance coverage for war or terrorism, (2001) 12(10) *Construction Law*, 27.

97 *The Times*, 27 February 2002, 29. Swiss Re is the ultimate reinsurer for the World Trade Center with a "sleep easy" policy, but litigation has arisen as to whether the loss resulted from one "occurrence" or two (see *SR International Business Insurance Co. Ltd. v World Trade Center* (2002) 222 F. Supp. 2d 385, which concluded there was just one occurrence, so limiting insurance liability to the property owners).

98 *The Times*, 7 September 2002, 18. In the 25 years prior to September 11, the highest third party loss in the aviation sector was $ 36 million paid to victims of the Lockerbie disaster. In comparison, $ 3.5 billion has been estimated as required to meet third party claims arising from 11 September. Similar problems are reported for commercial shipping following the Limburg incident (see below): Holman/Fenwick/Willan, War and terrorism: legal considerations, [2001] 8(2/3) *International Maritime Law*, 87.

99 *The Times*, 21 September 2001, 1.

100 *The Guardian*, 14 September 2001, 5.

101 It was authorised to carry on business under sec. 3 of the Insurance Companies Act 1982 from the 24 September 2001.

102 HC Debs. vol., col. 822w 25 February 2002 David Jamieson.

government to issue or arrange "war risks" insurance (sec. 1) or reinsurance (sec. 1) for ships or aircraft. Sec. 5 makes explicit that it is an arrangement underwritten by the Consolidated Fund (in other words, the Government). For these purposes, by sec. 10:

> "... 'war risks' means risks arising from any of the following events, that is to say, hostilities, rebellion, revolution and civil war, from civil strife consequent on the happening of any of those events, or from action taken (whether before or after the outbreak of any hostilities, rebellion, revolution or civil war) for repelling an imagined attack or preventing or hindering the carrying out of any attack, and includes piracy."

75 However, H.M. Treasury, on application under the Code on Open Government,[103] later revealed that the legal basis is claimed to be the default common law prerogative powers of the Crown, with those enabling action in emergencies perhaps being the most apposite.[104] The Maritime and Aviation Insurance (War Risks) Act 1952 was considered inappropriate because, first, the "war risks" referred to in sec. 10 are not generally applicable to terrorism risks[105] which must be excluded by a distinct clause[106] and therefore are beyond the scope of the 1952 Act. In addition, the 1952 Act relates to ships, aircraft and cargo and therefore could not be applied to a wider range of property (such as airports) or a wider range of services (such as those providing goods and services within the aviation sector).

76 The company was set up by the brokers, Aon (Chicago), Marsh (part of March & McLennan Companies, New York) and Willis (Nashville) and administered by Global Aerospace (a merger of the British Aviation Insurance Group (BAIG) and Associated Aviation Underwriters (AAU) in the USA). It offered cover for third party war and terrorism insurance for liabilities greater than $ 50 million (since this minimal level of cover remained available), with a limit of $ 2 billion.[107] At first, the government waived any premium, but from 8 November 2001 the airlines had to pay premiums to Troika based on passenger numbers (and also after August 2002 based on amount of cover). Airports and other ground service providers were charged a proportion of the premium they paid before cover was withdrawn. The European Commission issued guidelines on the level of these premiums to avoid unnecessary government

[103] Letter to author, 17 December 2002.

[104] *R v Hampden* 1637 3 *State Trials* (St Tr), 825 and *Burmah Oil v Lord Advocate* [1965] AC 75.

[105] See especially: *Spinney's (1948) Ltd. v Royal Insurance Co.* [1980] 1 *Lloyd's Law Reports* (Ll Rep), 406. Compare: *Pan American World Airways v Aetna Casualty and Surety Co.* 505 F 2d 989 (1974); *Holiday Inns v Aetna Insurance* 571 F Supp. 1460 (1983). For discussion see: J. Hirshleifer, War Damage Insurance, (2002–2003) 9:1 *Connecticut Insurance Law Journal*; P. Siegelman, Hirshleifer's War Damages Insurance After 50 Years: A Tribute & Reappraisal. (2002–2003) 9:1 *Connecticut Insurance Law Journal*; J. Hirshleifer, Comment on War Damage Insurance, (2002–2003) 9:1 *Connecticut Insurance Law Journal*; J.W. Stempel, The insurance aftermath of September 11th, (2002) 37 *Tort & Insurance Law Journal*, 817.

[106] See the sample clauses at http://www.iso.com/filings/update.htm.

[107] Aircraft hulls are usually covered for up to $ 200 million plus $ 500 million liability for passengers and $ 1 billion for ground damage and loss.

subsidies.[108] Insofar as the premiums failed to cover any losses, the Government agreed to provide an indemnity.

The scheme was extended on a couple of occasions. The initial scheme announced on 21 September expired on the 24 October 2002. It was then renewed to November, then to 22 January 2002 and then to the 20 March, then to 30 June, then to 29 August, then to 30 September. However, it drew to a close on the 31 October 2002, as required by the European Commission, by which time all commercial airlines had been able to arrange private cover.[109] The very strict time-limit set for the Troika scheme, as policed by the outside agency of the European Commission, is in contrast to the Pool Re scheme and seems to have encouraged the desired private sector initiatives. 77

In its response[110] to the House of Commons Transport, Local Government and the Regions Select Committee Report on the Air Transport Industry,[111] it is revealed that 78

> "The insurance industry withdrew almost all cover for third-party war and terrorism risks in September 2001. A number of companies now offer this type of cover, but at a higher price and with a significant restriction compared with that on offer before the terrorist attacks. In order to limit their exposure, insurers have restricted their cover to an aggregate limit rather than offering a per-occurrence basis.
>
> Since the inception of the Government-backed insurance scheme, Troika, HM Treasury has made clear in press announcements that the aim of Government was to intervene in the insurance market only as long as necessary. Treasury has progressively raised the price and/or the threshold at which cover would apply in order to encourage airlines and others to return to the commercial market.
>
> The Government is currently analysing possible long-term options. A number of international mutual insurance schemes have been proposed (one global, one for Europe, and one for USA), each relying on government support in the early years until sufficient funds have accrued to make them self sufficient. There have also been suggestions of a new international convention on air carrier third-party liability, and the International Civil Aviation Organisation has included this in its work plan over the next few years. It is possible that a proposed convention could include a cap on liability arising from war and terrorism which, depending on the limit agreed, could help to stabilise the insurance market.

[108] See C(2002) 591 final, 27 February 2002 and the European Commission Communication of the 2 July 2002 (COM (2002) 320 final; http://www.europarl.eu.int/meetdocs/committees/rett/20020909/com(02)0320_en.pdf).

[109] *The Times*, 1 November 2002, 29.

[110] http://www.aviation.dft.gov.uk/air-transport/index.htm, 30 October 2002.

[111] 2001–02 HC 484.

Taking into account the costs incurred in setting up Troika, Treasury has to date collected a little over £ 17 million in premiums from airlines, airports, ground service providers and other policyholders. Unless needed to meet claims, this money will be transferred to the Consolidated Fund."[112]

79 A further sequel to the unexpected financial windfall is that consideration is being given to regional or even global schemes for aviation insurance. The European Commission is debating both a scheme called Eurotime (based on an airline mutual fund)[113] while the International Civil Aviation Organisation is likewise hatching the Global Aviation War Risk Insurance Scheme.[114] The ideas revolve around indemnity support from governments while the fund is capitalised. Once premiums build up, the governments' responsibility for risk would fade away.

80 The influence of the Pool Re on these ad hoc arrangements for dealing with war risks is evident. While governmental intervention was unavoidable in view of the situation faced by the airline industry after September 11, the mechanisms adopted reflected once more the influences of managerialism and risk management. Once again, private institutions were heavily involved[115] and the government proved adept at moving out of the sector as speedily as possible.

V. Special Sectoral Liabilities

81 There is no special scheme relating to the victims of terrorism within the United Kingdom. There are various statutory schemes for compensation relating to personal injury,[116] but these correspond in large part to criminal injuries schemes elsewhere in Europe pursuant to the European Convention on the

[112] The accounts of the Troika Insurance Company Limited invariably reveal a nil profit/loss because the expenses precisely wipe out the modest net trading surpluses. They also reveal that no claims have been made under the insurance so issued.

[113] See http://europa.eu.int/luxembourg/docs/321-2002_fr.pdf. In the US, a scheme called Equitime (with the main participant airlines being Alaska, America West, American, Continental, Delta, Northwest, Southwest, United and US Airways) is estimated to have plans to reduce insurance costs by $ 500 million.

[114] Once implemented, the five-year scheme would provide third-party coverage for airline operators and other parties involved in civil aviation, through a non-profit insurance entity backed by state guarantees as a last resort. Coverage would be capped at U.S.$ 1.5 billion per insured and per occurrence, for claims in excess of U.S.$ 50 million: http://www.icao.int/cgi/goto.pl?icao/en/new.htm, 17 June 2002.

[115] The restrictions in the Restriction of Advertisement (War Risks Insurance) Act 1939 now seem anomalous in the circumstances.

[116] See for Northern Ireland: Criminal Injuries Compensation (Northern Ireland) Order 2002 SI no.796 (which repealed the 1988 Order SI no.793). See D.S. Greer/V.A. Mitchell, *Compensation For Criminal Injuries to Persons in Northern Ireland* (1976) and *Supplement* (1978). See for Great Britain: D.R. Miers, *Compensation for Criminal Injuries* (1990); D. Greer, *Compensation for Criminal Injuries* (1991); P.A. Duff, *Criminal Injuries Compensation* (1991); http://www.cica.gov.uk.

Compensation of Victims of Violent Crimes of 1983[117] and so will not be discussed further. It follows that liability is largely based on the general laws relating to the tort of negligence, but there are some variations in terms of strict liability.

A. *Fault Liability*

Liability arising from terrorist attacks on public facilities or public transport will in the main be settled by the law of torts. It would, of course, be possible to claim damages against the direct tortfeasors, the terrorists, but such actions are not common owing to the absence of resources held by them.[118] As for the liability of facility or transport owners and operators, circumstances such as the obviousness of the threat of attack, the level of security checks and inherent designs will affect the allocation of liability, if any. Liability will arise under the general laws of negligence. In addition, an occupier of land, fixed or moveable structures (including vehicles) has a duty under the Occupier's Liability Act 1957 to take such care as is reasonable to keep visitors reasonably safe. The liability can extend to the harm or loss caused by trespassers such as terrorists, but a high degree of foreseeability then seems to be required according to *Smith v Littlewoods Organization plc.*[119] In the words of Lord Griffiths:[120] 82

> "I doubt myself if any search will reveal a touchstone that can be applied as a universal test to decide when an occupier is to be held liable for a danger created on his property by the act of a trespasser for whom he is not responsible. I agree that mere foreseeability of damage is certainly not a sufficient basis to found liability. But with this warning I doubt that more can be done than to leave it to the good sense of the judges to apply realistic standards in conformity with generally accepted patterns of behaviour to determine whether in the particular circumstances of a given case there has been a breach of duty sounding in negligence."

This level of foreseeability has rarely been sustained, though one example is *Cunningham and Others v Reading Football Club Limited*, where the presence of football hooligans was dolefully predictable.[121] 83

[117] *European Treaty Series* (ETS) 116, 1983; Cm.1427, 1991. See C.N. Katsoris, The European Convention on the Compensation of Victims of Violent Crime, [1990–91] 14 *Fordham International Law Review*, 186; D.S. Greer (ed.), *Compensating Crime Victims* (1996) Part I.

[118] But there is a current attempt to sue members of the Real IRA who are alleged to be responsible for the death and injury resulting from the bombing in Omagh in August 1998: "Writs over Omagh delivered under grey Irish sky", *The Times*, 27 July 2002, 4.

[119] [1987] AC, 241. See also *P Perl (Exporters) Ltd v Camden London Borough Council* [1984] 1 *Queen's Bench Reports* (QB), 342; *King v Liverpool City Council* [1986] 1 WLR, 890; *Topp v London Country Bus* [1993] 1 *Weekly Law Reports* (WLR), 976; *Jeffrey v Commodore Cabaret Ltd* (1995) 128 *Dominion Law Reports* (DLR) (4th), 535. Compare: *Hosie v Arbroath Football Club Ltd* (1978) *Scottish Law Times* (SLT), 122. See D. Howarth, My brother's keeper? Liability for acts of third parties, (1984) 14 *Legal Studies*, 88.

[120] Ibid., 751.

[121] *The Times*, 22 March 1991.

84 To date, there have been no recorded instances of claims in the United Kingdom for damages against property owners or carriers arising from terrorism. However, cases in the United States include[122] the *Lockerbie* case, where Pan Am was held liable for wilful misconduct for failing to check baggage at Frankfurt Airport.[123]

85 Aside from the liability of public venue or transport owners and operators, there may be a residual duty of protection vested in the state. The state's recognition and protection of rights to life, liberty and property involve its most fundamental duties.[124] It is interesting to note that reminders from the insurance community of these types of duties were indeed in evidence during the crisis created by the IRA's City of London bombs in 1992–1993.[125] But do these broad normative considerations translate into legal duties? The answer would seem to be that protection by the state is a legitimate demand both in domestic law under the broad reach of the Royal Prerogative.[126] And one might reach similar conclusions in regard to international law. The focus here might first be turned towards the interpretation of the right to life under art. 2 of the European Convention on Human Rights and Fundamental Freedoms of 1950. The state must put in place laws, security personnel and security tactics such as can secure a reasonable amount of protection for all citizens.[127] This duty has now been reinforced domestically by the Human Rights Act 1998.

86 At the same time, there continues to be legal resistance to the eager application of fault liability to state coffers. The leading case in which the right to damages for negligence was tested was *Hill v Chief Constable of West Yorkshire*.[128] The

[122] See also *Sakaria v TWA* (1993) 8 F.3d 164; *Shah v Pan Am* (1999) 148 3d 84.

[123] *In re Air Disaster at Lockerbie, Scotland* (1994) 37 F3d 804, cert. denied, 513 U.S. 1126 (1995). Pan Am went bankrupt in 1991 but its insurers remain liable. Liability under the (Warsaw) Convention for the Unification of Certain Rules Relating to International Transportation by Air (1929) would otherwise be capped at $ 75,000 (art. 22). By art. 25: "the carrier shall not be entitled to avail himself of the provisions of this convention which exclude or limit his liability, if the damage is caused by his wilful misconduct or by such default on his part as, in accordance with the law of the court to which the case is submitted, is considered to be equivalent to wilful misconduct". The action against the airline was followed by several actions against the Libyan Government: *Rein v Socialist People's Libyan Arab Jamahiriya* (1998) 162 F. 3d 748. This case raised claims previously dismissed in *Smith v. Socialist People's Libyan Arab Jamahiriya*, (1996) 101 F.3d 239, *cert. denied*, 520 U.S. 1204 was built upon the Antiterrorism and Effective Death Penalty Act 1996 which amended the Foreign Sovereign Immunities Act by adding what is now 28 U.S.C. sec. 1605(a)(7). Under this new section, foreign states that have been designated as state sponsors of terrorism are denied immunity from damage actions for personal injury or death resulting from aircraft sabotage.

[124] P. Wilkinson, *Terrorism and the Liberal State* (2nd edn. 1986), 300–301.

[125] M. Kielmas, Minimizing terrorism losses, (1993) 27(29) *Business Insurance*, 17, 19.

[126] *Calvin's case* (1609) 77 English Reports (ER), 377; *Mutasa v Attorney General* [1980] Queen's Bench Reports (QB), 114; *R (Abassi and another) v Secretary of State for the Home Department, The Times*, 8 November 2002.

[127] *McCann, Savage and Farrell v United Kingdom*, (1995) Application no.18984/91, Series A volume 324, *The Times*, 9 October 1995; [1996] 21 *European Human Rights Reports* (EHRR), 97.

[128] [1989] AC, 53. But the possibility of liability to a suitable narrow category of persons (a prisoner known to be a suicide risk) was assumed in *Reeves v Metropolitan Police Commissioner* [2000] 1 AC, 360.

House of Lords concluded on grounds of public policy that it would be undesirable to impose civil liability on the police for failing to prevent further murders by a serial killer. It preferred to allow them to use their professional judgement in the allocation of resources and the direction of policies unworried by the threat of potentially endless civil actions by concerned or disgruntled citizens, even those within the most likely circle of victims (in this case, young women). The European Court of Human Rights in the case of *Osman*[129] later cast considerable doubt on any absolute exclusion of liability on grounds of public policy and required on grounds of due process the possibility of a claim to be considered case by case. However, it later understood, in *TP and KM v. United Kingdom*,[130] that these requirements of art. 6 of the European Convention are met by the approach of English law.

B. *Strict Liability*

In a recent risk assessment, the Security Service (MI5) identified 350 key terrorist targets, such as nuclear plants, telecommunications infrastructure, fuel depots, governmental and military centres.[131] Since commercial insurance coverage is often unavailable for these targets, insurance is provided through a mixture of Pool Re and other statutory schemes which have long recognised not so much their susceptibility to external attack but rather their inherent riskiness and potential for catastrophe. These schemes do not mean that private insurance is wholly absent,[132] but the insurance may be predicated on such state support. 87

The residual form of legal strict liability is that set out in the rule in *Rylands v Fletcher*,[133] by which:[134] "the person who for his own purposes brings on his lands and collects and keeps there anything likely to do mischief if it escapes must keep it at his peril, and, if he does not do so, is prima facie answerable for all the damage which is the natural consequence of its escape." Following consideration in *Cambridge Water v Eastern Counties Leather plc*,[135] the continued life of the rule is assured, but it is destined to live on at the margins of liability – confined to imposing strict liability for damage or loss caused by the "non-natural uses" of "dangerous things" already recognised as such and without prospect of creating a more general liability for ultra-hazardous activities or materials. 88

[129] *Osman v United Kingdom*, (1998) Application no.23452/94, Reports 1998-VIII, 29 EHRR, 245.

[130] *X v. Bedfordshire County Council* [1995] 2 AC, 633; *TP and KM v. United Kingdom* (2001) Application no. 28945/95, [2002] 34 EHRR, 2; *Keenan v United Kingdom*, (2001) Application no.27229/95, 33 EHRR, 38.

[131] *The Times*, 6 June 2002, 1.

[132] British Nuclear Fuels reported it had secured insurance in 2002: *The Times*, 6 June 2002, 3

[133] (1868) LR 3 HL 330. See W.V.H. Rogers, *Winfield and Jolowicz on Tort* (16th edn. 2002), chap.15.

[134] (1866) LR 1 Ex.265 at 279–280 per Blackburn J.

[135] [1994] 2 AC 264. Compare the abolition of the rule in Australia: *Burnie Port Authority v General Jones Pty Ltd* [1994] 120 ALR, 42.

89 Applying this form of liability to the releases of dangerous things as a result of attacks by terrorists, a number of limitations arise. While terrorist intervention will not count as an "Act of God" (a circumstance triggered by natural causes which no human foresight could provide against),[136] it will provide a defence to the property owner whose property then damages others in the form of the defence of an independent act by a third party, subject to it not being reasonably possible for the defendant to have foreseen and guarded against the intervention:[137]

> "If the mischievous, deliberate and conscious act of a stranger causes the damage, the occupier can escape liability."

90 Guarding against terrorist attack lies behind the compulsory audit scheme applied to laboratories under Part VII of the Anti-terrorism, Crime and Security Act 2001.[138] Part VII seeks to ensure that dangerous pathogens and toxins are held in circumstances of high safety and security, out of harm's way as far as terrorism is concerned. By sec. 67, it is an offence for occupiers of premises to fail, without reasonable excuse, to comply with any duty or directions, but no separate strict civil liability is created. Subject to these points, the occupier can be liable for an escape even if there is no negligence in foreseeing or preventing the escape. But a further requirement from the *Cambridge Water* case[139] is that the escape must at least be foreseeable, so that forms of novel attack by terrorists which result in the escape of dangerous things will again not result in liability. It is also probably the case that the tort does not allow for claims for personal injury but must relate to damage to land-owning interests.[140]

91 The foregoing discussion shows that *Rylands v Fletcher* liability is most unlikely to attach to terrorist attacks. But that observation does not exhaust the possibilities of strict liability, for there exist a range of statutes which relate to exceptionally dangerous substances or processes and any harm or loss arising from them.

92 The first such example relates to nuclear materials.[141] Under the Nuclear Installations Act 1965, sec. 7, there is imposed a strict duty to secure that there

[136] *Greenock Corporation v Caledonian Railway* [1917] AC, 556.

[137] *Perry v Kendricks Transport Ltd.* [1956] 1 WLR, 85 at 87 per Singleton LJ. See further *Box v Jubb* (1879) 4 Ex D, 76; *Richards v Lothian* [1913] AC, 263; *Northwestern Utilities v London Guarantee and Accident Co. Ltd.* [1936] AC, 108; *H & N Emanual Ltd v Greater London Council and another* [1971] 2 All ER, 835; *Ribee v Norrie* (2000) *The Times*, 22 November.

[138] C. Walker (supra fn. 1), chap.9.

[139] See W.V.H. Rogers (supra fn. 133), 554–555.

[140] Compare *Hunter v Canary Wharf* [1997] AC, 655.

[141] See H. Street/F.R. Frame, *Law Relating to Nuclear Energy* (1966); S. Tromans/J. Fitzgerald, *The Law of Nuclear Installations and Radioactive Substances* (1997); C.E. Miller, Radiological risks and civil liability, (1989) 1(1) *Journal of Environmental Law*, 10; M. Radetzki, Liability of nuclear and other industrial corporations for large scale accident damage, (1997) 15(4) *Journal of Energy & Natural Resources Law*, 317; M. Lee, Civil liability of the nuclear industry, [2000] 12(3) *Journal of Environmental Law*, 317; L.J.T. Horbach, Terrorism and nuclear damage coverage, (2002) 20(3) *Journal of Energy & Natural Resources Law*, 231.

is no injury, loss of life or damage to any property arising from the licensed use of a nuclear plant.[142] If there is a breach of that duty, then liability arises under sec. 12 provided the loss or damage is sufficiently proximate,[143] though other forms of legal action[144] are debarred (including against third parties such as suppliers of defective equipment). Liability for licencees is limited to 10 years under sec. 16 and claims must in any event be raised within 30 years. There is a defence under sec. 13 where the loss or harm arises from hostile action in armed conflict. Terrorism often does not qualify as within the meaning of "armed conflict" within the Laws of Geneva[145] and, given the general policy of the legislation, it is unlikely that there would be recognised any residual defence relating to problems caused by intervening third parties such as terrorists.[146] To ensure that claims can be met, the licensee must obtain under sec. 19 insurance up to a specified amount (£ 140 million is the figure currently set under the Energy Act 1983, sec. 27), though, under sec. 18, the government underwrites claims beyond that sum and claims after 10 years.[147]

The second sector involves poisonous pollution.[148] Should terrorist activity result in the deposit on land of any poisonous, noxious or polluting waste, then an offence is committed and civil liability arises under the Environmental Protection Act 1990, sec. 73(6): 93

> "Where any damage is caused by waste which has been deposited in or on land, any person who deposited it, or knowingly caused or knowingly permitted it to be deposited, in either case so as to commit an offence under section 33(1) or 63(2) above, is liable for the damage except where the damage –
>
> (a) was due wholly to the fault of the person who suffered it; or
>
> (b) was suffered by a person who voluntarily accepted the risk of the damage being caused;
>
> but without prejudice to any liability arising otherwise than under this subsection."

The liability attaches to any person who deposited waste or knowingly permitted it to be deposited. However, there is a defence under sec. 33(7) for one who can prove: 94

142 The UK Atomic Energy Authority, which, as the official agency, does not require a licence, is subject to the same liability under sec. 8.

143 Pure economic loss was not allowed in *Merlin v British Nuclear Fuels* [1990] 2 QB, 557.

144 An action under *Rylands v Fletcher* would seem otherwise possible: *Blue Circle Industries plc v Ministry of Defence* (1996), *The Times*, 11 December 1999, *Chancery Division Reports* (Ch) 289.

145 See C. Walker, Irish Republican Prisoners – Political Detainees, Prisoners of War or Common Criminals?, (1984) 19 *Irish Jurist*, 189.

146 Query whether loss or harm to the intervening third parties themselves might be blocked by the general principle, *ex turpi causa*.

147 Sec. 16, 18.

148 See S. Bell/D. McGillivray, *Ball and Bell on Environmental Law* (5th edn. 2000); J. Lowry/R. Edmunds (eds.), *Environmental Protection and the Common Law* (2000); D. Hughes, *Environmental Law* (4th edn. 2002).

"It shall be a defence for a person charged with an offence under this section to prove –

(a) that he took all reasonable precautions and exercised all due diligence to avoid the commission of the offence; or

(b) that he acted under instructions from his employer and neither knew nor had reason to suppose that the acts done by him constituted a contravention of subsection (1) above; or

(c) that the acts alleged to constitute the contravention were done in an emergency in order to avoid danger to the public and that, as soon as reasonably practicable after they were done, particulars of them were furnished to the waste regulation authority in whose area the treatment or disposal of the waste took place."

95 Another code on pollution relates to oil pollution from ships. Given the example of the alleged terrorist attack on the French super-tanker, the Limburg, off the coast of Yemen in October 2002,[149] one might consider the application of the Merchant Shipping Act 1995, Part VI.[150] Sec. 153 imposes liability on the tanker owners in respect of damage caused by contamination arising from the discharge or escape of oil. Liability extends to any damage caused as well as the costs of preventive measures and clean up operations. "Damage" is defined by sec. 156 and 170 as including loss, such as might be suffered by the fishing or holiday industries.[151] Owners of ships are required by sec. 163 to insure up to a set amount,[152] beyond which the International Oil Pollution Compensation Fund[153]

[149] *The Times*, 7 October 2002, 16.

[150] See D.W. Abencassis/R.L. Jarashow, *Oil Pollution from Ships* (2nd edn. 1995); H.N. Bennett, *The Law of Marine Insurance* (1996); A.R.M. Fogarty, *Merchant Shipping Legislation* (1994); N. Phillips/N. Craig, *Merchant Shipping Act 1995* (2001).

[151] Compare *Landcatch Ltd v International Oil Pollution Compensation Fund* [1999] 2 Lloyd's Rep, 316 which interpreted the Merchant Shipping Act 1974. The legislation is based on the International Convention on Civil Liability for Oil Pollution Damage (*Command Paper*, 1969). Though the range of recoverable economic loss has been widened by the 1995 Act, there must still be proof of causation: *Alegrete Shipping Co Inc v International Oil Pollution Compensation Fund* [2002] EWHC, 1095 (Admlty).

[152] Their liability is limited to that amount by s.157. There have also existed various voluntary compensation schemes, for example CRISTAL (Contract Regarding an Interim Supplement to Tanker Liability for Oil Pollution); TOVALOP (Tanker Owners Voluntary Agreement concerning Liability for Oil Pollution; see *ESSO Petroleum Co Ltd v Hall Russell & Co Ltd* [1989] AC, 643). These schemes terminated in 1997 because of the widespread acceptance of the International Oil Pollution Compensation Fund.

[153] See http://www.iopcfund.org; D. Wilkinson, Moving the boundaries of compensable environmental damage caused by marine oil spills: the effect of two new international protocols, (1993) 5(1) *Journal of Environmental Law*, 71; N. Gaskell, Oil pollution and the IOPC Funds 1971 and 1992, (1992) 6(7) *International Maritime Law*, 177. The IOPC Funds (the current version was constituted in 1992) arise from the International Convention on Civil Liability for Oil Pollution Damage (Cmnd, 1969) which establishes an international regime of liability and compensation for oil pollution damage caused by oil spills from tankers. The owner of a tanker is liable to pay compensation up to a certain limit for oil pollution damage following an escape of oil. Where the owner cannot meet all the claims, IOPC Funds can step in. The IOPC Funds are financed by levies on certain types of oil carried by sea. The levies are paid by entities which receive oil after sea transport, and normally not by States. Anyone who has suffered oil pollution damage may make a claim against the IOPC Funds for compensation.

will meet the claims under sec. 175. The defences in sec. 155 absolve the owner of liability from contamination which:

> "(a) resulted from an act of war, hostilities, civil war, insurrection or an exceptional, inevitable and irresistible natural phenomenon; or
>
> (b) was due wholly to anything done or omitted to be done by another person, not being a servant or agent of the owner, with intent to do damage; or
>
> (c) was due wholly to the negligence or wrongful act of a government or other authority in exercising its function of maintaining lights or other navigational aids for the maintenance of which it was responsible."

The formula in (b) will cover terrorist attack such as in the Limburg example. 96

The third sector relates to attacks on public utilities. For example, by sec. 209(1) of the Water Industry Act 1991,[154] "Where an escape of water, however caused, from a pipe vested in a water undertaker causes loss or damage, the undertaker shall be liable, except as otherwise provided in this section, for the loss or damage." In this case the liability extends to acts of third parties (unless the claim is by the person at fault for the loss or damage which has been sustained) and even Acts of God. Likewise,[155] under the Gas Act 1965, sec. 14, a "gas transporter shall be absolutely liable in civil proceedings in respect of damage caused by gas in an underground gas storage, or by gas in the boreholes connected with an underground gas storage, or which is escaping from or has escaped from any underground gas storage or any such boreholes." Again, the liability does not extend to a person who suffers the damage as the result of his own fault. 97

The fourth sector relates to aircraft. Aircraft are not considered "dangerous things" and so their use in attacks cannot *per se* give rise to *Rylands v Fletcher* liability.[156] However, strict liability is imposed by the Civil Aviation Act 1982, sec. 76(2), "where material loss or damage is caused to any person or property on land or water by, or by a person in, or an article, animal or person falling from, an aircraft while in flight, taking off or landing, then unless the loss or damage was caused or contributed to by the negligence of the person by whom it was suffered, damages in respect of the loss or damage shall be recoverable without proof of negligence or intention or other cause of action, as if the loss or damage had been caused by the wilful act, neglect, or default of the owner of the aircraft." The foregoing makes clear that there is no defence that the loss or damage is caused by a third party, though the owner may seek an indemnity from that nefarious third party. 98

[154] But no special civil liability is imposed by the Reservoirs Act 1975 (s.1(5)).
[155] There is no equivalent under the Electricity Act 1989.
[156] *Fosbroke-Hobbes v Airwork Ltd.* [1937] 1 All ER, 108.

VI. Final Reflections

99 Themes of late modernity and the responses to risk infuse this paper and provide critical points from which to analyse legal provision. These themes are also reflected in the targets of political violence. The point of attack becomes a global and private concentration of economic power. At the same time, the private commercial victim is a vital part of the public political economy and also exercises wide powers of self regulation which are not only used in the financial sector but are also very influential in the deployment of both public police officers and private security guards.

100 These strands are equally reflected in the contemporary legal response such as in the Reinsurance Act of 1993. It recognises that risk is to be managed rather than soothed away by the Keynsian welfare state. Moreover, management is a task for both public and private sectors of society. The broad conclusion must be that the state's role has changed over time and that it has moved, to use new public management symbolism, from "rowing to steering".[157] So, it becomes the role of the state to express sympathy and to encourage individual choice and responsibility in dealing with risk,[158] but these tasks are achieved through many tiers of agency, both governmental and non-governmental. It follows that calls to create forms of normative or even legal rights to compensation and protection for victims are likely to be met with considerable resistance in the risk society. The state can no doubt live with a duty to promote, as in the words of the Preamble to the European Convention on the Compensation of Victims of Violent Crime, "equity and social solidarity". But its relationship with individual potential claimants is likely to become, more rather than less distant, both for pragmatic and ideological reasons. Though there may be some benefits in terms of the encouragement of personal responsibility, it is also clear that social solidarity can be damaged through reliance on market choice. The reality, as illustrated by the cases of Docklands and Manchester, is that the market rarely works perfectly and that a public price must be paid for public benefits.

101 It may equally be possible to discern within the state's security responses the same late modern features and influences. This is illustrated by a familiar fragmentation of governance, including the mixing of public and private arrangements and an emphasis upon surveillance. After all, as Ericson and Haggerty contend: "Risk society is fuelled by surveillance".[159]

102 As a correction, there may be an ideological pull from the duties of protection which constrain the insouciance of the deregulatory state. That idealogical pull is provided by concepts of individual rights, which, in the United Kingdom at least, have been given a boost by the passage of the Human Rights Act 1998. But these rights are diminished or even inapplicable in the case of com-

[157] D. Osborne/T. Gaebler, *Re-inventing Government* (1992).
[158] N. Lewis, *Choice and Legal Order* (1996).
[159] R.V. Ericson/K.D. Haggerty (supra fn. 85), 450.

mercial victims, whose credit-worthiness may be offset by their target-worthiness.

Equally, the underlying tendency towards state withdrawal must be balanced against the factor of globalisation, which increases the range of risk and actually demands more concerted reaction to terrorism, of a kind only possible through state agencies.[160] As a result there is a tendency for policies to be replicated, a striking trend in the case of the United Kingdom's Reinsurance Act which has now influenced the US Terrorism Risk Insurance Act 2002.[161] In return for a deductible from direct earned premiums, all commercial insurers of buildings are required to begin offering terrorism coverage immediately, but in return the federal government must pay 90 percent of the cost of an attack by foreign terrorists after losses are greater than \$ 10 billion, up to a total of \$ 100 billion. The government will pay a smaller amount for losses less than \$ 10 billion.[162] 103

It may be concluded that terrorism has had significant impact in shaping civil liability and that, equally, "... the insurance industry has much to offer in the battle against terrorism."[163] Normal mechanisms to spread liability have been shown to be fragile in the case of meta-attacks. The result is the assertion of a stronger form of state sovereignty – and nothing can be a stronger signal than the threat of war. But even in these deadly circumstances, the state remains still reliant on private sector co-operation and forms of governance beyond legislation. 104

[160] See P. Hirst/G. Thompson, Globalization and the Future of the Nation State, (1995) 24(3) *Economy and Society*, 408; P. Hirst/G. Thompson, *Globalisation in Question* (2nd edn. 1999).

[161] S2600, PL 107–297. J.W. Stempel, (2002) 37 *Tort & Insurance Law Journal*, 817.

[162] The Act is set to expire at the end of 2004 but can be extended into 2005. To create incentives for a return to a commercial market, the deductible rises annually, as does the lower limit beyond the reassurance scheme. Actual losses will also trigger a 10% quota share participation for each insurer.

[163] G. Rappe, The role of insurance in the battle against terrorism, (1999) 12 *De Paul Business Law Journal*, 351 (353).

United States of America
Liability for Acts of Terrorism Under U.S. Law

Kenneth S. Abraham

I. Introduction

1 Two characteristics of tort law in the United States are so important that any analysis must begin with these characteristics as starting points. First, traditionally tort law is almost exclusively state law. That is, each of the fifty states and the District of Columbia make or enact their own tort law. Tort law is very rarely made by the federal government, and even then only within the limits of authority over interstate or international matters granted to the U.S. government by the Constitution. Thus, in a very real sense there is not one body of tort law in the United States, but fifty-one different bodies of tort law. Although over time these bodies of law have developed many similarities, differences sometimes remain both over points of significance and nuance. Second, tort law is largely common law. It is created by courts and evolves over time, rather than being enacted in statutes by legislatures. When statutes are enacted, they operate against a backdrop of common law decisions that apply unless overruled by statute.

2 It happens that in the case of liability for damages caused by terrorism, each of these different sources of tort law comes in to play, and that the federal government has enacted a number of special statutes governing liability for terrorism. Thus, special legislation, common law principles under applicable state law, and conceivably even international treaties and conventions would govern many of the different sorts of suits that might be brought to recover damages resulting from terrorist acts. This paper examines the application of these three separate sources of law to liability for terrorism, and then analyzes the hypothetical cases that each of the country-specific papers in this volume have been asked to address in common.

II. Special Legislation Creating Liability for Terrorist Attacks

3 Statutory liability for harm caused by terrorist acts falls into three separate categories: liability for state-sponsored acts of terrorism; liability of individuals and non-state-sponsored terrorist entities; and liability of the owners and operators of nuclear power plants.

A. Statutory Liability of States and State-Sponsored Entities for Terrorism

Until 1996 foreign governments were immune to suit in U.S. courts.[1] After this rule was applied to preclude suit against Libya and related entitities by representatives of those killed in the explosion of Pan American Flight 103 over Lockerbie, Scotland,[2] Congress enacted the Civil Liability for State Sponsored Acts of Terrorism Act, also known as the Flatow Amendment. The Act renders foreign states subject to U.S. jurisdiction in actions in which money damages are sought for personal injury or death that was caused by an act of torture, extrajudicial killing, aircraft sabotage, hostage taking, or the provision of material support for such an act, if engaged in by an official, employee, or agent of a foreign state while acting within the scope of employment.[3] The foreign state must be officially designated by the U.S. Department of State as a sponsor or terrorism. The foreign state is rendered liable under the Act in the same manner and to the same extent as a private individual would be under like circumstances, except for punitive damages, to which a somewhat different standard applies.[4] Further, any U.S. national injured by an act of international terrorism is given the right to bring an action therefore in a United States District Court and to recover treble damages plus the cost of suit.[5] These provisions have been applied in a series of cases, involving the downing of U.S. civilian aeroplanes,[6] terrorist bombings,[7] hostages,[8] assassination,[9] and Pan American Flight 103.[10] 4

[1] See Foreign Sovereign Immunities Act, 28 U.S.C. §1602 et seq.

[2] See *Smith v. Socialist People's Libyan Arab Jamahiriya*, 101 F.3d 239 (2d Cir. 1996).

[3] 28 U.S.C. §1605(a)(7).

[4] 28 U.S.C. § 1606.

[5] Id.

[6] *Alejandre v. Republic of Cuba*, 996 F. Supp. 1239 (S.D. Fla. 1997) (estates sued Cuba and Cuban Air Force; court awarded $ 17 million per estate compensatory and $ 45.9 million punitive damages).

[7] *Flatow v. Islamic Republic of Iran*, 999 F. Supp. 1 (D.D.C. 1998); *Eisenfeld v. Islamic Republic of Iran*, 172 F. Supp. 2d 1 (D.D.C. 2000) (estates and family members of two American students killed when bus attacked by suicide bomber sued Iran, MOIS, and various senior officials; court awarded compensatory damages totaling more than $ 27 million and punitive damages of $ 300 million); *Wagner v. Islamic Republic of Iran*, 172 F. Supp. 2d 128 (D.D.C. 2001) (estate and family of US Navy Petty Officer killed in 1984 Beirut embassy bombing sued Iran and MOIS; court awarded compensatory damages of more than $ 16 million and punitive damages of $ 300 million).

[8] *Cicippio v. Islamic Republic of Iran*, 18 F. Supp. 2d 62 (D.D.C. 1998) (three US citizens held hostage in Lebanon and their spouses sued Iran; court awarded compensatory damages totaling $ 55 million); *Anderson v. Islamic Republic of Iran*, 90 F. Supp. 2d 107 (D.D.C. 2000) (American journalist held hostage in Lebanon, his wife, and his daughter sued Iran and MOIS; court awarded compensatory damages totaling more than $ 41 million and punitive damages of $ 300 million); *Sutherland v. Islamic Republic of Iran*, 151 F. Supp. 2d (D.D.C. 2001) (Dean of American University of Beirut held hostage in Lebanon, his wife, and his children sued Iran and MOIS; court awarded compensatory damages of more than $ 53 million and punitive damages of $ 330 million); *Jenco v. Islamic Republic of Iran*, 154 F. Supp. 2d 27 (D.D.C. 2001) (estate and family members of Catholic priest held hostage in Lebanon sued Iran and MOIS; court awarded compensatory damages of more than $ 14 million and punitive damages of $ 300 million; court refused to award damages to priest's nieces and nephews); *Polhill v. Islamic Republic of Iran*, 2001 U.S. Distr. Lexis 15322 (D.D.C. 2001) (estate and family of American professor at Beirut University College held hostage in Lebanon sued Iran and MOIS; court awarded compensatory damages of more than $ 28 million and punitive damages of $ 300 million); *Daliberti v. Republic of Iraq*, 146 F. Supp. 2d 19 (D.D.C. 2001) (four U.S. citizens held hostage and their wives sued Iraq; court awarded compensatory damages totaling nearly $ 20 million).

5 The Act does have certain gaps. It applies only to personal injury or death resulting from "an act of torture, extrajudicial killing, aircraft sabotage, and hostage taking." Consequently, by its terms it would not apply to non-fatal personal injury resulting from such terrorist acts as bombing, or the use of chemical or biological weapons.[11]

B. Liability of Individuals and Non-State Entities

6 Several statutes create liability for damage caused by terrorist attacks by individuals or non-State entities.[12] First, the Anti-Terrorism Act creates a civil cause of action for U.S. nationals injured in their person or property by an act of international terrorism, defined broadly in the Act.[13] Arguably the Act creates a cause of action not only against individual terrorists, but also against individuals and organizations who have provided material support for terrorism. In *Boim v. Quranic Literary Institute*,[14] for example, parents of a victim of Hamas terrorism were held to have a cause of action against two non-profit organizations working in the United States and supporting Hamas.

7 Second, the Racketeer Influenced and Corrupt Organizations Act (RICO),[15] as amended by the Patriot Act of 2001,[16] creates civil (as well as criminal) causes of action for both U.S. and foreign nationals injured "in their business or property" by racketeering activity, including terrorism. To establish a RICO violation, the plaintiff must prove two or more acts constituting a "pattern" of racketeering activity, that the defendant invested in or associated with that enterprise, and that the enterprise engaged in or affected interstate commerce. Most terrorist activities that involve more than one individual would probably satisfy these requirements. But based on the terms of the Act, liability could be imposed only for property damage or economic loss, not for personal injury resulting from terrorism.

8 Finally, the Torture Victim Protection Act creates a cause of action for U.S. and foreign nationals for official torture and extrajudicial killings, when these

[9] *Elahi v. Islamic Republic or Iran,* 124 F. Supp. 2d 97 (D.D.C. 2000) (estate of American citizen assassinated in Paris sued Iran and OIS; court awarded compensatory damages of $ 11.7 million and punitive damages of $ 300 million).

[10] *Rein v. Socialist People's Libyan Arab Jamahiriya*, 162 F.3d 748 (2d Cir. 1998) (survivors and representatives of persons killed aboard Pan Am 103 over Lockerbie, Scotland sued Libya, the airlines, and individuals; court of appeals affirmed district court's denial of defendants' motion to dismiss, determining that 28 U.S.C. § 1605(a)(7) is constitutional as applied). For discussion, see B.F. Benson/J. Dahlmann Rosa, The Status of Pending Air Carrier Litigation, [2001] 66 *Journal of Air Law and Commerce* (J. Air L. & Com.), 1367, 1399.

[11] J. Goldsmith/R. Goodman, *U.S. Civil Litigation and International Terrorism* 29, in: J. Norton Moore (ed.), *Civil Litigation Against Terrorism* (forthcoming 2003).

[12] For the discussion in this section I have drawn very heavily on J. Goldsmith/R. Goodman (supra fn. 11).

[13] 18 U.S.C. §§ 2332–33.

[14] 2002 U.S. App. LEXIS 10724 (7th Cir. 10 June 2002).

[15] 18 U.S.C. §§ 1961–1964.

[16] 18 U.S.C. § 2332b(g)(5)(B).

acts are taken by persons acting under actual or apparent authority or color of law of any foreign government.[17] Only individuals, however, are subject to liability.

C. Nuclear Facilities

Nuclear power plants are subject to the standards of common law liability discussed below. Thus, their owners or operators are potentially liable for negligent failure to protect them against terrorist acts, and perhaps would be strictly liable for the escape of radioactive material on the ground that operation of a nuclear power plant is an abnormally dangerous activity. Under the Price Anderson Act,[18] however, the amount of liability that may be imposed for damages resulting from a nuclear incident is limited to the amount of liability insurance maintained by the plant in question (currently $ 200 million) plus the funds in what would be a retrospectively created industry wide pool, under which more than $ 9 billion in additional funds would be available. If the total amount of liability imposed exceeded this sum, any additional compensation would probably have to be provided by an Act of Congress. 9

III. Special Funds Providing Alternative Compensation for Victims of Terrorist Attacks

In the wake of the terrorist attacks on the United States on September 11, 2001, the U.S. Congress enacted the Air Transportation Safety and System Stabilization Act.[19] One portion of the Act, the "September 11 Victims Compensation Fund of 2001"[20] and the regulations promulgated thereunder,[21] creates an alternative compensation fund for the direct victims of the September 11 attack, and for certain indirect victims such as rescue personnel. 10

The Fund provides victims or their families with both economic and noneconomic ("pain and suffering") damages, offset by payments made to them by collateral sources of insurance. Any party who elects to accept such compensation, however, waives the right to file a civil action for damages sustained as a result of the September 11 attacks. 11

In addition, even if a victim or her family elects not to accept payment from the Fund, the liability of an airline, airline manufacturer, or person with a property interest in the World Trade Center for loss resulting from the September 11 attacks is limited to the amount of liability insurance maintained by that party. Finally, the liability of the City of New York is limited to the greater of $ 350 million or the amount of the City's liability insurance. 12

[17] Pub. L. No. 102–256. 106 Stat. 73 (1992).

[18] 42 U.S.C. § 2210.

[19] Public Law 107-42 (22 September 2001), 115 Stat. 230.

[20] Id., Title IV. at §§ 401–09.

[21] For promulgation of the final regulations and discussion by the Special Master appointed to administer the Fund, see 67 Fed. Reg. 11233 (13 March 2002).

13 Although the Victims Compensation Fund applies only to the September 11 attacks, its approach seems likely to serve as a model for compensating victims of future attacks. Any future attack that causes harm to substantial numbers of people is highly likely to elicit pressure for treatment that is equal to or at least the equivalent of what was provided to the September 11 victims. Moreover, this approach has the political benefit of providing a means of avoiding tort litigation in which American businesses are alleged to have negligently contributed to damage caused by terrorism. Despite the fact that U.S. tort law does appear to provide a potential avenue of recovery on this basis, litigation seeking such recovery could have the effect of undermining American political morale and the sense of unity in the fight against terrorism that has been generated since the September 11 attacks. Therefore, in the event of future attacks, the enactment of legislation that once again encourages victims and their families to stay out of court seems likely.

IV. Judicial Decisions Addressing Liability for Terrorism

14 As discussed above, American courts have addressed liability for terrorism in a number of cases. Probably the leading decision is *In re Air Disaster at Lockerbie, Scotland on December 21, 1988.*[22] This case affirmed a judgment in favor of the estates of persons killed in the crash of Pan Am Flight 103, against Pan Am and Alert Management Systems, Inc., for wilful misconduct in contributing to the crash. This is the principal decision imposing liability on third parties for damages caused by terrorist acts.

15 In addition, there are now a number of decisions imposing civil liability on foreign governments for acts of terrorism under the Civil Liability for Acts of State Sponsored Terrorism Act,[23] creating a new cause of action for state sponsored acts of terrorism,[24] and one important decision under the Anti-Terrorism Act supporting the use of the Act to impose liability on organizations providing material support for terrorist activities.[25]

V. The Influence of the September 11 Attacks on the U.S. Liability System

16 Without question the September 11 attacks have had a major effect on behavior and practices involving the prevention of terrorism in the U.S. First, the

[22] 37 F.3d 804 (2d Cir. 1994).

[23] 28 U.S. §1605 (a)(7).

[24] See, e.g., *Alejandre v. Republic of Cuba*, 996 F. Supp. 1239 (S.D. Fla. 1997) (for downing of U.S. civilian aeroplanes by Cuban Air Force in international airspace); *Flatow v. Islamic Republic of Iran*, 999 F. Supp. 1 (D.D.C. 1998) (awarding $ 2.5 million compensatory and $ 225 million punitive damages to estate of American student killed by suicide bomber in Israel); *Cicippio v. Islamic Republic of Iran*, 18 F. Supp. 2d 62 (D.D.C. 1998) (awarding total damages of $ 55 million to three U.S. citizens held hostage in Lebanon). See also *Rein v. Socialist People's Libyan Arab Jamahiriya*, 162 F.3d 748 (2d Cir. 1998) (upholding constitutionality of the Act in suit by representatives killed in Lockerbie crash against the government of Libya, the airline, and certain individuals).

[25] *Boim v. Quranic Literary Institute*, 2002 U.S. App. LEXIS 10724 (7th Cir. 10 June 2002).

U.S. government has taken over direct responsibility for airport security. Second, other parties involved in public transportation such as train and bus service have instituted more rigorous baggage checking and security precautions. Third, in the wake of the anthrax poisonings, post offices and other governmental buildings have adopted more exacting procedures for checking the safety of the mail and for the admission of individuals into buildings. Finally, there has been a widespread increase in security concerns and responsibilities on the part of private businesses and institutions generally. Undoubtedly some portion of this increased security is the result of a heightened awareness of the threat of liability for any harm that might result from the failure to exercise proper care and responsibility for security on the part of these institutions.

VI. International Conventions

The United States has signed and ratified ten international conventions associated with the prevention of terrorism;[26] it has signed but not ratified two other conventions.[27] By their express terms, none of these conventions creates civil liability for damage caused by terrorist acts. A number of the conventions do, however, create standards of conduct.[28] And without question a treaty or convention is the law of the land under the Supremacy Clause of the U.S. Constitution and is therefore binding on the federal courts and the individual states. But under U.S. law such international agreements do not create private causes of action for damages unless they are "self-executing." That is, if an agreement provides that signators shall enact law designed to comply with the terms of the agreement, then unless a statute is enacted giving the U.S. courts jurisdiction to enforce the provisions of the agreement in private lawsuits, there is no such cause of action. For example, if a convention provides that each contracting state will make the offenses specified in the convention pun- 17

[26] See Convention on Offences and Certain Other Acts Committed on Board Aircraft, 14 September 1963, 20 U.S.T. 2941, 704 U.N.T.S. 219; Convention for the Suppression of Unlawful Seizure of Aircraft, 16 December 1970, 22 U.S.T. 1641, 860 U.N.T.S. 105; Convention for the Suppression of Unlawful Acts against the Safety of Civil Aviation, 23 September 1971, 24 U.S.T. 565, 974 U.N.T.S. 177; Convention on the Prevention and Punishment of Crimes against Internationally Protected Persons, including Diplomatic Agents, 14 December 1973, 28 U.S.T. 1975, 1035 U.N.T.S. 167; International Convention against the Takings of Hostages, 17 December 1979, T.I.A.S. No. 11,081, U.N.T.S. 205; Convention on the Physical Protection of Nuclear Material, 3 March 1980, T.I.A.S. No. 11080, 1456 U.N.T.S. 101; Protocol for the Suppression of Unlawful Acts of Violence at Airports Serving International Civil Aviation, 24 February 1988, S. Treaty Doc. 100-19 (1988), 27 I.L.M. 627; Convention for the Suppression of Unlawful Acts against the Safety of Maritime Navigation, 10 March 1988, S. Treaty Doc. 101-1 (1989), 27 I.L.M. 672; Protocol for the Suppression of Unlawful Acts against the Safety of Fixed Platforms Located on the Continental Shelf, 10 March 1988, S. Treaty Doc. 101-1 (1989), 27 I.L.M. 685; Convention on the Marking of Plastic Explosives for the Purpose of Detection, 1 March 1991, S. Treaty Doc. 103-8, 30 I.L.M.

[27] See International Convention for the Suppression of Terrorist Bombings, 12 January 1998, S. Treaty Doc. 106-6, 37 I.L.M. 251; International Convention for the Suppression of the Financing of Terrorism, 10 January 2000, S. Treaty Doc. 106-49, 39 I.L.M. 270.

[28] See, e.g., Convention on the Physical Protection of Nuclear Material, 3 March 1980, T.I.A.S. No. 11080, 1456 U.N.T.S. 101, art. 3 (creating standards governing the transportation of nuclear material).

ishable under its own law, then the agreement is not self-executing. No statutes that would have the effect of creating a civil cause of action under the anti-terrorism conventions, however, have been enacted in the United States.

18 Similarly, a number of these conventions also seem to create duties on the part of private actors such as aircraft commanders.[29] But again, in the absence of federal statute enacted to execute the agreement, a civil action seeking to impose liability on a private actor based on breach of such a duty would probably be precluded. It should not be supposed, however, that the inability of a plaintiff to rely on the provisions of a treaty or convention would be a significant disadvantage. For the most part the anti-terrorism conventions create duties which probably would be found to coincide with, rather than to enlarge or contract, common law standards, in which case they would in fact have no operative effect even if applicable and probably would be regarded as largely superfluous.

VII. Common Law Principles

19 It should go without saying that under the tort law of all states, a terrorist would be liable in tort for all the damage that he intended to cause or that was a reasonably foreseeable result of actions he intended. Under the principles of foreseeability and duty that I discuss below, there might be some limit on the scope of a terrorist's liability for purely economic harm resulting from his act of terrorism, but I leave that issue aside.

20 The issues of real concern are whether and under what circumstances third parties could be held liable, either in strict liability or for negligence, for damages resulting from terrorist acts committed by others. The principles that bear on this issue concern not only these two different standards of care, but also doctrines governing duty, foreseeability, and proximate causation.

A. Strict Liability

21 In contrast to negligence, strict liability typically is imposed only for carrying on "abnormally dangerous" activities. Neither air transportation nor the maintenance of commercial buildings or facilities is regarded as abnormally dangerous, although a small minority of states hold that there is strict liability for ground damage (as distinguished from injury to passengers) caused by aviation. On the other hand, if the terrorism were directed at facilities carrying on abnormally dangerous activities (for example, a warehouse storing explosives), a suit seeking to impose strict liability on the party responsible for the facility would be possible. However, in contrast to negligence, strict liability generally does not apply when harm is caused by a third party who intentionally deprives the defendant of control over the activity causing the harm; in

[29] See, e.g., Convention on Offences and Certain Other Acts Committed on Board Aircraft, 14 September 1963, 20 U.S.T. 2941, 704 U.N.T.S. 219, art. 6 (creating standards for dealing with hijackers and hostage-takers).

addition, strict liability is limited to those harms that are characteristic of the defendant's activity.[30] Thus, a chemical manufacturer conceivably could be held strictly liable for harm caused from personal exposure to dangerous chemicals that escaped from its facility in the course of its ordinary operations. But this manufacturer would not be liable if the chemicals were stolen by terrorists and used to contaminate a municipal water supply.

B. Negligence: The "Enabling" Principle

There is a general duty to exercise reasonable care to avoid causing foreseeable physical harm to others or their property. In a variety of cases the courts have held that, under certain circumstances, one whose negligence enables a primary wrongdoer to cause harm may be held liable for the harm caused by that wrongdoer. For example, a party who negligently entrusts a motor vehicle to a driver whom he knows or should know is incapable of operating the vehicle properly may be held liable to those whom the driver injures. These so-called "enabling torts" contemplate liability not only when the primary wrongdoer is merely negligent, but also when the wrongdoer intentionally causes harm. For example, landlords have been held liable to tenants for negligently failing to secure premises so as to protect tenants against assault by third paties when there was reason to know that an assault might occur. Behind this form of liability is the clear recognition that often the primary wrongdoer is either unamenable to suit or judgment-proof, and that imposing liability on a "secondary" defendant who enabled the wrongdoer to cause harm will provide the plaintiff with a solvent source of recovery. 22

Nonetheless, liability is less likely to be imposed for enabling an intentional wrongdoer – including a terrorist – to cause harm, than for enabling someone to cause harm negligently. The principle that appears to be operating here is that, because the actions of an intentional wrongdoer are so much more blameworthy than those of a merely negligent party, the subsequent act of an intentional wrongdoer tends to break the "chain" of causation between the defendant's negligence and the plaintiff's harm. An exception is made, however, when the very risk that makes the defendant's act or omission negligent is the prospect of subsequent intentional wrongdoing by a third party. Sometimes this is addressed under the rubrics of duty and foreseeability, and sometimes as part of the doctrine of proximate cause. But regardless of the doctrinally categories employed, the principle remains the same. 23

Occasionally the courts create a categorical rule that there is "no duty" to avoid negligently causing certain forms of harm, and I suppose it is possible that the courts would create such a rule to govern liability for the consequences of terrorist acts. But I doubt it. The situations in which such liability might arise are too varied, and the existing rules governing acts of negligence that 24

[30] See American Law Institute, *Restatement of the Law, Torts: Liability for Physical Harm (Basic Principles)* (Tentative Draft No. 1, 28 March 2001), § 24 (b) and Comment a.

enable others to commit intentional wrongs are so analogous, that creating such a rule would be an exercise in activist judicial policymaking beyond what most American courts would be willing to undertake. In fact, I believe that one reason the Congress enacted the legislation providing compensation to the victims of September 11 was the unpleasant prospect that there would in fact have been extensive litigation over the responsibility of the airlines and the owner of the World Trade Center buildings for the damage that was suffered by these victims. The principle that one party can be liable for negligently enabling another to cause harm is too embedded in American tort law for such litigation to have been dismissed wholesale under a categorical "no duty" approach.

1. Application of the Principle

25 Clearly this "enabling" principle would be invoked in any of the vast number of tort actions that might be brought in the wake of a terrorist act. The vast array of parties who might be alleged to have been negligent in failing to prevent a terrorist act or mitigate its effects would be limited only by the facts giving rise to the harm: airlines, security companies, building designers, cargo inspectors, civil engineers, chemical storage facilities, owners of electrical power plants, etc. Each of these parties could be sued for negligently contributing to the personal injury or property damage resulting from a terrorist act, on the ground that their actions foreseeably enabled the terrorist act to occur. For example, at public facilities such as airports, train stations, and sports stadiums, the party who could be held responsible to assure that no terrorist enters and causes harm varies. Depending on the circumstances, the entity that runs the facility, enterprises that take advantage thereof (such as airlines or organizers of sports events), the state, or other persons might be liable.

26 It is not possible to resolve these cases with a single answer, both because management and supervisory responsibilities vary depending on local ordinances and state statutes, and because as a matter of common law the general principle that all parties owe a duty to exercise "reasonable care under the circumstances" potentially subjects each of these institutions and/or enterprises to liability, depending on the facts. Prior to September 11, airports and airlines were responsible for hiring security companies to maintain security at airports. Thus, the airports, the airlines, and the security companies could be held liable for their negligence under certain circumstances. The U.S. government, however, has now taken over security at airports; it is liable for the negligence of its employees under the Federal Tort Claims Act.[31] Responsibility for sports events and other gatherings varies, in part depending on who owns the stadium and who organizes the event held in it. Some stadiums are state-owned or municipally-owned, others are owned by separate public entities or authorities, and some are wholly private. The potential liability of state and local governments differs from the potential liability of private entities, because govern-

[31] 28 U.S.C. §§ 2671 et seq.

ments bear liability only to the extent that Tort Claims Acts waive sovereign immunity from liability. The scope of these waivers varies from state to state.

Even apart from these considerations, however, it is worth noting that the principles just discussed pertain to liability for physical harm and for the economic consequences of that harm to the party who suffers it. Separate rules apply to what is called "pure" economic loss – i.e., loss of profits or income that results from an act of negligence that has not caused any physical harm to the plaintiff or his property. With only very limited exceptions, there is no liability for negligently inflicted pure economic loss. Thus, for example, the owner of a building who negligently failed to secure it against terrorist damage would not be liable for profits lost by nearby businesses as a result of the building's destruction by a terrorist act. 27

2. Considerations of Foreseeability and the Role of the Jury

The outcome of suits against third parties for physical harm caused by terrorist acts would probably turn on two factors, the first a legal concept and the second a feature of the institutional structure of tort litigation in the United States. The legal concept is the notion of "foreseeability", and the institutional feature is the separation of the legal and fact-finding functions between judge and jury. 28

The rule that a party may be held liable for enabling another to cause harm is contingent on a number of factors. Only *reasonable care* to avoid contributing to foreseeable harm is required. So it would be a question in most cases whether the measures the defendant took in anticipation of possible terrorist acts were reasonable under all the circumstances. This would depend on the entire context. This context would include the burden and cost of precautions, the likelihood that they would prevent or reduce harm, the amount of harm that could be prevented, and the foreseeability that there would be a terrorist act. 29

Foreseeability is not a binary concept, but a question of degree. It is a matter of knowable probability. Other things being equal, the more foreseeable a terrorist act, the greater the obligation to invest in taking precautions to avoid the effects of that act. Consequently, it is difficult to go much farther in analyzing the application of this context-dependent concept at a general level, because most of the answers would depend on the particular facts of each case. Obviously, tall buildings designed long ago would be subject to a different standard than those designed after September 11, 2001. In addition, such matters as whether there had been specific rather than merely general foreknowledge of terrorist threats could also have a bearing. On the whole the foreseeability limitation on liability operates somewhat like the Act of God, *force majeure*, and unavoidable event defenses in other systems. In U.S. tort law, these defenses tend to apply only to natural events such as unusual weather and the like, but the requirement of foreseeability serves a similar function in limiting the scope of liability for the consequences of interventions by human agency. 30

31 All this, however, is merely an analytical prelude to the actual process of decision, which in the United States is allocated partly to the court and partly to the jury. The judge in a tort suit determines the law applicable to the suit. The judge then determines, based on the law and the evidence, whether there is a question appropriate for jury decision. In the analytical setting I have just described, the judge would have to decide whether, based on the law and the facts in evidence, reasonable people could disagree about whether the defendant exercised reasonable care to avoid foreseeable harm from a terrorist act. If not, then "as a matter of law" there would be no liability and the case would be dismissed. On the other hand, if the judge concluded that reasonable people could disagree about the issue, then it would be left for the jury to decide whether the defendant was negligent.

32 Thus, both the context-dependent character of the foreseeability requirement and the institutional allocation of decision-making responsibility between judge and jury make it impossible to state categorically whether and when liability might be imposed for negligently contributing to harm caused by terrorism. There is little doubt that liability *could* be imposed – the rules governing enabling torts make it clear that the imposition of liability is plausible – but whether liability would *actually* be imposed would depend very much on the facts. Indeed, the institutional structure of tort litigation in the United States depends so heavily on jury decision-making that it is possible that different juries would decide highly similar cases differently.

VIII. Hypothetical Cases

33 Analysis of the following hypothetical cases may help to illustrate the principles of American law discussed above.

1. A Terrorist Hijacks an Aeroplane and Crashes into

a) A Building or

b) A Nuclear Plant

34 In certain jurisdictions the airline might be strictly liable for ground damage caused by the aeroplane crashes. But in this situation the courts would probably apply the rule that because the placement of the bomb deprived the airline of control over the plane, there is no strict liability.

35 The owner of the building would potentially have liability for failing to exercise reasonable care to construct the building so as to secure it against foreseeable hazards. The designers of the building would also be potentially liable on this basis. However, a terrorist attack by aeroplane would not have been foreseeable at the time existing buildings were constructed. But damage from an unintentional striking by a passenger aeroplane to an extraordinarily tall building (e.g., one of the two or three tallest in a major city) might have been fore-

seeable. Consequently, a court might permit a jury to impose liability for harm resulting from a terrorist attack that would also have occurred if the collision had been unintentional.

As to buildings constructed since September 11, 2001, the foreseeability that a tall building would be struck by an aeroplane has increased substantially. Both the owner and designer could therefore be held liable for failing to take design or other precautions to make the building more secure than it would have been under prior standards against damage caused by such a crash. 36

Terrorist attacks on nuclear power plants probably would be found to have been somewhat more foreseeable, even before September 11. In addition, given the high risks involved, those who designed and own nuclear power plants could foresee the possibility that such plants would be accidentally struck by aeroplanes, and probably had a duty to design them so as to withstand strikes of foreseeability intensity. The extent of the precautions that should have been taken at the time the plants were built would have to be the subject of detailed inquiry. 37

2. A Terrorist Sets a Bomb Situated in an Aeroplane and the Plane Crashes into

a) A Residential Area or

b) A Nuclear Power Plant

The owner of the airline and the U.S. government (for its security operation) would be subject to potential negligence liability under the principles discussed above. In certain jurisdictions the airline might be strictly liable for ground damage caused by the aeroplane crashes. But in this situation the courts would probably apply the rule that because the placement of the bomb deprived the airline of control over the plane, there is no strict liability. However, even if the airline were liable (in negligence or strict liability) for conventional ground damage, it is a further question whether there would be liability for personal injury and property damage to those affected by damage to the nuclear power plant. While this sort of damage is a remotely foreseeable consequence of an aeroplane crash, it is sufficiently unlikely that it might be treated differently from ordinary ground damage. The owner of the nuclear power plant, however, would be potentially liable for this damage on the same basis as discussed above under Question 1. 38

3. A Terrorist Drives with Somebody's Car or Bus into a Crowd of People

In the absence of special facts putting a third party on notice of this particular risk, no third party owner of the car or bus would face liability under these circumstances. 39

4. A Terrorist Hides a Bomb in a Car Which Explodes Within a Crowd of People

40 In the absence of special facts putting a third party on notice of this particular risk, no third party would face liability under these circumstances.

Special Reports

Civil Litigation Arising out of the WTC Attacks

Kevin P. Hilliard*

The best illustration of third-party legal liability arising out of acts of terrorism in the United States is the civil litigation arising out of the terrorist attacks of September 11th 2001. Although The United States Government established the September 11th Victim Compensation Fund of 2001 (VCF), which allows victims to quickly receive compensation for wrongful death and personal injury claims without liability determinations, plaintiffs have filed lawsuits against the airlines, aviation security companies, airport operators, and various building-related defendants in the United States District Court for the Southern District of New York. The civil lawsuits arising from the September 11th terrorist attacks have been consolidated before Judge Alvin K. Hellerstein. 1

On September 22, 2001, the President of the United States signed into law the Air Transportation Safety and System Stabilization Act (ATSSSA), which established the VCF and sought "to preserve the continued viability of the United States air transportation system" by, amongst other measures, limiting the liability of the airlines for all claims to the extent of their liability insurance coverage. The Aviation and Transportation Security Act (Security Act) extended the liability limitation to aircraft manufacturers, airport sponsors, and persons with a property interest in the World Trade Center. The ATSSSA's liability limitation was again extended by the Homeland Security Act of 2002, which limited the liability of aviation security companies to the extent of their insurance coverage. However, the Homeland Security Act effectively did not extend the liability limitation to Argenbright Security, Inc. who has been named as a defendant in a number of September 11th lawsuits.[1] 2

[*] As Director of Claims of the North American operation of Global Aerospace the world's largest international aviation insurer, the author has had a twenty-four year involvement in numerous major aircraft accidents on behalf of insured aircraft operators and manufacturers including American Airlines on September 11, 2001.

[1] The Homeland Security Act's extension of the liability limitation does not extend to Argenbright Security, Inc. because Argenbright does not qualify as a person "that [has] contracted directly with the Federal Aviation Administration on or after and commenced services no later than February 17, 2002, to provide such security, and [has] not been or [is] not debarred for any period within 6 months from that date." Pub. L. 107–296, § 890(2), 116 Stat. 2135 (2002).

I. Status of the Litigation

3 To date, approximately, one hundred and fifty lawsuits have been filed against the aviation and building defendants, including American Airlines, United Airlines, non-carrier airlines (present at the relevant airports on September 11, 2001), aviation security companies, entities that contributed to the design and construction of the World Trade Center and entities with property interests in the World Trade Center (including the Port Authority of New York and New Jersey). Approximately seventy of these lawsuits name only the Port Authority of New York and New Jersey as a defendant and approximately fifty of the suits against the Port Authority are considered "dormant" actions. These actions are considered "dormant", due to timing considerations involving the VCF and the statutory notice requirement for suing the Port Authority.

4 The majority of the complaints filed thus far, allege claims for wrongful death and property damage against American Airlines and United Airlines based on their operation of American Flights 11 and 77 and United Flights 93 and 175 and the security screening for those flights. Four actions have been filed against "non-carrier" airlines that operated out of Newark International Airport on September 11, 2001 (the departure site of United Flight 93) based on their alleged joint responsibility for security at Newark International Airport. Similar allegations against non-carrier airlines have been made in a wrongful death ground victim action arising out of the crash of American Flight 77 into the Pentagon. Plaintiffs have made claims of negligent security practices against the relevant airport operators and aviation security companies and have named the parent corporations of the security companies in several complaints. Additionally, negligence claims have been brought against the engineers and architects involved in the design and construction of the World Trade Center buildings. Plaintiffs have also sued the Boeing Company alleging defective and negligent design of its aircraft and cockpit doors.

5 The extent of personal injury and wrongful death lawsuits that plaintiffs will file in the September 11th litigation is difficult to predict at this time because that number is linked to the number of VCF claims pursued. The deadline for filing a VCF claim is December 22, 2003. When a VCF claim is submitted, the claimant waives his or her right to file a civil action for damages arising out of the September 11th attacks (other than suits against the terrorists)[2]. It is important to consider the number of VCF claims submitted and the average and mean awards issued thus far because potential plaintiffs are carefully considering VCF award amounts when deciding whether or not to file civil lawsuits against the September 11th defendants. As of January 31, 2003, nine hundred seventy-two claims have been submitted to the VCF, one hundred

[2] The ATSSSA and the Final Rules for the administration of the VCF provides that a claimant waives the right to be a party to a civil action upon submission of a VCF claim. Pub. L. 107-42, § 405(c)(3)(B)(i), 115 Stat. 230; 104 CFR § 104.61. Neither the ATSSSA or the administrative rules explain what criteria must be met for a VCF claim to be considered "submitted" for purposes of waiving the right to file a civil lawsuit.

sixty-one award letters have been issued and one hundred ten acceptances have been made. The average VCF award as of January 31, 2003, after offsets for collateral source payments such as life insurance and pensions, is one million, five hundred forty-six thousand, thirty-six dollars ($ 1,546,036) and the median award after offsets is one million, two hundred eighty-five thousand, nine hundred forty-four dollars ($ 1,285,944).

A class action lawsuit has been filed which challenges the VCF Special Master's award calculations. This challenge to the VCF administration could result in an increase in VCF award amounts, thus making the VCF route more attractive to those with personal injury and wrongful death claims. Conversely, the lawsuit challenging the VCF administration can bring to the forefront the perceived under-valuation of VCF awards, thereby encouraging those who were injured or who have wrongful death claims to pursue litigation. 6

A. *Liability of Third-Parties to Ground Victims*

On January 17, 2003, the majority of the aviation defendants[3] moved to dismiss the claims brought against them by ground damage plaintiffs. The airport operators, including the Metropolitan Washington Airports Authority, the Massachusetts Port Authority and the City of Portland, Maine, also filed a motion to dismiss all claims, including passengers' claims, against them. The City of Portland, Maine also filed a separate motion to dismiss all claims against it based on plaintiffs' failure to comply with statutory notice requirements. The remaining defendants have until February 7, 2003, to file motions to dismiss the claims against them. 7

The ATSSSA requires that the substantive law applied to these suits be derived from the substantive law of the state in which the crash occurred, unless that substantive state law is inconsistent with or preempted by federal law.[4] It is not yet clear whether the court will apply New York's negligence case law or a federal standard of care based upon the regulations issued by the *Federal Aviation Administration* (FAA), to the aviation defendants' motion to dismiss. Regardless of which law the court applies, the aviation defendants have made a strong argument that the ground damage plaintiffs should not recover from the aviation defendants as a matter of law because none of the aviation defendants owed a legal duty to protect the ground damage plaintiffs from the terrorist attacks. 8

[3] The defendants who joined in the aviation defendants' January 17, 2003 Motion to Dismiss Ground Damage Claims are: American Airlines, Inc., AMR Corporation, Continental Airlines, Inc., AirTran Airlines, Burns International Services Corporation, Burns International Security Services Corporation, Globe Airport Security Services, Inc., Globe Aviation Services Corporation, Huntleigh USA Corporation and Pinkerton's, Inc.

[4] Pub. L. 107-42, § 408(b)(2), 215 Stat. 230.

1. Common Law Negligence

9 If the court applies New York's common law negligence principles, the aviation defendants' liability for the terrorist attacks will depend upon the court's determination of whether the aviation defendants owed a specific duty to the ground plaintiffs. An airline never has been charged with a duty that is designed to prevent the use of its aircraft as weapons; and the September 11th terrorist attacks were so unique that they cannot be analogized to previous pilot error or mechanical failure cases. Here the aviation defendants had no relationship to the ground damage plaintiffs who suffered their losses hundreds of miles from the intended flight paths of the seized aircraft. New York does not impose a duty to control the criminal conduct of third persons absent a special relationship existing between the defendant and the plaintiffs.

10 Further, New York courts have made clear that the existence and scope of a legal duty running from a defendant to a plaintiff is largely determined by policy considerations, including: (1) the reasonable expectations of the parties and of society; (2) the proliferation of claims; (3) the likelihood of unlimited or insurer-like liability; (4) disproportionate risk and reparation allocation; and (5) the expansion or limitation of new channels of liability. If the court places the appropriate weight on the overwhelmingly negative policy implications of creating a duty of care owed by airlines to ground plaintiffs for the criminal acts of terrorists who seized control of their aircraft, then the court should dismiss the ground damage claims.

2. Federal Standard of Care

11 The court may decide that federal law dictates the standard of care in the area of aviation security. Federal law governing aviation security makes it clear that the duty of the aviation defendants with respect to terrorism was to protect passengers and crew, not persons and property on the ground. Prior to September 11th 2001, the FAA's comprehensive set of regulations governing aviation security required that the aviation defendants implement certain security measures based on the federal government's terrorist threat assessments.

12 The FAA required that each airline adopt a mandatory *Air Carrier Standard Security Program* (A.C.S.S.P.). According to publicly available information, prior to September 11th, the FAA required airlines to follow a "common strategy" (which had the force of law) for dealing with terrorist attacks on civil aircraft. The "common strategy" required airlines to cooperate with the terrorists during a hijacking for the purpose of protecting passengers and crew from imminent danger. This required compliance with the "common strategy" was inconsistent with any purported duty to protect individuals on the ground. Prior to September 11th, cooperation with hijackers was expected to result in the safe landing of the aircraft, albeit at a potentially hostile location. Further, the ground damage caused on September 11th did not result from any negligence of the airlines' pilots flying the aircraft in the course of cooperating with the hijackers, the aircraft (except for United Flight 93) were flown intentionally into the ground targets by the terrorists. If the court applies federal law to the

motion to dismiss ground damage claims, the court should conclude that the aviation defendants were actually prohibited by law from responding to the September 11th terrorist attacks in any other manner.

3. Plaintiffs' Anticipated Arguments

Plaintiffs' opposition papers to the motions to dismiss are due on March 7, 13
2003. Plaintiffs will vigorously attempt to prevent the dismissal of this large group of lawsuits and potential lawsuits. Addressing the aviation defendants' common law negligence arguments, the plaintiffs likely would assert that no court has ever held that airlines do not owe a duty to ground victims. The plaintiffs would point out that victims of an aircraft crash caused by the negligence of an airline should recover damages regardless of whether the victims were injured on the aircraft's flight path or outside the scheduled flight path.

In opposition to the aviation defendants' arguments based upon federal law, 14
plaintiffs likely would argue that no federal aviation statute has ever been interpreted to exclude ground victims from the class of persons to whom an air carrier owes a duty. For example, plaintiffs likely would argue that FAA regulations are intended to keep civil aircraft safely in the air and are therefore intended to protect people and property on the ground. Plaintiffs would also point out that most provisions of the FAA regulations do not refer to any particular class of intended beneficiaries and are not intended to protect only passengers.

4. Expected Outcome of the Aviation Defendants' Motion to Dismiss Ground Damage Claims

In light of the unprecedented nature of the terrorist attacks giving rise to the 15
September 11th civil litigation, it is difficult to predict Judge Hellerstein's decision on the defendants' motions to dismiss ground damage claims. However, if Judge Hellerstein denies the aviation defendants' motion to dismiss, the United States Court of Appeals for the Second Circuit is likely to reverse such a decision on appeal. The Second Circuit generally is known to take a more academic approach in reaching decisions than the District Courts and will likely focus on the policy concerns, discussed above, which clearly favor the dismissal of the ground damage claims against the aviation defendants.

B. Passenger Claims

It would be difficult to obtain dismissal on the pleadings of the passenger 16
claims against the aviation defendants, particularly against the carrier airlines. No such motion to dismiss passenger claims against the carrier airlines has been filed. Courts generally hold that airlines, as common carriers, have a duty to exercise the highest degree of care for the safety of its passengers, New York has held that a carrier is to exercise the duty of care "which a reasonably prudent carrier would exercise under the circumstances."[5]

[5] *Gallin v. Delta Air*, 106 Misc. 2d 477, 480 (1980), *aff'd* 86 A.D.2d 782 (2d Dep't 1982).

17 The passengers' claims will likely hinge on foreseeability issues and the court will have few cases upon which to rely for guidance. Not since the First World War has an even remotely comparable attack given rise to civil litigation. In the matter of the sinking of the passenger ship, the *Lusitania*, by a German submarine, the Southern District of New York decided that the owner of the *Lusitania* was not liable in negligence for the deaths of its passengers.[6]

C. The United States Government's Intervention

18 While the claims arising out of the September 11th terrorist attacks are based on traditional tort claims, the information sought by plaintiffs through discovery involves a large quantity of material considered to be *Sensitive Security Information* (SSI). Only persons with an operational "need to know" are usually allowed access to SSI.

19 On June 28, 2002, the *Transportation Safety Administration* (TSA) through the office of the United States Attorney for the Southern District of New York moved to intervene in the September 11th civil litigation for the purpose of enforcing the nondisclosure requirements concerning aviation-related *Sensitive Security Information* (SSI). The court granted the TSA's motion and ordered discovery stayed in the action.

20 On September 12, 2002, the TSA submitted a report to the court in which it proposed discovery procedures that it viewed as necessary to protect SSI material from disclosure. The TSA's current position is that any disclosure of SSI material must be cleared by the government and any disputes arising from the government's decision to prohibit the disclosure of SSI should be referred to either the TSA for an administrative agency ruling or an appropriate Circuit Court of Appeals, possibly either the Court of Appeals for the Second Circuit or the Court of Appeals for the District of Columbia Circuit.

II. Going Forward After 9/11

21 As previously noted, the commercial aircraft operators involved in the 9/11 litigation should not be charged with a legal duty running to ground victims. Once a legal duty is established, the scope of that duty is determined by the reasonable foreseeability of the event. Therefore, even if the 9/11 aircraft operators were charged with a general legal duty running to ground victims, the courts, particularly at the appellate level, should determine that such a duty does not extend to the 9/11 attacks because prior to September 11, 2001, the use of commercial aircraft as weapons of mass destruction was not reasonably forseeable.

22 In civil litigation arising from a post-9/11 terrorist attack involving the use of a commercial aircraft, any negligence analysis would take into account the TSA's role in security screening and its exclusive responsibility in directing

[6] *The Lusitania*, 251 F. 715, 732 (S.D.N.Y. 1918).

law enforcement activity related to the safety of passengers on an aircraft involved in an aircraft piracy offense. The TSA's involvement in aviation security should reduce an aircraft operator's liability exposure for terrorist attacks because it would be difficult for victims to establish that the aircraft operators owed them a duty to protect from terrorist attacks because current federal regulations now charge the TSA with that duty. However, if a court did find such a general duty on the part of aircraft operators, that duty likely would be extended to require aircraft operators to protect against the risk of their aircraft being utilized as weapons because the unforeseeability argument is no longer available to the operators.

Terrorists might also utilize general aviation aircraft to carry out future attacks. For example, terrorists could purchase or lease an aircraft at relatively modest cost and take-off from a low use airport. The terrorists could utilize such an aircraft in a more severe manner than the 9/11 attacks by filling the aircraft with explosives or a "dirty bomb" and targeting such venues as high-rise buildings, power plants and open air stadia. The lessor of the aircraft could be susceptible to liability exposure; however, a commercial operator is not likely to be involved in such a scenario. 23

In addition to a tragic repeat of the 9/11 ground target attacks, the aviation industry is also susceptible to other forms of terrorist attacks. For example, the threat of attack on aircraft from shoulder launched *surface to air missiles* (SAMs) recently has become a reality. If terrorists successfully conduct an attack using SAMs launched from within an airport's perimeter, there should not be extensive, if any, liability exposure for the aircraft operator because the TSA in consultation with airport operators and law enforcement authorities has the ability to deploy personnel to ensure airport perimeter access security. Further, if a SAM were launched from outside an airport's perimeter, an aircraft operator should not be exposed to any liability because the security of such an area would presumably be the responsibility of law enforcement. However, there have been media reports that commercial operators could be required to equip their aircraft with apparatus that deflect SAMs. In the somewhat remote event that such a requirement were instituted, aircraft operators possibly could be charged with a duty to protect against SAM attacks for purposes of civil litigation. 24

The most important question an insurer must ask in determining whether it will ever again voluntarily participate in the aviation terrorist insurance market is how easily an aircraft can come under the control of terrorists or be targeted from the ground. In both instances, the liability exposure for the operator would be determined for the most part by the scope of the duty which a court determines that the operator owes to the victims in question. An American court applying post 9/11 federal law should find that the responsibility for maintaining commercial aviation security has been significantly removed from commercial aircraft operators and undertaken by the government. However, in the final analysis it is very difficult to predict a likely scenario of lia- 25 bility although that should not lead us to think a large liability exposure does not exist for the aviation industry. The events of 9/11 were certainly not predicted but they happened and there are still determined and calculating individuals out there focusing there minds to hatch the next plot.

III. Conclusion

26 In light of the inconceivable circumstances that characterized the September 11th attacks, the claims of ground damage plaintiffs are likely to be dismissed, probably following appellate review by the Court of Appeals for the Second Circuit. The dismissal of ground damage claims would significantly reduce the scope of the September 11th civil litigation.

27 The outcome of the passenger claims, particularly those claims against the carrier airlines, are not likely to be dismissed at an early stage of the litigation.

28 Even if negligence were established against the defendants by all possible claimants the statutory liability limitations as well as limited available insurance would make it impossible for such judgments to be paid in any appreciable amount.

29 The administration of the VCF will have a significant bearing on the eventual number of personal injury and wrongful death plaintiffs involved in the September 11th litigation. In particular, the outcome of the recently filed lawsuit challenging the method of calculating VCF awards could have a substantial bearing on the number of victims who pursue litigation. Further, Judge Hellerstein is moving the September 11th litigation along at an efficient pace which should allow personal injury and wrongful death victims to make well-informed assessments of their chances of success in civil litigation prior to the December 22, 2003 deadline for filing VCF claims.

THE SEPTEMBER 11TH VICTIM COMPENSATION FUND OF 2001

Peter H. Woodin*

The terrorist attacks in the United States on 11 September 2001, killed 2,998 people. The victims were citizens of more than 40 countries. Ten days after these terrible events, the United States Congress passed the *Air Transportation Safety and System Stabilization Act* (the Act). This legislation capped the liability of the airlines whose planes were used in the attacks at the limits of the airlines' liability insurance coverage, capped the liability of various other potential defendants at specified amounts, and established venue for all litigation arising out of the terrorist attacks in the federal court in New York City. 1

The legislation also created the *September 11th Victim Compensation Fund of 2001* (VCF). As set forth in the Act, the VCF is a no-fault, administrative compensation scheme designed to provide prompt and fair compensation to the victims of the September 11th attacks and their families. The VCF is no-fault in that claimants have no need to demonstrate liability on the part of any party in order to receive compensation. It is an administrative scheme in that the VCF operates entirely outside the court system. Under the Act, the VCF is structured to work in tandem with compensation received from other sources, such as governmental benefits and insurance proceeds, to assure that the September 11th victims are provided for financially. Those who choose to participate in the VCF are barred by statute from bringing any lawsuit to recover for their personal injury or wrongful death claims, and filing a lawsuit to recover on those claims waives the right to file a claim with the VCF. 2

The Act directed the U.S. Attorney General to appoint a Special Master to design and implement the compensation program. The Special Master was directed to promulgate governing rules for the VCF within 90 days of the passage of the Act, or by 21 December 2001. On 26 November 2001, Attorney 3

* Peter Woodin is Deputy Special Master of the September 11th Victim Compensation Fund of 2001. The opinions expressed herein are his own. Further information about the VCF, including the text of the enabling legislation, governing rules and regulations, and current claim statistics, can be found at www.usdoj.gov/victimcompensation/index.html.

General Ashcroft appointed Kenneth R. Feinberg as the Special Master of the VCF.

4 Drafted and passed in 10 days during a time of great national crisis, the Act is far from a model of legislative draftsmanship. Those provisions creating the VCF failed to address numerous issues and provided only very uncertain guidance on many others. During the two months prior to the Special Master's appointment, the *Department of Justice* (DOJ) made a tremendous effort to identify and address, at least on a preliminary basis, many of the issues that the Special Master would need to resolve in the process of creating the program. In October and November 2001, the DOJ promulgated extensive requests for comments from the public at large, seeking input on the many difficult issues the DOJ had identified. In response, the DOJ received thousands of submissions, from victims and their families, from lawyers, from businesses and insurers, from elected officials, and from many others.

5 On 21 December 2001, 25 days after his appointment, Mr. Feinberg promulgated interim regulations laying out in detail the VCF's structural and operational framework. While not final, the interim regulations permitted the VCF to begin operation immediately. At that time Mr. Feinberg also requested public comment on the interim regulations, and over the next two months he undertook an intensive process of reaching out to all parties with an interest in the VCF. A major part of this process included numerous meetings with the families of the victims, with elected officials, with the business community, with insurers, with lawyers and many other constituencies. The final regulations governing the VCF were promulgated on 13 March 2002.

6 In designing the compensation program, there were three fundamental components of the program that had to be addressed by the Special Master. These were eligibility, procedure and compensation.

7 Eligibility involves the determination of who should receive compensation from the VCF. The operative language in the enabling legislation directs that compensation should go to those who were "present" at the sites of the airline crashes either at the time of the crashes or "in the immediate aftermath", and who suffered "physical harm or death" as a result. There were three major issues involved in determining the scope of eligibility. The first was exactly what was meant by "present" at the site – exactly how wide a circle should be drawn? For the World Trade Center site, should it be Manhattan below 14th St., which was the portion of Manhattan evacuated and closed to public access in the immediate aftermath of the attacks? Should Brooklyn be included, because the debris plume from the fallen towers drifted across the East River and down on houses and streets in that borough? Or should it include the entire New York metropolitan area, where millions of people saw the events unfold as they watched from their windows or stood on street corners? The second eligibility issue involved "immediate aftermath" – how much time should constitute the "immediate aftermath" of the attacks? Is it hours, days, or for rescue

workers perhaps even weeks? And the third eligibility issue involved the definition of "physical harm". How serious must the harm have been to deserve compensation? Is smoke and dust inhalation sufficient? What about emotional distress, and what about latent injuries?

The final regulations embodied difficult choices. The term "present" was de- 8
fined as essentially presence within a zone of danger, i.e., a geographical area around each of the crash sites within which there was danger of injury or death as a result of the aircraft crashes or falling debris. The term "immediate aftermath" was interpreted to mean that a claimant must have suffered harm within 12 hours, and, for rescuers, within 96 hours. For "physical harm", the regulations require that the claimant must have sought medical treatment within 72 hours and injury must have resulted in at least temporary partial disability.

Procedure involves the process by which claims are filed, evaluated, deter- 9
mined and award proceeds distributed. Again, the statutory language provided uncertain guidance at best. Under the Act, a claim must be filed by the victim or, if the victim has died, by the Personal Representative of the victim. In cases involving deceased victims, who should act as the Personal Representative, and how should the award be divided up? And what about hearings – should every claimant have the opportunity for a hearing? If a claimant wishes, should he or she be able to have the claim processed without any hearing at all? How should the hearings be conducted, and should they be adversarial or non-adversarial? Although the statute provides that there is no appeal from the final determination of the Special Master, should there be some process for internal administrative review of eligibility and compensation decisions? A significant problem was also presented by the fact that, under the Act, the waiver of the claimant's right to file a lawsuit occurs upon the filing of a claim with the VCF. But, since each claim must be individually determined based upon the facts and circumstances of the victim, an individual claimant does not know what he or she will receive from the VCF until after the claim has been filed and any recourse to the courts has been waived. This created significant perceptions of unfairness – claimants would have to decide whether to file a claim with the VCF, or instead to preserve their right to file a lawsuit, without knowing what their ultimate recovery from the VCF might be.

The final regulations address these various issues. The VCF looks to state law 10
for the appropriate identity of the Personal Representative and for the distribution of the award. As for claim processing, the final regulations create two separate claim processing tracks, and claimants are free to choose one track or the other. In the first track, a claimant submits all of the required information and a "presumed award" is calculated pursuant to a complex formula based on a variety of factors relevant to the claim valuation determination. Under this track there is no hearing but, if a claimant is dissatisfied with the presumed award, the claimant can seek further review in a hearing before the Special Master or his designee. In the second track the claimant does not receive the offer of a presumed award, but instead proceeds directly to a hearing before

the Special Master or his designee. At the hearing, which is non-adversarial in nature, the claimant can submit additional information that might not be considered in the calculation of the presumed award, and can bring experts, economists, lawyers or anyone else to present evidence at the hearing. With respect to prefiling information about potential awards, the VCF regulations set forth comprehensive charts which give specific guidance concerning economic loss based, in cases where victims have died, on the victim's age, the number and the ages of dependents in the victim's family, the victim's annual income, and other factors. Additionally, Mr. Feinberg meets on an ongoing basis with individuals who have not yet decided whether to file claims, in order to discuss award parameters and other compensation issues. This is particularly useful for potential claims where the victim's income was higher than the top income level reflected on the presumed award compensation charts, which provide economic loss amounts based on annual incomes up to a maximum of $ 231,000 (the 98th percentile for U.S. incomes).

11 Compensation issues were perhaps the most difficult to resolve. The overarching challenge faced by the Special Master was how to devise a system that recognizes loss on an individual basis but that is fair and consistent across the universe of claimants.

12 The statute itself sets forth a three-part award determination. First, the Special Master is directed to determine "the extent of the harm to the claimant, including any economic and noneconomic losses". Second, the Special Master is directed to determine the amount of compensation "based on the harm to the claimant, the facts of the claim, and the individual circumstances of the claimant". And third, the Special Master is directed to reduce the amount of compensation "by the amount of the collateral source compensation the claimant has received or is entitled to receive" as a result of the terrorist attacks.

13 Again, the Special Master was faced with a number of difficult issues that had to be resolved. Non-economic loss is defined in the statute to include the traditional tort elements of pain and suffering, mental anguish, loss of enjoyment of life and all other types of non-pecuniary loss. But on what principled basis should the Special Master quantify, in dollars and cents, each victim's pain and suffering, particularly given the need for consistency across the universe of claimants? And whose pain and suffering and grief should be quantified – the victim's? – the surviving spouse's and the children's? And exactly how should economic loss be quantified – what elements of loss should be considered and whose economic loss should be included? The issue of collateral source offsets was extremely difficult as well. Collateral sources are defined somewhat circularly in the Act: "The term 'collateral sources' means all collateral sources, including life insurance, pension funds, death benefit programs" and governmental benefits paid as a result of the attacks. But what about all of the charitable support the victims have received and will receive? And what about situations where life insurance proceeds or other benefits are paid to individuals who might not share in the VCF award?

The Special Master's task was complicated by a fundamental tension embodied in the compensation provisions of the Act. Specifically, should the VCF operate more like a safety net, i.e. stepping in to ensure that everyone ultimately receives a fair and appropriate level of compensation when all sources are considered together? Or should it strive to provide a level of recovery more closely akin to what could be obtained as a full measure of tort recovery in the civil justice system, which in some cases might be $ 20 million or even more? Both approaches are reflected in different provisions of the statute, and the Special Master received a significant amount of public comment about this issue. 14

Ultimately, here again the final regulations embodied difficult choices. For non-economic loss in cases involving the victim's death, the Special Master set a flat amount of $ 250,000 for each victim's pain and suffering, a flat amount of $ 100,000 for the non-pecuniary losses suffered by a surviving spouse, and an additional $ 100,000 for the non-pecuniary losses suffered by each dependent of the victim. With respect to the calculation of economic loss, the Special Master used a traditional damages approach that relied on national data from the Bureau of Labor Statistics (e.g., average work life, general wage growth across all employment sectors etc.) to determine lost future earnings – i.e., a calculation of the victim's income plus benefits over the victim's estimated work life, adjusted for taxes and wage growth, and then discounted to present value in order to yield a lump sum amount. Certain favorable assumptions were built in to the economic loss formula. These include the assumption of a constant growth in income over the victim's working life, with no periods of negative wage growth or unemployment, and a constant level of benefits. For collateral source offsets, the Special Master determined that charitable contributions to victims and their families would not be deducted, and there would be no deduction for benefits paid to a non-beneficiary of the VCF award or for contingent benefits and self-funded programs such as 401(k) retirement accounts. 15

As of this writing (June 13, 2003), the VCF has been in operation for almost 18 months. It has received a total of 1,823 claims, of which 922 are claims on behalf of deceased victims and 901 are claims involving personal injury. The VCF has issued 521 award letters and received 409 responses: 323 claimants have accepted the award, 86 claimants have asked for a hearing, and 112 claimants have not yet responded to their award letters. The average award for deceased victims, after offsets have been deducted, is $ 1,438,646, and the median award for deceased victims, after offsets have been deducted, is $ 1,208,047. Awards for deceased victims have ranged from a low of $ 250,000 to a high of $ 6 million. 16

In the final analysis, the September 11th Victim Compensation Fund of 2001 is unique in American history. Compensation on this scale of magnitude, tax free and paid out of the federal treasury, is unprecedented, and Congress' passage of the Act reflected the same vast and immediate outpouring of support 17 that caused the American people collectively to give more than $ 1 billion in private charitable support for the victims in a matter of weeks. As well-intentioned as it was, however, the creation of the VCF raises difficult public policy issues that have provoked considerable debate. First and perhaps most fundamentally, is the VCF a good idea? While the U.S. government often steps in to assist the victims of disasters, never has it done so before on a scale such as this. Moreover, the victims of the 1993 World Trade Center bombing have never received similar compensation and in fact, more than 10 years later, their lawsuits are still wending their way through the courts. Nor has anything similar been paid to the victims of the Oklahoma City bombing, or to the victims of the U.S. embassy bombings in Kenya and Tanzania. Is that fair? And now, having created a program to compensate September 11th victims, has a precedent been established that will require similar compensation to the victims of future terrorist acts?

18 Other difficult issues are raised by the structure and operation of the VCF. Under the enabling legislation the Special Master has enormous discretion, essentially unreviewable by the courts, to set individual awards. Is this desirable? Does it promote a perception of equity and fairness, or is there too much danger that discretion can lead to arbitrariness and inconsistency? Earlier this year a small group of victims' families sued the Special Master, alleging that the rules and regulations he promulgated were arbitrary and inconsistent and did not fairly reflect the intent of Congress as expressed in the Act. In early May the federal trial court ruled that the Special Master had acted within the bounds of the discretion afforded him by Congress. Debate has also centered on a closely related issue, namely, instead of leaving it up to a Special Master to set individual awards which under the Act will necessarily vary greatly from individual to individual, whether it would be fairer for every victim and family to receive the same amount. This approach – a uniform award for all victims – is utilized in several other federal death benefit statutes, and many believe such an approach should have been adopted for the VCF.

19 Under the Act all claims must be filed with the VCF no later than December 22, 2003. A relatively low percentage of potential claims involving deceased victims – less than one third – have been filed through the first 18 months of VCF operation. Various explanations have been advanced, including that (1) the immediate financial needs of many victim's families have been met by private charities, which reportedly have distributed an average of more than $ 150,000 to each family, and thus there has been no immediate financial pressure to file for compensation; (2) the loss of loved ones is still relatively recent and grief remains strong, and families are simply not emotionally ready to accept the finality of loss which filing a claim with the VCF will necessarily entail; (3) issues of how to distribute the award among family members – e.g., how much to aging parents, how much to grown children, etc. – have the potential to be extremely divisive, and families do not want to confront these issues at a time when they are still looking to each other for emotional support; and (4) uncertainty about how the Special Master will apply the VCF rules

and regulations and exercise his discretion in determining final award amounts. At the end of the day, however, because he believes that the award amounts are fair and that the alternative – the delay, expense and uncertainty of litigation – is simply too unattractive, Mr. Feinberg expects that the vast majority of eligible claimants will ultimately decide to file claims with the VCF.

Developments in the Procedural Means for Resolution of Mass Tort Litigation in the United States

Linda S. Mullenix*

1 It is now generally recognized that mass tort litigation is a litigation phenomenon that has developed in the United States during the past twenty-five years. The first generation of mass tort litigation focused on a series of cases that are familiar to all practitioners in this area: litigation involving asbestos, Dalkon Shield, DES, Bendectin, and *Agent Orange*. This first wave of mass tort cases was succeeded by mass tort litigation dealing with an array of toxic exposure, medical devices, and pharmaceutical cases. This litigation dealt with products such as breast and penile implants, heart valves, orthopedic bone screws, albuterol, Fen/phen/redux, blood products, and hip replacements, to name a few. The 1991 Gulf War gave rise to an attempted mass tort litigation brought by veterans based on "Gulf War syndrome", with claims similar to those that formed the basis for the *Agent Orange* litigation. Finally, the events of September 11th, 2001 constituted a mass disaster for the twenty-first century.

2 As is equally well known, the American legal system has attempted to resolve these massive litigations through a variety of procedural and substantive mechanisms. The procedural mechanisms include class actions, consolidations, multidistrict litigations, claims facilities, alternative dispute resolution, and fund approaches. Mixed procedural and substantive mechanisms have included resolution of mass tort claims under bankruptcy auspices. Mass tort litigation also has expanded tort law to embrace theories relating to indeterminate plaintiffs, indeterminate defendants, various theories of enterprise liability, probabilistic proof, and the refinement of threshold standards for the admissibility of expert evidence (otherwise known as the problem of "junk science" in the courts).

3 Any understanding of the American judicial system's views about mass tort litigation must appreciate that the judicial system's attitudes have changed over time. The receptivity of American courts to innovative procedures, as well as the expansion of evidentiary and substantive tort law, has varied over

* Morris and Rita Atlas Chair in Advocacy, The University of Texas School of Law.

the past twenty five years. In addition, any appreciation of the problems of mass tort litigation must take into account the structure of the American legal system, which includes independent federal and state courts systems. Mass tort litigation in the United States has been additionally complicated by the intersection of the dual-system of federal and state courts, with overlapping and concurrent jurisdiction.

This paper is divided into three parts. Part I sets forth a general discussion of the time-frame in which mass tort litigation developed in the United States, and the ways in which the American legal system has adjusted to this new litigation phenomenon. The second section canvasses the variety of procedural means for possibly resolving mass tort litigation. This discussion is intertwined with the temporal framework suggested in Part I. The last portion of the paper contains some concluding remarks concerning the development of procedural means for resolving mass tort litigation in the United States, as these procedural means have evolved over three decades. These remarks also reflect on the possible consequences of the World Trade Center Victims' Compensation Fund for resolution of mass tort claims in the future. 4

I. American Mass Tort Litigation in a Temporal Dimension

A. *Distinguishing Mass Accident and Mass Tort Cases*

Conventionally, most contemporary mass tort litigation attorneys and judges distinguish between mass accident and "true" mass tort cases. Mass accident cases typically are characterized as "single site, single-event" disasters. The most prevalent forms of mass accident cases are aeroplane crashes, train wrecks, hotel fires, structural collapses, and the like. It is generally agreed that the American judicial system is capable of resolving most mass accident cases for a variety of reasons. Mass accident cases tend to be confined to a single site and single event, the numbers of claimants are known and manageable, problems of proof tend to be easier to resolve, there are no "future" claimants, and applicable law problems are not complicated or are *de minimus*. 5

"True" mass torts are characterized by a different cluster of attributes. Mass tort litigation typically is characterized by geographic dispersion of claimants throughout the entire United States, or in some instances, throughout the world. Mass tort claimants may be temporally dispersed, as well. Complex mass torts may include claimants who are exposed to toxic substances over a twenty or thirty year span, but who do not manifest injury until many years after exposure (for example asbestos claimants). Many mass torts may include latent-injury of "future" claimants, such as asbestos, or DES claimants. The *Agent Orange* litigation included claims for unborn children, arising out of alleged genetic defects. 6

In addition to geographic and temporal dispersion, mass tort litigation typically is characterized by significantly large numbers of claimants, numbering in 7 the thousands, tens-of-thousands, or hundreds of thousands. The proposed class of nicotine-addicted claimants in the *Castano* tobacco litigation presumably numbered upwards of fifty million American citizens.[1] The actual number of claimants may be unknowable, particularly if the claimant class includes "future" claimants. The actual size of the claimant pool presents a fundamental problem for resolving these types of mass torts. Both plaintiff and defense counsel have a high interest in determining the nature and scope of possible recovery. Plaintiffs' attorneys are interested in maximizing the size of the claimant pool to maximize recovery; while defense attorneys are interested in ascertaining the potential scope and duration of their liabilities. The inability to agree on the size of the claimant pool complicates negotiation and resolution of large mass tort litigation.

8 Another characteristic of "true" mass tort litigation are difficult problems of evidence and proof. Most medical device, products, pharmaceutical, and toxic exposure mass torts hinge on complex issues of scientific evidence and causation. Mass tort cases typically rely on the reports and testimony of expert witnesses. The state of scientific evidence in support of the causation element of a particular mass tort may be mature or immature. In the breast implant mass tort litigation, for example, the scientific evidence was immature to support claims for systemic auto-immune injuries. Nonetheless, some of the defendants settled this mass tort even in light of immature science. Difficult issues of scientific proof also complicated the Bendectin and *Agent Orange* litigations.

9 In addition, many mass tort cases are complicated by problems of indeterminate plaintiffs and indeterminate defendants. The DES mass tort litigation is a classic example of the problem of indeterminate defendants, where women who had used DES twenty years earlier were unable to identify which manufacturer's DES they had consumed. Viable and unique affirmative defenses also may complicate the prosecution of a mass tort litigation. Such defenses include, for example, sovereign immunity and the military contractor defense, both of which played a major role in precipitating the resolution of the *Agent Orange* litigation.

10 Finally, American mass tort litigation also typically is characterized by complicated choice-of-law problems. In the American legal system, under *Erie* doctrine, federal courts are obligated to apply state substantive law to tort claims that are aggregated in the federal system. Because there is no general federal common tort law, federal courts must apply the laws of the implicated states. The possible application of multiple states, or fifty states' laws, have frequently induced federal courts to conclude that federal mass torts are unmanageable. At the state level, state courts involved in multi-state mass tort litigations face the same complicated choice-of-law problems and analyses.

[1] See *generally Castano v. The American Tobacco Co.*, 160 F.R.D. 544 (E.D. La. 1995).

B. Mass Tort Litigation, A Decade-by-Decade Overview

Mass tort litigation began to develop in the United States in the mid-to-late 1970s. One useful way to understand the judicial system's reactions to the developing problems of mass tort litigation is to appreciate that the judiciary's response varied over time. The judicial system's responses may usefully be divided into three separate periods, each spanning approximately a decade. 11

1. The First Decade of Mass Torts Litigation, 1975–1985

The five seminal major mass tort litigations in the United States almost all developed in the mid-to-late 1970s and ran their course through the mid-to-late 1980s. These five seminal mass tort cases included litigation relating to asbestos, *Agent Orange*, Dalkon Shield, Bendectin, and DES. Each of these mass tort litigations began as individual lawsuits, then progressed through various procedural stages, including consolidations, multi-district litigation (MDLs), class actions, class action settlements, or bankruptcy procedures. *Agent Orange* was resolved through a class action settlement class. Dalkon Shield was resolved through class action and ultimately through bankruptcy auspices. Asbestos class settlements failed, and virtually all the asbestos manufacturers went into bankruptcy. Individual asbestos claims, as well as consolidated asbestos claims, continue to be litigated today. Bendectin and DES class actions failed; small numbers of individual Bendectin and DES claims subsequently were pursued to mixed results. 12

During this first decade of mass tort litigation, the federal courts generally were not receptive to efforts to aggregate mass tort claims. The federal courts generally agreed that these proposed mass tort class actions comprised disparate claims that were not susceptible of common classwide proof of liability or damages. Some courts recognized that choice-of-law or jurisdictional problems undermined or subverted manageability. Other federal courts concluded that proceeding as a class action was not a superior means for resolving the dispute. Moreover, numerous federal courts relied on the Civil Rules Advisory Committee Note to the 1966 amendment to Fed. R. Civ. P. 23 (the class action rule), as counseling against using the class action to resolve mass accident cases. Consequently, the federal courts rebuffed repeated efforts to certify mass tort class actions, particularly proposed asbestos, Dalkon Shield, DES, and Bendectin classes. The only proposed class action that was conditionally certified during this era was the proposed *Agent Orange* class. The *Agent Orange* class certification largely was the result of the efforts of the supervising managerial judge in the Eastern District of New York (Judge Jack Weinstein).[2] 13

2. The Second Decade of Mass Tort Litigation, 1986–1996

By the mid-1980s, the emergence of the new litigation phenomenon of mass tort litigation – as exemplified by the five seminal cases of asbestos, *Agent Or-* 14

[2] See *In re "Agent Orange" Prods. Liab. Litig.*, 818 F.2d 145 (2d Cir. 1987).

ange, Bendectin, DES, and Dalkon Shield – had become apparent. This decade was characterized by three separate initiatives, one coming from the major legal institutional organizations, and another set of initiatives from the judiciary itself. Yet a third set of initiatives would come from the American Congress, which also would begin legislative study and statutory proposals to deal with mass tort litigation.

15 During this decade, almost all the major institutional law reform organizations in the United States would undertake studying the mass tort litigation phenomenon, in order to define the problems and propose recommendations for resolving mass tort cases. This decade was characterized by a flurry of institutional and academic research and study of the mass tort litigation phenomenon. The purpose of these studies was to provide a working definition of mass tort litigation, as well as possible proposals for aggregating and resolving mass tort claims.

16 At the same time, a number of federal courts would take bold and innovative steps towards resolving what they perceived to be a mass tort litigation crisis in the courts. Because of the perceived crisis, a number of federal courts permitted various means of aggregating torts claims, either through consolidations, class actions, or MDL procedures. In justifying such actions, federal courts either repudiated prior precedents, or expanded the reading and interpretation of existing rules or statutes.

17 In terms of institutional reform efforts, the major judicial and extra-judicial organizations turned their attentions to the emerging problems of mass tort litigation. In 1986–87, the American Law Institute began its *Complex Litigation Project*, with the goal of proposing recommendations for reforming the multidistrict litigation statute (28 U.S.C. § 1407), and proposing a federalized choice-of-law regime. The *Complex Litigation Project* surveyed the problems of mass tort litigation, made several legislative proposals to Congress, and was ultimately completed and published in 1994.[3] In this same period, the ALI launched another project entitled the *Enterprise Responsibility for Personal Injury*, which *Reporters' Study* in 1991 included an analysis of the characteristics of mass tort litigation and a discussion of the possible means for aggregating and resolving mass tort cases.[4]

18 In 1987, the American Bar Association created a Mass Tort Commission, which similarly studied the emerging problems of mass tort litigation and made a report in 1989. The Commission's report included recommendations to the general membership. The A.B.A. Mass Tort Commission's proposals eventually were defeated by the general membership in 1990. In the late 1980s

[3] See American Law Institute, *Complex Litigation: Statutory Recommendations and Analysis* (1994).

[4] See American Law Institute, *Enterprise Responsibility for Personal Injury* (Reporters' Study 1991).

the Rand Institute for Civil Justice, a private think tank that conducts empirical research studies of the American legal system, embarked on a systematic study of mass tort litigation. In 1988 the Rand Institute published an analytical model for studying mass tort litigation, entitled: *Resolution of Mass Torts: Towards a Framework for Evaluation of Aggregative Procedures.*[5]

The United States Congress similarly began studying the problems relating to 19
mass tort litigation, with a view towards proposing statutory reforms. Beginning in 1988, the House of Representatives and the Senate introduced various pieces of legislation entitled the Multiparty, Multiforum Jurisdiction Act. The purpose of this proposed legislation was to amend Title 28 of the United States Code to add a provision on multiparty, multiforum jurisdiction, as well as a federal statutory choice-of-law provision. This bill was revised and reintroduced in several successive sessions of Congress through the late 1980s and into the 1990s.[6]

Finally, during this decade the federal courts reversed their previous refusal to 20
aggregate mass tort claims through class certification or the creation of mass tort MDLs. Reversing course, the courts began to permit certification of statewide or nationwide mass tort class actions. The most notable cases signaling this reversal was the Fifth Circuit Court of Appeals decision in *Jenkins v. Raymark Industries*,[7] upholding certification of a Texas class of asbestos claimants, and the Third Circuit Court of Appeal's affirmation of the class certification of a nationwide class of plaintiffs in the *School Asbestos Litigation*,[8] based chiefly on contract and property damage claims. The expansive holdings and interpretative language in these cases signaled a new receptivity in federal courts to allowing the class mechanism to aggregate and settle mass tort claims. In 1987, the Second Circuit Court of Appeals upheld the *Agent Orange* class certification and settlement class.[9] In 1991, the Judicial Panel on Multidistrict Litigation finally approved the creation of an asbestos MDL, after the Panel had previously rejected such an MDL on five previous occasions.[10] Following these precedents, a federal district court in the Eastern District of Louisiana certified a nationwide tobacco-addiction class of some fifty million claimants in 1995.[11]

[5] Mark A. Peterson/Molly Selvin, *Resolution of Mass Torts: Toward a Framework for Evaluation of Aggregative Procedures* (Rand, The Institute for Civil Justice, 1988).

[6] See e.g., The Multiparty, Multiforum Jurisdiction Act of 1993 (H.R. 1100, 103rd Cong., 1st Sess.); the Multiparty, Multiforum Jurisdiction Act of 1991 (H.R. 2450, 102nd Cong., 2d Sess.); the Multiparty, Multiforum Jurisdiction Act of 1990 (H.R. 3406, 101st Cong., 2d Sess).

[7] 782 F.2d 468 (5th Cir. 1986).

[8] 789 F.2d 996 (3d Cir. 1986).

[9] 818 F.2d 145 (2d Cir. 1987).

[10] *In re Asbestos Prods. Liab. Litig.*, 771 F. Supp. 415 (J.P.M.D.L. 1991).

[11] *Castano v. The American Tobacco Co.*, 160 F.R.D. 544 (E.D. La. 1995).

3. The Third Decade of Mass Tort Litigation, 1996-Present Trends

21 Through the early-to-mid-1990s, federal courts continued to be receptive to new and innovative ways of thinking about mass tort litigation. The academic literature and judicial opinions from this period reflect a growing consensus concerning a "crisis" in the courts created by the presence of large numbers of mass tort claims on court dockets. This "crisis mentality" inspired many state and federal judges to take charge of their dockets and to seek innovative means for resolving mass tort litigation.

22 By the mid-1990s, however, a third stage of reaction began to emerge in the federal courts. A precursor of this counter-revolution was anticipated in a Fifth Circuit Court of Appeals decision in 1991, in a case denominated *Cimino v. Raymark Industries.*[12] In this case the trial level court had approved a multi-phase class action trial plan which would include the trial of damages by statistical sampling. The Fifth Circuit rejected this concept, concluding that the proposed trial plan was not really a trial plan at all, and violated defendants' rights to due process and a fair trial.[13] Thus, the Fifth Circuit, which previously had endorsed the asbestos class in *Jenkins v. Raymark*, drew the line at innovative trial plans. However, on remand of that case, the trial court reconfigured the class action as a combination *Jenkins* class plus a Rule 42 consolidation. Subsequently, the multiphase trial of the *Cimino* case employed a statistical sampling methodology for trying damages.

23 By the mid-1990s, considered reaction against mass tort class actions began to emerge among the federal courts, in a landmark series of cases. In 1995, the Seventh Circuit Court of Appeals, in *In the Matter of Rhone-Poulenc Rorer, Inc.*,[14] repudiated a nationwide class action consisting of hemophiliacs infected by the AIDS virus as a consequence of using the defendants' tainted blood products. In that same year, the Third Circuit Court of Appeals rejected a so-called settlement class in *In re General Motors Corp. Pick-Up Truck Fuel Tank Prods. Liab. Litig.*,[15] a decision which set the stage for closer scrutiny of the concept of settlement classes. A few months later, in 1996, the Fifth Circuit Court of Appeals struck down the nationwide tobacco-addiction class in *Castano v. The American Tobacco Co.*,[16] the class that had been certified by the Louisiana trial court. In that same year, the Sixth Circuit Court of Appeals in *In re American Medical Systems, Inc.*,[17] struck down a mass tort class action based on defective penile implants, and the Third Circuit Court of Appeals rejected the global asbestos settlement class in *Georgine v. Amchem Prods. Inc.*[18]

[12] Order Certifying Class, December 29, 1989 (E.D. Tex. 1989)
[13] *In re Fibreboard Corp.*, 893 F.2d 706 (5th Cir. 1990).
[14] 51 F.3d 1293 (7th Cir. 1995).
[15] 55 F.3d 768 (3d Cir. 1995).
[16] 84 F.3d 734 (5th Cir. 1996).
[17] 75 F.3d 1069 (6th Cir. 1996).
[18] 83 F.3d 610 (3d Cir. 1996).

The federal judiciary's more careful scrutiny of mass tort initiatives culminated in two landmark Supreme Court decisions at the end of the 1990s: the Court's 1997 decision in *Amchem Products Inc. v. Windsor*,[19] and the Court's 1999 decision in *Ortiz v. Fibreboard Corp.*[20] In *Amchem*, the Supreme Court rejected a Rule 23(b)(3) global settlement class of asbestos claimants, and in 1999 the Supreme Court rejected a Rule 23(b)(1)(B) "limited fund" class settlement of asbestos claimants. The implications of both these decisions made it increasingly difficult for mass tort litigants to formulate, negotiate, and consummate mass tort settlement classes. The Supreme Court's pronouncements in both the *Amchem* and *Ortiz* decisions, with regard to class certification requirements, applied with equal force to the certification of litigation classes. As such, the two Supreme Court decisions made it more difficult for litigants to seek certification of mass tort class actions in the federal arena. 24

The consequence of these judicial decisions, beginning in the mid-1990s, is that it has become increasingly difficult (if not impossible) to pursue certification of a mass tort litigation class in federal courts. Likewise, it has become increasingly difficult to seek approval of proposed mass tort settlement classes. Nonetheless, at least four trends are discernible in the post-*Amchem* era. 25

First, the plaintiffs' mass tort bar has "regrouped" and chosen to pursue mass tort claims in state courts. The plaintiffs' bar now avoids federal courts generally, and instead seeks favorable state venues for filing and pursuing mass tort claims. Some efforts at the state court level have been successful either because such venues are plaintiff-favoring venues, or those courts have chosen not to follow federal rulings. Second, the federal judiciary remains receptive towards creating mass tort MDLs, in the hope that the creation of a mass tort MDL will lead to settlement or other resolution of the mass tort claims. Examples of recently-created MDLs involve litigation relating to the pharmaceuticals rezulin and baycol. Third, plaintiffs have chosen to resolve various mass tort claims not through litigation classes, but rather through the device of the medical monitoring class. The development of the medical monitoring class is a recent innovation on the American legal scene. Such classes are typically sought to be certified under the provisions of Fed. R. Civ. P. 23(b)(2). As discussed below, the development of the medical monitoring concept has been mixed. While most courts have rejected such efforts, particularly efforts to create medical monitoring classes for tobacco claimants, the Fen/phen/redux litigation ultimately was resolved by a medical monitoring class at the state level. Finally, bankruptcy had continued to be a means for resolving mass tort litigation into the twenty-first century. The breast implant litigation against the largest defendant, Dow Corning, ultimately has been resolved through bankruptcy auspices. 26

[19] 521 U.S. 591 (1997)
[20] 119 S. Ct. 2295 (1999).

27 Perhaps it is worth completing this current picture of the state of mass tort litigation in the United States by noting that the events of September 11th 2001 at the World Trade Center created a unique challenge for the American legal system. The immediate enactment of the legislation creating the Victims' Compensation Fund was motivated, in part, to avoid the creation of a new massive mass tort litigation. It remains to be seen how many World Trade Center claimants will avail themselves of the Fund auspices, and how many claimants will elect recourse to the ordinary tort system. Assuming that significant numbers of claimants opt-out of the Fund, then the judicial system will be faced with another mass tort.

II. Evolving Procedural Means for Resolving Mass Tort Litigation

28 The United States has experienced mass tort litigation for almost three decades, and the procedural means for collecting individual tort claims into an aggregate litigation are well-known and well-documented. In addition, the possibilities for post-aggregative procedures are also fairly well-known, well-tested, and well-considered. The following sections set forth these procedural possibilities, with some commentary on the evolving views of federal courts with regards to these procedural possibilities. It must first be acknowledged, however, that American courts continue to debate whether individual tort claims are susceptible to aggregation at all. Proponents of litigant autonomy insist that tort claims are tantamount to a natural law individual right, which natural law theory of tort prohibits any type of aggregative mass tort procedure. Proponents of judicial efficiency and economy, on the other hand, argue that justice demands the aggregative resolution of mass tort claims, lest claimants be denied relief through court congestion and delay.

A. *Mass Tort Class Actions (Fed. R. Civ. P. 23)*

29 Perhaps the most highly controverted problem of the last three decades has centered on the issue whether individual tort claims may be aggregated and resolved through the class action mechanism. This debate has itself centered on different problems at different times. The following discussion focuses on five areas of contention that have developed in class action arena regarding the suitability of the class action rule for resolving mass torts: (1) litigation classes, (2) settlement classes, (3) limited fund classes, (4) punitive damage classes, and (5) medical monitoring classes.

30 A quick primer of the American federal class action rule will assist understanding the context for these issues. Class action litigation is essentially *representational* litigation. As such the class is "represented" by a named plaintiff and class counsel. All other claimants are not parties to the suit, and are considered "absent" or "unnamed" class members. Because the absent class members are not actually present to oversee the conduct of the litigation and to supervise their own attorneys, class action litigation is imbued with due process concerns and due process protections for the absent class members.

Among these due process protections are the requirement that the court certify the proposed class action, evaluate the adequacy of class counsel and the proposed class representatives, provide notice in certain types of class actions, and approve any settlement before the case may be dismissed.

The American federal class action Rule 23 has been part of the Federal Rules of Civil Procedure since their enactment in 1938. The original class action rule was difficult to apply and was completely revised in 1966. The modern American class action rule has remained substantially unchanged since 1966 with one amendment in 1998 adding a provision for immediate interlocutory appeal of class certification orders. Other amendments to Rule 23 currently are pending, which amendments would add provisions for the court appointment of class counsel, determination of attorney fees, and enhancements to class settlement procedures. 31

Rule 23(a) currently contains four threshold requirements for class certification: numerosity, commonality, typicality, and adequacy. The adequacy requirement applies independently to require the court to assess the adequacy of class counsel and the class representative. If the threshold requirements of Rule 23(a) are met, then the proponents of the class certification must demonstrate to the court that the proposed class action may be certified under one of the provisions of Rule 23(b). There are three possible functional class categories in Rule 23(b), which are commonly known as (b)(1), (b)(2), and (b)(3) class actions. 32

Rule 23(b)(1) and (b)(2) class actions are mandatory classes. Any judgment reached in a Rule 23(b)(1) or (b)(2) class action binds all class members as a matter of *res judicata.* Class members may not exclude themselves, or "opt-out" of a (b)(1) or (b)(2) class action. These types of classes assume the homogeneity of the interests of the class members. Consequently, there is no requirement for notice, and no ability to opt-out of the class. Rule 23(b)(1) and (b)(2) class actions typically are not for monetary damages. The (b)(2) class is reserved for class actions that are predominantly seeking either declaratory or equitable relief. 33

The Rule 23(b)(3) class action category was created as part of the 1966 amendment to Rule 23. It is known as the damages opt-out class. This form of class action presumes heterogeneity among class members, and that not all class members will be situated exactly alike in the nature of their claims or damages. The major purpose for creation of the Rule 23(b)(3) class was to provide a vehicle for the so-called "negative value" or small-claims consumer class actions. That is, the Rule 23(b)(3) class was intended as a vehicle for permitting the aggregation of large numbers of claimants with very small claims, such that there is little or no economic incentive for an individual plaintiff to pursue legal relief, nor enough of an economic inducement for a plaintiff's attorney to undertake the representation. 34

35 In order to certify a Rule 23(b)(3) class action, the court must make two additional findings: that in the proposed class action common issues predominate over individual issues, and that pursuing the action through the class action mechanism is superior to any other means for resolving the dispute. In evaluating the "predominance" and "superiority" requirements, Rule 23(b)(3) lists four additional factors that a court may consider, which include consideration of whether the proposed class action would be manageable.

36 Finally, the Rule 23(b)(3) class action involves additional requirements that the Rule 23(b)(1) and (b)(2) classes do not. Rule 23(c)(2) requires that notice be provided to class members of the existence of the class, the nature of the claims and class counsel, the opportunity to appear by individual counsel, and the opportunity to exclude one's self from the class by a date certain. Any member of a Rule 23(b)(3) class who does not exclude him or herself by the cut-off date, is a member of the class and will be bound by the class judgment.

37 The remainder of the American class action rule, Rule 23(c), (d), and (e) deal largely with matters relating to the administration of the class action rule or settlement. These subdivisions provide for the possibility of subclasses, limited issues classes, orders governing the conduct of class actions, and judicial supervision of class actions. Rule 23(e) provides that no class action may be compromised or dismissed without the court's approval, which is a significant difference from ordinary litigation (where such court approval is not required). As a practical matter, American federal courts now routinely conduct "fairness" hearings as part of the Rule 23(e) settlement approval process. In addition, class members must receive notice of a pending fairness hearing, so that they may raise objections or appear at the hearing to voice those objections. The Supreme Court, in 2002, ruled that a person who wished to challenge the court's approval of a class action settlement must first have appeared at the fairness hearing and raised objections in order to have standing to bring an appeal. The Supreme Court rejected the argument that such an objector would have to formally intervene to subsequently bring an appeal.

1. Mass Tort Litigation Classes

38 The first locus of debate concerning the possible certification of proposed mass tort class actions centered on the problem of so-called "litigation" classes. A litigation class embodies the concept that a proposed class action is being certified in contemplation of actually being litigated and tried to a jury. By the end of the 1980s and into the 1990s, federal courts began to distinguish, in their judicial opinions, between the concepts of litigation classes and so-called settlement classes, which are discussed in the next section.

39 For approximately the first decade of mass tort litigation in the American courts, the courts fairly uniformly rejected the ability to certify proposed mass tort classes. Initially, courts viewed the Advisory Committee Note to the 1996 amendments, pertaining to the Rule 23(b)(3) class, as a bar or prohibition to

using the class action rule as a means for resolving mass accident cases. More expansive mass tort cases were presumed to come within this conceptual prohibition. In this period, when courts addressed the explicit rule requirements for class certification, the Rule 23(a) threshold requirements usually were accorded scant attention. Numerosity was seldom identified as a problem, since these early cases encompassed large numbers of claimants. However, various federal courts concluded that proposed mass tort class actions failed to satisfy the threshold requirements of commonality and typicality, because of differences among class members regarding the nature of their claims, the events giving rise to those claims, the nature and types of damages, as well as affirmative defenses. Even assuming that proposed mass tort class actions could satisfy these threshold requirements, federal courts almost uniformly held that the proposed class actions failed the more stringent predominance requirements, or were not a superior means for resolving the dispute. Many federal courts additionally recognized that difficult choice-of-law problems complicated the manageability of the proposed class actions.

In the second decade of mass tort litigation the federal courts substantially re- 40
versed course and began to approve proposed mass tort class actions. Prompted in part by a perceived "mass tort litigation crisis" on the federal court dockets, several federal judges were inspired to expansively read and apply the class action rule. During this period, one federal judge famously commented that modernity required federal judges to be creative and invent. This innovation was justified by the failure of Congress to enact substantive legislation resolving mass tort litigation, such as the asbestos crisis. Courts began experimenting with innovative, multiphase trial plans. In construing the class action rule, federal courts began formulating expansive, lenient standards for class certification. The Fifth Circuit Court of Appeals announced that "the threshold for commonality is not high",[21] and that the standard for satisfying typicality was equally lenient. Predominance problems were handled through the innovative trial plans, deferring individualized damage calculations to administrative procedures. In the alternative, some federal courts proposed novel damage sampling methodologies to permit classwide proof of damages.

Moreover, federal courts countenanced nationwide class actions by allowing 41
for the possibility of subsequent sub-classing by different state laws. During this period, federal courts looked to the Rule 23(c) provision permitting conditional or provisional class certification. In this view, courts could conditionally certify a class, allowing for the possibility that a proposed class might subsequently become unmanageable as the litigation developed. In such cases, if individual issues became problematic, or choice-of-law problems were rendered insolvable, then the courts could simply decertify the class.

In the third decade of mass tort litigation, the federal courts again reversed this 42
liberal trend towards certifying mass tort class actions. In a series of landmark

[21] See *Jenkins v. Raymark Industries*, supra n. 7.

decisions announced by the federal appellate courts in 1995–96, the federal courts clearly repudiated the possibility of certifying mass tort litigation classes. In reaching this conclusion, courts reverted to the same litany of reasons that characterized their decisions in the first decade of mass tort litigation, finding a lack of commonality, typicality, and predominance of common issues. In this third era, however, the federal courts articulated new, additional reasons for disapproving mass tort class actions.

43 In this latest era, federal courts have rejected the notion that the possibility of provisional or conditional certification permits certification of a class action with structural problems or defects (such as the failure to satisfy the predominance requirement). The Fifth Circuit Court of Appeals clearly stated the proposition that the possibility of conditional or provisional certification did not lessen the plaintiffs' burden at class certification to satisfy all the requirements for class certification.[22] The federal courts also began to reject innovative trial plans, particularly proposed trial plans that bifurcated the trial of liability and damages. Appellate courts rejected proposed mass tort trial plans because of Seventh Amendment right-to-jury problems, including the constitutional right not to have facts already determined by one jury re-examined by another.[23] The federal courts also rejected damage-by-sampling methodologies to prove up classwide damages.[24]

44 By the mid-1990s, the federal courts also recognized, in this period, the concepts of mature and immature mass torts. For these appellate courts, it was inappropriate for a court to certify a proposed immature mass tort, where the litigation track record of individual cases was indecisive, or the state of the scientific proof itself was uncertain.[25]

45 Finally, the federal courts reiterated the long-standing problems with ascertaining applicable law for a multistate or nationwide class action based on state law theories. The courts rejected the notion that federal courts could apply one law to an entire action, or that choice-of-law problems were susceptible of resolution by sub-classing or other means.[26]

2. Mass Tort Settlement Classes

46 By the end of the 1980s, a new debate surrounding mass tort class actions emerged with reference to so-called "settlement classes". This debate centered on whether Rule 23 authorized the creation and approval of class actions solely for the purpose of classwide settlement of claims, to be approved by the court without litigation. Related to this problem was the court's role in the timing of class certification, and ethical issues concerning whether an attor-

[22] See *Castano v. The American Tobacco Co.*, supra n. 16.
[23] See *In the Matter of Rhone-Poulenc-Rorer*, supra n. 14.
[24] *Cimino v. Raymark Industries*, 151 F.3d 297 (5th Cir. 1998).
[25] See *Castano*, supra n.16; *In the Matter of Rhone-Poulenc*, supra n. 14.
[26] Id.

ney-client relationship existed between class counsel and absent class members prior to certification and settlement.

Prior to the late 1980s, federal courts had routinely approved class action settlements, without much judicial scrutiny, comment, or analytical discussion. Settlement classes could develop in three possible ways. First, in the usual case, courts might certify a proposed class and then subsequently review and approve a proposed settlement. Second, courts might provisionally or conditionally certify a class for the specific purpose of negotiating a settlement (but without the prospect of actual litigation of the proposed class). Federal courts typically did not have many problems with class actions settlements that resulted from prior class certification decisions. However, with the emergence of the mass tort phenomenon and mass tort settlement classes, courts began questioning the authority for and legitimacy of so-called settlement classes. 47

By the early 1990s, a third type of settlement class developed, which proved much more troubling to the courts. In this scenario, plaintiffs' attorneys and defense counsel would negotiate a classwide settlement, and then simultaneously present the court with the proposed settlement and class certification decision. Thus, the court was asked to concurrently certify the class and approve the terms of the settlement. This procedure is sometimes called "back-ended" certification, because the class certification decision occurs at the back-end of the litigation, rather than at the outset. Since Rule 23 does not specify the exact timing of the class certification decision, there was no explicit reason, grounded in Rule 23, for not permitting back-end certification. 48

However, the possibility of back-end class certification in the context of a proposed settlement class raised disturbing questions about the ethical responsibilities of counsel prior to the court's certification of a class. Some argued that no attorney-client relationship exists prior to certification and therefore attorneys were free to negotiate and consummate any deal on behalf of the class. Others contended that a fiduciary responsibility exists to protect the interests of absent class members, and that the attorneys may not act on their own behalf to the possible detriment of absent class members. 49

In addition, a judicial debate arose concerning whether courts might relax the standards for certification when presented with a settlement class. The basic argument centered on the theory that because the settlement itself might be found to be fair, adequate, and reasonable, it was not necessary for the class to strictly satisfy all the requirements of certification as if the class were to be litigated. Another group of critics of the concept of the settlement class argued that Rule 23 itself makes no provision for the approval of settlement-only classes, and several federal judges ruled that they could find no provision in Rule 23 for such classes. 50

This array of issues concerning settlement classes converged in two landmark appeals to the United States Supreme Court at the end of the 1990s. In 1997, 51 the Court handed down its decision in *Amchem v. Windsor,*[27] a nationwide Rule 23(b)(3) opt-out global asbestos settlement class. Two years later, in 1999, the Court ruled in *Ortiz v. Fibreboard Corp.,*[28] a nationwide Rule 23(b)(1) limited fund asbestos settlement class. On both occasions, the Supreme Court addressed the general jurisprudence of settlement classes.

52 In *Amchem* and *Ortiz*, the Supreme Court recognized and endorsed the concept of settlement classes, as distinct from the concept of litigation classes. Although the Court did not identify any particular Rule 23 provision authorizing settlement classes, the Court recognized that the concept was implicit in the judiciary's authority to approve class settlements in Rule 23(e). The Court announced a number of important principles governing such settlement classes. First, there are no different or more relaxed standards for certifying settlement classes than there are for certifying litigation classes. The only possible exception to these standards regards the manageability criterion. Because settlements eliminate the need to proceed to trial, courts do not need to be satisfied that a proposed settlement class might be actually manageable as a trial matter. Second, the existence of a fair, adequate, and reasonable settlement was not sufficient, in itself, to ensure that the proposed class met class certification standards. In other words, the existence of a fair settlement could not "bootstrap" a finding of certifiability. However, courts were permitted to take into account the settlement agreement, when evaluating the class certification decision.

53 In both *Amchem* and *Ortiz*, the Court rejected the settlement classes on the facts of each proposed class. In *Amchem*, the Court held that the proposed asbestos settlement class could not have been certified as a litigation class, because the class failed the adequacy and predominance tests. The *Amchem* settlement class failed the adequacy standard because of the presence of intra-class conflicts between presently-injured claimants and exposure-only future claimants. Neither class counsel nor the class representatives could simultaneously represent these conflicting interests, without some structural safeguards to independently protect those interests. Moreover, even assuming structural due process safeguards could be created, the *Amchem* class could not have been certified as a litigation class because individual issues would predominate over common issues. This was particularly true because of the different types of asbestos injuries and damages among the members of the class. The Court found similar adequacy and predominance problems in the proposed *Ortiz* settlement class, a settlement class that was additionally reversed for failure to meet the standards for certification as a limited fund class action (see discussion below).

54 As a consequence of the *Amchem* and *Ortiz* decisions, the federal judiciary has recognized and validated the concept of the settlement class. Although the

[27] 521 U.S. 597 (1997)
[28] 119 S. Ct. 2295 (1999).

federal courts will permit back-end attempts to certify a class at the same time that a settlement is offered for court approval, such late certification decisions are greeted with some suspicion. In light of the significant ethical concerns raised by back-end certifications, the Court importantly held that such class certifications must meet the same standards as if the class had been reviewed for certification as a litigation class, earlier in the proceedings.

3. Mass Tort Limited Fund Classes

Rule 23(b)(1)(B) provides the functional category for limited fund class actions. The rule technically states that a court may certify a proposed class under this provision if 55

"adjudications with respect to individual members of the class which would as a practical matter be dispositive of the interests of the other members not parties to the adjudications or substantially impair or impede their ability to protect their interests". Thus, if individual lawsuits would threaten to exhaust a defendant's limited fund available to compensate all claimants against that fund, then the proposed class may be suitable for certification under this provision. Rule 23(b)(1)(B) classes are mandatory and any judgment is binding on all class members. This is no right to opt-out of a limited fund class action, and no right to receive notice of the certification of this type of class. 56

In the early 1980s through the end of the 1990s, plaintiffs' lawyers made numerous attempts to seek certification of Rule 23(b)(1)(B) classes in various mass tort cases. Primarily plaintiffs' attorneys sought certification of Rule 23(b)(1)(B) classes for punitive damages, on the theory that the multiple, repetitive award of punitive damages might ultimately exhaust a defendant's funds. In almost every instance, courts rejected certification of proposed Rule 23(b)(1)(B) punitive damage classes (see discussion below), chiefly because of the failure of the plaintiffs to prove the existence of a limited fund. Proposed punitive damage classes also failed because of disparities among the various states' law pertaining to the availability and determination of punitive damages. 57

In the mid-1980s, an asbestos defendant, the Keene Corporation, made an interesting attempt to seek certification of a limited fund class action against all prospective asbestos claimants. By reversing roles and assuming the role of plaintiff, the Keene Corporation sought to gather all asbestos claimants in a class action based on the theory that the Keene Corporation had limited assets with which to pay out claims. This innovative attempt by the Keene Corporation to strategically employ the (b)(1)(B) class to its own advantage, was subsequently repudiated by the Second Circuit Court of Appeals which rejected this as an illegitimate attempt by an asbestos defendant to circumvent the bankruptcy laws.[29] 58

[29] *In re Joint Eastern and Southern District Asbestos Litigation: In re Keene Corp.*, 14 F.3d 726 (3d Cir. 1993).

59 In 1999, the Supreme Court addressed the propriety of a Rule 23(b)(1)(B) asbestos settlement class that was previously approved by the lower federal courts. In *Ortiz v. Fibreboard Corp.*, the Supreme Court disapproved the settlement class because the proponents had failed to properly establish the existence of a limited fund. The Court's primary analysis focused on the evidentiary burden that the proponents of a limited fund must satisfy in order for the court to certify such a class. The Court indicated that a limited fund could not be established through an agreed-stipulation by the parties that insurance proceeds and other contributions from the defendant constituted a limited fund. Instead, the parties had an affirmative obligation to adduce evidence in support of proof of the limited fund. The Court also indicated that a limited fund could not be established where a defendant made a nominal contribution to the fund, but would continue to operate as a financially viable business after approval of the settlement. However, the Court did not go so far as to suggest that a defendant had to go into bankruptcy in order to prove the existence of the limited fund.

60 In addition to the Court's discussion of the history and nature of limited fund class actions and the evidentiary burden for establishing such a class, the Court reiterated the general principles governing settlement classes that the Court articulated two years earlier in *Amchem*. Thus, the Court reiterated that intra-class conflicts similar to those in *Amchem* defeated the ability to certify the proposed *Ortiz* class. In *Ortiz*, conflicts were present by virtue of the fact that some class members' claims were covered by insurance policies pre-dating 1959, while other claimants' claims came within the purview of post-1959 policies. Because of different policy provisions and coverage issues, some class members' claims were stronger than others. Hence, these differences raised material conflicts among class members which undermined the adequacy requirement and served to defeat class certification.

61 It is difficult to locate any mass tort class action actually certified and tried on a limited-fund basis. After *Ortiz*, Rule 23(b)(1)(B) limited fund mass tort class actions remain difficult to pursue. The Supreme Court was unclear concerning the precise evidentiary standards that proponents of such classes must satisfy to pursue limited fund mass tort settlement classes. Notwithstanding the Court's lack of clarity regarding the evidentiary burden for proving up a limited fund, a federal appellate court after the *Ortiz* decision approved a limited fund settlement class in the *Orthopedic Bone Screw* litigation. In approving that Rule 23(b)(1)(B) settlement class, the court relied on *Ortiz* principles.

4. Mass Tort Punitive Damage Classes

62 As indicated above, mass tort litigation in the early 1980s inspired some plaintiffs' attorneys to seek certification of Rule 23(b)(1)(B) punitive damage classes. The theory advanced in support of the punitive damage, limited fund concept was based on the extremely large punitive damage awards prevalent in many American jurisdictions. Theoretically, if individuals successfully pur-

sued punitive damage claims, at some point the defendants' assets would be exhausted by such multiple, repetitive claims. Therefore, to achieve equity for all claimants with equally valid compensatory and punitive damage claims, courts ought to certify such claims under the Rule 23(b)(1)(B) class category.

Although the theory underlying the limited fund, punitive damage class seems intuitively correct, courts generally have not permitted certification of such proposed classes. In virtually every case where such a punitive damage class has been proposed, courts consistently have found that the proponents have failed to prove up the existence of the limited funds.[30] After *Ortiz*, any proposed punitive damage class would need to meet *Ortiz* standards. In addition, proposed nationwide punitive damage classes have failed on choice-of-law grounds. Punitive damages are created by state law, and not every American jurisdiction recognizes punitive damages. The standards for the proof, award, and calculation of punitive damages vary from state to state. Some states cap punitive damages, while others do not. Because of the lack of uniformity of laws relating to punitive damages, applicable law has been another barrier to pursuing classwide punitive damages under Rule 23(b)(1)(B). This is particularly a problem in the mandatory class, where class members do not have the option to exclude themselves from the class. 63

5. Mass Tort Medical Monitoring Classes

Perhaps the most interesting class action development in the modern mass tort era is the creation of a new form of claim or relief – the "medical monitoring" class. Plaintiffs seek certification of a medical monitoring class when claimants have been exposed to a toxic substance or have used a medical device but may not manifest a medical condition until years later. Plaintiffs have sought medical monitoring in various mass tort cases, including cases of exposure to radioactive nuclear substances, polychlorinated biphenyls (PCBs), asbestos, lead paint and chemical contamination. Plaintiffs also have sought medical monitoring in actions related to heart valves, pacemakers and tampons. A very large number of plaintiffs have attempted to create tobacco-addiction medical monitoring classes. In seeking a medical monitoring class, plaintiffs request that the defendant create a fund to bear the expense of future medical monitoring of class members' conditions. 64

Throughout the 1980s and into the 1990s, courts have disagreed over whether medical monitoring is a substantive legal claim, equitable relief, a procedural device or an administrative mechanism. Plaintiffs usually seek certification of a medical monitoring class under Rule 23(b)(2), the provision for injunctive or declaratory classes. 65

Because medical monitoring classes involve a fund, courts have reached different conclusions on whether medical monitoring classes constitute equi-

[30] See e.g., *In re Northern District of California, Dalkon Shield IUD Prods. Liab. Litig.*, 693 F.2d 847 (9th Cir. 1982).

table or legal relief. Additionally, because medical monitoring classes embody a hybrid of legal and equitable elements, such classes implicate difficult Seventh Amendment right-to-jury problems.

66 Federal courts look to state law to determine whether the state recognizes a claim for medical monitoring. Some states, such as California, Louisiana, New Jersey, Pennsylvania and Utah, have authorized recovery for medical monitoring in the absence of physical injury, and some federal courts, predicting state law (for example, in Colorado), have reached the same conclusion. More than half the states now recognize claims for medical monitoring, although the elements of what constitutes a medical monitoring claim vary from state to state. The Fourth Circuit Court of Appeals, however, construing Virginia and West Virginia law, has held that medical monitoring expenses are only available if a plaintiff has sustained a physical injury.

67 The leading standards relating to medical monitoring class actions have been developed in Pennsylvania. The Third Circuit Court of Appeals, evaluating whether to certify a medical monitoring class of people exposed to PCBs, predicted that Pennsylvania would recognize a claim for medical monitoring.[31] The Pennsylvania Supreme Court then recognized a common-law action for medical monitoring, explaining that the "injury in a medical monitoring claim is the cost of the medical care".[32]

68 In 1997, the Pennsylvania Supreme Court, in *Redland Soccer Club Inc. v. Department of the Army*,[33] set forth the elements for stating a claim for medical monitoring. A plaintiff most show (1) that there is exposure greater than normal background levels; (2) to a proven hazardous substance; (3) caused by the defendant's negligence; (4) that as a proximate result of the exposure, the plaintiff has a significantly increased risk of contracting a serious latent disease; (5) that a monitoring procedure exists that makes the early detection of the disease possible; (6) that the prescribed monitoring regime is different from that normally recommended in the absence of the exposure; and (7) that the prescribed monitoring regime is reasonably necessary according to contemporary scientific principles.

69 The *Redland* court also indicated four policy reasons for recognizing a cause of action for medical monitoring. First, medical monitoring promotes the "early diagnosis and treatment of disease resulting from exposure caused by a tortfeasor's negligence". Second, "[a]llowing recovery for such expenses avoids the potential injustice of forcing an economically disadvantaged person to pay for expensive diagnostic examinations necessitated by another's negligence" and "affords toxic-tort victims, for whom other sorts of recovery might prove difficult, immediate compensation for medical monitoring needed as a result

31 *In re Paoli R.R. Yard PCB Litigation*, 916 F.2d 829 (3d Cir. 1990) (*Paoli I*).

32 *Simmons v. Pacor Inc.*, 543 Pa. 664, 647 A.2d 232 (1996).

33 *Redland*, 548 Pa. 178, 696 A.2d 137, 14647 (1997).

of exposure". Third, medical monitoring "further[s] the deterrent function of the tort system by compelling those who expose others to toxic substances to minimize risks and costs of exposure". Finally, medical monitoring is in harmony with "the important public interest in fostering access to medical testing for individuals whose exposure to toxic chemicals creates and enhances risk of disease".[34]

Pennsylvania's criteria for establishing a medical monitoring claim incorporate elements of common-law negligence. Many other states that have developed either common law or statutory claims for medical monitoring incorporate similar lists of elements in order to establish a claim for medical monitoring. In Pennsylvania and elsewhere, defendants have challenged medical monitoring classes as disguised attempts to seek legal relief because medical monitoring closely resembles a negligence-based claim for future medical expenses. If a medical monitoring class is merely a disguised attempt to recover compensatory damages, then certification is not permissible under Rule 23(b)(2). 70

Federal courts grappling with this issue have concluded that a medical monitoring claim may be either equitable or legal in nature. Courts, therefore, must carefully scrutinize a plaintiff's request for a medical monitoring class to determine whether the claim may be accurately characterized as legal or equitable. In a seminal decision concerning medical monitoring claims, Judge S. Arthur Spiegel explained that a medical monitoring claim may be satisfied in different ways.[35] For example, a court may order a defendant to pay the plaintiff money, and the plaintiff may or may not choose to use the money to have his or her medical condition monitored. Alternatively, a court might order the defendant to pay the plaintiff's medical expenses directly, so that the plaintiff might be monitored by a physician of the plaintiff's choice. Neither of these forms of relief constitutes equitable or injunctive relief under Rule 23(b)(2). 71

If, however, the court established a medical monitoring program of its own, financed by the defendant but managed by court-appointed or supervised trustees, in which the plaintiffs were monitored by particular physicians and the medical data were used for group studies, this program would constitute injunctive relief under Rule 23(b)(2). Thus, the use of a medical monitoring fund to administer medical surveillance payments would be an exercise of the court's equitable powers.[36] 72

In the wake of Judge Spiegel's distinction in *Day v. NLO*, federal courts have indicated that the dispositive factor in assessing whether a medical monitoring claim can be certified as a Rule 23(b)(2) class is to determine what type of relief the plaintiffs actually are seeking. If the plaintiffs seek relief that is a 73

[34] *Id.*, 696 A.2d at 154.
[35] See *Day v. NLO Inc.*, 144 F.R.D. 330, 335–36 (S.D. Ohio 1992).
[36] *Id.*

disguised request for compensatory damages, then the medical monitoring claim can only be characterized as a claim for monetary damages. "In contrast, if plaintiffs seek the establishment of a court-supervised medical monitoring program through which the class members will receive periodic examinations, then the plaintiffs' medical monitoring claim can be properly characterized as a claim seeking injunctive relief".[37]

74 A further complicating issue in medical monitoring classes is whether such claims require a jury trial. Under prevailing Seventh Amendment jurisprudence, if a medical monitoring claim is deemed equitable in nature, then there is no right to a jury trial. On the contrary, if the medical monitoring claim is deemed legal, then the defendant is entitled to a jury trial. Because medical monitoring claims are certified under Rule 23(b)(2), it would seem that such claims would not go to the jury, but in many federal courts, the opposite is true. Thus, several federal courts have sent medical monitoring claims to the jury to decide the issue of liability or the plaintiffs' need for medical monitoring.[38]

75 Medical monitoring claims thus present a vexing conundrum, and the way in which a plaintiff pleads the medical monitoring claim often is critical. If the plaintiffs seek a lump-sum award for the medical monitoring claim, then they would be barred from seeking injunctive relief. In theory, the plaintiffs have an alternative adequate remedy at law – the lump sum of compensatory damages to pay for future medical expenses. If the plaintiffs seek relief in the form of a medical monitoring fund, however, such a remedy invokes the equitable powers of the court, and a plaintiff is not required to show an inadequate remedy at law.

76 In analyzing the tension between the Seventh Amendment and Rule 23(b)(2) medical monitoring classes, a Pennsylvania district court (in a tobacco medical monitoring class subsequently decertified) held that "the nature of relief sought under the plaintiffs' medical monitoring fund, for the purposes of the Seventh Amendment analysis is inherently both legal and equitable".[39] The court concluded that the constitutional right to a jury trial could not be made to depend upon the choice of words used in the pleadings.[40] The court reconciled the apparent conflict between a Rule 23(b)(2) equitable medical monitoring class and providing a jury trial: "Thus, in order to establish a right to a Rule 23(b)(2) certification, it need only be shown that the relief requested is not predominantly for damages. This inquiry has nothing to do with whether

[37] *Barnes v. American Tobacco Co. Inc.*, 989 F. Supp. 661 (E.D. Pa. 1997); but see *Barnes v. American Tobacco Co.*, 161 F.3d 127, 146 (3d Cir. 1998) (affirming decertification of medical monitoring class).

[38] See e.g., *In re Paoli Railroad Yard PCB Litigation*, 35 F.3d 717 (3d Cir. 1994); *Paoli I,* supra, 916 F.2d 829; *Herber v. Johns-Manville Corp.*, 785 F.2d 70 (3d Cir. 1986); *Fried v. Sunguard Recovery Services Inc.*, 925 F. Supp. 372, 375 (E.D. Pa. 1996) (reserving the power to structure the medical monitoring fund); *Day v. NLO Inc.*, 851 F. Supp. 869 (S.D. Ohio 1994).

[39] *Barnes v. American Tobacco Co. Inc.*, 989 F. Supp. 661, 668 (E.D. Pa. 1997).

[40] Citing *Dairy Queen Inc. v. Wood*, 369 U.S. 469 (1962).

one's constitutional right to a jury trial has been implicated by the underlying nature of the claim. Indeed, the bar for determining whether the nature of a claim is equitable or legal for Seventh Amendment purposes is much higher than it is under Rule 23(b)(2) analysis."

In the court's view, "[u]nder Seventh Amendment analysis, the right to a jury trial must be upheld even if the legal issues are characterized as 'incidental' to equitable issues...For this reason, decisions holding that medical monitoring claims may be certified under Rule 23(b)(2) are not dispositive for the purposes of a jury trial. In theory and practice, courts can certify a class pursuant to Rule 23(b)(2) and yet find the parties are entitled to a jury under the Seventh Amendment".[41] 77

The general development of medical monitoring classes has been erratic. Although earlier decisions certified such classes, many appellate courts have reversed certification of medical monitoring classes. Virtually all attempts to certify tobacco-related medical monitoring classes have failed, due to the lack of homogeneity among the class members' life and medical histories, and events giving rise to the possible medical monitoring claims. On the other hand, the Fen/phen/redux mass tort litigation recently was successfully settled as a medical monitoring class. 78

B. Multidistrict Litigation: MDLs (28 U.S.C. § 1407)

Another common method for aggregating mass tort claims has been through use of the "MDL" or multidistrict litigation procedure. Unlike the class action model, the multidistrict litigation procedures are provided for by federal statute 28 U.S.C. § 1407. The MDL statute provides that; "When civil actions involving one or more common questions of fact are pending in different districts, such actions may be transferred and consolidated for coordinated or consolidated pretrial proceedings". Congress enacted the multidistrict litigation statute in 1968, largely as a consequence of the federal judiciary's experience handling electrical products antitrust litigation during the early 1960s. 79

The MDL statute essentially is a federal transfer of venue statute. The statute permits the transfer of individual cases that have been filed throughout the federal judicial system, to all be transferred to one particular federal court for aggregative procedures. After approval of an MDL and designation of the MDL court and MDL judge, all cases that come within the description of the MDL order will be transferred. The great utility of the MDL statute is that it permits coordinated discovery that is common to all the individual cases to occur under the supervision of one court. 80

The Judicial Panel on Multidistrict Litigation determines whether an MDL will be created. The Judicial Panel on Multidistrict Litigation consists of seven 81

[41] *Barnes*, 989 F. Supp. at 668.

federal judges who are appointed by the Chief Justice of the United States Supreme Court. Litigants may petition the MDL panel to create an MDL, or the judges may *sua sponte* determine to create an MDL if the Panel is aware of a developing number of similar cases across numerous federal dockets. The Judicial Panel may receive briefing on the desirability to create a specific MDL, and may hear oral argument from counsel and various interested parties prior to making that determination. The Panel will entertain recommendations for the best venue to designate as the MDL forum, as well as possible judges to supervise the MDL.

82 Once the Panel creates an MDL by order, all cases are transferred to the MDL forum. The MDL judge typically will organize the MDL litigation by designating litigation committees, and lead and liaison counsel for each side. MDL judges assume a managerial role over the litigation, and will work closely with counsel to create scheduling orders and agreements concerning the conduct of discovery.

83 The MDL statute, by its own terms, does not permit a joint or consolidated trial of the transferred cases in the MDL forum. The Supreme Court affirmed this statutory prohibition in 1998, in *Lexecon v. Milberg Weiss Bershad Hynes & Lerach.*[42] The statute requires that once the coordinated pretrial proceedings have been completed, the MDL court must remand the individual cases back to the original forums, for trial in those original forums. While this restriction on MDL procedure would seem to undermine the utility of the transfer-and-consolidation procedures, empirical studies of MDL litigation has indicated that a very high percentage of cases that are accorded MDL treatment settle. In order words, the creation of an MDL and subsequent transfer and coordinated proceedings usually suffice to induce the parties to settle as the evidentiary basis for the litigation is developed.

84 As the statutory language indicates, the standard for the creation of an MDL is not very exacting; the Panel merely needs to find that individual cases currently pending in various federal courts share "one or more common questions of fact". Clearly, the standards for creation of an MDL are much less exacting than for certification of a class action. Notwithstanding this lax standard, in the late 1970s and early 1980s the Judicial Panel on Multidistrict Litigation was hesitant to create MDLs that were proposed for various mass tort litigations. For example, in 1976 the Panel refused to create a multidistrict Litigation for DES cases, and beginning in 1977 the Panel refused to create an asbestos MDL.[43] This initial resistance towards creation of mass tort MDLs has largely dissipated over time. Now, the Judicial Panel frequently takes the lead in creating mass tort MDLs, as a precursor to resolution of these cases.

[42] 118 S.Ct. 956, 140 L.Ed.2d 62 (1998).

[43] *In re Asbestos and Asbestos Insulation Material Prods. Liab. Litig.*, 431 F. Supp. 906 (J.P.M.D.L. 1977).

Perhaps the most famous example of the Judicial Panel's reluctance to create a mass tort MDL relates to the Panel's history with asbestos litigation. Between 1977 and 1991, the Panel rejected creation of an asbestos MDL on five occasions. In the most significant decision rejecting creation of an asbestos MDL, the Panel delineated numerous reasons why asbestos cases failed to satisfy even the minimal threshold requirement for common questions of fact. By 1991, however, with a mounting asbestos litigation crisis in the federal courts, the Judicial Panel finally approved the creation of an asbestos MDL.[44] In so doing, the Panel recognized that the litigation crisis, and the failure of Congress to legislatively act to provide some relief from the situation, impelled the Panel finally to agree to create an asbestos MDL. The federal district court for the Eastern District of Pennsylvania was designated as the MDL forum, and the ill-fated *Amchem* global asbestos settlement, which the Supreme Court struck down in 1977, ultimately was generated from this MDL. 85

The pattern of mass tort cases that have been processed through MDL procedures is varied and it is difficult to explain why the Panel authorizes MDLs for some mass torts, but not for others. Among the five seminal mass torts, the Panel authorized creation of MDLs in four of those five mass torts. In 1975, the Panel created a Dalkon Shield MDL; in 1979 the Panel authorized an *Agent Orange* MDL; in 1982 the Panel created a Bendectin MDL; and finally in 1991 the Panel authorized an asbestos MDL. Only the DES litigation was denied MDL status. In this same early era of mass torts, the Panel denied creation of MDLS in the MER/29 pharmaceutical litigation as well as cases relating to thalidomide. 86

Among second and third generation mass torts, the Panel's approval or disapproval of mass tort MDLs has been varied. The panel has approved MDLs for mass torts relating to: breast implants, norplant, benzene, orthopedic screws, tainted blood products, swine flu vaccine, fen/Phen/redux, TMJ implants, J-pacemaker leads, felbatol, latex gloves, baycol, and rezulin. The Panel has denied creation of MDLs for mass torts involving: tobacco, radiation-HRE, radiation fallout, heart valves, computer repetitive stress syndrome, lead and lead paint, penile prostheses, and tampons. 87

The creation of a mass tort MDL often is the precursor to other procedural developments. After some period of pretrial discovery and motions practice, attorneys often attempt to certify mass tort classes in the MDL forum. In some instances, class certifications in the MDL forum have been repudiated or reversed on appeal. For example, MDL Judge John Grady certified a nationwide class in the HIV tainted blood products litigation. In that case, Judge Grady approved a classwide generic trial plan in the MDL forum, followed by a remand of individual cases to the originating forums for individual trials on liability and damages. The Seventh Circuit Court of Appeals subsequently struck 88

[44] *In re Asbestos Prods. Liab. Litig.*, 771 F. Supp. 415 (J.P.M.D.L. 1991).

down this trial plan.[45] Similarly, attempts to certify pacemaker lead class actions, in the context of MDL proceedings, similarly have failed.

89 However, a number of mass tort litigations have been settled on a classwide basis, as an outgrowth of MDL proceedings. Among the mass tort cases that have accomplished classwide settlements after MDL proceedings are *Agent Orange*, breast implants, orthopedic screws, and Fen/phen/redux. The tainted blood products litigation, after its initial unsuccessful attempt at a nationwide litigation class certification, ultimately was settled on a classwide basis. This resolution grew out of the MDL proceedings.

90 The multidistrict litigation procedure has both values and obvious limitations as a means for resolving mass tort litigation. The major value in creating a mass tort MDL is that this facilitates transfer, consolidation, and coordinated pretrial discovery that otherwise would result in expensive and repetitive practice. Additionally, creation of an MDL facilitates organization of the litigation under the managerial supervision of one judge, who will gain expertise in the particular litigation, and assist the attorneys in brokering a negotiated settlement. Perhaps the primary virtue of MDL proceedings is the empirical reality that the creation and development of an MDL, in a very high percentage of cases, does result in settlement of the litigation.

91 On the other hand, the statutory prohibition preventing trial of the consolidated cases removes the threat of a joint trial in the MDL forum. Because of this obvious limitation, almost all major law reform organizations, beginning in the mid-1980s, have urged various recommendations to Congress to amend the current multidistrict litigation statute. These proposals have also been combined with proposals for Congress to enact a federalized choice-of-law provision, that would be applicable to cases transferred and proposed for trial in an MDL forum. To date, none of these legislative proposals have been enacted by Congress.

C. Consolidation (Fed. R. Civ. P. 42)

92 Rule 42, the federal consolidation rule, provides a third procedural option for aggregating and resolving mass tort cases in the federal court system. Because almost all mass tort cases are treated either through MDL procedures or through attempted class actions, there are very few examples of mass tort litigation resolved through use of the consolidation rule. Rule 42 provides: "When actions involving common questions of law or fact are pending before the court, it may order a joint hearing or trial of any or all matters in issue in the action; it may order all the actions consolidated; and it may make such orders concerning proceedings therein as may tend to avoid unnecessary costs or delay." Similar to the MDL statute, the standards for consolidation under Rule 42 is much more lax than the standards for class certification, requiring only that the cases share common questions of law or fact.

[45] See *In the matter of Rhone-Poulenc-Rorer*, supra n. 14.

In order for cases to be subject to Rule 42 consolidation procedures, the individual cases must all "be pending" before the court. Therefore, in federal practice, Rule 42 often is used in combination with the general federal transfer provision, 28 U.S.C. § 1404(a), which permits the transfer of civil actions to any judicial district where the cases could have originally been brought. Alternatively, Rule 42 consolidation may be used in coordination with MDL procedure, and a Rule 42 consolidation may be accomplished after cases have been transferred and collected in an MDL proceeding. Indeed, many mass accident cases, such as aeroplane crashes, combine MDL and Rule 42 procedures to resolve these cases.[46] 93

Unlike class action litigation, cases consolidated under Rule 42 each retains its individual identity; that is, each case retains its separate plaintiffs and attorneys. Consolidation under Rule 42 does not create a representational litigation. And, unlike MDL procedure, cases that are consolidated in one federal forum may be tried in that forum. There are few examples of mass torts that have been aggregated and resolved using Rule 42 consolidation procedures, largely because the consolidation rule was not promulgated with the prospect of consolidation of thousands or hundreds of thousands of claims which characterize the modern mass tort. Rule 42 was originally designed to permit federal courts to consolidate and try small numbers of similar cases in one court. Hence mass accident cases, with fewer numbers of claimants, provide examples of a type of mass tort that has been susceptible to resolution under this rule. 94

With the exception of mass accident cases, there are fewer examples of true dispersed mass torts that have been resolved through Rule 42 auspices. On the other hand, the failure of an attempted Rule 42 mass tort consolidation may lead to the demise of a nascent mass tort. For example, in 1992, Judge Jack Weinstein in the Eastern District of New York approved a consolidation of forty-four pending repetitive stress injury cases. The plaintiffs also sought creation of an RSI multidistrict litigation, which the Judicial Panel on Multidistrict Litigation denied. On appeal of the Rule 42 consolidation, the Court of Appeals for the Second Circuit vacated the consolidation order, finding that the RSI cases failed to mean the threshold rule requirement of sharing common questions of law or fact.[47] After rejection of the attempted MDL and Rule 42 consolidation, the RSI cases were tried individually. After plaintiffs lost several of these RSI cases, the nascent mass tort failed to develop. 95

Large aggregations of mass tort claims under Rule 42 also may lead to complicated and confusing jury trials and attempts to actually litigate consolidated mass tort cases in a consolidated trial may result in unfair and unreasonable jury verdicts. In 1991, a joint federal court in the Eastern and Southern Dis- 96

[46] See e.g., *In re Air Crash Disaster at Detroit Metro Airport on August 16, 1987*, 737 F. Supp. 391 (E.D. Mich. 1989).

[47] *In Re Repetitive Stress Injury Litig.*, 11 F.3d 368 (2d Cir. 1993).

tricts of New York tried a consolidated mass tort consisting of over 600 individual asbestos tort claims. The trial lasted for more then six months, resulting in jury verdicts for 45 of the plaintiffs and an aggregate award of over $ 94 million dollars. One defendant, the Keene Corporation (which was assessed a percentage of liability for the joint damages), appealed on the grounds that the court's original Rule 42 consolidation order constituted prejudicial error. The Second Circuit Court of Appeals agreed that the Rule 42 consolidation, and resulting trial, had compromised the defendant's rights to a jury trial under the Fourteenth Amendment.[48]

97 Although Rule 42 consolidation has been the least useful mechanism in federal courts for resolving true, dispersed mass torts, the possibility of consolidated procedures has re-emerged as a potential technique. During fall 2002, plaintiffs' attorneys brought a significantly large consolidated asbestos action in state court in West Virginia, against some 200 defendants. The plaintiffs proposed, and the West Virginia state court approved, a massive consolidated trial of asbestos claims. The defendants appealed to the United States Supreme Court for expedited review of the proposed state court procedures, but the Supreme Court refused to grant review and to intervene in the state court case. After the Supreme Court refused review, all defendants except one settled with the plaintiffs. The consolidated case ultimately went to trial against the single remaining defendant, and it appears likely that the state's novel consolidated trial procedures will again be appealed to the United States Supreme Court.

D. Fund Approaches

98 Another possible means for resolving mass tort claims is through fund approaches. The fund approach to resolving mass tort claims is more common in European and civil law countries, and is more rarely used in the United States. The recent events at the World Trade Center, resulting in Congressional legislation to address victims' claims, present a somewhat unique instance of the United States employing a fund approach to resolve a mass tort litigation

99 Notwithstanding the seemingly novel enactment of the World Trade Center Victims' Compensation Fund, Congress has, in the past, enacted other statutes to create funds for resolving mass tort claims arising from various different events. These previous fund approaches entail many of the same types of goals, rationales, and provisions similar to those incorporated in the Victims' Compensation Fund legislation. Generally, Congress has enacted fund legislation to protect certain industries from the consequences of massive tort litigation and to restrict the liability of potential defendants. In order to assist claimants with the fair, efficient and expeditious compensation of claims, such legislation typically relaxes the requirements for proof of claims. Thus, such legislation typically eliminates the need for proof of causation or negligence.

[48] *Malcolm v. Nat'l Gypsum Corp.*, 995 F.2d 346 (2d Cir. 1993).

Counterbalancing these concessions, plaintiffs typically waive defenses and agree to caps on damages. Some fund legislation provides for exclusivity of remedies, or limits alternative access to the judicial system in order to adjudicate claims. Also characteristic of legislative fund approaches are the use of tables of claim values to determine awards. Finally, the financing of pervious legislative fund schemes has come from various sources, but a common approach has been for the particular industry to finance such funds.

In addition to the WTC Victims' Compensation Fund, Congress has enacted a 100
number of other fund approaches in the past. Examples include the National Childhood Vaccine Injury Act, which created a fund to guarantee the supply of childhood vaccines by protecting manufacturers from the costs associated with products liability litigation. The legislation also was intended to ensure that injured consumers would expeditiously receive adequate compensation for any injuries resulting from such vaccines. In 1976, Congress enacted the National Swine Flu Act, with a similar purpose and intent. In 1969, Congress enacted the Black Lung Benefits Act and Black Lung Disability Trust Fund, to provide benefits, in cooperation with the states, to coal miners who are totally disabled due to black lung disease (as well as to their surviving dependants). The Price-Anderson Act, enacted in 1957, is one of the oldest examples of a fund approach to potential mass tort litigation. This legislation was intended to encourage entry by private industry into the field of nuclear energy, by ensuring that funds would be available to compensate for injuries and damages sustained by the public in event of a nuclear accident. The Longshore and Harbor Workers' Compensation Act, another historical fund legislation, created a federal no-fault compensation scheme for occupational injury and disease claims. More recently, the state of California has enacted legislation creating an AIDS Vaccine Victims' Compensation Fund, also to encourage manufacturers to develop an AIDS vaccine. Similar to other such federal vaccine-fund legislation, the purpose is to compensate parties injured by AIDS vaccines manufactured and marketed in California.

In addition to Congressionally-enacted funds, fund approaches also have been 101
instituted and administered as a consequence of judicial resolution of mass tort events. For example, the Agent Orange class action settlement, which was approved by the federal judiciary, was implemented through a fund administered by a special master, claims administrator, and advisory board.

E. *Bankruptcy*

In addition to class action settlements and MDL procedures, bankruptcy has 102
proved to be one of the major mechanisms for resolving mass tort claims. Obviously, bankruptcy law implicates both procedural and substantive law. In the procedural realm, various federal statutes provide the means for transferring and aggregating claims before the bankruptcy court. In addition, federal bankruptcy law provides an important means for staying any parallel state court litigation, an important feature of bankruptcy in a system where mass tort claims

frequently are simultaneously pursued in both state and federal court. Federal bankruptcy law and its intersection with mass tort litigation, is too vast a subject to be encompassed in this paper. The following sections provide a basic outline describing how bankruptcy procedures facilitate resolution of mass tort claims, as well as special issues in using bankruptcy auspices to resolve mass tort claims.

103 The general bankruptcy laws of the United States are collected in Title 11 of the United States Code. 28 U.S.C. § 1334(a) grants federal district courts original and exclusive jurisdiction over bankruptcy claims. A bankruptcy case, as well as related to cases, may be venued in a single forum. The bankruptcy statutes contain two transfer provisions. One of these provisions may be used to transfer tort cases to the bankruptcy venue. The bankruptcy statutes also allow the transfer of a case for all purposes, including trial. Bankruptcy courts have their own rules of procedure, but these rules frequently parallel the Federal Rules of Civil Procedure.

104 There are many different forms of bankruptcy, but the prevalent form of mass tort bankruptcies is pursuant to "Chapter 11" bankruptcy provisions. Bankruptcy proceedings may begin if the debtor files a petition (a voluntary proceeding) or if a certain number of creditors file a petition (an involuntary proceeding). A Chapter 11 bankruptcy is the chief vehicle which allows a corporation to restructure its operations. The United States trustee chooses a creditors' committee at the outset of the bankruptcy proceedings, and the creditors' committee plays a role in the bankruptcy plan and implementation. The debtor in possession continues to run the business, rather than the trustee. A reorganization plan will be generated and needs to be approved by the bankruptcy court.

105 A Chapter 11 bankruptcy reorganization plan must identify the separate classes of creditors' claims and equity interests. The plan must specify what treatment is to be accorded to each of these claims and interests within a particular class, and to provide for equal treatment within classes. The reorganization plan may not benefit the corporation's director, officers, and trustees at the expense of creditors and interest holders. The bankruptcy principle of absolute priority ensures that tort claimants will receive the value of their claims prior to the interest of equity claimants for their interests in the company.

106 The bankruptcy principle of "the best interests of the creditor" requires that a Chapter 11 bankruptcy plan may not be confirmed over the objections of a single creditor (a dissenting member of the class) who would receive a better return in a Chapter 7 liquidation case than a proposed Chapter 11 reorganization. The bankruptcy code requires the court to approve or confirm a bankruptcy reorganization plan. The bankruptcy court will conduct a hearing to ascertain whether a proposed reorganization plan satisfies thirteen statutory requirements, that the plan is feasible and in the best interests of the creditors. The court may approve the reorganization plan even if an impaired class of claims or interests votes not to accept the plan.

Similar to problems presented in mass tort settlement classes, issues relating to the resolution of "future claims" have greatly complicated the bankruptcy resolution of mass torts. Generally, the bankruptcy laws provide a broad definition for the term "claims". In order for future claims to be treated equally with those of other creditors, future claims would need to be included in a reorganization plan. Moreover, without inclusion of future claims, the debtor could not achieve final resolution of liability for such claims through the bankruptcy. However, a major legal dispute has arisen regarding how to determine when claims arose for the purpose of having rights determined under a bankruptcy plan. Bankruptcy courts have approved different tests for resolving the "future claims" problem, and institutional law reform groups have suggested various approaches for dealing with the treatment of future claims in bankruptcy. In addition, the inclusion of possible future claims in a bankruptcy reorganization plan also greatly complicates the estimation process, which is necessary to determine how large a bankruptcy trust will be needed to pay such claims either fully or to provide a pro rata share. 107

Notwithstanding the complex problems generated by the bankruptcy resolution of mass torts, a large number of mass tort defendants have elected Chapter 11 bankruptcy to resolve their mass tort exposure. Mostly prominently, a large number of asbestos manufacturers have elected bankruptcy to resolve their mass tort liabilities, beginning with the Johns-Manville Company in 1982. The Dalkon Shield litigation was resolved when the A.H. Robins Co. elected bankruptcy, and the breast implant global settlement collapsed after the major defendant in that litigation - Dow Corning – also went into bankruptcy. In addition, a number of the smaller implant manufacturers similarly chose to enter bankruptcy to resolve their potential mass tort liabilities. 108

III. Concluding Remarks on Procedural Developments: Mass Torts After and Beyond the WTC Victims' Compensation Fund

The problems relating to mass tort litigation which have emerged during the past three decades have persisted into the twenty-first century. What these decades teach us is that the experience of mass tort litigation has evolved over time. Indeed, our recognition of this phenomenon, and our understanding of the nature of mass tort cases has become more sophisticated with each passing decade. In this period, judges, attorneys, commentators, the business and insurance communities, and other actors have developed a vocabulary and analytical constructs to describe the mass tort phenomenon. We now recognize mass tort litigation as a separate litigation phenomenon, complete with a descriptive "life cycle" developing through stages of immaturity to maturity. 109

During this same period, the judicial system's willingness and ability to deal with mass tort cases also has changed and evolved. The debate between litigant autonomy and aggregative justice persists to the present. In the judicial realm, a period of initial skepticism concerning aggregative procedure gave way to a decade of judicial experimentation, followed by another decade of re- 110 trenchment and resistance to collective means for resolving mass tort events. Against this backdrop, bankruptcy has emerged as a major auspices for resolving the mass tort liabilities of many corporate defendants.

111 The resolution of mass tort litigation in the United States remains a work-in-progress. Perhaps the most striking characteristic of these efforts to resolve various mass tort crises has been the inventiveness of the practicing bar in developing new theories of pleading, consolidation, and aggregation to package mass tort cases for resolution. In turn, as courts have considered and rejected various options, the practicing bar has been endlessly creative in rethinking the mass tort problem. Thus, the practicing bar has taken the lead in spurring the judiciary to consider whether old rules can be used to handle new and changed legal problems, at first by pressing the class action rule into use for collecting individual mass tort cases. And, as the mass tort phenomenon evolved, both the plaintiff and defense bars have joined forces to rethink the possible utility of such mechanisms as the limited fund class for resolving tort liabilities, or the punitive damage class to provide equity for all persons claiming such damages. The American plaintiffs' bar is responsible for inventing the concept of the medical monitoring class. And the practicing bar has been responsible for the development of the concept of the settlement class. With each generation of new mass tort cases, both the practicing bar and the judiciary has become increasingly more sophisticated in refining what techniques will work, and which techniques violate fundamental due process or other jurisprudential constraints.

112 The events at the World Trade Center, and the legal context for the resolution of those events, are but a piece of this evolving legal landscape. There are two fundamental points about the Victims' Compensation Fund that should be stressed. First, the Victims' Compensation Fund is but another fund approach to resolving tort claims without fault or liability, similar to other such programs that Congress has enacted in the past. Having said that, the specific terms of the Victims Compensation Fund legislation are *sui generis*, and will not be precisely replicated should another catastrophic mass tort phenomenon like the WTC events occur in the future. In fact, all past fund approaches to mass tort litigation events have each differed in the details.

113 It is impossible, at this juncture, to speculate about the consequences for the judicial system concerning those claimants who elect not to take compensation through the Victims' Compensation Fund. It is even difficult to speculate whether the remaining universe of claimants will constitute their own mass tort litigation. The exact numbers of those persons who decline to take compensation through the Fund will be determined at some date certain, when the Fund application cutoff becomes effective to bar further claims against the Fund. After that point, claimants will then have to make the decision whether to retain counsel and pursue relief through ordinary tort litigation, in the judicial system. Initially, such lawsuits will be individual suits. Whether plaintiffs' attorneys will collect claimants, or will pursue aggregative litigation, remains to be seen.

The Victims' Compensation Fund specifies that any such litigation must be brought in the federal court in the Southern District of New York. Beyond that threshold jurisdictional mandate, we can only guess at the procedural form such litigation might take, or the substantive legal issues that will be involved in those cases or claims. Because all such tort cases must be brought in the Southern District of New York, it is a fair bet that the Judicial Panel on Multi-district litigation will swiftly create an WTC MDL. But beyond the creation and supervision of a WTC MDL, we cannot know whether, in the fashion of *Agent Orange* or DES or asbestos (or any other mass tort), a managerial judge will cram down a class settlement. It also is interesting to speculate whether and to what extent such a possible class settlement would mimic the terms of the Victims' Compensation Fund (with the necessary added provision for payment of attorneys' fees). Finally, it seems likely that pursuit of WTC claims will involve difficult questions such as the identification of the universe of viable defendants, as well as the identification of the legal theories to support such litigation. However, one has absolute confidence in the American plaintiff bar's ability to identify such defendants and theories. Whether such creative pleading will support the tort claims, however, remains an open question. But it is worth remembering that even the existence of problematic defendants, coupled with problematic legal theories, did not prevent the *Agent Orange* litigation from being resolved on a classwide basis through a classwide, court-supervised fund. 114

It is now well-recognized that in 1966, when the Advisory Committee on Civil Rules completely redrafted the American class action rule, that the distinguished jurists on that Committee did not anticipate the emergence of mass tort litigation as we know it today. It is equally well-recognized that those jurists' lack of psychic predictive abilities had consequences when mass tort litigation finally emerged as a distinctive litigation phenomena, because the rules they drafted dealt poorly, if at all, with the new types of litigation that they did not foresee. In the intervening years, mass tort litigation has continued to evolve through forms, procedures, and substantive problems that we could not have predicted, and still cannot envision. Who, fifteen years ago, would have predicted the advent of the medical monitoring class? Mass tort litigation is an evolving phenomenon, and the experience of each new mass tort case pushes the borders of known jurisprudence, and inspires creative new means for resolution. The only thing of which we may be certain is that we cannot now know what mass tort litigation will look like in twenty-five years, and how the judicial system, the tort lawyers, the insurance industry, or any other actor in the system will resolve these cases. 115

General Reports

Liability and Insurance in Cases of Damage Caused by Terrorist Attacks – Economic Analysis

Israel Gilead*

I. The Questions

1 The emerging threat of large-scale terrorist attacks aimed at civil targets in North America and the EU raises, from the perspective of tort and insurance law, three major questions:

1. *Efficient Prevention – Primary Cost Reduction (Avoidance)*. The first question is that of efficient prevention, or, in Calabresi's terms, that of primary cost reduction. Could and should tort law be used in order to prevent and ward off terrorist attacks in a way that minimizes the primary costs: the costs of prevention and the *irreducible expected* costs of "successful" attacks?[1] Drawing again on Calabresi's terminology, the question is: who is the best "attacks' primary cost *avoider*"?

2. *Cost Bearing – Secondary Cost Reduction (Avoidance)*. The second question is how to deal with the damage *actually* caused by "successful" terrorist acts in a way that will reduce its *reducible* costs.[2] This is the question of secondary cost reduction, in Calabresi's terms. As we shall see, this question has two aspects. First, who can incur the costs of this damage, in a way that will secure the availability of funds needed for damage repair and its containment, to avoid costs of deteriorating damage (direct secondary costs). Second, who can provide these funds, without being exposed to economic dislocation or financial collapse (collateral secondary costs)? The question, to sum up the two aspects, is who is the best "attacks' cost *bearer*"?

* Bora Laskin Professor of Law, The Law Faculty, The Hebrew University of Jerusalem

[1] A "successful" terrorist attack, like any accident or damage causing occurrence, involves two kinds of costs: The expected inevitable or irreducible costs of the damage caused by the attack, and costs that are avoidable or reducible if the damage caused is properly handled. In the following discussion reference to primary costs of the damage caused by an attack is to these expected and irreducible costs. The reducible costs of the damage actually caused by a terrorist attack are referred to as "secondary costs" – see below.

[2] Ibid.

3. *Relation between Primary and Secondary Cost Avoidance.* The third question looks to the interrelation between the former two. Should the decision as to who should be the "cost bearer" take into account the latter's ability to function as a "primary cost avoider", or should cost avoidance be regarded only as one consideration among others, or even be disregarded altogether?

The following sections elaborate on these questions.

II. Primary Cost Avoidance (Reduction) – Minimizing the Overall Costs of Attacks and Their Prevention

Avoidance by Tort Law. The overall primary costs of terrorist attacks and their 2
prevention may be minimized by various methods, some of which are obviously unrelated to tort law. To start with, terrorism may be prevented by the resolution of the conflicts– political, national, or religious – that feed it in the first place. Alas, such a solution is often the result of wishful thinking, rather than being particularly practical (or attainable) in the foreseeable future. Military attacks on terror bases in the countries that harbor and support it is another complicated mode of active prevention. International cooperation, intelligence work, restrictive immigration and visa policies are other methods.

Our analysis, however, is restricted to those activities, bodies or individuals, 3
that may be held liable in tort. It concentrates on those who are subject to tort liability and who may be induced by such liability (or its absence) to take preventive measures to reduce the primary costs of terrorist attacks and the cost of their prevention (primary cost avoidance).[3]

The Best Cost Avoider. According to basic economic analysis regarding damage 4
prevention, tort liability should be imposed on the best primary cost avoider. Primary costs are, on the one hand, the expected irreducible costs of a "successful" terrorist attack,[4] and on the other hand, the costs of preventative measures taken against such attacks. A primary cost avoider is, accordingly, an activity, a body, or an individual that can, directly or indirectly, lower primary costs by taking preventative measures that are less costly than the expected costs of the preventable attack.[5] The best cost avoider is the one that can minimize primary costs – minimize the overall costs of the attacks and their prevention.[6] Tort liability is to

[3] The role of tort liability in encouraging the potentially liable to take preventive measures is often described in terms of "deterrence". Tort law functions as a deterrent. Yet, the notion of deterrence is more suitable with regard to tort liability imposed on those who actively inflict losses on others. When liability is imposed on those who fail to prevent others, third parties, from inflicting loss, as in our case, the term "deterrence" seems less appropriate.

[4] See supra fn. 1.

[5] This is illustrated by Posner's Hand Formula. When the expected primary costs of an attack (PL) exceed the costs of prevention (B), this is a cost avoidance situation. The cost that can be efficiently avoided is the *difference* between PL and B.
Under the Hand Formula "L" (loss) denotes the primary costs caused by the accident and "P" denotes its probabilty. "PL" denotes accordingly the expected primary costs of the attack. "B" denotes the burden, the costs of the preventive measures.

[6] The best cost avoider would minimize the total costs of PL+B.

be imposed on this best primary cost avoider in order to encourage it to take the efficient preventive measures that minimize primary costs.

5 There are situations in which the greatest reduction in primary costs would be brought about by preventative measures taken by more than one cost avoider. In such situations, where there are some best cost avoiders, tort liability is to be imposed in a way that would encourage each of them to avoid "his share" of the primary costs.

III. The Cost Avoiders

6 The cost avoiders of terrorist attacks include the following:

- *Governmental and Municipal Authorities.* Different public authorities may be held liable for failure to detect terrorists or to prevent them from executing their vicious plans. These include: border/immigration police, the secret services, the police and other governmental authorities in charge of security and anti terrorism activity (such as seaport, airport and transportation authorities), public health authorities in charge of biological warfare etc.
- *Occupiers or Others in Charge of Premises Open to the Public.* Terrorist attacks often take place in crowded places – malls, theaters, hospitals, cafes, schools, indoor parking lots etc. Close scrutiny of those who enter the premises at risk may prove to be a most effective measure, as demonstrated by the Israeli experience. Indeed, attacks that take place aboard means of public transportation, such as buses, trains and planes, can also be prevented by security measures taken at the terminals, and on the public transportation means by the operators.
- *Providers of Private Security Services.* Security services flourish in times of terrorist threats. Failure of the providers of security services to prevent terrorist acts may generate liability in contract and tort toward the beneficiaries of these services, such as clients and third parties.
- *The Victims* of terrorist attacks may also take some preventive measures against such attacks by protecting themselves as potential victims. They may, for example, purchase security services or security products, avoid risky places, be alert and attentive, and report suspicious activities or persons. Potential victims are induced to take preventive measures because they are personally subjected to the damage. Denying them the right of compensation wholly or partially (contributory negligence) would strengthen their self-protection motives.

IV. Cost Bearing – Secondary Cost Avoidance Distinguished from Primary Cost Avoidance

7 *Cost Bearing – The Two Aspects.* Who should incur the costs of terrorist attacks? Who should be the cost bearer? As mentioned, the primary cost avoidance role of tort law is predicated on the assumption that tort liability induces

potential primary cost avoiders to take efficient preventive measures to prevent terrorist attacks. From the primary cost avoidance perspective, then, the cost bearer of terrorist attacks should be the best primary cost avoider. Cost bearing is the means to create incentives for primary cost reduction.

Yet, as emphasized by Calabresi, primary cost avoidance is only one aspect of tort law's role as a promoter of efficiency. Deciding who shall bear the costs has another major aspect – the reduction of the other kind of damage-related cost – secondary costs. These costs, as well, should be reduced in an efficient manner. Choosing the best avoiders of primary costs as cost bearers would efficiently reduce primary costs, but may result in secondary costs that should be avoided. The decision concerning the cost bearer should therefore take into account, not only the effect of such a choice on primary cost reduction, but also its effects on secondary cost reduction. 8

What are these avoidable, reducible, secondary costs? These are costs associated with the need to efficiently prevent the damage directly following the terrorist act from growing. There are two kinds of secondary costs – first-order cost and collateral cost. 9

Direct Secondary Costs. The starting point of secondary cost analysis is that, unfortunately, terrorist attacks do occur and may recur, causing substantial damage. Some costs, previously referred to as primary costs, are unavoidable or irreducible. Some costs, however, secondary costs, are avoidable or reducible. A given damage, to body, property and even to economic interests may often expand, causing more costs, if not treated or otherwise contained. Any given bodily injury, for example, may deteriorate without proper medical treatment. A loss of earning capacity due to bodily injury may become permanent, unless the injured is trained in another occupation. Economic loss caused by a damaged car or machine may grow if the car or the machine are not fixed and cannot produce earnings. To avoid such secondary costs there is a need to take preventive measures in the form of medical treatment, vocational training, fixing damaged property etc. Secondary cost avoidance is efficient whenever the costs involved in the repair or the containment of a given damage are lower than the avoided secondary costs. The best avoider of these direct secondary costs is the one that can provide the necessary funds for efficient repair and containment in a way that minimizes these overall costs. 10

Collateral Secondary Costs. Financial ability to provide for efficient preventive measures of secondary costs, however, is only one aspect of secondary cost avoidance. Repair and containment of damage may involve large costs, as is often the case with regard to damage caused by terrorist acts. As emphasized by Calabresi, when these costs amount to a substantial portion of the cost bearer's resources, the burden may bring about the bearer's financial collapse or economic dislocation. These costs of collapse or dislocation are another kind of secondary costs, collateral secondary costs, that should also be avoided or minimized. 11

12 *Secondary Loss Avoidance – An Overview.* The conclusion, then, is that secondary cost avoidance has two aspects:

- A loss bearer has to have the ability to incur the costs of efficient prevention of direct secondary costs – ability to pay for medical treatment, lost earnings, vocational training, repair of damaged property etc.
- The loss bearer should be able to incur the above costs without being susceptible to the collateral secondary costs of financial collapse and economic dislocation.

13 These two goals can be attained by the following methods: "deep pocket", and loss spreading. The mechanisms that spread loss are insurance, either first-party or third party insurance, and market prices

V. Cost Bearing – "Deep Pocket" and Loss Spreading

14 *Deep Pocket.* A "deep pocket" is a potential cost bearer sufficiently wealthy to incur the costs of efficient prevention of secondary costs of terrorist attacks without being subjected to its collateral secondary costs of financial collapse or economic dislocation.

15 *Loss Spreading – Kinds of Insurance.* The major mechanism for secondary cost reduction is loss spreading. The loss spreader is a potential cost bearer who has the ability to spread the costs among many bearers, so that each bearer incurs only a small share of the total costs. Loss spreading reduces both direct secondary costs by providing sufficient funds to repair and contain damage, and collateral secondary costs, by avoiding financial collapse or economic dislocation. The major method of loss spreading is insurance – either liability insurance or first party insurance. Where the potential cost bearer is a liable tortfeasor, the relevant insurance is third-party insurance, liability insurance, unless the liable entity has a "deep pocket", which actually means self-insurance. The loss is spread over those insured – the potential group of tortfeasors. Where the potential loss bearer is the victim, the relevant insurance is first party insurance. The loss is spread over the potential group of insured victims.

16 *Loss Spreading – Market Prices.* A third method of loss spreading is through market prices. Where the potential cost bearers are tortfeasors that conduct activities susceptible to terrorist acts, the prices of these activities may be raised to cover the costs of liability. In this way the costs of terrorist acts are shifted, at least partially, to consumers of the threatened activities.

17 *Costs of Loss Spreading.* The operation of insurance mechanisms is costly. Contracting, classification of the insured according to risk, handling claims, payments – all these involve costs that from an economic point of view should be taken into account when considering the efficiency of different loss spreading mechanisms. Liability insurance, for example, may prove to be less costly

than first party insurance if the risks of the insured group are specific risks that are easy to assess, and if premiums are easier to collect.

Combination of Different Methods. The different methods of loss spreading are not mutually exclusive. On the contrary, they can be integrated. For example, some costs of terrorist attacks may be spread by liability insurance over the susceptible activities, including consumers, and other costs spread through first party insurance of the victims. 18

The Best Cost Bearer. Given the different aspects of loss bearing, the different methods of loss spreading and the "deep pocket" option, the best cost bearer is the one that can: 19

- Provide the necessary resources required for efficient prevention of direct secondary costs.
- Do so while avoiding, or minimizing, the collateral secondary costs of financial collapse or economic dislocation.
- Attain the above two goals with minimal costs.

VI. Cost Avoidance and Cost Bearing – Interrelation

Notably, there is an inherent tension between primary cost avoidance on the one hand, and secondary cost avoidance through loss spreading on the other hand. Primary cost avoidance is premised on the assumption that it is the burden of potential liability that would induce the cost avoider to take efficient measures to prevent damage for which the cost avoider would otherwise be liable. In our context, it is the burden of having to incur the costs of terrorist attacks that is supposed to encourage the cost avoider to minimize the overall primary costs of terrorist attacks and their prevention. But if, however, the primary cost avoider is also a cost bearer that meets the requirements of secondary cost avoidance by way of loss spreading, this negatively affects the incentives for primary cost avoidance. Once premium is paid, and tort liability of the insured is covered, the sanction of tort liability becomes less effective, if at all, and the insured's incentives to take costly preventive measures are reduced or even disappear. This is the "moral hazard" aspect of insurance. There are, however, methods to encourage the insured to take efficient preventive measures despite insurance coverage. These include deductibles, premiums rise when claims are filed, and, more importantly, requiring the insured to take preventive measures as a pre-condition to coverage. Such preventive measures include alarms, bars, employment of security personnel etc. This insurance-induced prevention may offset the moral hazard effect, but not always, and usually to a limited degree. 20

On the basis of the above, let us now examine the potential avoiders of primary and secondary costs of terrorist attacks. 21

VII. Governmental and Municipal Authorities – Cost Avoidance

22 Governmental and municipal (public) authorities are "natural" primary cost avoiders of terrorist attacks. Prominent examples, as mentioned, include border/immigration police, the secret services, the police, other governmental authorities in charge of security and anti-terrorism activity such as seaport, airport and transportation authorities, public health authorities in charge of biological warfare etc.

23 Is there a need to impose tort liability on public authorities in order to induce them to take efficient measures to minimize the primary costs of terrorist attacks? This is doubtful. It is argued that the conventional cost avoidance analysis can hardly be applied to public authorities the way it is applied to "private" tortfeasors. The main difference has to do with the "externalities" economic justification of tort liability. Tort liability is imposed on a "private" tortfeasor on the assumption that, otherwise, the latter would externalize the costs that his tortious activity inflicts on others. Being a rational maximizer of one's own utility, a "private" tortfeasor tends to ignore, to externalize, the negative effects of his activity on potential victims whenever his own utility is not affected. Tort liability is called upon to "internalize" these externalities. The risk of being liable for the victim's loss renders this loss a "private" cost of the tortfeasor's activity. This analysis is much less applicable to public authorities. Assuming that public authorities, through public officials, do not seek their own, "private", utility, but rather the common good, they have no reason to externalize costs of their activity to others. On the contrary, such costs are supposed to be taken into consideration in the first place. Where there are no externalities there is no need for tort law to "internalize" activity costs to potential tortfeasors. These costs are already internalized.

24 Of course, one should not be naive. Public authorities and public officials do not always pursue the public good. They may often have their own personal or organizational interests that may lead them to externalize costs. There is certainly a degree of externalization in the public service activity that calls for remedial internalization by tort law. Yet, the existence of such externalities should be examined in each relevant context. With regard to terrorist attacks, it appears that the degree of externalization, if it exists at all, does not call for internalization by tort law. For various reasons, public authorities and public officials seem to be well motivated to prevent terrorist attacks. To start with, the general tendency is to morally condemn these acts, given their horrific outcomes, so that those who can prevent terrorist attacks are genuinely inclined to do so. Moreover, as terrorist attacks disrupt daily life, threatening the most basic values and ways of life, there are immense political pressures to fight them. These pressures intensify where terrorist acts are conducted on the background of national, racial, or religious conflicts, posing a threat to national security and to the very fabric of society. In Israel, for example, terror attacks are perceived as a threat to national existence.

The conclusion, then, is that public authorities are sufficiently motivated to function as primary cost avoiders of terrorist acts. It is doubtful whether the imposition of tort liability on public authorities in this regard would significantly improve primary cost avoidance. Even if it would improve it, arguably on the margin, the social costs of litigation (tertiary cost reduction in Calabresi's terms) may well exceed the value of such improvement. Moreover, at least two difficult legal questions may complicate the judicial tort process. First, in many countries public authorities enjoy different degrees of immunity against tort liability, especially where the authorities exercise wide discretion. Second, claimants may find it problematic to establish the causal link between the alleged failure of the authority and the successful attack. 25

VIII. Public Authorities – Loss Bearing

Public authorities, in our case the state or municipalities, are obviously very suitable cost bearers. They actually combine "deep pocket" with loss spreading capacities. The public budget is usually "deep" enough to cover the costs of terrorist attacks, and, if not, can be enlarged to that end by changing priorities, increasing taxes, or otherwise. Moreover, public authorities, that become the cost bearer, have the ability to spread the costs of terrorist attacks on taxpayers. In this way the necessary funds for secondary costs avoidance would be available with no collateral secondary costs of financial collapse or economic dislocation. 26

There are three additional advantages to making the public budget the major cost bearer of terrorist attacks: 27

The costs of this mechanism of loss bearing and loss spreading are relatively low, as this mechanism already exists and functions. 28

There is hardly any tension between primary and secondary cost avoidance in this regard. The public authorities are committed, according to the above observations, to the prevention of terrorist acts, regardless of tort liability. The ability to spread the costs of terrorist attacks over taxpayers would not undermine this commitment. On the contrary, functioning in this regard as "deep pocket", the public authorities would have an incentive to reduce secondary costs by reducing the primary costs, namely, to prevent the attacks in the first place. Making the public authority the cost bearer provides an important incentive to primary cost reduction. 29

Economic analysis should not ignore considerations of justice and fairness. Victims of terrorist attacks are often innocent victims who just happen to be at the site of the attack. Terrorist attacks threaten the social order, especially when motivated by national, religious or racial ideologies. It is therefore fair and just that the public, as a whole, incur the costs of such attacks. This is actually the law in Israel, where the state incurs the costs suffered by victims of acts of hostility, including terrorist attacks. The same approach was taken in 30 the U.S. after the September 11 attacks. Nowadays, when states are declaring and waging war against terrorism, the victims of terrorism are victims of war.

IX. Conclusion – Public Authorities Should be Made Cost Bearers

31 The above discussion indicates that public authorities are "natural" primary and secondary cost avoiders. They are sufficiently motivated to minimize primary costs. They are effective cost bearers able to minimize all sorts of secondary costs. Making them cost bearers is not only fair and just, but also serves as another stimulus for primary cost reduction.

32 Making public authorities the bearers of the costs of terrorist attacks is actually equivalent to the imposition of strict, or even absolute, liability on them.

33 *Caps and Restrictions.* This "no-fault liability" of public authorities, the outcome of becoming the cost bearer, may be restricted by caps or exclusion of certain kinds of losses. Should such restrictions be imposed? And if so, who should incur the costs uncovered by public authorities? These questions are tackled below, as the discussion extends to examine tort liability and cost bearing with regard to other primary cost avoiders.

X. Occupiers or Others in Charge of Premises at Risk Open to the Public – Fault-Based Liability

34 *Primary Cost Avoidance.* As mentioned, terror attacks often take place in crowded premises – malls, theaters, hospitals, cafes, schools, indoor parking lots etc. The Israeli experience clearly demonstrates that close scrutiny of those who enter premises at risk (including public means of transportation) and the presence of security personnel prove to be a most effective preventive measure that deters and prevents terrorist attacks.

35 Should tort fault-based liability be imposed on occupiers and others in charge of endangered premises, including operators of means of transportation for failure to take such measures? In this regard fault-based liability is to be imposed whenever the costs of preventive measures are lower than the expected primary costs of terrorist acts, and a causal link can be established between a successful terrorist attack and the failure to take these preventive measures.

36 It appears, on the one hand, that the imposition of tort liability upon those who control premises open to the public and means of transportation may well encourage them, as cost avoiders, to take efficient preventive measures. Without such liability the costs of the attacks may be externalized to the public in the absence of incentives to pay the costs of preventive measures. It may be argued, on the other hand, that such incentives exist anyway. Why? Because if preventive measures are not taken, the public may refrain from entering unsecured premises or using unsecured means of transportation. The ensuing expected loss of revenues may well serve as a major consideration that actually internalizes the costs of attacks to occupiers and others in charge of risky pre-

mises and means of transportation. Moreover, the latter may find it relatively easy to cover the costs of these preventive measures. Security is a commodity or service for which the public is ready to pay. In Israel coffee shops, restaurants, hotels, and theatres add a small amount to the cost of the service to cover the costs of additional security measures. This is actually an example of the operation of the "Coase Theorem": customers are "bribing" the occupiers to take security measures by being ready to pay the costs of such measures.

Still, there would be cases in which occupiers and others in charge of premises 37
open to the public do externalize the costs, or at least some of the costs, of terrorist acts. This may be the case where potential victims are not potential customers. Imposition of tort liability may seem appropriate to internalize this externality and create incentives to take preventive measures. Given the huge costs of a successful terrorist attack, occupiers and others, especially if risk averse, would tend to take these preventive measures in order to avoid liability, even where the probability of such an attack is very low. Furthermore, they would certainly wish to protect themselves against such liability by acquiring liability insurance, and it stands to reason that such coverage would be conditional upon the taking of preventive measures. This insurance-induced prevention may generate the same kind of prevention induced by tort liability not backed by liability insurance.

In sum, imposition of tort liability on occupiers and others in charge of endan- 38
gered premises and public transportation means may prove to encourage efficient prevention of primary costs.

Cost Bearing – Secondary Cost Avoidance. Although those in charge of endan- 39
gered premises and means of transportation are primary cost avoiders, their suitability to serve as cost bearers is questionable. Given the expected high costs of terrorist attacks, it is doubtful whether liability insurance will be available or affordable. This depends on the probability of such attacks in terms of frequency and scale. It appears that no private insurer will undertake to cover the risk of frequent, large scale, attacks. Where the risk is remote and attacks are expected to be limited in scale, insurers may be ready to offer coverage for affordable premiums. The problem, however, is that the probability of terrorist attacks in terms of frequency and scale is hardly predictable, and insurers may avoid such coverage as a policy.

XI. Occupiers or Others in Charge of Premises at Risk Open to the Public – No-Fault Liability

An alternative to the above fault-based liability is the imposition of no-fault li- 40
ability. Liability in this regard is strict or absolute if imposed despite the occupiers and others taking reasonable or efficient preventive measures, or despite the absence of an established causal link between the failure to take such measures and the success of an attack. Such liability would certainly strengthen incentives to take preventive measures, especially if occupiers and others are

risk averse. The problem, obviously, lies with the cost bearing aspect, as it seems not many occupiers could withstand the burden of strict liability, and it is doubtful whether liability insurers would be ready to cover the risks of such no-fault liability.

XII. Liability of Occupiers or Others in Charge of Premises at Risk Open to the Public and "Liability" of Public Authorities – The Interrelation

41 Previously identifying public authorities as fitting cost avoiders and cost bearers, the question is how should this cost bearing, on the one hand, and tort liability of occupiers and others, on the other hand, be accommodated, assuming that the latter could also be made cost bearers? Should both bear the costs of attacks? And if so, how should the burden be apportioned between them?

42 From a primary costs avoidance perspective, joint liability seems appropriate. Public authorities, on the one hand, and occupiers and others in control of premises, on the other hand, often specialize in different aspects of attacks' prevention. Scrutiny of those who enter private premises at risk, for example, is a preventive measure that should and could be taken by occupiers and others and not by public authorities. Each of the two should be induced to take preventive measures within its "specialty", and it is the combined effort of the two that would lead to the best results.

43 Yet, the victim's entitlement to damages and benefits from both sources would require adjustment of entitlements and apportionment. The mechanisms of adjustment and apportionment, as well as the availability of two venues of suits, may prove to be expensive.

44 More importantly, it is doubtful, as emphasized, whether occupiers and others in control of premises, although cost avoiders, can serve as cost bearers given the problem of unavailability or the non-affordability of insurance coverage.

XIII. Residual Liability?

45 An interesting option is to render the liability of occupiers and others in control of premises towards the victims residual, namely, liability limited to those losses not covered by public authorities, assuming that the latter's liability is indeed restricted by caps or exclusion of some kinds of loss. Actually, in the first place, such restrictions may be aimed at allowing cost bearing by occupiers and others liable in tort. Such residual liability may, on the one hand, induce occupiers and others to take preventive measures in which they "specialize". On the other hand, such liability, being limited to residual costs not covered by public authorities, can be backed and spread by liability insurance, so that occupiers and others, as well, may serve as residual cost bearers.

46 It may be argued that rendering the liability of occupiers and other cost avoiders residual may weaken their incentive to take preventive measures. This can

be rectified by subjecting them to indemnity or contribution claims by public authorities, once it is established that the failure to prevent a terrorist attack amounts to gross negligence or recklessness (indifference).

XIV. Providers of Private Security Services

The Israeli experience proves that security services, of all kinds, flourish in times of terrorist threats. Failure of providers of security services to prevent terrorist acts may be the source of tort liability to the victims. Under doctrines such as "protective" contracts or third party beneficiary, providers may also be held contractually liable to these victims, despite the lack of contractual privity, 47

The above analysis regarding liability of occupiers is applicable to this group of potential tortfeasors. 48

XV. The Victims

As mentioned, victims of the attacks may also take preventive measures against terrorist attacks by protecting themselves as potential victims: avoiding risky places, being alert and attentive, reporting suspicious activities or persons, and purchasing security services or security products. Victims are cost bearers by default: if no one else is liable, victims will incur the costs of the attacks. If made cost bearer, victims would try to spread their loss through first party insurance. 49

Primary Cost Avoidance. Should liability arrangements be used to encourage potential victims to take self-protection preventive measures? Such encouragement could be attained by exposing victims to the costs of attacks, either wholly, by denying the liability of others, or partially, through the contributory negligence defence. 50

Although potential victims do "specialize" in some aspects of preventive measures, being at the site of a targeted area, it is doubtful whether tort liability arrangements should be used to encourage primary cost avoidance by them. For starters, where bodily injury may be involved, potential victims are well motivated to do everything they can to protect themselves. It is doubtful whether exposing them to the financial burden of such injury would add much to efficient prevention by them. On the contrary, such exposure may lead to overreaction, for example, people staying at home, hysteria etc. With regard to risks of damage to property and to economic interests, these risks are often the outcome of the same terrorist acts that threaten bodily integrity, so that self-protection motives exist anyway. 51

Moreover, it seems unfair to "punish" victims of terrorist attacks for failing to prevent such attacks even when they behave carelessly. This risk of terrorist attack is of the kind that should be borne by society at large. 52

53 *Victim as Cost Bearer – Residual Loss Spreading.* If potential victims are made cost bearers of terrorist attacks, they will try to spread the expected costs through first party insurance covering all or part of the risks.

54 As with regard to liability insurance of occupiers and providers of security services, it is doubtful whether such comprehensive first party insurance would be available or affordable. This depends on the expected frequency and scale of such attacks, but insurers may be reluctant to cover even the risks that seem remote.

55 The residual liability option, discussed with regard to occupiers and providers of security services, may prove to be useful in this regard as well. If, for example, victims would have no right of compensation for some types of losses, or only limited entitlement to compensation for other losses, they may be willing to purchase first liability insurance to cover the uncovered risks. As these risks are only residual, insurers may be ready to provide such coverage for affordable premiums. To this end insurers can extend existing life insurance, accidents, disability, fire, property damage and so on to cover terrorist acts for reasonable premiums.

XVI. Conclusions

56 Public authorities are both cost avoiders and cost bearers. The major burden of primary and secondary cost avoidance of terrorist acts should be imposed upon them as "strictly liable", and in a way that would strengthen their incentive to take efficient preventive measures. On the other hand, such "liability" may be restricted by caps and by exclusion of some types of damage. Such restriction would induce other cost avoiders to take preventive measures in which they specialize.

57 Occupiers and those in charge of endangered premises, including operators of means of public transportation, as well as providers of security services, may be held liable for the residual costs uncovered by public authorities. Such residual, fault-based liability, would create or strengthen the incentives of these cost avoiders to take preventive measures in which they specialize. Being residual, such liability may well be covered by affordable liability insurance. Moreover, to fortify the incentives to take preventive measures, these cost avoiders may be exposed to indemnity claims of public authorities for gross negligence and recklessness in preventing terrorist attacks.

58 Victims as well may be induced to spread the costs of the residual costs uncovered by public authorities by denying their entitlement to compensation for residual costs. These costs could be spread by victims through the extension of first party liability insurance.

59 Whether residual costs are better handled by liability insurance, namely by the imposition of tort liability on cost avoiders other than public authorities, or by

first party insurance of victims with no such residual tort liability, is a question that should be further examined. Possibly, the best method could be a combination of the two to cover these residual costs.

Liability Insurance for Acts of Terrorism?

Christian Lahnstein

I. Insurance of the Person, Property and Liability Insurance

1 Acts of terrorism have always been an issue in insurance, and this is true of most classes of insurance. September 11th highlighted the accumulation of losses from different classes in a striking way. The classes most affected were insurances of the person: life, disability and workers' compensation insurance; property insurance, more specifically material damage and business interruption insurance; and finally, liability insurance, particularly the liability insurance of the airlines involved as decisive links in the causal chain. But the question of the liability of other parties also arose – and were masked by the Victim Compensation Fund, which was quickly established by the Federal Government. This Fund has so far served its purpose of avoiding having to answer these questions of liability; to avoid, as Kenneth Abraham put it in the US country report "undermining American political morale and the sense of unity in the fight against terrorism".[1]

2 Aviation insurance – like marine insurance – involves a specific insurance market. It comprises property insurance, insurances of the person and liability insurance. Aviation liability differentiates between the liability of airports and of airlines. It also distinguishes between liability towards passengers, its own employees, and liability towards third parties. Since September 11th, airlines' liability towards third parties and the liability of airport operators have been the subject of worldwide debate and various solutions, often differing from country to country.[2]

3 For insurances of the person, there is widespread agreement that the risks of terrorism are included in the cover and will continue to be so. One of the reasons is that social security, which in fact is primarily responsible for compensating bodily injury, has to cover terrorism risks, as well as war risks – this is true of pension and health insurance, and also of workers' compensation. September 11th – an attack on a working city – made it clear that the working environments in expensive office complexes at the heart of major cities are ex-

[1] K. Abraham, USA (supra 204), no. 13.

[2] B.A. Koch/S. Strahwald, Compensation Schemes (infra 293), no. 65 et seq.

posed targets for terrorism. Against this social-law background, private insurers of the person are not inclined to exclude terrorism. Besides, they know that, in relation to the total volume of life, health and workers' compensation insurance, the risk is lower than it might seem to an occasionally nervous public – not a bad underlying situation for sales. However, the accumulation risk, for example in the case of group accident insurances, is now rated higher.

With property insurance, the most striking difference compared to insurances of the person is that the background of state provision and state social security is largely absent. It is well known that in the 20th century, the world's governments tried, not always successfully, to establish Bismarck- or Beveridge-style models of pension, health and workers' compensation insurances. Certain historical models of using property insurance as social insurance were largely forgotten. Property insurance is, accordingly, the domain of private insurance. 4

Now it is precisely the risks of natural hazards (like an earthquake or flood) and political risks, like terrorism, where the need for government involvement in compensating property damage is also seen. Appropriate measures may be developed on an ad hoc basis, leading to one-off arrangements. Such ad hoc solutions may be welcome from the political point of view: to isolate a problem and to demonstrate initiative and efficiency in a state of emergency, instead of struggling with boring, commonplace structural problems. An example is the flood situation in Germany summer 2002 in the middle of an election campaign. Or these systems are institutionalised, as in the various specific terrorism pools, mostly with mixed state and private involvement, such as "Extremus" in Germany or "Gareat" in France, or the Spanish Consorcio-model introduced in 1941 after the Civil War. With the US "Terrorism Risk Insurance Act" of 2002, the US government became involved not by participating in a pool, but directly, in a tax-based model. This Act covers all property and casualty classes of business and workers' compensation, but is limited to a few years. As far as implementation of this US law is concerned, the cost of administration is considerable. 5

Whereas with insurances of the person, the risk of terrorism is largely covered, in property insurance different solutions are being found. But what about liability insurance? Unlike providers of first-party insurances, liability insurers, as third-party insurers, can leave the question to be dealt with by tort law. At the same time, liability law is influenced by the existence and scope of any first-party insurances. This happens in different ways. 6

In most cases, liability law is only masked by first-party insurance. First party insurers pay out and then subrogate against the liable parties. This is what happens with Extremus, Gareat and the other European property insurance pools. Gareat, however, expressly waives subrogation against motor insurers. So, if a building collapses as a result of a car bomb, Gareat will not subrogate against the motor insurer. But it can subrogate against the architect's liability insurers, if miscalculations by the architect have contributed to the building's collapse. 7

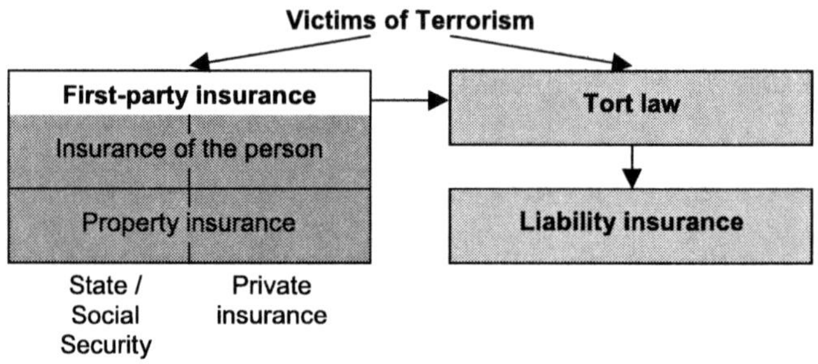

8 Liability practice changes however, simply because in the case of subrogation, the victim protection aspect is not relevant. The purposes of subrogation are thus reduced to sensible apportionment of costs and penalties for fault. For administrative reasons too, with such arrangements between organisations – first-party insurers and liability insurers – liability mechanisms other than those in direct relation to the victim develop.

9 To some extent, liability law is not only masked by first-party or similar insurance constructions, but also replaced or abolished to a greater degree. Quantitatively unlimited liability is replaced by quantitatively limited insurance cover, as in the case of the USA's Victim Compensation Fund. Here, the compensation is set at a high level, in order to get victims to forego any liability claims. As far as considerations on replacing liability by insurance cover are concerned, different trends are observable.

10 On the one hand, the systematic expansion of the first-party cover provided by welfare-state schemes has long been discontinued, or is in decline worldwide. Instead, particularly in the case of bodily injury, tort law has been increasingly developed to protect victims. With terrorism, unlike with industrial accidents or road accidents, there is no possibility of replacing the liability of the main responsible parties with insurance. The reason is simply that, unlike car drivers or employers, terrorists are not suitable for financing the insurance of their victims.

11 On the other hand, there is a trend towards the merging of first-party insurance and full compensation under tort law in a number of more or less clearly defined areas: for example, in compulsory motor insurance, or – as currently proposed in France and the UK – in industrial accidents and occupational diseases. This is also the case on the basis of non-compulsory insurance, as in the French insurance model *accidents de la vie* (life accidents). These are optimum solutions from the point of view of the protection of victims. The question is whether developments of this kind are also being seen in respect of the victims of terrorism, and how the question of sensible apportionment of costs is to be answered.

12 Compulsory cover of road accidents or industrial accidents thus also includes the compensation of victims in terrorism situations. The costs are borne by the

community of motorists or employers in the framework of differently structured and differentiated risk tariffs. *Accidents de la vie*, on the other hand, is a model of voluntary self-insurance for the potential victims of accidents in which it is assumed either that no liability exists, or that the question of liability is at least unclear. Examples are accidents in the home, or terrorist attacks. Given the high level of compensation corresponding to "droit commun" – tort law –, the broad scope of cover and the non-compulsory basis, the premiums are considerable. Marketing of this cover – which is largely done through banks – nevertheless appears to be successful. 10% of the French population now have such cover. A similar model restricted solely to terrorism, and thus cheaper, is therefore not unrealistic (see the comments made by Gilead on voluntary self-insurance for people who see themselves as being at risk from acts of terrorism).[3]

II. Specific Questions Regarding Liability Insurance

A. *Exclusion of Intent*

Considerations about liability insurance for acts of terrorism should not conceal one quite obvious aspect, namely liability insurance on the part of the perpetrators. This comes into consideration in many ways. For example, as part of compulsory insurances in road, air and shipping traffic. Perpetrators can also be employees in insured companies. Or they may be members of families with personal liability insurance who are of age or still minors. Companies themselves can be considered joint perpetrators, for example in connection with the manufacture of weapons or hazardous substances. The transition between deliberate perpetrators and negligent third parties is, in any case, fluid. States and companies can be accused – if not of supporting – of inadequate supervision or control, while individuals can be prosecuted or sued under both criminal and tort law for not passing on information. 13

In such cases, the liability insurer involved will invoke the exclusion of intent, a core principle of any private insurance. Some questions arise, however: 14

The exclusion generally applies to intent on the part of the policyholder. Often though, the wilful act is carried out by other persons. The owner, keeper, driver or thief, the pilot or hijacker of an aircraft or vessel, or the operator of a motor vehicle, need not be the same as the policyholder. The same goes for employees, freelancers or subcontractors in corporate liability insurance, and for family members or employees in personal liability and professional indemnity insurance. 15

With compulsory liability insurances, victims are usually allowed to claim against the liability insurer direct. In some countries – France Spain and Poland, for instance – this applies also in general liability insurance. The insurer 16

[3] I. Gilead, Economic Analysis (supra 271), no. 49 et seq.

can then enforce certain objections from the insurance contract only against the policyholder, but not against the victim. This applies usually also to the intentional act exclusion. The victims of car bombs may so be indemnified by motor liability insurers. For British motor insurers, this did not become a problem during 30 years of IRA activity. The rule applying in German motor liability insurance is somewhat different. In Germany, direct claims by injured parties are not allowed in cases where policyholders have acted with intent. Instead, "Verkehrsopferhilfe" – "help for the victims of road accidents" comes into play up to the amount of the minimum sums insured.

17 It is clear that, for motor liability insurance as a whole, which in the countries of the EU has to cope with providing compensation for more than 40,000 fatalities and half a million seriously-injured people each year, the problem of terrorism is negligible. However, car bombs and the transportation of dangerous goods, accidents in tunnels and train crashes are still among the major loss scenarios that have to be taken into account in connection with high or unlimited sums insured in motor liability insurance.

18 Finally, there is a fluid transition between "dolus eventualis", "contingent intent" – which continues to be excluded – and gross negligence which remains covered; for example, where a bomb goes off early and causes bodily injury, although only property damage was intended.

B. Traditional Exclusion of Common Perils (Natural Hazard Risks, Political Risks) in Standard Wordings

19 An international survey of standard wordings shows practice to be inconsistent, with traditional exclusions of natural hazards like earthquakes or floods, and of political risks like war, civil commotion or terrorism, being understood differently. Often though, liability and coverage considerations overlap. This is particularly true of countries that have not acquired intensive experience of the phenomenon, and so have not developed specific systems of compensation.

20 Such exclusions are often lacking in liability insurance – sometimes even because of the assumption that no liabilities exist in this context. Or these exclusions are used, but based on the same assumption, and in the belief that the exclusions are then only declaratory, to be used for clarification.

21 In some cases, such exclusions only crop up in special covers relating to strict liability under special legislation – in Germany, for example, as part of the special covers in environmental liability insurance, or for radiation risks. The reasons for this are not always coherent either. On the one hand, even basic covers include liability based on fault in connection with acts of terrorism; on the other hand though, strict liability under special legislation does not always extend to terrorism situations.

C. *Specific Exclusion of Liability in Connection with Acts of Terrorism: Criteria*

In the wake of September 11th, slightly varying lists of liability risks considered to be particularly exposed were drawn up. According to a circular from the German Association of Insurers, as regards general liability insurance, these were as follows: security companies, bridges, dams, stadiums, exposed buildings, chemical and pharmaceutical industry, major hospitals, big events, food manufacturers, local and long-distance public transport (including railway stations and airports), pipelines, tour operators and hotel chains. 22

While nuclear pools and aviation insurers generally see themselves as exposed, marine insurers fear the following scenarios first and foremost: destruction, hijacking, or use of chemical and biological weapons on a cruise liner; dirty bombs on a cargo vessel (e.g. in containers), with damage to cargo and bodily injury, contamination of port facilities and warehouses; ship as a weapon after hijacking (gas tanker collides with selected targets); a deliberate oil disaster caused by a tanker (following attack or hijacking), or some other provoked accidents involving the transport of hazardous substances. 23

Consideration may be given to absolute exclusions of terrorism, or relative exclusions combined with special covers. These can be placed in international special markets, like the war risks and terrorism markets in marine and aviation insurance. Alternatively they may be concentrated in market-wide pools. Sublimits in catastrophe situations are widespread, especially since September 11th. Typical sublimits are: US$ 50m or € 60m in respect of airlines' third party liability and US$ 200m in marine insurance. There are also corresponding sublimits in respect of exposed major industrial liability risks. The general limits of these major risks – now slightly reduced – still reach a billion or more (having approached some years ago the capacity limits of the nuclear pools). 24

With specific terrorism exclusions, problems of definition inevitably arise. All definitions ultimately tend to go further than intended. No-one would see a well-intentioned Greenpeace attack as an act of terrorism, even if went wrong, although it does have the same specific symbolic nature in order to influence governments and the public. Difficulties also arise when it comes to distinguishing terrorism from war and other political risks, or from other criminal acts; or in differentiating organised terrorism from unorganised madness, as in the case of the recent attack on the metro in Korea; and finally, in distinguishing terrorism from normal traffic accidents or normal industrial accidents.[4] 25

In view of these questions of definition, the property insurance pools and also the US Terrorism Risk Insurance Act make provision for decision-making bodies, which usually also ensure political influence. Political interests can 26

[4] Cf. the suspicion of terrorism that was never cleared up in connection with the sinking of the ferry Estonia in the Baltic Sea in 1994.

differ from one case to the next. It may serve the interests of both corporate management and the government to blame a terrorist group for an accident in a state-owned industrial enterprise that is prone to disasters. Conversely, it may be in the public interest not to pursue the suspicion of terrorism in order to avoid hysteria; for example when there is a time link to a terrorist attack, as in the case of the industrial accident in Toulouse 2001 which occurred ten days after September 11th.

27 Cover or exclusion of terrorism in liability insurance also has an influence on decisions whether liabilities that are otherwise dubious or difficult to enforce are identified and realized.

28 When is this effect desired – on the part of liability insurers, victims, liable parties or other stakeholders? When is it undesired because it leads to liabilities being shifted to the wrong parties, for instance provoking first-party insurers subrogation that would otherwise not have been realized? Or because sensible methods of limiting contractual liability are being undermined?

29 Gilead describes the situation of a restaurant owner in Tel Aviv, who has the option of guaranteeing higher safety standards and having his clients pay for them, thus reducing the risk within his restaurant whilst increasing his liability in the event that something happens anyway.[5] The options available to liability insurers are thus set against the backdrop of the policyholders' options.

30 The amounts of compensation are influenced by the available liability insurance limits. The fact that there is disagreement regarding the amount of compensation to be granted to victims of terrorist acts plays a role in this context. In the various social security systems, victims of terrorist acts are sometimes privileged, in general or under ad hoc funds that are occasionally established; sometimes they are discriminated against. Under tort law, they are sometimes put in the same category as victims of road accidents; sometimes they receive less or less systematic protection. There are examples where generous compensation is paid by the liable "enabling states", either involuntarily as in a number of US cases[6], or voluntarily as in the ongoing negotiations between Libya and the Lockerbie and other terrorism victims.[7] Given the high capacities involved in enterprise liability insurance, sub-limits are agreed, and in motor liability insurance, unlimited cover has become increasingly questionable.[8]

31 On the other hand, politically motivated kidnappings of tourists have sparked a debate on whether or not the hostages should pay part of the costs for their

[5] I. Gilead, Economic Analysis, no. 36.

[6] See B.A. Koch, Comparative Analysis (infra 318), no. 11 et seq.

[7] Libyan diplomats originally offered to compensate the German victims in accordance with the table for pain and suffering compensation released by the German ADAC for victims of road accidents. Their offer was rejected on the ground that they had not been victims of a road accident. The sums offered have risen significantly in the meantime.

[8] Supra no. 24 and 17.

release. The question arises whether tour operators can also be held liable. A first-party policy to be funded by the tourists seems to be a suitable solution in this regard. There remains the problem, however, that the extortion of ransom money should not be encouraged neither by first-party insurance nor the liability of third parties and their insurance.

Compensation Schemes for Victims of Terrorism

Bernhard A. Koch and Stefan Strahwald

I. Introduction

1 Apart from traditional tort law, and in addition to social security, all jurisdictions covered offer some alternative scheme which provides compensation to at least certain victims of terrorist attacks. While these systems may differ in many aspects, they are presented in the following overview according to the degree of state control, intervention or participation: On the one hand, there are schemes which are based predominantly on the notion of welfare rather than distribution of loss among all potential victims. These include compensation schemes protecting crime victims in general, or specific funds which are only open to those harmed by terrorist attacks in particular. On the other hand, insurers, either upon their own initiative or backed by some sort of state support, offer payments to victims which are financed at least in part by insurance premiums collected from specific risk groups. There are of course also combinations and variants of these notions.

II. State Compensation Schemes

A. Schemes Aimed Specifically at Victims of Terrorism

2 Some countries have introduced state compensation schemes which are specifically designed for the protection of victims of terrorist attacks. Within their respective scope, such special schemes invariably supersede any other more general system which aims at crime victims at large. The former will therefore be dealt with first before turning to the latter. One should note at the outset, however, that neither variant will compensate all possible harm resulting from terrorist attacks, so that the remainder will have to be borne by alternative funds (such as private insurance) to the extent available.

1. France

In addition to a general crime victim compensation system[1], France has set up a special scheme for the victims of terror attacks[2]. Only the latter shall be described here. It offers compensation to any victim of such attacks committed on French territory for both physical injuries and mental suffering. French citizens are also eligible for compensation if the attack was committed abroad[3]. In fatal cases, the surviving dependants of the deceased may claim compensation for their economic loss[4]. Property damage is not covered by this system, except for a certain limited additional compensation for damage to, or loss of, clothing[5]. After an application has been made, the Fund must – within three months – make an offer to the victim, who need not accept it. If she does, she thereby enters into a binding and enforceable agreement with the Fund. If the victim rejects the offer, she may file a claim before the civil courts[6]. Victims of terrorism are granted the status of war victims, which leads to additional advantages, including free access to medical care and a special pension[7]. 3

The French system is funded by levies on the premiums paid to insurance companies for the compensation of property damage[8]. 4

2. Spain

Spain also has both a general crime victim compensation scheme[9] and a special system for the compensation of victims of armed gangs and terrorist groups[10]. Again, only the latter will be addressed in the following. 5

Victims of terrorist acts committed in Spain will receive state compensation for their bodily and mental injuries. Property damage is only covered to the extent it is not reimbursed by other funds (in particular insurance)[11], and only certain heads of damages are eligible for such subsidiary protection. This includes damage to dwellings, to certain vehicles, or to commercial and indus- 6

1 See J. Mikaelsson/A. Wergens, *Repairing the Irrepairable. State compensation to crime victims in the European Union* (2001), 63–75.

2 *Fonds de garantie pour les victimes d'actes de terrorisme et d'autres infractions* (FGTI). See *Code des assurances*, art. L 126-1 and L 126-2, L 422-1 to L 422-5 (legislative part), R 422-1 to R 422-10 (regulations) and A 422-1 (byelaws); *Code de procédure pénale*, art. 706-3 to 706-14 (legislative part) and R 50-1 to R 50-28 (regulations). See O. Moréteau/F. Lafay, Liability for Acts of Terrorism Under French Law (supra 29, in the following: O. Moréteau/F. Lafay, France), no. 6–15.

3 O. Moréteau/F. Lafay, France, no. 7.

4 O. Moréteau/F. Lafay, France, no. 8.

5 O. Moréteau/F. Lafay, France, no. 8. Such loss may, however, be covered by some (private) insurance (see O. Moréteau/F. Lafay, France, no. 3).

6 As to the application procedure see O. Moréteau/F. Lafay, France, no. 9–11.

7 O. Moréteau/F. Lafay, France, no. 15.

8 O. Moréteau/F. Lafay, France, no. 6.

9 See J. Mikaelsson/A. Wergens (supra fn. 1), 123 et seq.

10 M. Martín-Casals/J. Ribot, Liability for Acts of Terrorism Under Spanish Law (supra 88, in the following: M. Martín-Casals/J. Ribot, Spain), no. 16 et seq.

11 M. Martín-Casals/J. Ribot, Spain, no. 26. As to the Consortium see no. 59–60 below.

trial facilities[12]. The amounts paid out correspond to those that the actual wrongdoer would have to pay under the provisions of tort law. Payments are only made as long as the tortfeasor himself has not yet paid, and the victim assigns her claims against the wrongdoer to the state. Thus the state effectively only reinsures the victims of terror attacks against the risk of insolvency of tortfeasors[13].

3. Italy

7 Though Italy has not (yet) established a general crime victim compensation scheme, special provisions offer limited indemnification to victims of terrorism and organised crime[14]. Any person who suffers a permanent disability as a result of such crimes committed in Italy is eligible for compensation proportionate to the degree of her disability, the percentage of which serves as a multiplier of a specific amount[15]. Victims with a permanent disability reducing at least two thirds of their working ability may opt for a lifetime annuity instead of a single payment[16]. If they have lost at least one quarter of their working ability, victims are eligible for another flat-fee monthly payment regulated by a separate statute[17]. In fatal cases, the surviving family members are eligible for compensation[18].

B. Schemes Based on the 1983 European Convention

1. The European Convention on the Compensation of Victims of Violent Crimes

8 The 1983 European Convention on the Compensation of Victims of Violent Crimes[19] entered into force on 1 February 1988. It obliges the contracting states to develop compensation schemes for victims of intentional and violent offences resulting in bodily injury or death. Art. 2 of the Convention contains a certain principle of subsidiarity, holding that the states shall "contribute" to compensation if it is "not fully available from other sources". Moneys obtained from other sources (including social security, some insurance, or the offender himself) shall be deducted from the amount paid out in accordance with this Convention (art. 9).

[12] M. Martín-Casals/J. Ribot, Spain, no. 18.
[13] M. Martín-Casals/J. Ribot, Spain, no. 22.
[14] Law no. 302/1990 of 20 October 1990. See A. Zaccaria/G. Bisazza, Liability for Acts of Terrorism Under Italian Law (supra 57, in the following: A. Zaccaria, Italy), no. 1–15. For the historic development of this scheme see id., no. 1–5.
[15] One percentage point thereby corresponds to € 774.68 (the maximum available amount of compensation is therefore € 77,468). A. Zaccaria, Italy, no. 5.
[16] A. Zaccaria/G. Bisazza, Italy, no. 5.
[17] A. Zaccaria/G. Bisazza, Italy, no. 6.
[18] A. Zaccaria/G. Bisazza, Italy, no. 7.
[19] Signed at Strasbourg on 24 November 1983, *European Treaty Series* (ETS) – No. 116, available on the internet: http://conventions.coe.int/Treaty/en/Treaties/Word/116.doc.

Eligible for such payments are persons who have sustained serious bodily injury or impairment of health directly attributable to an intentional crime (art. 2 subs. 1 lit. a), or, in fatal cases, the surviving dependants of direct victims (art. 2 subs. 1 lit. b). Compensation shall be paid – even if the offender is unknown – by the state on whose territory the crime was committed to the nationals of all contracting parties and to nationals of other member states of the Council of Europe if they are permanent residents in the country where the crime was committed (art. 3 lit. b). 9

As a minimum, loss of earnings, medical and hospital expenses, funeral costs and – as regards surviving dependants – loss of maintenance shall be covered (art. 4). The Convention leaves it open to the participating countries to decide whether they set upper limits or minimum thresholds for any or all elements of compensation (art. 5). They can also specify a certain period of time within which an application must be filed (art. 6). Compensation can be reduced or even refused altogether in light of the financial situation of the victim (art. 7) and on account of the victim's or the applicant's conduct before, during or after the crime, or with respect to the injury or death (art. 8 subs. 1). Compensation may further be limited or denied if the victim was involved in organised crime (art. 8 subs. 2), or if compensation would be contrary to the sense of justice or to public policy (art. 8 subs. 3). 10

Among those countries covered by this publication, France, Germany, Spain, Sweden, Switzerland and the United Kingdom have ratified the Convention. To the extent these jurisdictions have not yet been addressed by this overview, they will be presented in the following. 11

As the individual systems still differ in many important aspects, the Convention's aim to achieve common minimum standards[20] has not (yet) been reached, even though many of the elements envisaged by the Convention have been adopted by countries who themselves have not ratified it[21]. 12

2. Germany

In Germany, the *Opferentschädigungsgesetz* (Victim Compensation Act, OEG) of 1976[22] entitles direct victims as well as mere bystanders of intentional and wrongful attacks[23] who have suffered serious bodily or psychological injuries to claim compensation from the *Bundesländer* (Federal States) or in certain 13

[20] See the preamble of the Convention: "Considering that the aim of the Council of Europe is to achieve a greater unity between its members … Considering that it is necessary to establish minimum provisions in this field".

[21] Infra C.

[22] *Bundesgesetzblatt* (BGBl.) 1976 I 1181 as amended on 6 December 2000 (BGBl. 2000 I 1676). See U. Magnus, Liability for Acts of Terrorism Under German Law (supra 60, in the following: U. Magnus, Germany), no. 2–4; J. Mikaelsson/A. Wergens (supra fn. 1), 76 et seq.

[23] Intentional poisoning and – at least negligently – causing a danger for others through a criminal act committed with means dangerous to public safety, are treated alike (§ 1 subs. 2). For the group of persons eligible for compensation see J. Mikaelsson/A. Wergens (supra fn. 1), 82.

cases from the Federal Republic of Germany. Compensation can also be sought by a person who has been injured in legitimate defence against such acts, while it is doubtful whether bodily injuries of the police or firemen and other rescuers are covered[24]. In fatal cases, the surviving dependants are eligible for compensation.

14 The injury resulting from the crime must have been sustained on German territory (§ 1 subs. 1)[25]. Eligible for compensation are only German citizens, the citizens of other Member States of the European Union, or the citizens of third countries which either also grant compensation to Germans injured on their respective territories (reciprocity), or whose inhabitants have to be treated equally due to Community provisions. Citizens of countries that do not fulfil these criteria can claim compensation only if they have either been legally resident in Germany for a certain period of time, or in cases of hardship[26].

15 Compensation is granted in accordance with the provisions of the Federal Act on Pensions for Victims of the War[27]. There are no minimum or maximum awards, except for loss of earnings[28]. Pain and suffering is not indemnified[29]. Benefits under the OEG are unavilable if the victim caused the damage, or if her behaviour disqualified her from compensation for other reasons[30].

3. Sweden

16 Compensation for crime victims in Sweden is regulated by the recently amended *Criminal Injuries Compensation Act* 1978:413 (CICA)[31]. Direct victims of intentional criminal offences, in fatal cases their surviving dependants, as well as persons injured in the course of such a crime, are entitled to compensation[32]. Under certain circumstances also damage to property and pecuniary loss is indemnified: This is not only true for goods carried by the victim when the crime was committed which are essential to her such as spectacles or hearing aids, but also for damage to property and pecuniary loss that arise from property crimes where the offender had escaped from an institution, furthermore for cases where the applicant's ability to support herself is seriously jeopardized as a result of the damage, or if compensation otherwise appears to be of vital importance[33]. If certain requirements are met, pure economic loss may also be compensated[34]. Where the victim is incapacitated as a result of

[24] U. Magnus, Germany, no. 2.
[25] For the territorial scope of application see J. Mikaelsson/A. Wergens (supra fn. 1), 83.
[26] J. Mikaelsson/A. Wergens (supra fn. 1), 83.
[27] *Gesetz über die Versorgung der Opfer des Krieges* (BVG), Act of 20 December 1950 (BGBl. 1950 I 791) as amended.
[28] J. Mikaelsson/A. Wergens (supra fn. 1), 81.
[29] J. Mikaelsson/A. Wergens (supra fn. 1), 85.
[30] See § 2 OEG.
[31] See J. Mikaelsson/A. Wergens (supra fn. 1), 133 et seq.
[32] An English translation of the Swedish law can be found in J. Mikaelsson/A. Wergens (supra fn. 1), 354 et seq.
[33] J. Mikaelsson/A. Wergens (supra fn. 1), 141–142.
[34] See art. 3–4 CICA.

the offence, she can claim damages for pain and suffering. Offences against personal freedom and criminal molestation make the victim eligible for compensation for violation of personal integrity ("moral damage")[35].

17 To qualify for compensation the crime must have been committed on Swedish territory[36]. In case of personal injury, also offences committed outside Sweden are covered if the victim has a Swedish domicile and there is no way of receiving compensation under foreign law. The Act does not apply where it appears to be unreasonable to compensate a victim out of Swedish funds due to the fact that neither the offender nor the victim have sufficient ties with Sweden[37]. To qualify for state compensation, which strictly follows the principle of subsidiarity, the victim must have unsuccessfully tried to receive compensation from other sources such as the wrongdoer himself or from private insurance[38].

18 There are maximum awards for certain heads of damages[39]. Compensation may be denied or at least reduced in cases of contributory negligence, or if the victim intentionally or carelessly increased the risk of injury or loss[40].

4. Switzerland

19 Any crime victim is entitled to claim compensation under the *Opferhilfegesetz* (Victim Assistance Act) in cases of damage to physical, sexual or mental integrity, even if the tortfeasor is unknown, on the condition that the crime was committed in Switzerland[41]. If a Swiss person is the victim of a crime committed abroad, she can nevertheless seek compensation in Switzerland if this is her place of residence unless she is sufficiently compensated under foreign law (art. 11). In cases where the effect of a crime committed in Switzerland takes place in another country[42], financial support is only granted if equitable support cannot be achieved under the law of that country (art. 11). The amount of compensation depends both on the damage and on the financial situation of the victim[43]: If the victim's post-crime income exceeds the maximum sum of the so-called "Lebensbedarf", a sum of money determined by the *Bundesgesetz über Ergänzungsleistungen zur Alters-, Hinterlassenen- und Invalidensicherung* (Act on supplementary achievements concerning the security of old age pensions, surviving dependants and invalidity, ELG), the award is reduced accordingly. If the income is four times the *Lebensbedarf* or higher, no compensation is awarded at all. Independent from the respective income, a person

[35] J. Mikaelsson/A. Wergens (supra fn. 1), 143.
[36] For the territorial scope of application see J. Mikaelsson/A. Wergens (supra fn. 1), 140.
[37] Sec. 1 subs. 2 sent. 2 CICA.
[38] J. Mikaelsson/A. Wergens (supra fn. 1), 139.
[39] See J. Mikaelsson/A. Wergens (supra fn. 1), 137.
[40] Sec. 9 CICA.
[41] See Th. Lörtscher/C. Parizzi/S. Gutzwiller, Liability for Acts of Terrorism Under Swiss law (supra 128, in the following: Th. Lörtscher/C. Parizzi/S. Gutzwiller, Switzerland), no. 2.
[42] This is, for example, the case when a letter bomb is sent abroad from a destination in Switzerland.
[43] See art. 11–12 *Opferhilfegesetz*.

severely affected can seek compensation for pain and suffering if this is justified by all the circumstances. A victim who negligently contributed to the loss may have to bear part of it herself.

5. United Kingdom

a) Great Britain[44]

20 The Criminal Injuries Compensation Act of 1995 replaced a non-statutory scheme in force in Great Britain since 1964 and introduced the so-called Criminal Injuries Compensation Scheme.

21 The most striking feature of this scheme is a tariff system which lists more than 400 different injuries and allots 25 levels of compensation to them, depending on the severity of the injury and ranging from £ 1,000 (level 1, about € 1,400) to £ 250,000 (level 25, about € 360,000). "Additional compensation", i.e. compensation for loss of earnings and so-called "special expenses"[45] can raise the total payment up to a maximum amount of £ 500,000 (about € 720,000)[46]. Apart from bodily injuries (including fatal injuries), mental harm is also compensated, but only if the applicant was put in reasonable fear of immediate physical harm, or if she had a close relationship of love and affection with the crime victim[47], or if she was the non-consenting victim of a sexual offence[48]. According to the definition of "criminal injury" in § 8 of the scheme, not only intentional crimes are covered but there is, under certain circumstances, also the opportunity to seek compensation for injuries caused by recklessness[49]. For injuries sustained accidentally by persons engaged in law-enforcement activities or any other activities directed to containing, limiting or remedying the consequences of any crime, compensation is only payable if the injured person was taking an exceptional risk justified under all the circumstances (§ 12).

[44] See J. Mikaelsson/A. Wergens (supra fn. 1), 147 et seq.; Criminal Injuries Compensation Authority (ed.), *Guide to the Criminal Injuries Compensation Scheme 2001*, available on the internet: http://www.compensationni.gov.uk.

[45] They cover the cost of medical treatment that cannot be provided by the National Health Service, the costs of adaptations that have to be made to a victim's house etc.

[46] Loss of earnings are only paid if the victim has lost earnings/the ability to earn for longer than 28 weeks. "Special expenses" are paid from the date of the injury, but only if the victim has lost earnings/the ability to earn for more than 28 weeks. See Criminal Injuries Compensation Authority (supra fn. 44), 5 no. 20.

[47] The relationship must still subsist (unless the victim has since died) and the applicant must have been present when the crime was committed and witnessed the injury of the beloved person, or have been involved in the immediate aftermath. While it is easy to decide whether or not a person was present when the crime was committed, the decision if the constituent facts "close relationship of love and affection" and "immediate aftermath" are fulfilled, can only be made from case to case. (Criminal Injuries Compensation Authority (supra fn. 44), 20 no. 10).

[48] For the main types of incident and injury, which compensation may be awarded for, see §§ 6–12 of the Compensation Scheme.

[49] See Criminal Injuries Compensation Authority (supra fn. 44), 22 no. 20.

The scheme offers compensation to direct victims and their surviving dependants or relatives as defined by law[50]. It also covers persons with a close relationship of love and affection as well as people who try to stop criminals or to prevent the commitment of a crime. Injuries must have been suffered on British territory[51]. The applicant does not have to be a British citizen, however. Applications must be filed within two years after the crime has been committed[52]. The offender need not be identified[53]. Awards may be refused or at least reduced[54] not only due to the lack of cooperation with the relevant authorities[55], but also in cases where the behaviour of the victim caused or significantly contributed to the incident in which she was injured. The criminal record of a person may lead to the same consequences. 22

b) Northern Ireland

i) Personal Injury

The Criminal Injuries Compensation (Northern Ireland) Order 2002[56], applying to all incidents occuring on or after 1 May 2002, has changed the previous system of crime victim compensation in Northern Ireland, which had been regulated by the provisions of the Criminal Injuries (Compensation) (Northern Ireland) Order of 1988. The new law introduced a tariff system like the one just presented for Great Britain[57]. It now also allows payments for loss of earnings or "special expenses" in certain cases. The new system is very similar to the above-mentioned British scheme and thus will only be described very briefly here. Victims of violent crimes (including arson or an act of poisoning) are compensated for physical and/or mental harm directly resulting from those crimes, but these injuries must be serious enough to fall at least under the minimum tariff. The application time limit is two years (subject to certain exceptions). Failure to inform or cooperate with the relevant authorities[58], the victim's conduct before, during or after the crime, as well as the victim's criminal record may lead to a reduction or refusal of the compensation. 23

[50] This includes persons who – at the time of the victim's death – were the deceased's husband or wife, unmarried but long-term partner of either sex, parent, son or daughter, or the former husband or wife who had still been financially supported by the victim. See § 38 Criminal Injuries Compensation Scheme (2001).

[51] That is England, Scotland and Wales. Northern Ireland has its own compensation scheme, which will be described below.

[52] Criminal Injuries Compensation Authority (supra fn. 44), 34 no. 1. Under certain circumstances late applications are accepted. It has to be reasonable and in the interests of justice to do so (see Criminal Injuries Compensation Authority (supra fn. 44), 34 no. 2 et seq.).

[53] Criminal Injuries Compensation Authority (supra fn. 44), 18 no. 3.

[54] See Criminal Injuries Compensation Authority (supra fn. 44), 24 et seq.

[55] These are the police and the Compensation Authority.

[56] See The Compensation Agency (ed.), *A Guide to the Northern Ireland Criminal Injuries Compensation Scheme 2002*, available on the internet: http://www.compensationni.gov.uk.

[57] The Northern Ireland system has 29 levels of compensation, ranging from £ 1,000 (level 1, € 1,400) to £ 280,000 (level 29, € 400,000).

[58] These are the police and the Compensation Agency.

ii) Property Damage

24 Under the Criminal Damage (Compensation) (Northern Ireland) Order 1977[59], a person can claim compensation for losses suffered as a result of physical property damage caused unlawfully, maliciously or wantonly by three or more persons, unlawfully, riotously or tumultuously assembled together, or by acts of terrorism. Harm must have been incurred within Northern Ireland, but compensation is not restricted to British citizens. To qualify for compensation, an applicant must have a specific interest in the damaged property[60] and have suffered a loss of more than £ 200 (€ 285). Where an applicant planned, assisted in, or actively and willingly facilitated the act resulting in the damage, or was associated or connected with the wrongdoer, no compensation will be awarded[61]. The same exclusion applies to any person who – at any time – was a member of an unlawful association or engaged in the commission, preparation or instigation of terrorist acts[62]. Failure to cooperate with the police may lead to a reduction or even refusal of compensation[63]. Generally speaking, whether and to what extent compensation will be paid depends upon the victim's behaviour before, during and after the crime. No compensation is payable in respect of damages to or theft of coins, bank notes, postal orders, money orders and the like, articles of personal adornment, including watches, jewellery and the like, and property taken from a damaged vehicle or house[64].

C. Other State Compensation Schemes

25 Whereas the following examples will present crime victim compensation schemes introduced by countries which have not yet ratified the above-mentioned European Convention, one should note at the outset that the image may not be complete. As the Austrian country report has indicated[65], victims of traffic accidents caused intentionally (e.g. by a terrorist running a car into a group of pedestrians) may be eligible for compensation under the applicable traffic victim compensation scheme. The same or similar alternative schemes may apply in other countries, though this will not be elaborated further in the following.

26 South Africa is not listed since no crime victim compensation scheme has been set up there due to budgetary restraints[66]. The estimated annual amounts

[59] See C. Walker, Liability for Acts of Terrorism: United Kingdom Perspective (supra 138, in the following: C. Walker, UK), no. 9 et seq.; The Compensation Agency (ed.), *A Guide to Criminal Damage Compensation in Northern Ireland*, available on the internet: http://www.compensationni.gov.uk.

[60] In case of a damaged building, for example, this constituent fact will usually be fulfilled by either the owner, the landlord, or even a tenant responsible for carrying out repairs under the terms of lease: The Compensation Agency (supra fn. 59), no. 8.

[61] The Compensation Agency (supra fn. 59), no. 17 lit. b.

[62] The Compensation Agency (supra fn. 59), no. 17 lit. c.

[63] The Compensation Agency (supra fn. 59), no. 17 lit. d.

[64] The Compensation Agency (supra fn. 59), no. 10.

[65] See B.A. Koch/H. Koziol, Liability for Acts of Terrorism Under Austrian Law (supra 5, in the following: B.A. Koch/H. Koziol, Austria), no. 9.

[66] See M. Ovens, Assisting Victims of Crime, http://www.aqpv.ca/diffusion/textes/mnopgr_t/ovens_m.pdf; L. Camerer, What About the Victims?, [1999] Nedbank ISS Crime Index 3, available on the internet: http://www.iss.co.za/Pubs/Crimeindex/99vol3no2/victims.html.

the state would have to pay under such a system are as high as R 5 billion (about € 600 million) a year[67].

1. Austria

a) Compensation for Crime Victims[68]

If an Austrian citizen is injured or killed either as a direct victim or as a passer-by of an intentional crime (sanctioned by a minimum sentence exceeding six months of imprisonment), the victim or – in fatal cases – her dependants may claim compensation from the state for the consequences of bodily harm, including serious psychological injury, under the so-called *Verbrechensopfergesetz* (Act on granting aid to crime victims, VOG)[69]. This is possible even in cases when the offender is unknown, or if the crime was committed abroad. However, compensation is unavailable to the extent that the applicant is eligible for indemnification under the laws of a foreign state. Citizens of other countries participating in the *European Economic Area* (EEA) are also entitled to compensation if the crime was committed on Austrian territory; if it took place abroad, EEA citizens are only eligible for awards under the VOG if they have their permanent place of residence in Austria 27

There are no minimum or maximum awards under the VOG, except for loss of earnings and loss of maintenance. Pain and suffering is not indemnified under this regime. Victims who either participated in the crime, incited the wrongdoer, or exposed themselves to the danger with gross negligence are excluded from receiving compensation under the VOG[70]. Failure to assist the authorities in prosecuting the wrongdoer may have the same consequences. 28

b) Compensation for Victims of Lawful Police Actions[71]

A person harmed by weapons used in the course of legitimate coercive measures by the Austrian police authorities (e.g. in the course of chasing a terrorist) can recover damages for personal injuries[72] as well as property damages from the Federal Republic under the *Polizeibefugnis-Entschädigungsgesetz* (Law on compensation for damage caused by lawful police actions, PolBeG) if she is not compensated by any insurance or under the VOG. No compensation is available if the victim unlawfully induced the police actions herself. If she negligently contributed to the damage, she has to bear a part of the loss proportionate to her contribution. There is the possibility of mitigating the damages in cases where the harmful measures were taken for the prevailing 29

[67] South African Press Agency, Crime victim payouts cost SA R 5bn a year, http://www.dispatch.co.za/2001/05/09/southafrica/CPAYOUT.HTM.

[68] See B.A. Koch/H. Koziol, Austria, no. 6.

[69] Type and extent of the compensation are regulated by very detailed provisions (§§ 2 et seq. VOG).

[70] As to the exclusions see § 8 VOG.

[71] See B.A. Koch/H. Koziol, Austria, no. 7.

[72] There is no compensation for pain and suffering.

interest of the injured party, while in such a case, property damages are not recoverable at all.

2. USA[73]

30 In the USA, there is no single federal program governing compensation for crime victims, but all 50 states, the District of Columbia, Guam, and the Virgin Islands have set up separate crime victim compensation schemes. These systems are in most cases funded by the state[74] and supplemented by federal sources[75]. Special ad hoc solutions such as the September 11th Victim Compensation Fund[76] will be disregarded in the following.

31 In most states, not only direct victims but also so-called "secondary" or "derivative" victims can seek compensation. To this second group of eligible persons belong the surviving dependants and the estate of a deceased, "good samaritans", and people who provided victims with funds and/or services that would be covered by compensation. Out-of-state residents, victims of drunk drivers, as well as state residents who are victims of terrorism abroad are covered by all state schemes[77].

32 A victim must have suffered physical harm to qualify for state compensation, but few exceptions are made, for example payments for psychological counselling and treatment for homicide survivors or for children who have witnessed crimes. Typically, these schemes do not compensate loss of property[78], pain and suffering, or loss of future income.

33 In general, victims who participated in the crime are excluded from state compensation. Such exclusion may also apply to people with long criminal records, or people who fail to prove that they are in financial need. The different schemes strictly follow the principle of subsidiarity, which means that the states only pay to the extent benefits cannot be achieved through other sources[79].

34 In every state, there are caps on the overall amounts to be paid per victim as well as per category of recoverable damage. The average maximum of com-

[73] The following information on crime victim compensation in the USA is derived from the homepages of the National Association of Crime Victim Compensation Boards (http://www.nacvcb.org) and of the National Center for Victims of Crime (http://www.ncvc.org/gethelp/compensation).

[74] Most of the state funding comes directly from convicted offenders, who either pay special fines, assessments, or penalties, or whose earnings from "in-prison-work" are collected.

[75] The *Federal Crime Victim Fund* (VOCA), funded by federal criminal fines and fees, provides additional grant funds for each state.

[76] See P. Woodin, The September 11th Victim Compensation Fund of 2001 (supra 197).

[77] Nevada is the only state that refuses to accept claims of non-residents.

[78] Except for items essential to the victim like glasses, hearing aids, medical equipment etc.

[79] Medical and auto insurance, employee benefits etc.

pensation lies between $ 10,000 (about € 8,800) and $ 25,000 (€ 22,000). Some states require a minimum loss of $ 100 (about € 88).

D. Comparative Remarks[80]

1. Eligibility

While it is obvious that all schemes offer compensation to direct victims, i.e. to persons towards whom the crime was directed, also dependants of homicide victims are eligible, though the relationship to the deceased required by the different systems may vary. Bystanders, i.e. persons accidentally hurt when a crime was committed, and so-called "good samaritans", i.e. persons who helped the victim and/or the police to prevent the crime or to apprehend an offender, cannot seek compensation in all countries. In Austria, for example, bystanders are covered, but "good samaritans" are excluded, whereas in the UK and all American states, the latter are eligible for compensation. 35

2. Territoriality, Citizenship, Nationality

In most countries, namely in Italy, France, Northern Ireland, Sweden, Switzerland, the UK, and in most American states, the victim's nationality is not relevant as long as the crime was committed on the respective jurisdiction's territory. In Germany and Spain, non-EU nationals are only covered if they have their permanent residence there, or if their countries offer reciprocity. Austria, France, Sweden, Switzerland and every state of the USA offer, under certain restrictions, compensation to their nationals in cases where they have been injured abroad. 36

3. Losses Covered

Medical expenses are covered under all schemes, whereas expenses incurred for transportation to and from the hospital are only compensated under some systems (such as Austria, Germany, Northern Ireland, Sweden, and the UK). Sweden compensates both transportation expenses and loss of earnings of relatives who visit the victim in hospital. 37

Loss of earnings is covered in all countries except for Italy. Compensation for loss of maintenance or financial support is granted to surviving dependants of a deceased person in all countries. Funeral costs are also covered under all schemes but Italy. Compensation may furthermore cover items damaged in the course of the commitment of a crime, for example torn clothes, broken spectacles, or medically essential items, though not in Italy, Spain, and Switzerland. Northern Ire- 38

[80] Part of the information presented here has already been provided above. Additional information is taken: for Austria, Germany, Sweden and the UK from the comparative remarks of the European Commission, *Green Paper on Compensation to Crime Victims*, COM(2001) 536 final, 28 September 2001; for France, Italy, Spain, Sweden, Switzerland, Northern Ireland and the USA from the international resources available on the homepage of the Office for Victims of Crime: http://www.ojp.usdoj.gov/ovc/intdir/intdir.htm.

land is exceptional as it is the only country in which there is a special statutory scheme for property damages incurred in the course of criminal acts.

39 Compensation for pain and suffering is granted in France, Northern Ireland, Sweden[81], the UK and Switzerland, but not in Austria, Germany, Italy, Spain or the USA.

4. Thresholds and Caps

40 Maximum awards limit compensation in Austria (but only for loss of earnings or of maintenance), Germany (for loss of earnings), Sweden (for personal injury, life annuities and property damage), Switzerland (as determined by the *Bundesrat*), the UK (highest amount payable under either tarriff scheme is £ 500,000 or € 712,000), and the USA (varying from state to state, ranging from $ 10,000 to $ 100,000).

41 Some jurisdictions require a certain minimum harm, either defined by type of injury (such as in the UK) or by the amount of compensation (such as in some U.S. states).

5. Formal Criteria and Advance Payment

42 In all countries, victims are required to co-operate with the relevant authorities. Applications must be filed within a certain period of time, which can usually be prolonged due to different factors. The time limits for filing applications are between one year (USA), two years (Northern Ireland, Spain, Sweden, Switzerland and the UK), and ten years (France and Italy). Time limits run from the commitment of the crime, except for Sweden, where it is set from the ending of court proceedings.

43 An advance payment for victims in need of prompt help is available in Austria, France, Italy, Northern Ireland, Spain, Switzerland, the UK, as well as in some states of the USA.

E. Future Perspectives for the European Union

44 After preparatory works started in 1998[82] and encouraged by the conclusions of the European Council's meeting in Tampere 1999[83], the Commission has

[81] Sweden offers additional compensation for "moral damages" in case of particularly offensive attacks.

[82] See point 51 (c) of the Vienna Action Plan of the Council and the Commission, OJ C 19, 23.1.1999, 1, and the Communication from the Commission to the Council, the European Parliament and the Economic and Social Committee. Crime victims in the European Union – reflections on standards and actions, COM(1999) 349 final, 14.7.1999. These actions were preceded by a resolution of the European Parliament on victims of violent crimes in 1989, where it had already called for the harmonisation of the extent of compensation (A 3-13/89 C 256/32, 12.09.1989).

[83] Tampere European Council 15 and 16 October 1999, Presidency Conclusions, point 32: "[M]inimum standards should be drawn up on the protection of the victims of crime, in particular on crime victims' access to justice and on their rights to compensation for damages, including legal costs. In addition, national programmes should be set up to finance measures, public and non-governmental, for assistance to and protection of victims."

undertaken "to ensure that all EU citizens and all legal residents in the EU can receive adequate compensation for the losses they have suffered in case they fall victim to a crime within the EU"[84]. An assessment of the current situation[85] made clear that even though 13 Member States have so far introduced a general scheme of state-funded compensation for crime victims[86], these national systems differ substantially both with respect to eligibility of victims as well as the types of losses covered[87].

The Commission therefore produced a "Green Paper on Compensation to Crime Victims" in September 2001[88] and sponsored further discussions, which culminated in the publication of a "Proposal for a Council Directive on Compensation to Crime Victims"[89] in October 2002[90]. 45

This draft shall not only introduce minimum standards for state compensation schemes similar to the ones in force for road victims[91], but also ensure that crime victims will benefit from such schemes irrespective of the place where the crime was committed within the European Union. The proposal consequently foresees a system of interstate co-operation which shall allow victims to file applications in their country of residence, even if injured in another Member State[92]. The draft insofar goes further than the 1983 Convention presented above, which did not address such cross-border issues. 46

As far as substantive rules are concerned, the planned minimum standard only applies to personal injury and death resulting from intentional crimes, so that neither negligently inflicted bodily harm nor damage to and loss of property is covered (recital 15 of the preamble and art. 2 of the draft). Member States may further exclude minor injuries from the scope of their implementing regimes (art. 6), which is in line with several systems already in force. 47

[84] Proposal for a Council Directive on compensation to crime victims, COM(2002) 562 final, 16.10.2002, OJ C 45, 25.2.2003, 69, Explanatory Memorandum (sub. 3.1).

[85] See the comparative study on this topic sponsored by the Grotius programme: A. Wergens, *Crime victims in the European Union* (2000). See also J. Mikaelsson/A. Wergens (supra fn. 1).

[86] Apart from those already presented above, this includes Belgium, Denmark, Finland, Ireland, Luxembourg, the Netherlands, and Portugal.

[87] See the Explanatory Memorandum of the new Draft Proposal (supra fn. 84), sub. 4.1, and the Green Paper on Compensation to Crime Victims, COM(2001) 536 final, 28.9.2001, 11–19.

[88] See the citation in fn. 87. On the Green Paper, see B.A. Koch, European Union, in: H. Koziol/ B. Steininger (eds.), *European Tort Law 2001* (2002), 473 (no. 25–30).

[89] See the citation in fn. 84. The preamble thereto lists all preparatory works on which it is based.

[90] On the draft, see B.A. Koch, European Union, in: H. Koziol/B. Steininger (eds.), *European Tort Law 2002* (2003), 444–446 (no. 47–54).

[91] Cf. Explanatory Memorandum sub. 5.5: "The current proposal will ensure that victims of crime do not find themselves in a less fortunate situation than victims of road accidents, by introducing provisions based on – to a large extent – similar principles as these Directives." Note that the preamble repeatedly states that harmonisation beyond setting a minimum standard is not a goal of this draft.

[92] See art. 16 of the draft.

48 While compensation under this scheme shall be adjudicated and administered according to the respective national laws of each Member State[93], the draft nevertheless requires that non-pecuniary loss must always be covered, even if suffered by dependants or close relatives of a deceased victim[94]. According to art. 4 para. 3 of the draft, Member States may introduce caps to compensation under such a scheme, but these limits may not be less than € 60,000 per victim. A system of advance payments shall be introduced in order to speed up the functioning of such schemes (art. 5).

49 In a series of equally optional provisions, the draft further leaves it open to the Member States whether they require prior efforts by the victim to go after the offender (art. 8), whether they deduct third-party payments to the victim (such as insurance or other benefits) in order to avoid double compensation (art. 9), or even whether they would like to be subrogated to the victim's tort law claims to the extent these have been satisfied (art. 10). The introduction of time limits for filing applications is also purely discretionary under this draft, though art. 13 at least prescribes a minimum limitation period (if any) of two years[95].

50 While one may even question the Community's authority to regulate this matter[96], the draft may not be an adequate solution to its objectives. After all, most provisions of this draft directive are purely optional, which reduces the suggested minimum standard to a minuscule one[97]. It would nevertheless improve the position of crime victims throughout Europe who could take advantage of the easier access to compensation in cross-border cases.

III. Insurance solutions

51 While the above-mentioned state compensation schemes offer quite a considerable spectrum of protection to victims of terrorist attacks, property damage is mostly excluded or recoverable only to a very limited extent. Insurance ar-

[93] See in particular art. 4 para. 2 of the proposal:
"2. The amount of compensation shall be determined:
(a) on a case-by-case basis where the compensation, taken as a whole, does not deviate significantly from what has been or could be expected to be awarded in damages to the applicant in accordance with civil law in the member state responsible for paying the compensation; or
(b) in accordance with pre-defined tariffs, for the entire compensation or for some or all of the individual items of losses that is covered by the compensation.
The tariffs referred to in point (b) shall reflect the average of what would be awarded in damages for similar losses as those suffered by the applicant, in accordance with civil law in the member state responsible for paying the compensation."

[94] Recital 18 of the preamble reads: "The compensation must cover non-pecuniary losses, in particular to ensure adequate compensation to victims of serious crimes and to dependants and close relatives of victims who have died as a result of a crime." This has been worked into art. 4 para. 1 of the draft.

[95] This period shall run "from the end of the police investigations or the end of the criminal proceedings instituted as a result of the crime, whichever comes latest", in the absence of either formal steps the two years shall run "from the date of commission of the crime".

[96] See B.A. Koch (supra fn. 90), no. 53.

[97] This was also criticised by the EESC in its opinion on the proposal, SOC/132, 26.2.2003, in particular with respect to the extent of compensation as regulated by art. 4.

rangements are found in some countries whose administrations participate therein to a greater or lesser degree[98].

A. Insurance Schemes with State Participation

1. France

As the French country report has elaborated in further detail[99], a co-reinsurance pool called Pool GAREAT[100] was created jointly by insurers, reinsurers and the state-backed *Caisse centrale de réassurance* (Central Reinsurance Fund, CCR) to cover direct property damage and business interruptions caused by terrorist acts. It has been compulsory for insurers to cover such acts since 1986[101]. The relevant provisions, originally requesting full coverage, were amended by a Decree of 28 December 2001[102] and since then allow the offerage of partial coverage[103]. All insurance companies that are members of the *Association of French Insurers* (FFSA) must participate in the Pool. Other insurance companies that are either resident in France or operate under the European freedom of service arrangements, carrying out direct insurance in France, are free to participate. GAREAT, reinsured first by member insurers, secondly by reinsurers, and lastly[104] by the CCR, enables insurers to globally cede all terror-related risks if they meet certain requirements. GAREAT covers large risks only, i.e. those insured for more than € 6 million. Insurers charge a special premium on behalf of the Pool, the amount of which is determined in relation to the premium charged for the natural catastrophe cover. 52

2. Germany

In Germany a special insurance company called Extremus AG was established[105], which offers coverage for terror-caused property damage and business interruption with an insured sum exceeding € 25 million. The total capacity of Extremus is currently € 13 billion, limited to € 1.5 billion per insured. The shareholders of Extremus are 16 German insurers and reinsurers as well as international reinsurers. Only risks situated in Germany are covered, which 53

98 See a recent study published by Swiss Re (ed.), *Terrorism risks in property insurance and their insurability after 11 September 2001* (2003), which concludes that a state "should be more than merely a supervisor and regulator. It should also take on the role of an insurer or reinsurer" (24).

99 O. Moréteau/F. Lafay, France, no. 23; see also B. Raoul, The French GAREAT – First Post-WTC Terrorism Insurance Pool, http://www.ercgroup.com/gpc/resource_center/exposure/expo10_en/e02_gareat.html#cre; Th. Masquelier, French solutions to hyperterrorism, 134 [2001] Assurer, 2, available on the homepage of the *Fédération Francaise des Sociétés d'Assurances*: http://www.ffsa.fr.

100 This is an abbreviation for "Gestion de l'assurance et de la Réassurance des risques Attentats et Actes de Terrorisme".

101 Art. R 126-1, R 126-2 and L 126-2 *Code des assurances* (French Insurance Code).

102 Decree 2001-1337 of 28 December 2001.

103 See O. Moréteau/F. Lafay, France, no. 23.

104 In case aggregate losses exceed € 1.5 billion.

105 For detailed information see their homepage: http://www.extremus-online.de, where the full standard terms of business are provided (http://www.extremus-online.de/pdf/atb.pdf).

is regarded a disadvantage for enterprises with cross-border operations[106]. The reinsurance capacity of Extremus is funded through three layers: German first party insurers and reinsurers provide € 1.5 billion. The next € 1.5 billion are written by international reinsurers. If the losses covered exceed that sum, the German federal state provides up to another € 10 billion. Certain risks are excluded, among them nuclear risks, contamination with toxic substances, damage to aeroplanes, boats, pieces of art, harm caused by virus attacks, and in cases of business interruption, so called *Rückwirkungsschäden*[107]. Extremus offers only policies which automatically expire at the end of the respective year. Enterprises wishing to insure with Extremus have to take out full coverage.

3. United Kingdom[108]

54 In immediate response to serious bomb attacks hitting the city of London at the beginning of the 1990s, reinsurance – and as a consequence – insurance cover for terror incidents was no longer available. The UK government felt a strong need to react and initiated the founding of Pool Reinsurance Company Limited, commonly referred to as Pool Re, a mutual insurance company, authorized only to write reinsurance relating to terror risks[109] on commercial property insurance in the UK[110]. Pool Re itself reinsures with the UK government. The cover that it provides has recently been extended from "fire and explosion only" to an "all risks basis" with an exclusion for damage caused to electronic components by hacking and virus[111]. A previous exclusion for damage caused by nuclear devices has been deleted[112]. There have been no changes to the existing war risks exclusion and the type of losses covered (only commercial property damage and business interruption costs).

4. South Africa[113]

55 The South African Special Risks Association (SASRIA) was incorporated in 1979 in terms of the Companies Act 1973, providing insurance coverage

[106] R. Oelßner/G. Schlicht, Extremus AG – ein neuer Versicherer, http://www.dvs-schutzverband.de/aktuells/extremus_ag.cfm.

[107] These include e.g. the losses of a deliveryman caused by his contracting partner's business interruption.

[108] See C. Walker, UK no. 39 et seq.; Tillinghast-Towers Perrin, Pool Re and Terrorism Insurance in Great Britain, Update October 2001, http://www.tillinghast.com/tillinghast/publications/publications/till_update_uk/Uk_Pool_Re_and_Terrorism/2002052111.pdf, 2 et seq., especially on how the Pool operates, 3.

[109] "Acts of Terrorism" are defined by the Reinsurance (Acts of Terrorism) Act 1993. § 2 subs. 2 reads: "In this section 'acts of terrorism' means acts of persons acting on behalf of, or in connection with, any organisation which carries out activities directed towards the overthrowing or influencing, by force or violence, of Her Majesty's government in the United Kingdom or any other government de jure or de facto".

[110] Not only damage to property itself but also consequential losses are covered.

[111] C. Walker, UK, no. 61; Changes to Pool Re (Summary paper) (supra fn. 120), 2.

[112] See C. Walker, UK, no. 61.

[113] See J. Neethling, Liability for Acts of Terrorism Under South African Law (supra 72), no. 4; The preamble of the Conversion of SASRIA Act 134 of 1998, http://www.polity.org.za/html/govdocs/legislation/1998/act134.pdf.

against property damage caused by political acts. The Reinsurance of Damage and Losses Act 56 of 1989 extended SASRIA's business to defined political as well as unpolitical acts, named "special risks" (such as riots or strikes). Terror attacks fall – *inter alia* – under these "special risks" and are therefore covered by SASRIA. The government recognised that the insurance industry was not prepared to underwrite these risks and agreed in the public interest to act as a reinsurer of last resort. It conferred monopoly status on SASRIA for the supply of insurance coverage for "special risks" and exempted it from tax until the 1996 tax year. This allowed SASRIA to accumulate substantial reserves, but being a section 21 company under the Companies Act 56 of 1973, it was not allowed to distribute these. This is why SASRIA was converted into a public company with a share capital[114] through the Conversion of SASRIA Act 134 of 1998. The monopoly status will be retained until the Reinsurance of Damage and Losses Act 56 of 1973 is repealed. The State may terminate (all or part of) its shareholding and thereby its reinsurance duty.

5. Spain[115]

Direct damage to insured[116] residents of and/or property located in Spain[117], 56
caused violently by – *inter alia* – acts of terrorism[118] committed in Spain, as well as loss of profits resulting therefrom[119], are to be compensated by the *Consorcio de Compensación de Seguros* (Consortium for Insurance Compensation, CCS). This public corporation in the Ministry of the Economy shall cover certain "extraordinary risks" defined in its statute. Its members are insurers and reinsurers. Coverage is integrated into private insurance policies. CCS covers the amount corresponding to the insured sums. The different insurance companies collect special premiums on behalf of CCS in all accident and property damage policies[120]. It is obligatory for insurers operating in Spain to participate in that system and to pay the CCS premium, even if they reinsure these risks privately.

In cases where the insurance policy includes terror risks, insured persons are 57
compensated by the insurer and CCS provides subsidiary coverage only, which means that its intervention is limited to the case of an insurer's bankruptcy. In practice however – except for loss of profits[121] – terror risks are

[114] All shares are held by the state.

[115] See M. Martín-Casals/J. Ribot, Spain, no. 9 et seq.; Swiss Re (supra fn. 112), 4.

[116] The policy must be still in force, but exclude the terrorism risk. See M. Martín-Casals/J. Ribot, Spain, no. 10.

[117] I.e. Automobiles registered in Spain, real estate located in Spain, and chattels placed in immovable property located in Spain. See M. Martín-Casals/J. Ribot, Spain, no. 10.

[118] The definition of these acts can be found in art. 4 *Real Decreto* 2022/1986, *de 29 de agosto* (BOE no. 235, 1.10.1986). See M. Martín-Casals/J. Ribot, Spain, no. 10.

[119] Compensation for loss of profits has been introduced in the aftermath of September 11. See M. Martín-Casals/J. Ribot, Spain, no. 12.

[120] M. Martín-Casals/J. Ribot, Spain, no. 9.

[121] After the September 11 attacks, insurers operating in Spain had to seek the intervention of CCS to get reinsurance for those risks.

hardly ever covered by insurance policies, and this is where the *Consorcio* steps in[122].

6. USA

58 In response to the actual unavailability of property and casualty insurance on the market in the immediate aftermath of the WTC attack, the U.S. Congress passed the Terrorism Risk Insurance Act (TRIA), which became law in November 2002[123]. The Act is intended to provide temporary federal support to the U.S. insurance industry allowing it to re-develop "the systems, mechanisms, products, and programs necessary to create a viable financial services market for private terrorism risk insurance".[124]

59 This shall be achieved by a federal reinsurance scheme which will be in force until the end of 2005. While insurers falling under the statute[125] are required to offer coverage for certain terrorism risks as certified by the Secretary of the Treasury[126], their overall risk is cushioned: 90% of their losses exceeding a per insurer deductible[127] will be directly reimbursed by the federal government. Since the insurer has to recoup the federal government for payments made up to a certain annual limit, federal funding effectively only covers large-scale

[122] M. Martín-Casals/J. Ribot, Spain, no. 13.

[123] See, e.g., S. Lowe/S. Shah, Tillinghast-Towers Perrin Update December 2002, http://www.tillinghast.com/tillinghast/publications/publications/till_update_us/Terrorism_risk_ins_act/Update2_12_02.pdf.

[124] § 101 (a)(6) TRIA.

[125] According to § 102 (6) TRIA, this includes in particular all insurers "licensed or admitted to engage in the business of providing primary or excess insurance in any State" as well as those "approved for the purpose of offering property and casualty insurance by a Federal agency in connection with maritime, energy, or aviation activity".

[126] See § 102 (1) TRIA which defines "act of terrorism" as follows:
(A) Certification. The term "act of terrorism" means any act that is certified by the Secretary, in concurrence with the Secretary of State, and the Attorney General of the United States
- (i) to be an act of terrorism;
- (ii) to be a violent act or an act that is dangerous to
  - (I) human life;
  - (II) property; or
  - (III) infrastructure;
- (iii) to have resulted in damage within the United States, or outside of the United States in the case of
  - (I) an air carrier or vessel described in paragraph (5)(B); or
  - (II) the premises of a United States mission; and
- (iv) to have been committed by an individual or individuals acting on behalf of any foreign person or foreign interest, as part of an effort to coerce the civilian population of the United States or to influence the policy or affect the conduct of the United States Government by coercion.

(B) Limitation. – No act shall be certified by the Secretary as an act of terrorism if –
- (i) the act is committed as part of the course of a war declared by the Congress, except that this clause shall not apply with respect to any coverage for workers' compensation; or
- (ii) property and casualty insurance losses resulting from the act, in the aggregate, do not exceed $ 5,000,000. …

[127] This deductible is calculated on the basis of the respective insurer's direct earned premium in covered lines and increases annually throughout the duration of the program.

losses, whereas the bulk of smaller losses still has to be absorbed by the market. This is alleviated by the fact that insurers must charge separately for the terrorism coverage they offer. They furthermore have to collect a policyholder surcharge, which can be compared to a temporary federal premium tax and which may not exceed three percent of the premium (for the policy as a whole).

Federal support is currently capped at an overall annual limit of $ 100 billion 60
(about € 88 billion), though Congress may decide to release additional funds if necessary.

B. Insurance Systems Without State Participation

In some countries, the insurance industry has not yet concluded negotiations 61
with the state in order to establish an arrangement of the kind just presented. In the interim, Austrian insurers, for example, have entered into a pooling agreement without state participation (though it was always made clear that this was and still is the ultimate goal)[128]. The so-called Terror Pool, which went into operation on 1 October 2002 and started covering risks on 1 January 2003, consists of both first party insurers and international reinsurers, and grants affordable property cover. The policies are issued by direct insurers, coverage is capped at € 5 million per single event and year, with a possibility for every insurer to increase the amount to € 25 million for the payment of extra premiums. All premiums are ceded to the pool, which provides the compensation. The pool has an overall capacity of € 200 million, one quarter of which is paid by the primary insurers according to each insurer's market share, whilst the rest is borne by the reinsurers. Only direct business interruption is covered, while the system does not include business interruption caused by mere threats of terror attacks.

C. Excursion: Insurance in the Aviation Sector[129]

Following the tragic events of 11 September 2001, the insurability of aviation 62
risks and ultimately the viability of the airline industry as a whole became doubtful since such cover was no longer obtainable on the market. After all, private insurers stepped out of the scene almost entirely in the immediate aftermath (as they did in other lines of insurance). Even though they gradually returned by offering at least some cover (though at significantly higher prices), in the meantime the question had been raised to what extent states should step in also in this field, either temporarily or on a mid- to long-term basis.

[128] See B.A. Koch/H. Koziol, Austria, no. 5; H. Koziol, Haftung für Terrorschäden, [2002] *Die Versicherungsrundschau* (VR), 225 (233); the website of the Austrian Insurance Association (http://www.vvo.at) and Th. Klöckner, Terror pool in Austria – Review of risk management approach to terrorism, http://www.converium.com.

[129] See European Commission, *Communication from the Commission on Insurance in the Air Transport sector following the terrorist attacks of 11 September 2001 in the United States*, COM(2002) 320 final, 2 July 2002; European Commission, *Commission Staff Working Paper. Analysis of aviation insurance schemes*, SEC(2002) 1030, 27 September 2002.

63 This matter was also discussed by the European Union, where the Council had allowed temporary protective measures by the end of September 2001[130]. The Council subsequently asked the Commission to examine all proposals of aviation insurance schemes which had been introduced in response to the new situation, in particular the "Globaltime" scheme of the International Civil Aviation Organisation (ICAO), the "Equitime" proposal by the American Air Transport Association (ATA) and the AEA (Association of European Airlines) initiative called "Eurotime". All three are based upon a combination of funds created from premiums charged to those covered as well as government guarantees backing up worst-case scenarios[131].

64 The Commission analyzed all three schemes in its "Communication on Insurance in the Air Transport sector following the terrorist attacks of 11 September 2001 in the United States"[132]. While the "Eurotime" proposal was commented favourably, the Commission made it clear that it preferred a more global scheme as proposed by ICAO since the latter not only would allow all airlines (including those of non-EU countries which fly into European airspace) to take out insurance cover, but would also spread the risk among the higher number of participating countries[133]. The Commission consequently produced a "Co-ordinated response" to the ICAO's request for feedback to the "Globaltime" proposal[134] and further published an "Analysis of aviation insurance schemes"[135].

65 At the same time, the European Commission decided to introduce new insurance requirements for airlines and submitted a proposal for a "Regulation of the European Parliament and of the Council on insurance requirements for air carriers and aircraft operators"[136] on 24 September 2002. The draft shall introduce uniform minimum insurance requirements that all air carriers and aircraft operators[137] have to observe when flying into, out of or within European Community airspace, irrespective of their country of origin[138].

130 This was decided at the ECOFIN Informal Council in Liège on 22 September 2001. See also COM(2001) 574 final, 10.10.2001.

131 On all three schemes, see the Commission's "Communication on Insurance in the Air Transport sector following the terrorist attacks of 11 September 2001 in the United States", COM(2002) 320 final, 2.7.2002, no. 21 et seq. (sub 3.2). The ICAO and AEA proposals are more thoroughly compared in the Commission Staff Working Paper SEC(2002) 1030 cited infra fn. 145.

132 Citation supra fn. 131.

133 The Communication concluded that all Member States "should indicate a favourable attitude in principle" to the ICAO proposal, subject to the condition that its largest members (in particular the U.S. and Japan) also contribute thereto: COM(2002) 320 final, 2.7.2002, no. 58.

134 "Co-ordinated response to the ICAO State Letter (LE 4/64-02/55) on the establishment of a global aviation war risk insurance scheme", Commission Staff Working Paper SEC(2002) 1031, 27.9.2002.

135 SEC(2002) 1030, 27.9.2002.

136 COM(2002) 521 final, 24.9.2002, OJ C 20, 28.1.2003, 193.

137 The draft covers all flights whether commercial or non-commercial, scheduled or not, whether operated with or without a licence, including flights by state aircraft (art. 2 of the draft).

138 This is expressed by art. 1 of the draft; see also no. 4 of the Explanatory Memorandum thereto. Air carriers registered in third countries may substitute the required insurance cover with certain other securities (see the list of alternatives in art. 5 para. 2 of the draft, which is modelled after art. 15 para. 4 of the Rome Convention).

The draft refers to common liability standards introduced by the Montreal Convention and Council Regulation (EC) No. 2027/97 (as amended). However, the proposed insurance requirements may nevertheless go beyond these standards since the Explanatory Memorandum holds it necessary "to clearly state that insurance regarding passenger, baggage, cargo and mail liability shall also cover acts of war and/or terrorism"[139], whereas art. 18 para. 2 (b) of the Montreal Convention, for example, excludes liability for acts of war or armed conflict in case of damage to cargo[140]. 66

139 Explanatory Memorandum, no. 12 (see also no. 15). This is executed by the definition of "incident" in art. 3 (f) of the draft, which is in turn used for defining "insurance". The definition reads:
"'incident' shall mean the occurrence or series of occurrences having the same origin, in which an aircraft causes damage to passengers, baggage, cargo, mail and/or third parties on the surface and/or in the air. … Incidents shall be understood to cause accidentally damage to passengers, baggage, cargo, mail and/or third parties on the surface and/or in the air, or because of acts of war, terrorism, hijacking, act of sabotage, unlawful seizure of aircraft, civil commotion or labour disturbances; …"

140 On details of the proposed regulation, see B.A. Koch (supra fn. 90), no. 19 et seq.

COMPARATIVE ANALYSIS OF LIABILITY FOR ACTS OF TERRORISM

Bernhard A. Koch

I. Loss Allocation

1 It is clear from the outset that traditional fault liability alone will not lead to satisfactory solutions for all scenarios of losses caused by terrorist acts. The problem in that respect is not, however, that the notion of responsibility for wrongful and faulty behaviour were unfit to handle such cases properly, quite the contrary: It is actually very easy to thereby identify a wrongdoer who should bear the loss – the terrorist. The problem becomes only apparent at the very end of the story: The victims will typically not be able to collect damages from this tortfeasor, even if they succeeded in bringing him into court. Liability for acts of terrorism therefore turns into a topic of debate not because of intricate difficulties of tort law, but because of the empty pockets of the most obvious defendant.

2 The primary focus should therefore not be responsibility, but rather loss allocation. The following shall sketch a roadmap for allocating the losses produced by terrorist acts, thereby presenting how tort law vehicles from all jurisdictions covered would move along. This roadmap will necessarily be incomplete and cannot indicate all detours, side alleys and dead ends of this map, which has not grown organically, and which does not always point into the right direction. What can be said from the outset, however, is that drivers from all ten jurisdictions covered will probably find their way around rather easily, because the solutions in their home countries are remarkably similar (considering the degree of differences found in other tort law scenarios).

A. Default Loss Bearer – The Victim

3 The most basic rule of tort law, which is often forgotten (or rather deliberately ignored), says that the loss should lie with the victim unless there are convincing reasons to relieve him from such burden. The question is therefore whether the victim of a terrorist attack should bear his entire loss all by himself, or whether he should be able to find compensation elsewhere. Even though this seems to be a rhetoric question, it is not: The answer thereto depends upon the

weight of the reasons to shift the loss, and is therefore not a clearcut "yes" or "no". While there is clearly much more sympathy with the victim in these cases as compared to a person – say – who spills hot coffee by his own carelessness, sympathy alone cannot suffice: If we take away the loss from the victim, it does not simply vanish, but ends up with somebody else, and the former question therefore turns into a follow-up enquiry whether it is truly fair and reasonable that the new addressee should ultimately compensate all or at least parts of the damage. This truism has to be mentioned since it sometimes seems to fade away in recent discussions on this topic, particularly in the media and unfortunately also in legislative debates.

Before entering the various routes to shift the loss away from the victim, one should note that this journey will for the most part focus on the so-called "innocent" victim, thereby ignoring blameworthiness or specific risks in his own sphere. Not only will therefore the losses of the dependants of a suicide bomber be left aside, but also – and more importantly – instances of contributory negligence or the like. 4

B. Route 1: The Terrorist Act

1. Terrorists Themselves

The first and most obvious route to pass on the victim's damages leads to the terrorist(s), but it does not end there. While it is clear that the terrorists themselves are liable for their intentional acts in all jurisdictions, even though their intent very often will not exceed *dolus eventualis*, their assets (or estate) will typically not suffice to cover all claims from those injured by their acts. 5

2. Terrorist Organization

In some cases, however, it could be promising at least to some extent to aim at the assets of the terrorist organization backing up the ultimate wrongdoers. To the extent that the attack was directly supported by such an organization, it is not difficult to extend the chain of causation and to establish its liability. But even if a member of a terrorist group performs an illegal activity which is covered by the organization's general scheme or strategy, even though it did not specifically direct the performance of this very act, the group will nevertheless be liable for ensuing losses. As Horton Rogers puts it, "it would be difficult to reject liability in a person who procures or participates in the planning of intentional wrongdoing, just as the criminal law extends liability to 'secondary parties' as well as those directly engaged in the crime".[1] 6

[1] W.V.H. Rogers, Comparative Report, in: W.V.H. Rogers (ed.), *Unification of Tort Law: Multiple Tortfeasors* (forthcoming 2004), no. 8.

3. Sponsors of Terrorism

a) Individuals or Organizations

7 Another step further away (but still) on the chain of causation may lead to people or entities sponsoring terrorist individuals or organizations. Again, it seems to be unproblematic to bring them into the ballgame if they were aware of the (at least potential) use of their means.[2]

A recent U.S. case may illustrate the issue[3]:

8 In June 2002, the 7th Circuit denied defendants' motions to dismiss a lawsuit filed by the estate of David Boim, who was killed by Hamas terrorists in Israel in 1996. His parents had sued (amongst others) the Chicago-based Quranic Literacy Institute, an organization which officially promoted the translation of Islamic texts, but allegedly (and in part even admittedly) funded Hamas activities in Israel. The action was based on the 1991 Antiterrorism Act (18 U.S.C. § 2333)[4], which introduced a federal tort claim for U.S. victims of an "act of international terrorism". Previously, this provision was interpreted to cover only "active involvement in planning and executing terrorist activities"[5]. The *Boim* court claimed, however, that "Congress purposely drafted the statute to extend liability to all points along the causal chain of terrorism"[6]. Therefore, it also extends to cases where defendants merely support those who actively execute attacks as long as defendants knew about those operations and intended

[2] Cf. art. 5 of the 1999 UN Convention for the Suppression of the Financing of Terrorism, which suggests civil liability as one of the possible measures to be taken by the signatories.

[3] *Boim v. Quranic Literacy Institute*, 291 F.3d 1000 (7th Cir. 2002).

[4] The relevant provisions read:
"§ 2333. – Civil remedies
(a) Action and Jurisdiction. –
Any national of the United States injured in his or her person, property, or business by reason of an act of international terrorism, or his or her estate, survivors, or heirs, may sue therefor in any appropriate district court of the United States and shall recover threefold the damages he or she sustains and the cost of the suit, including attorney's fees.
§ 2331. – Definitions
As used in this chapter –
(1) the term "international terrorism" means activities that –
(A) involve violent acts or acts dangerous to human life that are a violation of the criminal laws of the United States or of any State, or that would be a criminal violation if committed within the jurisdiction of the United States or of any State;
(B) appear to be intended –
(i) to intimidate or coerce a civilian population;
(ii) to influence the policy of a government by intimidation or coercion; or
(iii) to affect the conduct of a government by assassination or kidnapping; and
(C) occur primarily outside the territorial jurisdiction of the United States, or transcend national boundaries in terms of the means by which they are accomplished, the persons they appear intended to intimidate or coerce, or the locale in which their perpetrators operate or seek asylum; ...".

[5] Seventh Circuit Recognizes Implied Action for Aiding and Abetting Terrorism, [116] *Harvard Law Review* (Harv. L. Rev.) 713 (2002) at fn. 3.

[6] *Boim*, at 1020.

to support such goals (even though this need not have been the exclusive purpose backing their support).

The court further argued that this provision 9

> "... would have little effect if liability were limited to the persons who pull the trigger or plant the bomb because such persons are unlikely to have assets, much less assets in the United States, and would not be deterred by the statute. ... *The only way to imperil the flow of money and discourage the financing of terrorist acts is to impose liability on those who knowingly and intentionally supply the funds to the persons who commit the violent acts*".[7]

Even without a statute to the point, it is quite likely that European courts 10
would go equally far in extending the chain of causation, particularly if plaintiffs succeeded in bringing forward convincing evidence of the defendants' intent to support terrorist activities. After all, the *Boim* court made clear that funding alone would not suffice to state a claim: It required "funding that meets the definition of aiding and abetting an act of terrorism",[8] so in the continued trial, the Boim family will have to convince the court that "that the defendants knew about the organization's illegal activity, desired to help that activity succeed and engaged in some act of helping".[9]

b) Foreign States

A special problem in that respect concerns a very particular group of sponsors, 11
namely foreign states: There is quite considerable case law in the United States affirming the liability of countries such as Libya, Iran or Iraq for terrorist acts performed by organizations such as Hamas, which is based on the Foreign Sovereign Immunities Act as amended.[10] Apart from the jurisdictional problem of how to bring those countries into court, the more intricate question is to what extent the plaintiffs will be able to collect their potential awards (which are quite likely since such defendants will rarely ever apear in court, so that plaintiffs will obtain a default judgment).

In one such case against Iran, for example, brought by the parents of two U.S. 12
students who were killed – again in Israel – by Hamas suicide bombers, plaintiffs were awarded almost 330 million US dollars in compensatory and punitive damages[11]. While the solvency of such countries is not an issue as long as the oil and gas market does not collapse, it seems to be impossible to seize assets of such countries as a private party: Even if they had such funds in the U.S., these had already been blocked or frozen by Executive order of the U.S. President.

[7] *Boim*, at 1021.
[8] *Boim*, at 1028.
[9] *Boim*, at 1028.
[10] See the cases cited in K. Abraham, Liability for Acts of Terrorism Under U.S. Law (supra 176, in the following: K. Abraham, USA), no. 4.
[11] *Eisenfeld v. Islamic Republic of Iran*, 172 F. Supp. 2d 1 (D.D.C. 2000).

13 However, tables turned in October 2000 (immediately before the end of the Clinton administration) when Congress and the President finally succumbed to effective lobbying of certain selected plaintiffs[12]: In an ad hoc legislation Congress passed the "Victims of Trafficking and Violence Protection Act" which only applied to this very small group of particular plaintiffs, thereby discriminating against all other victims of terrorism in the U.S., even if they had already obtained judgment but failed to join those lobbyists. This unique statute satisfied the compensatory damages awards of those few totalling almost 400 million US dollars to be paid by the U.S. Treasury (and therefore ultimately by U.S. taxpayers). Plaintiffs thereby subrogated these claims to the U.S., which – accidentally or not – held funds in exactly the same amount which had been paid by Iran for military equipment that was never delivered by the U.S.[13] The Flatows, by the way, collected US$ 26 million out of this jackpot.

14 This case is therefore a perfect real-life example of how governments and legislators can substantially influence the distribution of loss by such ad hoc measures, thereby to a large extent disregarding a broader perspective of the phenomenon and succumbing to the political influence of a rather accidental selection of victims. While the validity of their claims shall not be questioned (at least not in this context), one must always bear in mind that such extraordinary measures may not be taken in a follow-up case, which makes the outcome of such quests for compensation even more unpredictable.

C. Route 2: Lack of Security

15 A second route does not lead to the behaviour of terrorists, but focuses on deficiencies in the prevention of their acts – misbehaviour that is attributable to third parties who are not affiliated to the terrorists themselves. This route is still based upon the notion of culpable wrongdoing, even though fault may at least in some instances be presumed.

16 To a large extent (if not exclusively), the defendants along those lines will not have actively done something wrong[14]. In order to hold them liable for omissions, however, the plaintiffs first need to establish a duty to act or – in this scenario – show that the defendants were under an obligation to prevent the terrorists from putting their plans into action.

[12] See S. Mangan, Compensation for "certain" victims of terrorism under section 2002 of the Victims of Trafficking and Violence Protection Act of 2000: Individual payments at an institutional cost, [42] *Virginia Journal of International Law* (Va. J. Int'l Law) 1037 (2002).

[13] The so-called *Foreign Military Sales* (FMS) Trust Fund, see S. Mangan, [42] Va. J. Int'l Law 1051 (2002).

[14] There may of course be cases where third parties have actively contributed to the terrorist act, either by negligently transporting packages that should have rendered them suspicious, or by providing terrorists with weapons or know-how (e.g. training them to steer a large passenger aeroplane).

Such an obligation may be rather general or very specific, for example, if there are actual threats against a particular target, which certainly raises the standard of care. Furthermore, such obligations may exist from the outset, which is typically the case, or be induced by an attack that has already taken place. 17

1. State

The most obvious addressee of such duties is the state. In any country governed by the rule of law, it is primarily the state which has to maintain law and order.[15] 18

This does certainly not mean, however, that the mere occurrence of an act of terrorism will per se lead to liability of the state, quite the contrary. In France, for example, there is case law denying state liability unless expressly provided for by statute.[16] Furthermore, potential French plaintiffs will even have to prove gross negligence of those acting on behalf of the state in order to succeed against the latter.[17] In the United Kingdom, there seems to be equal reluctance to hold the state liable for lack of police security.[18] Other countries apply ordinary standards of negligence[19], if not tighter ones (such as Spain[20] or Switzerland[21]). 19

While there will typically be a statutory or regulatory regime describing a state's duty to provide for adequate safety measures in more or less detail[22], this has to be read in light of the given fact that intentional criminal acts of others cannot be predicted with certainty, and that it is flatly impossible in a liberal society to tighten security safeguards in an Orwellian way. As Magnus has put it, "secret preparation and unexpected commission is characteristic" for terrorist attacks[23]. 20

[15] B.A. Koch/H. Koziol, Liability for Acts of Terrorism Under Austrian Law (supra 5, in the following: B.A. Koch/H. Koziol, Austria), no. 50 et seq., U. Magnus, Liability for Acts of Terrorism Under German Law (supra 128, in the following: U. Magnus, Germany), no. 24, A. Zaccaria/G. Bisazza, Liability for Acts of Terrorism Under Italian Law (supra 57, in the following: A. Zaccaria/G. Bisazza, Italy), no. 53, 57, M. Martín-Casals/J. Ribot, Liability for Acts of Terrorism Under Spanish Law (supra 88, in the following: M. Martín-Casals/J. Ribot, Spain), no. 53; C. Walker, Liability for Acts of Terrorism: United Kingdom Perspective (supra 138, in the following: C. Walker, UK), no. 85.

[16] O. Moréteau/F. Lafay, Liability for Acts of Terrorism Under French Law (supra 29, in the following: O. Moréteau/F. Lafay, France), no. 39. See also M. Martín-Casals/J. Ribot, Spain no. 45–47.

[17] O. Moréteau/F. Lafay, France no. 40.

[18] C. Walker, UK no. 85–86.

[19] B.A. Koch/H. Koziol, Austria no. 52–53, U. Magnus, Germany no. 23, K. Abraham, USA no. 26 (though rules vary from state to state).

[20] M. Martín-Casals/J. Ribot, Spain no. 42 (liability is strict in cases of "normal or abnormal operation of public services"), but see also no. 54.

[21] P. Widmer, Liability for Others under Swiss law, in: J. Spier (ed.), *Unification of Tort Law: Liability for Others* (2003), no. 12.

[22] Cf. B.A. Koch/H. Koziol, Austria no. 50 et seq., J. Neethling, Liability for Acts of Terrorism Under South African Law (supra 72, in the following: J. Neethling, South Africa), no. 20.

[23] U. Magnus, Germany no. 23.

21 A very rough rule of thumb may therefore conclude that the state's duties to protect individuals against such an offence are going further the more is known about its likelihood, but the reverse is equally true. While one can hardly deny an obligation of the state to investigate this probability, complete surveillance of all individuals is virtually impossible.

22 Furthermore, the budgets of all countries are limited, which very often leaves the police and other security forces understaffed and underequipped. However, apart from a massive undermining of their resources, it will hardly ever be possible to blame the state for not providing sufficient funds.[24]

23 And even if absolute control were technically and financially feasible, one would still have to consider civil rights issues: How much intrusion into their privacy do law-abiding individuals have to forbear in order to contribute to the state's strive for safety? While this it not the place to develop this issue further, one should only consider current plans to install security scanners at airports which would depict every person passing through naked.

24 Should these conclusions relieve the state from further duties to provide for financial cover to victims? I think not. After all, it is not only the state's general duty to protect its citizens as mentioned before, but the state also stands for the community of those at risk, which renders the state a possible addressee for pooling considerations, apart from the fact that acts of terrorism are by definition very often directed against the state as such. Still, this does not mean that tort law should be stretched beyond its systematic boundaries in order to achieve loss distribution via the state.

25 Another example of arbitrary legislation has been mentioned by the Austrian country report: As described in more detail there[25], a recent amendment to the Austrian law on the prevention of criminal acts against the security of civil aviation has reduced state liability for failure to provide for adequate safety measures to the amount of one million Euros (as compared to unlimited liability before). This maximum figure is truly ridiculously low, but illustrates how legislators tend to run amok in response to events such as 9/11.

2. Private Company – Organization – Institution

26 Other possible defendants who may be liable for the lack of adequate security are private companies to whom the duty to provide for safety measures has been shifted either by law or by contract.

27 In the aforementioned Austrian example, the state enters into a contractual relationship with security firms who thereby assume the responsibility to perform security checks at the airport, for instance. Such contracts with private

[24] Cf. B.A. Koch/H. Koziol, Austria no. 53, O. Moréteau/F. Lafay, France no. 40.
[25] B.A. Koch/H. Koziol, Austria no. 54–56.

security providers will not only be concluded by governments, but also by individuals and other companies who seek to protect their lives, property or businesses.

These contracts by their nature have to be qualified as "Verträge mit Schutzwirkung zugunsten Dritter", as a German concept would say, which means that the protective scope of the contract not only includes the parties thereto, but also third parties who are affected by the contractual duties covered. In the Austrian example, passengers, airport visitors and personnel will therefore have a direct claim against these companies if they should fail to perform as could have been expected. However, possible victims may still be tempted to go after the state first to the extent it can be held vicariously liable for their losses. 28

Private companies and institutions may further be obliged to provide for the protection of individuals by statute or regulation: National laws governing public events may require organizers thereof to ensure that a certain level of safety is guaranteed. Similar duties may affect the proprietors of public buildings such as sports stadiums, theatres, concert halls or the like. Depending on the nature of the event, it is not always clear to what extent terrorist attacks would be a risk covered by such rules. There may neveretheless be events which may be considered possible targets like the Olympic Winter Games at Salt Lake City in the immediate aftermath of the WTC attack or the 2002 Ski World Championship in Switzerland, where particular safety measures in light of the looming war against Iraq were extensively discussed. Even without the fear of actual terrorist threats, organizers of rock concerts or football games with large crowds attending will have to screen people entering the location and should thereby be able to detect bombs or weapons. If a terrorist were able to use such deadly instruments inside a sports stadium, for example, liability of those in charge of security will certainly be an issue despite the fact that their target group will rather be hooligans than people with political motivations. 29

Another aspect of potential liability for inadequate security measures does not address the prevention of terrorist acts themselves, but facilities which should step in once such attacks have taken place: While institutions such as fire brigades or rescue services may only be liable for the aggravation of loss if they should be unprepared for reacting to terrorist acts, one need only think of the anthrax menace or threats of other biological attacks which might require hospitals and similar institutions to stock sufficient vaccines and antidotes, particularly if the type of offensive agent is known in advance. Even though these are measures to be taken before the attack occurs, such duties are not aimed at fighting off the terrorist himself, but rather the consequences of his act. 30

While there may be quite a variety of arguments on which victims may build a claim against private institutions or companies, the more practical issue will concern their solvency and the extent of their insurance cover, which again brings the deep-pocket argument into the game, as undesirable as this may be. 31

3. Private Person

Prevention of terrorist acts or damage resulting therefrom

32 Individuals are in general not obliged to take an active role in preventing terrorist attacks.[26] Nevertheless, there may be a duty to react or intervene if someone gains knowledge of possible future terrorist activities or witnesses such criminal acts. While failure to warn authorities or to lend assistance to victims may indeed lead to civil (and not just criminal) liability of such persons[27], this is only the case if such action could reasonably be expected, which naturally depends upon the circumstances of the case. Factors considered may include the foreseeability of harm as well as a weighing of the respective interests.

4. Victim

33 As indicated earlier, contributory negligence matters will only be mentioned rather than elaborated extensively, though they certainly need to be considered when deciding upon loss allocation. Indeed, preventive security measures, for example, belong to an area where deficiencies may very well also lie within the sphere of the plaintiff, which may counter-balance arguments to shift the loss away from him. Not just after 9/11 should people be alert of certain dangers, though this should not lead to hysterical cocooning. Certain people, businesses or institutions should nevertheless also contribute to protect themselves if they belong to a group of likely targets, and even more so the more concrete the threat of an attack has become.

D. Route 3: Risk Inherent in Target

34 Apart from cases of misbehaviour, another route to relieve the victim from his losses takes a detour around the fault requirement and leads to instances of strict liability, which can be found in all jurisdictions covered.

1. Aircraft Operator

35 In the WTC scenario, the most obvious defendants will be the airlines, which were the first (though not the ultimate) targets of the terrorists. Liability of airlines is of course predominantly governed by international conventions or agreements. Therefore, the focus of this part will be on only one particular problem where national laws still play a decisive role, and that is ground dam-

[26] B.A. Koch/H. Koziol, Austria no. 66, U. Magnus, Germany no. 24, A. Zaccaria/G. Bisazza, Italy no. 52, J. Neethling, South Africa no. 14, 26, Th. Lörtscher/C. Parizzi/S. Gutzwiller, Liability for Acts of Terrorism Under Swiss Law (supra 128, in the following: Th. Lörtscher/C. Parizzi/S. Gutzwiller, Switzerland), no. 27.

[27] B.A. Koch/H. Koziol, Austria no. 66–67, O. Moréteau/F. Lafay, France no. 43, J. Neethling, South Africa no. 15–26, M. Martín-Casals/J. Ribot, Spain no. 62–63, Th. Lörtscher/C. Parizzi/S. Gutzwiller, Switzerland no. 27–29. But see U. Magnus, Germany no. 24 (neglect of such duty does not trigger civil liability).

age to non-passengers, which leads to the first case hypothetical of the questionnaire: A hijacker steers an aeroplane into a building (Case 1).

While strict liability for ground damage is clearly the predominant regime in a comparative survey[28], most jurisdictions will nevertheless not hold the airline liable for the damage to the building or its occupiers unless it can be blamed for contributing to the hijacking. If the terrorist could therefore take over control of the aircraft without any negligence within the sphere of the airline, the latter will be exonerated under most regimes.[29] This is not true, however, in France, South Africa, Switzerland and the United Kingdom, where the airline cannot avail itself of such a defence and therefore remains strictly liable.[30] 36

The latter solution becomes the predominant one, however, if the aeroplane was not hijacked, but if the terrorist blew it up with a bomb (Case 2): While it may come as no surprise that the airline remains strictly liable for ground damage in those four countries where hijacking did not serve as a defence, this second case is solved differently in Austria, Germany, Italy, Spain and Sweden.[31] In such case, it is argued that the terrorist did not take over control of the aircraft, which would constitute a defence under the wording of some aviation liability statutes, so that the carrier remains liable. 37

Kenneth Abraham assumes, however, that even in those U.S. jurisdictions where airlines can still be held strictly liable, courts may acknowledge the defence that they were deprived of control over the aircraft even in the bomb case.[32] 38

At first sight, it does indeed sound odd that the airline turns liable if the terrorist did not hijack the plane, but used a bomb instead. If the key to this solution should be whoever is in control of the aircraft, it certainly does not seem to be the airline if there is a bomb aboard which blows up at the will of the terrorist, whereas a sole hijacker may still be overpowered while aboard. 39

One of the major reasons for holding the airline liable in the first place is the danger brought about by the aeroplane flying at high speed and at extraordinary heights, which results in substantial danger to those on the ground if it 40

[28] B.A. Koch/H. Koziol, Austria no. 26, O. Moréteau/F. Lafay, France no. 29, U. Magnus, Germany no. 12, A. Zaccaria/G. Bisazza, Italy no. 33–34, J. Neethling, South Africa no. 8, M. Martín-Casals/J. Ribot, Spain no. 39–40, B. Bengtsson, Liability for Acts of Terrorism Under Swedish Law (supra 118, in the following: B. Bengtsson, Sweden) no. 9, Th. Lörtscher/C. Parizzi/S. Gutzwiller, Switzerland no. 14. But see K. Abraham, USA no. 21, 34.

[29] B.A. Koch/H. Koziol, Austria no. 25–28, U. Magnus, Germany no. 25, A. Zaccaria/G. Bisazza, Italy no. 58–59, M. Martín-Casals/J. Ribot, Spain no. 67–69, B. Bengtsson, Sweden no. 9, 36, K. Abraham, USA no. 21, 34.

[30] O. Moréteau/F. Lafay, France no. 29, 31, 45, J. Neethling, South Africa no. 8, Th. Lörtscher/C. Parizzi/S. Gutzwiller, Switzerland no. 30, UK no. 98.

[31] B.A. Koch/H. Koziol, Austria no. 73 (but see fn. 108), U. Magnus, Germany no. 27, A. Zaccaria, Italy no. 64, M. Martín-Casals/J. Ribot, Spain no. 76, B. Bengtsson, Sweden no. 38.

[32] K. Abraham, USA no. 38.

should come down extraordinarily. However, this argument should count equally irrespective of a possible hijacker who purposefully steers the aeroplane earthbound in order to cause harm. Whether or not he uses a bomb, the airline has only very limited means to avoid touchdown. It is therefore rather remarkable that those two cases are resolved so differently.

2. Keeper of Motor Vehicle

41 While strict liability for aeroplanes is only denied in certain U.S. jurisdictions, there is more inconsistency in the case of motor vehicles, where also the U.K. and South Africa resort to traditional fault concepts. This difference is not reflected in the outcomes of two further hypotheticals addressed by the above country reports:

42 In the example of a terrorist who takes the car of somebody else and purposefully drives it into a crowd of people (Case 3), all jurisdictions are in accord that the keeper of this car will not be strictly liable for the injuries of these victims.

43 Of those countries where no-fault liability would be possible, the arguments raised may not always be identical, particularly when it comes to the question whether such a harmful event would fall under the notion of "accident" as required by their statutes[33], or whether the car was "in operation" at the time[34]. All agree, however, with the solution that the terrorist has taken over control of the vehicle, and if the keeper is not to blame for losing control, he will not be liable for the subsequent acts of the terrorist.[35]

44 The Swedish solution only appears to be different at first sight: While the Swedish traffic insurance will still pay even under such circumstances[36], the same is true, for example, for the Austrian *Verkehrsopferfonds* (a fund which covers losses caused by car accidents where, for example, the driver is unknown, or if he causes harm intentionally)[37].

45 A true (and insofar single) exception can be found in Swiss law which (at least at face value) holds the keeper jointly and severally liable with someone who has taken away the car for the sole purpose of using it, which would include the terrorist in this case since he does not seem to be interested in keeping the car. While this harsh rule does not apply if the car was actually stolen before

[33] Accident confirmed: B.A. Koch/H. Koziol, Austria no. 19 (even if terrorist acted intentionally), accident denied: O. Moréteau/F. Lafay, France no. 50,

[34] Car in operation (within the meaning of the statute): B.A. Koch/H. Koziol, Austria no. 18, U. Magnus, Germany no. 10, car not in operation: M. Martín-Casals/J. Ribot, Spain no. 36–37 (no "hecho de la circulación").

[35] B.A. Koch/H. Koziol, Austria no. 76–77, O. Moréteau/F. Lafay, France no. 50–51, U. Magnus, Germany no. 29, J. Neethling, South Africa no. 30, M. Martín-Casals/J. Ribot, Spain no. 80, Th. Lörtscher/C. Parizzi/S. Gutzwiller, Switzerland no. 34 (if car was stolen, see below at fn. 38), K. Abraham, USA no. 39.

[36] B. Bengtsson, Sweden no. 17–18, 40.

[37] B.A. Koch/H. Koziol, Austria no. 9.

the attack, the Swiss authors suspect that the courts would not apply it anyhow to such drastic cases as the one at hand.[38]

Agreement of all jurisdictions can also be found in the final case example (Case 4), which is a variety of the former: There, the terrorist does not drive the vehicle into his victims, but uses it as a cover for a bomb which later explodes. In this case, even the reasonings coincide: Using a car as a mere hiding place for a bomb does not trigger statutory provisions which require the "operation" of the car: A stationary vehicle in a situation like this is not different from any other object or cover (such as, for example, a wastebin), so that the typical risk of a car is not involved, whereas in the prior case, the terrorist was actually using the car as such (though not in the way its designers had wanted it to be used).[39] 46

3. Operator of Nuclear Power Plant

There is further widespread accord (but with the opposite result) when it comes to nuclear facilities: If terrorists should attack an atomic power plant, either by using rockets or by steering a hijacked aeroplane into it, most reporters agree that the operator of the nuclear facility will be strictly liable for all harm resulting from the radiation which is thereby set free,[40] though certain limits may apply – either by statutory caps (such as in France[41] or Spain[42]) or effectively by limits to the required insurance coverage (such as in Germany[43], the United Kingdom[44] or the United States[45]). This follows from the laws on nuclear liability in the countries covered, of which most are based upon the Paris Convention. Even though the latter includes a war defence (art. 9[46]), it is not interpreted to include acts of terrorism[47]. The only exception thereto may 47

[38] Th. Lörtscher/C. Parizzi/S. Gutzwiller, Switzerland no. 8, 34.

[39] B.A. Koch/H. Koziol, Austria no. 78, O. Moréteau/F. Lafay, France no. 53, U. Magnus, Germany no. 30, J. Neethling, South Africa no. 31, M. Martín-Casals/J. Ribot, Spain no. 85, B. Bengtsson, Sweden no. 40, Th. Lörtscher/C. Parizzi/S. Gutzwiller, Switzerland no. 35, K. Abraham, USA no. 40.

[40] B.A. Koch/H. Koziol, Austria no. 72, 74, O. Moréteau/F. Lafay, France no. 47, U. Magnus, Germany no. 26, 28 (but see no. 14: defence of utmost care in cases not within the scope of the Paris Convention), J. Neethling, South Africa no. 28, M. Martín-Casals/J. Ribot, Spain no. 75, B. Bengtsson, Sweden no. 13–14 (but possibly applicable war defence), Th. Lörtscher/C. Parizzi/S. Gutzwiller, Switzerland no. 19, 31, C. Walker, UK no. 92, K. Abraham, USA no. 9, 37, 38.

[41] The current limit is 23 million Euros: O. Moréteau/F. Lafay, France no. 47.

[42] Up to 150 million Euros: Spain no. 75.

[43] Up to 1 billion Euros.

[44] Currently about 200 million Euros (£ 140 million: UK no. 92)

[45] Currently US$ 200 million: K. Abraham, USA no. 9.

[46] It reads:
"The operator shall not be liable for damage caused by a nuclear incident directly due to an act of armed conflict, hostilities, civil war, insurrection or, except in so far as the legislation of the Contracting Party in whose territory his nuclear installation is situated may provide to the contrary, a grave natural disaster of an exceptional character."

[47] B.A. Koch/H. Koziol, Austria no. 43, O. Moréteau/F. Lafay, France no. 46, U. Magnus, Germany no. 20, J. Neethling, South Africa no. 8, M. Martín-Casals/J. Ribot, Spain no. 74, B. Bengtsson, Sweden no. 14, Th. Lörtscher/C. Parizzi/S. Gutzwiller, Switzerland no. 31, K. Abraham, USA no. 37.

be found in Italian law, where such an exclusion may be held applicable even in cases of terrorism.[48]

4. Owner of Building – Architect – Construction Company

48 As the WTC attack has shown, there may be cases where two (or more) separate risks coincide: Apart from the afore-mentioned aeroplanes, the buildings themselves may have had an inherent danger that at least contributed to the overall losses. In this particular case, the typical dangerousness of aeroplanes was used to trigger the typical dangerousness of skyscrapers (which for the time being of course neglects the symbolic value of the two towers that were attacked).

49 The discussions following these tragic events soon turned to deliberations whether the towers had been constructed properly in order to withstand such an enormous impact, whether the emergency equipment (in particular for the evacuation of the building) were adequate or the like. The underlying allegations were that these buildings had some inherent danger which was not brought about but just realized by the attack of the terrorists.[49]

50 While there may certainly be fact constellations where the loss might be shifted to people responsible for the building or its construction, the reason therefor will not be a risk of the object per se, but rather the misbehaviour of those in charge, even though the way to holding them liable may be somewhat less problematic since some jurisdictions might reverse the burden of proving fault in such cases[50]. Furthermore, architects of skyscrapers in the future will have to consider the WTC scenario, and the owners of such buildings might have to adjust their security or maintenance policies[51].

51 But still: Unless they have failed to meet current standards which can reasonably be expected from them, it is rather unlikely that victims will be awarded damages for the losses sustained in their buildings, and even if they do, the calculation will only consider harm suffered just because of the deficiencies in the construction or its maintenance and not for injuries that they would have incurred anyhow[52].

5. Risk of Becoming a Target of Terrorism?

52 One risk should, however, never be the decisive reason why those concerned should be held strictly liable, even though it is quite frequently brought up in recent discussions: While it is undeniable that certain persons or objects are

[48] A. Zaccaria/G. Bisazza, Italy no. 36–37.

[49] Cf. e.g. the report in the New York Lawyer, September 11, 2002, After 9/11: Victims' Suits Filed to Meet One-Year Time Limit (available online at http://www.nylawyer.com/news/02/09/091102e.html).

[50] Cf. B.A. Koch/H. Koziol, Austria no. 40.

[51] Cf. K. Abraham, USA no. 30.

[52] H. Koziol, [2002] *Die Versicherungsrundschau* (VR), 225, 228.

more likely to be attacked by terrorists, does that particular risk per se constitute ample reason to shift the loss into the sphere of those in charge of such potential targets? (This question shall not concern heightened duties of self-protection or the like which merely raise the standard of care.)

Some people would answer the question in the affirmative: The mere fact that 53
aeroplane hijacking stimulates immediate and broad-scale media attention leads them to conclude that airlines are automatically liable for operating such possible targets – not because of the dangers of flying, but for the very reason that there is a certain likelihood that terrorists would pick an aircraft rather than a taxi when deciding how to cause the kind of commotion they are aiming at.

These arguments are extremely weak, to say the least: In such case, banks would 54
under all circumstances have to compensate passer-by victims of robberies (because it just so happens that banks are sometimes robbed)[53]. Public transport systems would be strictly liable for pickpocketing in subways because it is a given fact that public mass transportation is an attractive scenario for thieves.

We are all aware that this is not the case. After all, where would this reasoning 55
end? Should McDonald's be held liable for the harm of customers who were injured in an attack on some foreign branch of this worldwide chain just because McDonald's is commonly associated with the United States, so that terrorists believe that attacking McDonald's stands for an attack on the U.S. as a whole? This would necessarily also lead to the further conclusion that all people injured in an attack on some American embassy could sue the United States for damages because their "war against terrorism" makes their foreign representations likely targets of terrorists.

6. General Issues of Strict Liability

As one could see, mere allegations of a pre-existing "risk" do not necessarily 56
support a claim based upon strict liability, even if the legal system should be more generous in that respect. While certain objects are considered to be so inherently dangerous that fault is not decisive on the way to compensation, the list of such objects in various jurisdictions is certainly not identical.[54] One only needs to reconsider the aeroplane example: While strict liability for aircraft all across Europe is virtually undisputed (not even in England), the number of U.S. jurisdictions considering aeroplanes to be "abnormally dangerous" is apparently declining.[55]

[53] Cf. G. Schmidt-Räntsch, Fragen der Haftung des Luftfrachtführers für Schäden durch widerrechtliche Entführung von Luftfahrzeugen, [1979] *Zeitschrift für Luftrecht und Weltraumrechtsfragen* (ZLR), 429 (432).

[54] See, e.g., the inventory of strict liabilities listed by B.A. Koch/H. Koziol, Comparative Conclusions, in: B.A. Koch/H. Koziol (eds.), *Unification of Tort Law: Strict Liability* (2002), 395 (no. 4 et seq.).

[55] G. Schwartz, United States, in: B.A. Koch/H. Koziol (eds.), *Unification of Tort Law: Strict Liability* (2002), 351 (no. 17).

57 If applicable laws do provide for no-fault liability for the dangerous object involved in a terrorist attack, victims will still not automatically succeed: First of all, the scope of the risk will have to be determined. As could be seen in the car case, using a motorized vehicle as a mere shelter for a bomb does not bring the case within the ambit of the applicable road accident legislations.

58 Even if this were the case, one would still have to consider defences available to the defendant, the most important ones in this context being the defence of *force majeure*, of an unavoidable event, or of third-party intervention.

59 The availability of these defences depends upon the weight of the risk which serves as the foundation of the special liability regime in the first place: In the case of nuclear facilities, the scenario under which the operator may be exonerated is very tightly drawn, if a defence is available at all. Therefore, pointing at the intentional harmful act of terrorists will not exonerate the operator.

60 In other cases, the external unavoidable influence exerted by terrorists on the dangerous object may already have been considered at an earlier stage: Since the car bomb case is outside the scope of traffic liability legislation, the behaviour of the terrorist who had placed the bomb does not serve as a defence in the technical sense, but "ruins" the victim's case before it has started.

E. Route 4: Deficiencies in Responding to the Terrorist Act

61 One final route shall only be indicated rather than elaborated: In some cases, there may be misbehaviour in the aftermath of terrorist attacks, for example wrongdoings of rescue workers or specific risks triggered particularly by the clearing works such as improper disposal of hazardous waste. If at all, liability would not extend to the whole damage, but rather to the part which was aggravated due to such ex post deficiencies. Still, they may thereby have to absorb at least some of the victim's loss.

II. Subsidiary Resources

62 We have so far seen at least some ways to shift the loss from the victim to some other person who is held liable in tort for at least parts of the loss. For the following, we need to take one step back and look at the scenario from a slightly different perspective, thereby including information summarized earlier on alternative compensation schemes[56].

63 In tort law, one primarily focuses on the two parties of the action – the victim as the claimant and the tortfeasor as the defendant. Their relationship may be connected with a shorter or longer chain of causation, and the reasons for shifting the loss from one to the other vary in weight. From a legal policy perspective, there are, however, further players who need to be considered in this game before deciding where the loss shall lie in the end.

[56] See B.A. Koch/S. Strahwald, Compensation Schemes for Victims of Terrorism, supra 293.

On the victim's side, one first needs to consider social security, which at least in most European countries absorbs the most pressing needs of the victim, i.e. medical costs and other consequences of personal injuries and death. Since the victim's claim against the tortfeasor is thereby passed on to the social security carrier, the risk of collecting on that claim is spread within the pool of those covered. 64

Furthermore, the victim may have taken out life, accident or property insurance and thereby covered the losses in his own pocket by shifting them into the balance sheets of insureres. While it seems unpopular to require such cover at first sight, from an economic point of view, this might not always be the worst solution[57]. 65

Finally, the state may also intervene in favour of the victim by providing him with assistance other than social security, for example by awarding payments out of general funds designed for crime or terror victims, or by installing ad hoc funds like the September 11th Victims Compensation Fund. The state may further participate in pooling arrangements with the above-mentioned first-party insurers. 66

On the side of the tortfeasor, there are further actors who might step in and contribute to the victim's indemnification out of their own pockets. 67

One group of payors is not the most obvious, but still very important particularly in the terrorism scenario: As presented above, there are many possible defendants in tort law if all its tracks are followed, and the victim's claims against them will very often concern the same damage. While this is not the place to elaborate on issues of multiple tortfeasors and questions of internal recourse[58], one should bear in mind that some defendants who are jointly and severally liable may effectively serve as alternative loss bearers if the victim cannot collect from the most obvious tortfeasor, which is almost the rule in cases of terrorist acts. While those alternative defendants may theoretically have a right of recourse, they will most likely not be more successful than the victim and thereby end up with the entire loss that they have at least in part prefinanced for other possible defendants. This may not always reflect the original intention of tort law – and if it were, this objective should very well be laid out in the open. 68

Spreading the risk on the defendants' side through liability insurance systems will also have to be considered when deciding where the overall loss should lie at the end of our deliberations. 69

[57] See I. Gilead, Liability and Insurance in Cases of Damage Caused by Terrorist Attacks – Economic Analysis (supra 238, in the following: I. Gilead, Economic Analysis), no. 6, 49 et seq.

[58] See the contributions to W.V.H. Rogers (ed.), *Unification of Tort Law: Multiple Tortfeasors* (forthcoming 2004).

70 Finally, the state may equally intervene on the tortfeasors' side, for example if it joins liability insurers in forming a pool, thereby again effectively serving as a kind of reinsurer of last resort . The policies behind such state intervention can of course not be separated from the aforementioned assistance granted directly to the victim.

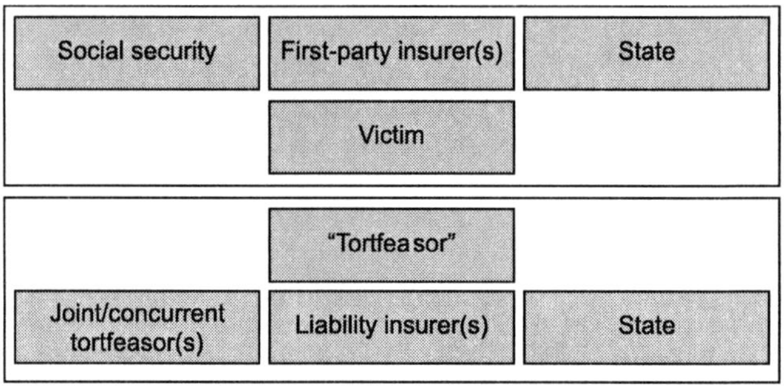

III. Concluding Remarks

71 From the perspective of tort law, terrorist attacks would not pose any noteworthy problem if the clear-cut solutions it offers in theory for such intentional harmful acts could be realized in practice: The tortfeasor would need to be brought before a court of law, and his realizable assets would have to be sufficient in order to fully indemnify his victims.

72 The problems start where this theory fails to correspond to real life, and any alternative solution found beyond this borderline is necessarily based on weaker reasons to attribute the loss. While there may be deficiencies in security and prevention measures which should be sanctioned, for example, one should bear in mind that it is always the terrorists who trigger the need for such measures in the first place.

73 Seen from this perspective, any alternative compensation scheme which focuses on the position of the victim appears to be more honest as it clearly disregards retribution for the sake of reparation. However, the range of such compensation schemes in a comparative perspective is rather broad, with varying degrees of overlap[59]. One may wonder in particular why such schemes draw their funds from such different sources as property taxes or insurance premiums or tax-like additions thereto, and why the risks are therefore spread among those contributors rather than any other possible members of the risk-group. Furthermore, any state participation, which is of course in many respects desirable and justifiable in this field[60], may provoke the critical and probably unwelcome question why these peculiar hazards of life deserve such

[59] See B.A. Koch/S. Strahwald (supra fn. 56).
[60] See I. Gilead, Economic Analysis, no. 22–33.

special attention whereas other risks are not even addressed yet at all by comparable public initiatives.

What tort law can do is to offer several ways for the victim of a terrorist attack to obtain compensation, some may be dead ends, some may be difficult to follow, and some may be detours and short cuts. What tort law cannot accomplish, however, is to point into one single direction which should always be followed, but this is not a flaw in the system of tort law: Terrorist attacks are by and large unpredictable, and this is equally true for the chances to place the loss where it should lie: with the terrorists. 74

Conclusions

Helmut Koziol

I. Introduction

1 In the wake of the terrorist attacks on the United States on September 11, 2001, the whole world discusses the problem of terrorism and how to control it. The United States seem to be prepared to go to any lengths in fighting terrorism, thereby even risking violating international law and bringing disaster upon hundreds of thousands of civilians, not shrinking back from endangering the lives of her own soldiers and from spending billions of dollars – and all that, as it seems from the outside, without having sufficient proof of the opponent's dangerousness and its decisive connection with terrorism. But this topic is loaded with emotions and we do not have to deal with it.

2 As we are lawyers, we want to discuss the special problems of tort law and insurance in cases of terrorist attacks. Nevertheless, I deem it useful at least to some extent not to ignore these emotions entirely but to proceed from them and to put some questions at the beginning which may seem surprising or improper or even impertinent. But I do hope that the answers to these questions will help us to realise the peculiarities of our topic and to justify the degree of intensity of this topic's discussion.

3 Of course, everyone who saw the pictures of the terrorist attacks on September 11, 2001, and who remembers the deaths of more than 3000 innocent people will feel quite some understanding for the current public sentiment in the United States. But, on the other hand, it appears rather one-sided. One has to recall that in the period from 1965 to 2000, more than 65 million people were injured and almost 1.5 million people were killed by road accidents in the U.S.A.. In the year 2000 alone, 41,821 people died on the roads in the United States. Even the horrifying number of 3200 victims on September 11 in Washington and New York seems to go pale in light of these shocking figures. However, there is nearly no public reaction to these millions of killed and injured persons, and comparatively little is done by authorities against these immense numbers of deaths and injuries. This seems all the more astonishing as one has to highlight the following: It is absolutely sure that the roads will always remain "battlefields" leaving behind innocent victims, whereas there is no comparable certainty that singular attacks compared to the year 2001 will be repeated as often or even at all in the future.

II. A First Answer to the Questions

The decisive question is what the reasons are that lie beneath these inconsistent reactions. I feel that the following factors are relevant: First of all, we have got used to the bloodshed on the roads and, furthermore, nearly everyone of us is not only a potential victim but also a possible offender. Without doubt, the latter puts a damper on the emotions against the responsible parties. Furthermore, all in all road traffic still has to be considered useful, while terrorist attacks, of course, are not. But the latter is also true for natural phenomena, nevertheless the responses thereto are quite different as compared to terror attacks. Still, one has to consider that intent to cause harm always and rightly so arouses special emotions. In the end decisive, in my opinion, is the following reason: Road traffic as well as natural phenomena such as flood disasters or strong earthquakes may have terrible results, but they do not put at risk the system of our society and the existence of our state. The subversive activities of terrorists intend to do so. Clive Walker[1] starts his report on the law of the United Kingdom with the sentence: "The sub-form of political violence known as 'terrorism' should be viewed as at the pinnacle of risks and liabilities, for it seeks to perpetrate harms which threaten not just single enterprises or individuals or even groups of them linked either by location or type but the entire population and the political economy." There is consequently no doubt that terrorism and control over terrorists has to be one of the most pressing issues in our societies. 4

Still, while all this underlines the seriousness of terrorism, it cannot fully explain why lawyers and especially tort and insurance lawyers are discussing this topic with such passion. One could say that the legal situation is very simple since it is equally beyond doubt that the terrorists are liable for the damage they have caused as it is generally useless to address this question because they will either be dead or unable to compensate the loss[2]. Furthermore, one does not have to think about terrorists' liability insurance – not even the so-called rogue states worry about that. 5

However, on the one hand, there is at least a slight chance to recover damages from terrorists if there is a claim against organisations who have provided material support for them[3], and in some countries also in cases of state-sponsored terrorism[4]. Furthermore, Lahnstein[5] pointed out that liability insurance must not be disregarded. On the other hand, the country reports show impressively that there are still quite some problems in the area of liability for terrorist attacks, especially when looking at "enabling torts",[6] or when considering such questions as for ex- 6

[1] Cf. also Dahlke, Terror als Schadensursache, [2002] *Versicherungsrecht*, 25.

[2] But there are some exceptions, see e.g. O. Moréteau/F. Lafay, Liability for Acts of Terrorism Under French Law (supra 29, in the following: O. Moréteau/F. Lafay, France), no. 16 et seq.

[3] K. Abraham, Liability for Acts of Terrorism Under U.S. Law (supra 176, in the following: K. Abraham, USA), no. 6.

[4] See K. Abraham, USA, no. 4 and 14 et seq.

[5] Ch. Lahnstein, Liability Insurance for Acts of Terrorism? (supra 252, in the following: Ch. Lahnstein, Liability Insurance).

[6] Cf. K. Abraham, USA, no. 22 et seq.

ample whether the keeper of an aeroplane is liable for the damage caused by terrorists who used his plane for destroying a sky scraper, whether the keeper of a nuclear plant or a refinery may become liable for insufficiently guarding the plant and thus giving the terrorists an opportunity to blow it up, whether the company which is in charge of airport security checks has to compensate the owner's damage caused by the blasting of the aeroplane and for the loss of the passengers' dependants if its employees acted negligently. Last but not least the question of states' liability for insufficient control of terrorism is also under discussion.

7 Of course, these are very interesting and demanding problems. But one has to admit that most or even all of them are topics of a rather general nature and are of equal relevance in other areas of tort law. Therefore, they should be discussed under a broader angle, and I even have to add that they must not be discussed solely with a view to terrorist attacks. For example: We have heard that under many legal systems the question arises whether in the area of strict liability terrorist attacks should be qualified as *force majeure* and whether the keeper of an aeroplane, a motor car or a factory should have a defence in such cases. But it is a general question concerning the whole area of strict liability whether such events should be accepted as a defence at all and if so, to what extent, and whether they bar liability or only reduce the obligation to compensate[7]. It is obvious that such fundamental questions cannot be solved from the isolated perspective of strict liability for terror attacks.

8 I think we have reached the core of the matter if we bear in mind the following: In his comparative report Bernhard Koch points out the different solutions under the respective legal systems, and such comparative work gives profitable incentives to further all the legal systems and to fill possible loopholes in their laws. Nevertheless, one has to be aware of the fact that there is not a single legal system which offers full and effective compensation to all victims of terrorism under tort law. To a large extent, only the terrorists will be liable who will, however, not be able to pay compensation. Under the principle that everyone has to bear the risks in his own sphere if there are not sufficient reasons to pass on the loss to another person, the victim then has to suffer his loss. It seems that widespread opinion opposes such an outcome.

9 Of course, one has to take into consideration that there is a very effective social security system in Europe operating side by side with tort law. Therefore, in cases of personal injuries, the victim does not have to pay for medical treatment, his loss of earnings is compensated, and after the victim's death the persons who are entitled to maintenance will receive support. Nevertheless, not all losses are absorbed by the social security system, especially not non-pecuniary loss. Furthermore, there is no such compensation system in case of damage to property[8].

[7] Cf. to all these questions B.A. Koch/H. Koziol, Comparative Conclusions, in: B.A. Koch/H. Koziol (eds.), *Unification of Tort Law: Strict Liability* (2002), 395 (no. 109 et seq.).

[8] Cf. C. Walker, Liability for Acts of Terrorism: United Kingdom Perspective (supra 138, in the following: C. Walker, UK), no. 45.

It is a matter of policy whether in cases of harm caused by terrorist attacks tort and social law are considered to be sufficient for indemnifying the victims or whether one thinks that protection is incomplete. 10

I think that in cases of damage caused by terrorists there are weighty reasons which speak in favour of additional compensation of victims beyond the contributions offered by tort and social law. This is the point where some ideas mentioned in the beginning may play a role. 11

In defining terrorism it is frequently pointed out that terrorists aim at influencing the state, the public or parts of the public, and that the victims are chosen at random. In this sense the United Kingdom's Terrorism Act 2000 specifies that the use or threat of action is designed to influence the government or to intimidate the public or a section of the public. To quote again Clive Walker:[9] "The attack is symbolic, and the real impact is to be on the state." He deduces from this observation about the nature of terrorist-related torts that there should indeed be a state response, and experience shows that to some extent the public sector follows this opinion. One only needs to refer to the English example and to the September 11 Victim Compensation Fund in the United States. 12

I strongly support this idea[10]: If the terrorists' action is designed to harm the state or the public, injuring the individual victim is only a means to the end. This is an important difference to cases in which the tortfeasor causes damage to a person without aiming at a third person, but also to cases of harm caused by natural events. It seems reasonable that the institution whose impairment is the terrorists' true goal has to compensate the innocent victims who have to suffer as substitutes for the public sector. Therefore, in the end the idea that terrorism puts the system of our society at risk as well as the existence of our states, and that it does not aim at injuring individuals, seems to be an argument of some weight in favour of establishing a duty to compensate the victims affected by the terrorists. I think the same idea is only expressed in other words if one refers to the principle of solidarity towards the victims[11]. 13

One further argument for such a duty may be that under many legal systems it is a duty of the state to control terrorism and to maintain the safety of the members of its society[12]. One could therefore conclude that the state should be 14

[9] C. Walker, UK, no. 4.

[10] In the same sense I. Gilead, Liability and Insurance in Cases of Damage Caused by Terrorist Attacks – Economic Analysis (supra 238), no. 30. Cf. also Rohde-Liebenau, [2002] *Zeitschrift für Versicherungswesen*, 71.

[11] M. Martín-Casals/J. Ribot, Liability for Acts of Terrorism Under Spanish Law (supra 88, in the following: M. Martín-Casals/J. Ribot, Spain), no. 17.

[12] Cf. B.A. Koch/H. Koziol, Liability for Acts of Terrorism Under Austrian Law (supra 5), no. 50 et seq.; J. Neethling, Liability for Acts of Terrorism Under South African Law (supra 72), no. 22 and 25; C. Walker, UK, no. 85. See also M. Martín-Casals/J. Ribot, Spain, no. 14 and 53 et seq.

liable if it fails in doing so. But I have to admit that some legal systems such as France[13] are going the other way by introducing remarkable hurdles on the victim's way to hold the state liable for breaching its duty to ensure safety, where gross negligence has to be proven. Furthermore, one has to admit that the argument in favour of states' liability is not very convincing as long as the authorities actually did all they should and could have done, and if no negligence is attributable to their sphere.

15 One has to further consider that the idea of prevention may favour the solution that the victim has to bear his own loss: Everyone will watch out more carefully to avoid damage if there is nobody else who might step in to compensate the harm. On the other hand, one has to admit that the individual citizen hardly ever has a chance to prevent damage caused by terrorists.

16 There is yet another idea which has to be considered, namely that the citizens could insure their risk. It certainly needs to be discussed whether this or any other way to indemnify the victim is more advantageous and reasonable.

17 These brief hints already show that there are several reasons for intensively discussing the question whether victims of terrorism should enjoy supplementary compensation, and if so by whom, or if this is not the case, whether the current system in combination with the possibility to insure one's own risks is sufficient. We will cast a short glimpse on all these difficult questions.

III. Outlook

18 In summary a comparative overview shows that there are some attempts to expand the tortious liability of the state. Nevertheless, according to widespread opinion, victims of terrorist attacks should receive some compensation beyond what is offered by tort law and also by social security law. But the various countries have created different systems: Compensation by the state, by funds or by first-party insurers who are supported by the public sector. It is obviously a rather technical question whether compensation has to be paid out by the state or by a fund nourished by the state. But there is a difference in substance whether citizens have a claim against the state or whether they themselves have to make provisions by taking out some first party insurance cover.

19 Nevertheless, all these solutions indicate that additional compensation of victims can only be provided by the public sector or at least with its support. I feel that this is in accordance with dogmatic arguments which also point rather into the direction of the public sector. But I have to admit that these clues are not very strong, and that they do not have enough weight by themselves to introduce a general strict liability of the state for damage caused by terrorists. The clues may be supported by the general idea of tort law's preventive purpose which is accepted under some legal systems and which is given special emphasis by the economic analysis of law.

[13] O. Moréteau/F. Lafay, France, no. 40.

But Gilead's convincing statements based on such an economic analysis do not only point to the state alone as the exclusive bearer of his subjects' losses, but also consider further persons who may have to contribute to compensation. As long as there are no other strong dogmatic arguments, the economic analysis may give the decisive impulse for future regulations. Therefore, I think we have to go back to Gilead's conclusions: 20

He argued that the major burden of primary and secondary cost avoidance of terrorist acts should be imposed upon the public sector, the latter being "strictly liable", and all that in a way that would strengthen the incentive to take efficient preventive measures – I agree with this result, but I would prefer not to speak about "strict liability": I feel it is not a matter of liability but rather of solidarity or assumption and spreading of risk. 21

Gilead further recommends to restrict such compensation by caps and by exclusion of certain types of damage. Such restriction would induce other cost avoiders to take preventive measures in which they specialize. 22

Moreover, Gilead would hold occupiers and those in charge of endangered premises liable for the residual costs not covered by public authorities since such fault-based liability would strengthen the incentives of these cost avoiders to actually take preventive measures. As Gilead points out, being residual, such liability may well be covered by affordable liability insurance. Moreover, to fortify these incentives to take preventive measures, the cost avoiders may be exposed to indemnity claims of public authorities for gross negligence and recklessness in preventing terrorists attacks – I would like to add that, of course, liability in case of gross negligence should be unlimited as there is no reason at all to release such tortfeasors from liability established by tort law. Further, I am of the opinion that even in case of slight negligence the tortfeasor should not always – apart from his residual liability to the victims – be fully released from indemnification[14]: According to tort law, he would be fully liable, and a restriction of this liability should only be conceded if compensation would exceed his financial capacities, taking into account insurability. Except for the unforeseeability of damage caused by terrorist attacks I cannot see a reason for treating such tortfeasors better than others. Therefore, I am not in favour of constraining the applicant's right to file a claim for damages caused by the terrorists as the September 11 Victim Compensation Fund explicitly does, and what Congress is considering as a general restriction of tort actions in case of future attacks. Finally – but that is a rather technical question – the same argument of equal treatment speaks out against only residual liability. But, of course, it makes it easier for the victim if he has a claim without many prerequisites against the state and the public authorities have to claim indemnity. 23

[14] I think this is true even if we take into consideration – as Ch. Lahnstein, Liability Insurance, no. 8, rightly pointed out – that in case of insurer's redress the idea of victim's protection is not at stake.

24 Last but not least, Gilead suggests that victims themselves may be induced to spread the costs which public authorities do not cover by denying their entitlement to compensation for residual costs. These costs could be spread by victims through the extension of first party liability insurance[15]. I think that one should not cut off the victims' claims for residual costs against persons who are liable on the basis of tort law because of their faulty behaviour or their strict liability.

25 Finally, Gilead suggests that the question whether residual costs are better handled by liability insurance or by first party insurance of victims should be further examined. He feels that possibly the best method could be a combination of these two.

26 I would like to add that it seems very important to discuss where compensation by the public sector should begin and how to lay down restrictions of such compensation. I am in favour of solutions which restrict the state's ex ante involvement as far as possible and reasonable, and the English example leads into the same direction[16]. Therefore, I would propose to provide for first party and liability insurance as far as economic circumstances allow. Of course, there are quite some difficulties since losses arising out of terrorist attacks can hardly be predicted. Furthermore, the chance of very large single-event losses is rather high. It may help to reach this goal by establishing "terror pools" by the insurance companies, as is already done in some countries. Further, one should consider the proposal of Swiss Re to provide for mandatory insurance for damage caused by terrorist attacks. Thus the risk community would become much broader and insurance would be more compatible with the means. In this way, and maybe by supporting the insurability by playing the role of a "reinsurer of last resort", the public sector can restrict its duty to directly compensate the victims of exceptional cases.

27 One last remark: I have to point out that it would not be reasonable or even possible to draft a plan for compensating victims of terrorist attacks that were meant to be applicable all around the world. The reason is that the legal systems which have to be the obvious starting point differ quite considerably. You only need to think of the availability of social security which in some countries is as generous as to cover nearly all personal injuries. As a result, the need for additional compensation is much less pressing in Europe than in the United States. Furthermore, the broader the area of strict liability and the less the keepers' defences, the more limited is the need for special provisions in regard of harm caused by terrorists. Therefore, as even in Europe strict liability differs to an astonishing degree[17], the starting point in the various European countries is anything but homogenous.

[15] Espoused by Ch. Lahnstein, Liability Insurance, no. 12.

[16] With good reasons against ex ante involvement of the government A. Gron/A. Sykes, Terrorism and Insurance Markets: A Role for the Government as Insurer?, *Chicago John M. Olin Law & Economics Working Paper No. 155 (2d Series),* available at http://www.law.uchicago.edu/Lawecon/index.html.

[17] See B.A. Koch/H. Koziol (supra fn. 7).

Although we cannot offer a general rule of compensation in cases of terror attacks I strongly feel that the country reports, the comparative report, the economic analysis and the paper on liability insurance aspects are very useful in addressing the peculiar problems of each jurisdiction: We receive quite some food for thought and valuable stimulation by all of them, and the experience in other countries helps us to avoid wrong decisions and to come to satisfactory results quicker and more safely. 28

Index

The numbers refer to marginal notes, the letters to the individual contributions. The country reports are marked by the international letter symbols: A stands for Austria (supra 5), CH for Switzerland (supra 128), D for Germany (supra 47), E for Spain (supra 88), F for France (supra 29), I for Italy (supra 57), S for Sweden (supra 118), UK for the United Kingdom (supra 138), US for the United States of America (supra 176), ZA for South Africa (supra 72). The special reports are abbreviated as follows: CL stands for the report on "Civil Litigation Arising out of the WTC Attacks" (supra 189), VCF for the report on the September 11th Victim Compensation Fund (supra 197), and MTL points to the presentation on mass tort litigation issues (supra 204). The abbreviations used for the general reports are: EA for the economic analysis (supra 238), LI for the report on liability insurance (supra 252), CS for the summary of compensation schemes (supra 260), CA for the comparative analysis (supra 282), and C for the conclusion (supra 300).

Publications

Principles of European Tort Law

Volume 1: *The Limits of Liability: Keeping the Floodgates Shut.*
Edited by Jaap Spier.
Kluwer Law International, The Hague. Hardbound.
ISBN 90-411-0169-1. 1996, 162 pp.

Volume 2: *The Limits of Expanding Liability. Eight Fundamental Cases in a Comparative Perspective.*
Edited by Jaap Spier.
Kluwer Law International, The Hague. Hardbound.
ISBN 90-411-0581-6. 1998, 244 pp.

Volume 3: *Unification of Tort Law: Wrongfulness.*
Edited by Helmut Koziol.
Kluwer Law International, The Hague. Hardbound.
ISBN 90-411-1019-4. 1998, 144 pp.

Volume 4: *Unification of Tort Law: Causation.*
Edited by Jaap Spier.
Kluwer Law International, The Hague. Hardbound.
ISBN 90-411-1325-8. 2000, 161 pp.

Volume 5: *Unification of Tort Law: Damages.*
Edited by Ulrich Magnus.
Kluwer Law International, The Hague. Hardbound.
ISBN 90-411-1481-5. 2001, 225 pp.

Volume 6: *Unification of Tort Law: Strict Liability.*
Edited by Bernhard A. Koch and Helmut Koziol.
Kluwer Law International, The Hague. Hardbound.
ISBN 90-411-1705-9. 2002, 444 pp.

Volume 7: *Unification of Tort Law: Liability for Damage Caused by Others.*
Edited by Jaap Spier.
Kluwer Law International, The Hague. Hardbound.
ISBN 90-411-2185-4. 2003, 335 pp.

Volume 8: *Unification of Tort Law: Contributory Negligence.*
Edited by Ulrich Magnus and Miquel Martín-Casals.
Kluwer Law International, The Hague. Hardbound.
ISBN 90-411-2220-6 (forthcoming).

Tort and Insurance Law

Volume 1: *Cases on Medical Malpractice in a Comparative Perspective.*
Edited by Michael Faure and Helmut Koziol.
Springer, Vienna/New York.
Softcover. ISBN 3-211-83595-4.
2001, 331 pp.

Volume 2: *Damages for Non-Pecuniary Loss in a Comparative Perspective.*
Edited by W.V. Horton Rogers.
Springer, Vienna/New York.
Softcover. ISBN 3-211-83602-0.
2001, 318 pp.

Volume 3: *The Impact of Social Security on Tort Law.*
Edited by Ulrich Magnus.
Springer, Vienna/New York.
Softcover. ISBN 3-211-83795-7.
2003, 312 pp.

Volume 4: *Compensation for Personal Injury in a Comparative perspective.*
Edited by Bernhard A. Koch and Helmut Koziol.
Springer, Vienna/New York.
Softcover. ISBN 3-211-83791-4.
2003, 501 pp.

Volume 5: *Deterrence, Insurability and Compensation in Environmental Liability. Future Developments in the European Union.*
Edited by Michael Faure.
Springer, Vienna/New York.
Softcover. ISBN 3-211-83863-5.
2003, 405 pp.

Volume 6: *Der Ersatz frustrierter Aufwendungen. Vermögens- und Nichtvermögensschaden im österreichischen und deutschen Recht.*
By Thomas Schobel.
Springer, Vienna/New York.
Softcover. ISBN 3-211-83877-5.
2003, 342 pp.

Volume 7: *Liability for and Insurability of Biomedical Research with Human subjects in a Comparative Perspective.*
Edited by Jos Dute, Michael G. Faure and Helmut Koziol.
Springer, Vienna/New York.
Softcover. ISBN 3-211-20098-3.
2003, approx. 400 pp. (forthcoming).

Volume 9: *Pure Economic Loss.*
Edited by Willem H. van Boom, Helmut Koziol and Christian Witting.
Springer, Vienna/New York.
Softcover. ISBN 3-211-00514-5.
2003, approx. 320 pp. (forthcoming).

Volume 10: *Liber Amicorum Pierre Widmer.*
Edited by Helmut Koziol and Jaap Spier.
Springer, Vienna/New York.
Softcover. ISBN 3-211-00522-6.
2003, 376 pp.

European Tort Law Yearbook

European Tort Law 2001.
Edited by Helmut Koziol and
Barbara C. Steininger.
Springer, Vienna/New York.
Softcover. ISBN 3-211-83824-4.
2002, 571 pp.

European Tort Law 2002.
Edited by Helmut Koziol and
Barbara C. Steininger.
Springer, Vienna/New York.
Softcover. ISBN 3-211-00486-6.
2003, 596 pp.

Springer-Verlag and the Environment

WE AT SPRINGER-VERLAG FIRMLY BELIEVE THAT AN international science publisher has a special obligation to the environment, and our corporate policies consistently reflect this conviction.

WE ALSO EXPECT OUR BUSINESS PARTNERS – PRINTERS, paper mills, packaging manufacturers, etc. – to commit themselves to using environmentally friendly materials and production processes.

THE PAPER IN THIS BOOK IS MADE FROM NO-CHLORINE pulp and is acid free, in conformance with international standards for paper permanency.